D

ROAD COMPANY.

# STEELWAYS of NEW ENGLAND

LITHOGRAPHED POSTER (ABOUT 1880) SHOWING THE WEST
PORTAL OF THE HOOSAC TUNNEL AND A WAGNER SLEEPING CAR.

# STEELWAYS
## of
# NEW ENGLAND

## By ALVIN F. HARLOW

NEW YORK
CREATIVE AGE PRESS, INC.

DESIGNED BY JEROME MULCAHY

PRINTED IN THE UNITED STATES OF AMERICA
AMERICAN BOOK—STRATFORD PRESS, INC., NEW YORK
55

# Contents

1. The Sad State of New England     3
2. The First Railroad     14
3. The Dawn of Private Enterprise     36
4. The First Charters     71
5. Massachusetts Produces Triplets     80
6. Over the Hills to the Hudson     116
7. The Birth of the Boston & Maine     143
8. New Haven Becomes a Railroad Center     170
9. Ghost Train and Ghost Road     196
10. "In the Land of the Pine and the Cranberry Bog"     215
11. The Fitchburg and the Great Bore     236
12. The Forty Years' War in Vermont     259
13. Concord and Discord in New Hampshire     285
14. From Kittery to 'Quoddy     308
15. Twentieth-Century Epilogue     329
16. The Thin-Gaugers     339
17. Operation by Trial and Error     350
18. Comfort and Elegance     379
19. More Yankee Ingenuity     403
20. New England, Mother of Railroads     411
    Acknowledgment     433
    Bibliography     435
    Index     449

# STEELWAYS of NEW ENGLAND

# The Sad State of New England

"IS OLD Massachusetts in her palsied dotage?" demanded "Shadrack," an anonymous letter-writer to the *American Traveller* of Boston in 1825. "Is her sun of prosperity . . . setting, to rise no more? This sun with increasing splendor is irradiating the hills of Hudson and fertile vales of New York. Where are the thousand ships of the Bay State, her accumulated wealth of two centuries? Has the building of a few roads and the cutting of *one* canal, or rather, *ditch* of inconsiderable distance satisfied her ambitions and put her 'at ease in her possessions'?"

Shadrack's diatribe, wrung from an anguished heart by the triumphant completion of New York's Erie Canal, did not fail, it will be observed, to hurl a poisoned barb at the Middlesex Canal, "or rather, ditch," once Boston's pride and hope. Built between 1793 and 1803, this twenty-seven-mile waterway from Boston to the Merrimac River was designed principally to bring the products of New Hampshire directly and more cheaply to Boston than if they went out through the mouth of the Merrimac and around to Boston by sea. But in two decades of operation, it had lost money for its stockholders, and had not aided the city as was expected. The state, by way of aid, had given it two townships of land in Maine, then still a province of Massachusetts, but the canal company couldn't sell the land and scarcely knew where it was, so that was no help.

Now that westward expansion of the nation had begun and was proceeding with a rush, New England, to her dismay, found herself an isolated eddy, apparently left behind in the swelling tide of national expansion. A Boston editor called attention to the fact that from the first United States census in 1790 to 1820, Massachusetts had increased its population by only 30 per cent, while the whole nation had increased by 150 per cent. Bigness, ant-hill augmentation ("Watch Bung-town grow!") was becoming an American gauge of progress. Big businessmen everywhere now began to think more of national than of local trade; and "national" in 1825 meant something many times larger than it had a few years before.

Boston in particular, in the decade of the 1820's, squirmed unhappily under her unpleasant predicament. She had once considered herself the leading city in America—Nordic America, that is; Latins didn't count. But upstart villages like Dutch New York and Quaker Philadelphia had arisen, become great and challenged her supremacy; in fact, New York had already far outgrown her. Still, New England, with Boston as a center, held a certain leadership in thought and action, as she had done from the beginning. The first attempt at a federal government in Anglo-Saxon America had been the loose organization of the little settlements in Massachusetts, Connecticut and, later, Rhode Island, known as the United Colonies of New England, or the New England Confederation, established in 1643 and continuing for forty years. Boston had the college that was greatest—and oldest by more than half a century—in the British colonies. She, with Samuel Adams as her mouthpiece, was the first to protest—in May, 1764—against England's proposed Stamp Tax on America, and the first to deny—at this same town meeting—that the old country had the right to tax the colonies without their consent. She was the first to take the tea tax problem by the horns eight years later and throw a cargo of tea into the ocean. She, or her yeoman neighbors, fired the shot heard 'round the world, which began the Revolution.

For three decades after the Revolution, Massachusetts held supremacy in shipping. The sails of Boston, Salem and New Bedford ranged the seven seas, carrying furs to Chinese mandarins and coming back with tea, silks and—whisper it!—opium;

bringing in fish, whale oil, rum and tropical products, either for consumption here (too true as to the rum!) or for reshipment in Yankee bottoms to Europe. Then came the War of 1812, which New England deplored. Seemingly, she should have been as angry as the rest of America over the British blows at our shipping trade, the searching of our vessels and impressment of seamen, and so she was at first. But when war was declared by a radical Republican (Democratic) President—New England being still largely Federalist—when all her ports were blockaded, her merchant vessels either captured and sunk by the enemy or lying idle in her harbors, her sea fisheries almost completely halted, she lost her temper. After two years of suffering from it, she even plotted against the war in secret at Hartford, or so it was charged, in a manner regarded by the rest of the country as bordering on the treasonable, or worse.

Well might she fume over the situation, for somehow she never quite recovered her shipping supremacy thereafter. All coast cities suffered from a depression after this war; but De Witt Clinton and other wise men of New York realized that new forces were awaiting release, that the interior trade was hereafter going to be one of the most important of all transportation activities. Times were changing. The nation's expansion was now the marvel of the age. The frontier was rolling westward, brushing the Indians aside, to and beyond the Mississippi River. Our flatboatmen by thousands were floating down the Mississippi and all its tributaries to New Orleans, and steamboats had appeared upon those waters. Our trappers were in the Rocky Mountains, yes, even to the mouth of the Columbia; for we had bought at a bargain price from a trumpery French Emperor a vast, ill-defined area of land extending to the shores of the Pacific.

George Washington—whose stature, despite the popgun attacks of petty publicists, increases as we recede from him in time—had realized the necessity of transport connection with the West and had invested in and encouraged two canal projects to connect the Potomac and the James with the Ohio. He also foresaw the usefulness of the Erie Canal, a project which

Jefferson at the time denounced as impossible. But other eminent minds, foremost among them that of De Witt Clinton, continued to agitate the subject of western waterways, and at last, in 1817, largely as a result of Clinton's tireless promotion, the State of New York began building the Erie Canal, to connect her Hudson River and, through it, her metropolis, with the Great Lakes and the West.

Even as the big ditch crept slowly across the state during the next few years, the development of the country along its route was so remarkable that envy gnawed the souls of all other northeastern commonwealths. Just after the Erie was completed, it was reported in Boston that Lyons, New York, which five years before had consisted of only two houses, now had a courthouse, three meeting houses, six inns, ten stores and about a thousand inhabitants.

After eight years of toil and bickering, the canal was an accomplished fact; and starting at Buffalo on October 26, 1825, a celebration was staged surpassing anything hitherto seen in America. Clinton, then governor, and other dignitaries, in a convoy of "elegant" canal boats, passed theatrically through the waterway with rhetoric and ecstatic uproar at every town and hamlet—eastward to Albany, thence down the Hudson to New York City, where the climax of ceremonial fanfare and enthusiasm was reached. Long and largiloquent speeches competed with the booming of cannon, the blare of bands, the sputter of fireworks, the guzzling of banquets, the parades so dear to every American heart, and other ceremonies which seem faintly absurd to us now and appeared even more so at the time to other less fortunate cities on the seaboard. Thinly veiled sarcasm was heard from Philadelphia and New England over the delirium and the "Roman pomp and parade" of the occasion.

But there was envy back of these sneers, as so often happens. New England, and especially Boston, had now begun to wrestle with some unpleasant facts. The six northeastern states, the cradle of liberty, once so important a part of the nation, now realized that they were a small geographical unit, frustrated by nature, separated from the rest of the country by a mountain wall—a minor barrier today but a major one then—and being left behind as the other eastern states turned their faces westward, preparing to do business with the new hinterland. North and south along the western boundary of Massachusetts and Connecticut rambled that long range of low mountains known variously as the Berkshire Hills, the Taconic, the Hoosac, and as it heaved higher and farther northward, the Green Mountains. It is no serious impediment to the modern engineer, but in 1825 it was terrific. A few rough, tortuous roads crawled through it; there was no east-west waterway save Long Island Sound along the southern coast. And New England's only real road connection with the rest of the nation—though even that was nothing to boast of—was the old Post Road from Boston to New York, hugging the shores of the Sound as it approached Gotham, wriggling around or ferrying across the numerous inlets and estuaries.

You could travel by stagecoach from Boston to Albany in two days—two very full days, that is. You were dragged out of bed and left Boston at two o'clock in the morning, reaching Northampton, on the Connecticut River, at six o'clock on the evening of the same day, though it must have seemed more like a week. Then, after a none-too-long night's sleep at a tavern—and heaven knows, you needed it!—you took another coach early next morning, though not quite so early, and joggled through the hills to Albany in rather less time than the day before. Returning, you had to leave Northampton at the same unholy hour of two. There was another route via Athol and Greenfield which took longer.

Now New York had dug a canal which immediately became a rival of the Mississippi River system as the nation's most important traffic artery, and Pennsylvania, alarmed by the prospect, was discussing the project of building a great state canal system which would tap all her coal regions and connect Philadelphia with the Ohio River and Lake Erie. Two New England canal projects had just been begun: the Blackstone, to connect Worcester with Providence, and the Hampshire-Hampden-Farmington, running from Northampton to New Haven—a New Haven scheme, artfully by-passing Hartford. But a few wise heads saw at a glance that these would be a detriment to New England in general, drain-ing business away to Rhode Island and Connecticut, and thence to New York.

Northern Vermont tended to trade with Canada, though, since the completion of the Erie Canal, many Vermonters laid their commercial courses southward and westward through Lake Champlain, the Champlain Canal and the Erie. There were little grouches, grudges and jealousies between states. Vermont and New Hampshire weren't any too fond of each other or of proud Massachusetts, which, in turn, hadn't quite forgotten the loss of a strip of boundary land to New Hampshire through the arbitration of a British king. Maine had been freed from Massachusetts and set up as a state on her own as recently as 1820, and was beginning to feel her oats. She, too, was inclined to seek commercial relations with Can-ada. Her young metropolis, Portland, was already becoming a bit jealous of Boston. That little porcupine, Rhode Island, probably with an inferiority complex because of its size, didn't get along well with anybody.

Not only were other states forging ahead of New England commercially, but her own children were leaving her in con-siderable numbers. One to two centuries of cultivation of hillside farms had brought to the surface more stones than were dreamed of at the start, and many gaunt agriculturists had tired of building walls of them or just piling them in heaps and plowing around them. And then there were the small merchants, the young doctors, lawyers, clerks, even preachers, who saw visions of vastly greater opportunity in the new, rich, level, booming country beyond the sunset and a fine avenue leading to it in the new Erie Canal. So west-ward by horseback or in covered wagons along the serpentine roads through the hills, or in boats up Lake Champlain and the branch canal to Troy they came, to embark on the Grand Canal, along with thousands of citizens of New York State in the next two or three decades, and set the whole upper Middle West—northern Ohio, Indiana, Illinois, southern Wisconsin and nearly all of Michigan—a-twang with Yankee nasal speech. Indeed, Michigan, one of the major goals of the northeastern emigrant, might almost be called the child of New England. Of her first fourteen governors, six came from New York and six from New England; while her religion, her local government and mores bear traces of New England ancestry to this day. In the 1830's they were singing a ballad as they floated westward, one stanza of which ran:

Then there's old Varmount, well, what d'ye think of that?
To be sure, the gals are handsome and the cattle very fat.
But who among the mountains 'mid cloud and snow would stay,
When he can buy a prairie in Michigam-i-ay?
          Yea, yea, yea, in Michigam-i-ay!

The *Boston Advertiser* declared in 1829 that in a decade it was estimated 100,000 persons had emigrated from Massachusetts alone—a figure which appears exaggerated. This westward migration was but a normal American phenomenon, affecting other eastern states as well as those of New England and causing no great depopulation of Yankeedom; but to pessimists like Shadrack it appeared as a handwriting on the wall, a fit accompaniment to other ill omens and cataclysms, such as the ruin of the Federalist Party, plus the simultaneous rise in the West and South of roughneck, backwoods Republicanism (later called Democracy, but in New England often contemptuously referred to as Jacksonism), and the great religious upheaval which had been going on in New England for some years past. That area was the last remaining stronghold of the Federalists, though Jacksonians were increasing in number there. That New England was not entirely hidebound, a thrall of tradition, is proved by such facts as her early abolition of slavery and her giving birth to a new religion, of which William Ellery Channing was the chief apostle. Scores of Congregational and Episcopal churches, not to mention many individual members of these and other denominations, had broken with the old orthodoxy and gone over to the new cult of Unitarianism, repudiating the Trinity and the vicarious atonement, denying the divinity of Jesus, original sin and everlasting punishment.

Despite the gibes at them, New Englanders were in some important respects liberal. Sir Charles Lyell, traveling there, was amazed to find that "so large a population united great earnestness of religious feeling with so much real toleration." He thought the excellent public school system must be largely responsible. Friends told him that about one-fifth of all New Englanders were Nothingarians: latitudinarian, used in the best sense, appeared to be the meaning of the word, "for a Nothingarian, I was informed, was indifferent whether he attended a Baptist, Methodist, Presbyterian or Congregational Church, and was often equally inclined to contribute money liberally to any or all of them."

Culturally, New England was approaching that flowering of which Van Wyck Brooks has written so winsomely, though Shadrack and his ilk feared that, economically, it was in its Indian summer. Ralph Waldo Emerson, in the middle 1820's, was a young clergyman, just beginning his ministry. Bronson Alcott was teaching school in Boston, and young fellows named Hawthorne, Whittier, Longfellow, Bancroft and Prescott were trying their 'prentice pens. Over in the lovely village of Litchfield, Connecticut, a girl in her middle teens, daughter of a bluff, fiery Presbyterian parson named Beecher, was learning the demure art of being a lady, never dreaming that she was destined to write America's most famous novel or that her younger brother Henry would some day be the nation's most noted and then its most notorious clergyman. That sterling son of Massachusetts, John Quincy Adams, elected on the first national fusion ticket, had just taken his seat in the White House. Dynamic Josiah Quincy—otherwhiles Congressman, prolific author and President of Harvard —was Mayor of Boston and was literally making the fur fly: razing noisome tenements, giving the city streets their first real cleaning in two centuries, filling tidal marshes and otherwise amply justifying his incumbency and his existence.

New England was building a literary hierarchy and tradition which would hold sway for generations. Public education was the best in the country, and there seemed to be a desire for self-education and reading which did not obtain elsewhere then, and is rarely seen anywhere now: the sort of thing which enabled an overalled farmer, giving a pail of water to Charles Eliot Norton's buggy horse half a century later, to correct that great scholar when he attributed a quotation to Montaigne, snapping unexpectedly, " 'Tweren't Montaigne said that; 'twere Montes-ki-ew." And Norton admitted that he was right. The mill girls of Lowell wrote worthy poetry and affixed it to the walls of their factory buildings, and European travelers, Dickens among the rest, went to gaze at them in wonder. At a hotel in Franconia Notch, two "ladies" were pointed out to Lyell as chambermaids at a hotel in Maine. A friend engaged them in conversation and proved to Sir Charles that "they had been well taught at school, had read good books and could enjoy a tour and admire scenery as well as ourselves." At another inn en route, where a great many mechanics took their noon meal, Lyell observed that after dinner they sat a while in the parlor, reading newspapers and books before going back to their work. "On looking at the books they laid down," says he, "I found that one was D'Israeli's Coningsby, another Burns' Poems and a third an article just reprinted from Frazer's Magazine on 'The Policy of Sir Robert Peel.' . . . There is a general feeling of selfrespect in the New-England States," adds Lyell in another place, "which enables those who rise in the world, whether in political life or by suddenly making large fortunes in trade, if they have true gentility of feeling, to take their places in good society easily and naturally."

Slavery had long since been eliminated in New England, and abolitionism was a growing cult. There was still no little of the Puritan inhering in the old stock, though it often spent its bias on small matters, and its consciences were sometimes flexible, as consciences always have been and are yet everywhere—in fact, the conscience has become a minor factor in the modern unmoral world. In the seventeenth century, Boston had wondered whether tea might not be a menace to morals, but consumed quantities of West India rum. The deacon whose ships did not disdain a shipment of opium could sing and pray in church on a Sabbath morning without unease. Connecticut in 1825 was still producing, and her Sam Slicks were peddling, clocks with wooden works which didn't always work.[1]

In 1824 a man was arrested and fined two dollars for smoking a "segar" on the street in Boston; but drunkenness, though now declining, was still a curse, as it was the country over—mostly rum in New England, whisky in the South. Thomas Jefferson said that of all agencies within his knowledge, liquor had been the greatest detriment to the public's business in America. But drunkenness in New England was now declining noticeably: the Temperance movement was having its effect, promoted ardently by dry periodicals such as the *Taunton Dew Drop*, which in 1848 was merged with the similarly teetotal *Massachusetts Cataract*, thereafter to function at Worcester under the appallingly concatenated name of *Massachusetts Cataract, Worcester County Waterfall, Temperance Standard and Dew Drop.*

The old piety still obtained. Here and there in libraries you may still find today a sheet of fine white paper about eighteen by twenty-four inches in size, containing a New England governor's spring Fast Day proclamation, sometimes set for Good Friday, though others considered that date too popish. It was a day for "reviewing their past lives, repenting of their transgressions . . . and to beseech the Almighty of His infinite love to enable them to forsake their sins and walk in the

---

[1] The following appeared in an Easton (Pa.) newspaper in 1831:

NOTICE

Whereas, Henry Lewis, a Yankee Wooden Clock Pedler, some time in December, 1831, sold to the subscribers a number of Wooden Clocks which he guaranteed as patent and to keep good time—and took in payment therefor our notes of hand which will become due about the latter part of the present month. Now this is to give notice to all persons not to buy said notes, as we are determined not to pay them unless compelled by law—the said Clocks not performing in the manner warranted.

Robert Newel<br>Abraham Levering<br>John Merwine<br>Sarah Sox

Mount Pocono, Dec. 15th, 1831.

paths of wisdom." It was distinctly a day for "Humility,
Prayer and Fasting. . . . All servile labour and vain recreation
on the said day are by law forbidden." [2]

New England still preserved much of its early quaintness.
An obituary in a Boston newspaper in 1824 read, "In Tor-
ringford, after undergoing the distresses of twenty thousand
fits, Jannet M. Tolles, aged 9 years." That ancient functionary, the weathercock tender, still performed his no doubt
arduous duties in some rural districts, for we read that Jim
Bagley was removed from such a job in a New Hampshire
town in 1829. The local government so favored, and rightly,
by Thomas Jefferson still inhered in New England: the town
meeting was still the most vital legislative body and the town
*see*-lectmen the most important statesmen. Some of that in-
dividualism and love of home rule still burns in many New
England hearts and hamlets, and here is at least one writer,
not a Yankee, who honors them for it and wishes we had
more of the like elsewhere in the nation.

[2] Proclamation of Governor of Connecticut, 1832.

# The First Railroad

SUCH was the New England and, more particularly, the Boston, which was taking stock of its economic situation in 1825. There was a plenty of evidence to the effect that it needed bettering. In 1824, when plans were being studied for improving the navigation of the Connecticut River—which cuts across Massachusetts from north to south, considerably west of the center of the state—the *Vermont Republican* said the movement "originated with the mercantile interests of the City of Hartford, and will no doubt be seconded by the same interests in New-York." There was, continued the editor, "a strong combination of interests in its favor." (Vermont, of course, was for it.) In addition to New York and Hartford, the canal companies and "the Banking interest on the river" would probably pull for it. "It will give an extensive circulation to their bills. At present, they cannot loan to merchants who trade to Boston, in consequence of the measures taken by the merchants of that place, through the agency of their Banks; and of necessity they can loan only to those who trade at New-York. The same reason will have a direct tendency to divert the trade." Vermont's natural tendency, he said, would be to trade with Boston, "yet interest must and will govern." In other words, Boston and the Connecticut Valley, as represented by their bankers and merchants, were in effect boycotting each other—engaging in the Spartan diversion anciently known as cutting off the nose to spite the face.

A Portsmouth, New Hampshire, editor reported, after the

New York canals were opened, that "a gentleman of Caledonia, Vt.," had said that he could send the produce of his farm to New York, 350 miles away, cheaper than he could to either Boston or Portsmouth, though they were only 170 and 150 miles distant, respectively. He was 80 miles from Burlington, on Lake Champlain, and it cost him $16 a ton to have his produce hauled there. Thence it was carried 270 miles by water—through Lake Champlain, the Champlain Canal and the Hudson River—to New York City for only $5 a ton, a total of $21; whereas, to carry his goods overland to Boston or Portsmouth cost $20 per ton for every hundred miles— that is, $34 to Boston and $30 to Portsmouth. Was it any wonder that he traded with New York?

Boston journalists also called attention to the fact that one must pay eight dollars a ton to send goods by water or wagon between Boston *or* Providence and western Massachusetts— "water" meaning around Cape Cod by sea and up the Connecticut River; which competition kept the wagon rates down.

Necessity is the mother, not so often of invention as of enterprise. Boston's realization that she was in a parlous state commercially drove her to being the pioneer city of America in the promotion and building of railroads in a large way. But first she had to go through a more or less unwilling and painful course of education, covering several years, starting with the firmly established thesis that canals were the only solution, and gradually working around, with more or less acrimony between teachers and pupils, to an understanding of the inevitability of railroads and the proper manner of promoting them. The important thing to observe is that New England, or shall we say Massachusetts, did not go off the deep end and build a system of canals such as almost ruined Pennsylvania and made her bonds a byword and a hissing in the money marts of Europe. Thackeray, in one of his funniest contributions to *Punch* (August 15, 1846), burlesquing the joyous hullaballoo in Constantinople when Mehemet Ali, Viceroy of Egypt, visited the Sultan of Turkey, pictures the parades, the fireworks, the officials throwing coin into the crowds, while "the American Minister flung about showers of Illinois and Pennsylvanian bonds; [1] which, however, were received with utter disregard by the Turks—for the most part unable to read and ignorant of their value"—a final satirical fillip which was like a scorpion's sting under the epidermis of the citizens of those two commonwealths.

The Erie Canal was the admiration of New England and completely dazzled the eyes of many leaders of thought in Boston; a city now—according to the private census of Mayor Quincy in 1825—of 58,000 population, street-lighted by gas, as were some other large cities in New England, but—save for a thin trickle to one quarter of it through wooden pipes from a near-by pond—with no public water supply, practically all its citizens drinking from wells and cisterns. In January, 1825, ten months before the Erie was completed, the Massachusetts Legislature, at its winter session, had appointed a committee to study the idea of building a canal from Boston to the Connecticut River. Governor Levi Lincoln recalled that this was not the first time such a project had been considered. Big, fat General Henry Knox, who had left his bookshop to become a useful soldier in the Revolution, had conceived the idea as far back as 1791, and in the following year had obtained a charter for himself and associates under the name of "The Proprietors of the Massachusetts Canal." But as Governor Lincoln put it, in his multiloquent way, "It is not understood that any other obstacle presented itself to the accomplishment of the object at that time than the absorption of the money of the country by concerns of more pressing occasion"—which was just the governor's elegant manner of saying that the country was miserably poor in those days, and General Knox couldn't raise the wind.

In his message to the summer session on June 2, 1825, the Governor, with characteristic delicacy, alluded to New York and its canal:

The spirit of enterprize which has already accomplished great and valuable results in other parts of the Union, and

[1] The former issued to build state railroads, the latter to build state canals.

more especially in a neighboring State, has also animated the people of Massachusetts to the unequivocal manifestation of a desire that some public effort should be made to secure a participation in the benefits which are to be derived from *internal improvements*, and the facilities to communication and the transportation of produce and of articles of trade and consumption to the places respectively of demand and of market.

That was a verbose age, especially on the part of politicians, editors and authors, and Governor Lincoln, who gave no man odds in the matter of verbosity, admitted when recommending a canal across the state that in the case of the Middlesex Canal, "the pecuniary investment has been unproductive of personal advantage," though he maintained that the public had received "rich returns for the sacrifices occasioned by its execution to its spirited and persevering proprietors."

On the seventeenth of that same month of June, an event took place which has an important bearing on our story. This was the laying of the cornerstone of that plain, sturdy obelisk which still stands, commemorating the Battle of Bunker Hill. It was done with elaborate ceremony, the elderly Marie Joseph Paul Yves Roch Gilbert Motier, Marquis de Lafayette, now bulky and stiff with age, depositing a trowelful of mortar on the foundation with his gouty fingers, and Daniel Webster rumbling through one of his big, thunderous orations. Another, more humble and almost unnoticed, yet important personage present was one Gridley Bryant, who officiated as Master Builder. Born in Scituate, Mass., Bryant was now thirty-six, a building contractor by trade but also a self-educated—"jackleg," as the old idiom had it—engineer. He had the contract to supply the stone for the monument, and he had bought a ledge at Quincy from which to get it. The quarry was more than three miles from the seashore, and it was by water that he planned to carry his stone up to Charlestown, the site of the famous hill; yes, and to Boston, too, where it later went into many buildings. Hauling to the waterfront by wagon seemed too arduous and costly a process. He had read of George Stephenson's first railroad experiments in England—horse railroads, that is—and decided to turn the idea to account in his own case.

And here we are confronted with the usual touchy problem. To put one's finger on a certain spot and say, "Here was the first railroad in America," is risking future embarrassment. But the first use of rails that we can discover took place nowhere else than in Boston, and before 1800. The west slope of Beacon Hill, from Beacon Street to what is now Pinckney Street, was once a meadow belonging to John Singleton Copley, the artist. Copley, then living in England, sold it in 1796 to a syndicate of four men who proceeded to cut it into new streets and lots and promote that beautiful quarter of the so-called Brahmins, whose buildings stand almost unchanged today. They sliced six feet off the highest peak of the hill, just back of the State House, and hauled the earth down the slope on a little gravity tramway, to fill the tidal marshes at the bottom, through which Charles and other streets now run.[2]

J. A. Ringwalt, in his *Development of Transportation Systems in the United States*, is one of those who claim that there was another tramway built on Beacon Hill in 1807, and list four constructed before Bryant's at Quincy. There was one running to a landing place on Crum Creek, in Delaware County, Pa., built in 1809 and 1810, and another, about a mile long, built almost simultaneously, to serve a powder mill near Richmond, Va.—which eventually blew up, as powder mills usually did in those days. A fourth, with wooden rails, was constructed at a furnace in Armstrong County, Pennsylvania, in 1818, and a fifth "probably," says Ringwalt, at Nashua, N. H., in 1825.

Did that little Nashua tramway stir some vague beginning of an idea in the New Hampshire consciousness? We do not know, but it is curious that the first suggestion I have discovered of railroads as a possible solution of New England's commercial problem is found, not in up-and-coming Massa-

[2] This is usually and erroneously spoken of as a tramway for hauling brick. The facts here cited are taken from an article in the *Boston Gazette* for January 6, 1889, supplied to the writer by Warren Jacobs.

chusetts, but in New Hampshire, which later proved to be most backward of all in giving railroads a chance for existence. A pamphlet published in Boston reveals that in April, 1825, some "highly respectable gentlemen who dwell in the interior of New Hampshire" (apparently it always had to be emphasized that a movement or a project was respectable) went down to Boston to confer with such persons as they could muster who might be interested in the promotion of a canal across New Hampshire, uniting the Connecticut River with the Merrimac and the ocean; a project well calculated to appeal to Boston, as it would draw the commerce of the upper Connecticut Valley in her direction.

That meeting was encouraging, and as a result, in May there was a "numerous and respectable meeting at Concord" (N. H.) with several Bostonians, all no doubt very respectable, in attendance. The delegates viewed with concern the facts that a considerable portion of Vermont's and western New Hampshire's trade went down the Connecticut to Hartford and New York, and that New York was conniving at having the obstructions cleared from the Connecticut, with a view to annexing all the trade of that river's valley. As for New Hampshire, the delegates thought it was now time for the state to pull itself together and join the march of progress.

The meeting admitted that doubts were being expressed by some as to the feasibility of a canal's climbing the watershed between the Merrimac and the Connecticut, and suggested waveringly and without much apparent confidence in the idea, that "the invention of RAIL-WAYS may come in aid, and surmount difficulties which occur in the *water-way*." But it was evident that canals were their chief hope, though railroads were mentioned twice more in the document: "From some experiments which have been made, and which may be relied on, carrying on a canal or rail-way, must be at least *one-third* less, than the cost of carrying on wheels, in New-England"; and New Hampshire, they concluded, could not realize her destiny as a manufacturing state, "unless the WATER-WAY or the RAIL-WAY can be established." Nothing came of this convention, and oddly enough, eighteen years later, New

Hampshire was still arguing with herself about railroads and had so far blocked their progress that the state had almost no rail mileage.

A few days after the Concord meeting, Governor Lincoln, in his June message to the Massachusetts Legislature, gave considerable wordage to advocacy of the building of the canal which, by order of the previous legislative session, was then being surveyed westward across the state. He conceded that another means of communication had been suggested, namely, railways. In England, he continued, they had been "approved in practice," but he wondered whether "the severe frosts of our climate, by increasing their expense or endangering their security," would not be a drawback. However, the Governor, though a canal supporter, was fair in conceding that railroads should be given study.

A few others were beginning to notice the subject, as is proved by occasional bits in the newspapers. The *Boston Patriot* on November 30, 1825, carried an item clipped from some other source which read, "The inquiry is often made as to the manner in which the summits of our hills can be surmounted by carriages on railroads. It is suggested in answer to this inquiry, that stationary steam engines may be placed on their summit levels, to assist the locomotive engine in passing over such hills."

The idea had at last begun to penetrate American brains. Oliver Evans of Philadelphia had in 1786 invented a steam carriage for roads, and followed it in 1804 by a little steamboat which, after demonstrating it on the water, he put on wheels and ran through the streets of Philadelphia. But he could get no backing, in the way of either cash or franchise, moneyed men as well as legislators thinking him a crank. In 1812 he offered to build a steam carriage that would run fifteen miles an hour on rails, which made him seem crazier still. Perhaps he had heard that over in England Richard Trevithick had invented a locomotive in 1804, and that rails three or four feet long had been made and used on a road in Leicestershire as far back as 1767.

Evans died unrecognized, but while he was still battling

against hidebound ignorance, another pioneer arose, Colonel John Stevens of Hoboken, N. J., pre-Fulton promoter of steamboats. He began about 1810 to urge the construction of railways and in 1811 applied to the Legislature of New Jersey for America's first railway charter, which was finally granted after four years of delay; and then he could get no support for it. He was always for steam engines, never for horses. He appealed to Congress for aid, but the lawmakers, frequently referred to by journalists as solons, thought the subject unimportant.

Unlucky John Fitch, too, had tinkered with the railroad idea, as well as making a practical steamboat that nobody would believe in. In 1819 Benjamin Dearborn of Boston tried vainly to interest Congress in the subject of "carriages propelled by steam on level railroads," and mentioned a possible speed of a mile in three minutes, which of course ruined any chance he might have had of obtaining recognition. Finally, Stevens built in his dooryard at Hoboken a little locomotive and track that actually worked, to the amazement of all beholders, and aided him in obtaining a charter from the Pennsylvania Legislature in 1823 to build a railroad from Philadelphia to the Susquehanna River, which eventually became a link in the state canal system.

Meanwhile, over in England in 1814, George Stephenson had built his first locomotive for use at a coal mine, and in 1825 he was called upon to give Parliament his opinion as to the possible velocity of such machines. When he ventured to predict twelve miles an hour, members smiled at each other and denied the pending petition for a railway charter between Liverpool and Manchester. Two books on railroads, by Tredgold and Wood, had just appeared, each author having the assurance to call his work a Practical Treatise; and these probably influenced Parliamentary thinking. Tredgold wrote: "Locomotives must always be objectionable on a railroad for general use, where it is attempted to give them a considerable degree of speed." That passengers would ever ride faster than ten miles an hour or thereabouts he thought "extremely improbable."

Wood refused to sanction "the ridiculous expectations, or rather professions, of the enthusiastic speculator," who predicted "twelve, sixteen, eighteen or twenty miles an hour. Nothing could do more harm towards their general adoption and improvement than the promotion of such nonsense." The learned Dionysius Lardner, who was looked up to in Britain as an all-around scientist, declared that if such speeds were attempted, "the wheels would merely spin on their axles, and the carriages would stand stock still." English periodicals joined in the chorus of ridicule.

The State of Pennsylvania in that year and the next was in a state of agonized befuddlement. It was committed to the building of a vast system of canals, but the granting of Stevens' Philadelphia-Columbia railroad charter had become as a fly in the pudding. Voices began to be heard, saying that canals were already outmoded—that even the Erie would soon be superseded by a railroad. The newly organized Pennsylvania Society for the Promotion of Internal Improvements sent William Strickland to Europe in 1825 to collect information on canals, railways, bridges, steam engines and other new devices, especially railways, because "of the mode of constructing them and of their cost, nothing is known [here] with certainty." He must find out everything about them, especially as to the "locomotive machinery," which *"is entirely unknown in the United States."*

Up in Massachusetts, from spring to autumn of 1825, the survey of the Boston-Albany canal was going on under the direction of Colonel Loammi Baldwin, a Massachusetts man and Harvard graduate, lawyer and self-taught engineer, whom some have called the Father of Civil Engineering in America. Yet there was one man in the state who wasn't interested in canals. Gridley Bryant, master builder and quarryman, didn't have to go to Europe to discover what he wanted—a railroad from his quarry to the water front. But he had used his cash and credit in buying the quarry, and he needed more means to build the railroad. In this emergency he called upon some moneyed acquaintances, chief among them being Colonel Thomas Handasyde Perkins, and they agreed to risk the cash, which Bryant thought would be at least $35,000 and which eventually proved to be nearer $50,000. "These gentlemen," wrote Bryant in later years, "thought the project visionary and chimerical, but being anxious to aid the Bunker Hill monument, consented that I might see what could be done." But in the end, "only by the munificence and public spirit of Col. Perkins" was the road built, for the other four men who had promised to go in on the project "never paid any assessments, and the whole stock finally fell into Col. Perkins's hands."

A corporation was necessary, of course, in order to procure a right of way. Massachusetts law had long since given turnpike corporations the privilege of condemning a strip of land for their roads through anyone's property, paying a fair price for the same, as determined by agreement, by arbitration or in extreme cases by litigation. So application was made to the General Court, as the State Legislature was still being called, for a charter.

The winter session of that body opened on January 4, 1826, with Governor Lincoln in his Message again reminding the lawmakers of the canal project. He declared that the Erie Canal was already drawing business away from the western part of the state, carrying "westward the traffic of the green hills of Berkshire and the rich valley of the Housatonic." He pointed out that the Hampshire-Hampden and Blackstone Canal projects, then just getting under way, would only open new and easy communication to ports of adjoining states, and thus do Massachusetts harm rather than good.

Shortly after the session opened, it heard the report of the Commissioners appointed by the previous winter's session to study the project of a canal from Boston to the Hudson. Colonel Baldwin had chosen a route which reached the Connecticut River at the mouth of the Deerfield, a tributary coming down from the northwest, and followed up the valley of that stream, veering toward the Vermont line as it reached the Hoosac Mountain barrier. There, where the ridge must be crossed or penetrated to connect with the westward-tending valley of the Hoosac River, the Colonel encountered his worst problem. If the canal was to climb over the mountain, he found that it would require the appalling number of 220 locks in 18 miles of channel, taking two days for a boat to pass through and costing some $2,090,000.

As an alternative he suggested a tunnel, which a canal boat might traverse in an hour and twenty minutes, "provided it is furnished with a towing path, which should be the case." The cost of this bore, said Baldwin, "it is difficult to ascertain with much exactness, although great exertions have been made to collect information on the subject." His estimates varied from a minimum of $370,000 to the highest he could imagine as possible, $920,832, which he thought the outside one "beyond a doubt." Charles Francis Adams, II,[3] considers Colonel Baldwin's report "one of the curiosities of engineering literature." He thinks it doubtful that with nothing for tools but hand drills and gunpowder, the mountain could have been tunneled at any cost. David Henshaw, a prominent Democratic politician, argued in the columns of the *Boston Courier* that on one basis of estimate the time required to complete the work would be 52 years, on another, 182 years. "The last estimate," commented Adams dryly, "would probably, under the circumstances of the time, have proved the more nearly accurate of the two had the work been attempted, which, fortunately, it was not." It may be interesting to pause here and remark that when the Hoosac Tunnel was bored for a railroad many years later, precisely where Baldwin had envisioned his canal tunnel but with far better equipment than they had in 1825, its cost was somewhere near $20,000,000!

Baldwin estimated the entire cost of the canal from Boston to the Hudson, including the tunnel, at $6,023,172—a figure which so frightened the commissioners that they recommended the construction of the canal only as far as the Connecticut, which the engineer thought could be done for $3,000,000. The Legislature could not look even that sum in the face, and so tabled the report—forever, as it was eventually

[3] In his fine chapter on railroads in Justin Winsor's *Memorial History of Boston*.

proved. Governor Lincoln's adjuration to "do now what the present or future age will certainly execute" fell on deaf ears.

The canal project, however, had friends who continued to be vocal and rhetorical. A letter-writer to the *Boston Patriot* said on January 4 that Governor Clinton favored the canal, "because he looks not with a narrow view at the metropolis of his own State, but with a noble and liberal mind, consults the good of the whole nation.". . . "An intelligent gentleman of Vermont," said the *Patriot*, urged that the canal approach the Vermont line and strike the Connecticut at the mouth of Miller's River, thus avoiding the payment by boats from above of the high lock tolls on the Miller's Falls Canal and below, and effectually diverting the traffic toward Boston. "The weak and timid, the miserably selfish and contracted," remarked this gentleman bitingly, "will gaze at the magnitude of the undertaking and turn away sick"; the courageous and inevitably successful would go on. But a mass meeting of Berkshire County citizens at Becket in May voted for a canal crossing the Connecticut far below Miller's River and traversing the southeastern part of the county to reach the Hudson.

Perhaps none of these people had ever heard of Gridley Bryant or Colonel Tom Perkins; perhaps none heard of the petition which was unostentatiously introduced in their behalf, asking for a charter for a little railroad down in Norfolk County. But that petition was fundamentally more important than all their canal schemes and was destined to start a revolution in all New England's thinking about transportation.

Colonel Perkins had to do some intensive lobbying to overcome what Bryant later described as "every delay and obstruction that could be thrown in the way." There was strong opposition to their enterprise, especially from country members in the House. "What do we know about rail roads?" they demanded. "Who ever heard of such a thing? Is it right to take people's land for a project that no one knows anything about? We have corporations enough already." But finally a bare majority was mustered, and the Granite Railway Company was granted its charter in March, not long before the session adjourned. There were certain restrictions. Many of the legislators detected a strong odor of monopoly about the proposition. They thought a corporation which was given the right to take citizens' land for a right of way should be compelled to give service to the public, instead of hauling nothing but its own products. So they inserted a provision to the effect that "any person shall be entitled to have stone carried on the said cars and vehicles at pleasure, on payment of toll as aforesaid." That sentence was cited in later years, as we shall show, in support of the contention that a railroad track was not private but a public highway, upon which anyone had a right to operate his own vehicles, just as on a turnpike.

Bryant lost no time. He surveyed several routes for his line, decided upon one and began work in April; that was 1826. The course lay through the towns of Milton and Quincy; and here it might be apropos to explain—having in mind the bare possibility that some non–New Englanders may read this book—that a town in Yankeedom may cover, let us say, as much territory as a township in the Middle West, and may embrace several villages and/or a city. It is, however, a quite different organization from the Middle Western township, which has no political power whatsoever; the New England town is an important governing unit, really more important than the county. All this is preliminary to recording that progressive Milton, in town meeting held April 3, 1826, voted "unanimous and cordial consent" to the Granite Railway to build through the town, "so long as said corporation indemnifies and protects the town against charge, prosecution or damages caused by said railway's crossing the public highways. . . . And said Town offers the corporation its best wishes for the success of the enterprise."

Although Bryant had followed the reports of Stephenson's work attentively and knew that the English engineer was developing a steam engine, he did not venture to try steam on the Granite Railway. To begin with, the locomotives were too expensive, so he chose horsepower. Had he made the more ambitious venture of steam, says Adams, he might have ruined his enterprise and given the whole railroad idea in Massachusetts a severe backset. Down in Maryland, where the Baltimore and Ohio Railroad was being organized, its backers had the full intention of using horsepower; steam was as yet a bit too adventurous for the American mind.

As for Bryant's track: "The foundation," we are told, "was formed by digging a trench two feet wide and about the same depth, which was filled with stone, compactly laid, without mortar." The foundation was made so deep to avert the danger of the buckling of the track by frost, which was so much feared in New England, and in this it was successful. Across the two trenches filled as above described, granite sleepers or cross-ties, ten by twelve inches in thickness and seven and one-half feet long, were laid about eight feet apart. On these, pine "rails," six inches thick and twelve inches high, were laid, being fastened to the stone ties by iron stays sunk three inches into the granite. On top of the pine timber was a strip of oak, three inches wide and two inches thick, and this was protected by a strap-iron plate a quarter-inch thick and covering the oak rail's full width of three inches. The horse path was not quite filled from rail to rail, in order to keep the wood from contact with the earth and so avoid decay. The path did not need to be wide, anyhow, as only one horse was used to a "train." The laborers who built the road, by the way, received twelve dollars a month and board—fairly good pay for those days.

As Bryant toiled away at his railroad that summer, the majority of the inhabitants of Boston appeared to have heard little or nothing about it. The major question agitating the public mind at the moment was the projected building of bridges to Cambridge or Charlestown and South Boston, and whether they should be free or toll bridges. On this subject weighty editorials, letters sometimes one or two columns long from "Civis," "Veritas," "Common Sense" and other well-known scribes, filled the papers. But many legislators and other public men were aware of the new project, and a railroad party was gradually forming in the Legislature, showing its teeth at the Boston-Albany canal project.

The canal advocates, however, were still numerous and well entrenched. Look at the rest of the country, they advised: Pennsylvania and Ohio were starting to build their own canal systems; private enterprise at that very moment had such great undertakings as the Delaware & Hudson, the Morris, the Union, the Chesapeake & Ohio, the Lehigh and the Chesapeake & Delaware Canals well under way; the Schuylkill was already completed. Would these astute men waste their money in something so soon to be superseded, as their opponents claimed, by a gimcrack thing which was more in the nature of a toy?

There were two men, however, who led the railroad party most ably, and were in fact chiefly responsible for it. One was Dr. Abner Phelps, a member of the Legislature; the other, Nathan Hale, an editor. Hale, destined soon to become the leading champion and apostle of railroads in New England, was a nephew of the young hero who gave the only life he had for his country. This younger Nathan taught mathematics for a few years in his twenties at Phillips Exeter Academy, then studied and practiced law in Boston for a while. In 1814, when he was thirty, he bought the *Boston Advertiser*, the first newspaper to be established in the city, and owned and edited it for forty years. It became in the best sense the leading railroad organ of New England.

But there were other journalistic boosters, too. The rising tide of interest in railroads is clearly shown in the more frequent and more extensive references to them in the newspapers. In March, just before Bryant obtained his charter, the *American Traveller* of Boston announced, "that we may not be behind our neighbors in the good work of communicating information," it had "incurred considerable expense to procure an engraving of an English Rail road, together with the mode of transportation thereon by steam carriages." This, a picture of an engine and train on the Hetton Railway in England, it presented, together with a description, in its issue of March 7, devoting a whole page to the feature—a remarkable bit of journalistic enterprise in those days when newspapers were only four-page affairs. This paper had to relinquish more than a third of a day's advertising revenue in order to accomplish it.

The type matter was mostly taken from the work of Thomas Tredgold, the English "authority" on railroads. Among other things, Tredgold said that he could not recommend a greater speed than six miles an hour, "for at higher velocities, the risk of accidents must be very considerable. The engine must be proportioned for a particular velocity, and it does not admit of much variation of speed, either greater or less, without a loss of effect."

As to passenger cars:

. . . None such have yet been tried in practice, and some means of softening down the shocks which take place among the carriages at every stoppage or change of velocity must be adopted, before they will be rendered fit for passengers, or, indeed, for some species of merchandise.

He thought springs between the cars might answer this need.

But the editor could not resist quoting De Witt Clinton in opposition. The Governor, having built the now highly prosperous, traffic-thronged Erie Canal, couldn't see much good in railroads. In "throwing out" some "desultory intimations," Mr. Clinton quoted with relish Tredgold's estimate of £5,000 per mile as an average cost of building a railroad—as much as or more than the cost of a canal, and with far less traffic capacity. "As to revenues," the Governor said delicately, "I believe it will not be pretended that it will be as productive by rail roads as by canals." Railroads might cost even more to build in this country than in England: "Our frosts are more severe—our snows are more frequent." Furthermore, a short private road under the control of individual interests, "principally for the conveyance of one article, would be easily managed; but in a great public road, through which immense regions send and receive commodities and merchandize, the greatest confusion and embarrassment must exist."

And now inventors began to pop out of their lairs, devising "improvements" for a species of apparatus which they had never seen and of whose ultimate possibilities and limitations they knew almost nothing. The *New England Farmer* in May of that year told its readers that "we have seen a model of an improvement in Rail Ways, invented by Messrs. John Brown and George W. Robinson of Providence," which promised "great utility":

> It consists in raising and lowering loaded teams by a balance and lever power, similar to a scale beam. The carriages running on these railways will proceed at perfect levels, except at certain places on platforms, in which, by the operation of levers and weights, the carriages, etc., are raised or lowered, as the case may require, from one level to another. This is effected in two minutes by a simple process, requiring less strength than one man can conveniently exert. The horses will travel beneath the carriage, and thus be protected from rain or snow.

How many a poor street-car horse in later years must have wished that somebody had put something of this sort into practice!

The *Palladium* gave further elucidation of the grade-elimination device:

> It is calculated to overcome with rapidity all irregularities in a road, from four feet to any height. The wagons are always to carry the same burden (which can be regulated by weights added to the load when necessary), which the elevators are to be arranged to balance so exactly that less than a pound weight will turn them, when the load and counterpoise are 20 tons. A slight pulling of a string, by the driver, will secure the benefit of an elevator, as often as one is arrived at. The inventors calculate that their carriages for passengers and for burdens will travel at the rate of seven miles an hour, and that goods can be delivered at that rate of speed. The carriages will glide over the Rail-way with such ease that lady passengers may attend to their sewing, if they please, or they and other passengers may read and write, if agreeable.

What a pity that this consummation was not reached! Reading on a train is still hard on the eyes, and penmanship on train-board, even today, is nothing to boast of.

The chief value of these quotations, it would seem, lies not so much in their quaintness, the now ludicrously wild shooting at targets which the experimenters could scarcely see, but in their demonstration of how completely even supposedly well-informed Americans were in the dark as to the nature, the requirements and latencies of railroads, and by contrast, how quickly they learned, when once they had begun to grasp the fundamentals.

When the Legislature convened for its June session, Governor Lincoln in his message gave recognition to the increasingly acute debate between canal and railroad advocates and denied that he had taken any decided stand on the subject. "Canals and railroads," said he, "have each their respective advocates, and the election in most cases, must be decided entirely by a regard to the surface of the earth over which their construction is promised. . . . The more extended and beneficial influences of canals in the general improvement of the country seem to me too important and decisive to be lightly regarded." He was still dubious as to railways, but did not wish to be understood as intending any discouragement to their construction, "wherever the situation and the character of business giving occasion to transportation, may warrant their adoption."

As the session got under way, it appeared that the railroad party had captured control of the House of Representatives; the august Senate remained conservative. A petition was presented by Colonel Perkins and others, urging that surveys for a line be made from Boston to the Hudson and the project be given legislative study. Dr. Phelps, one of the representatives from Boston, moved that a joint committee be appointed, to sit during the recess and "consider the practicability and expediency" of the state's building such a line. The bill was passed, but the Senate refused to concur, and the committee represented the House alone. It consisted of Dr. Abner Phelps, George W. Adams of Boston—a son of John Quincy

Adams—and Emory Washburn of Worcester, later governor. This action was highly significant, as being the first concerted move toward the building of railroads in New England. C. F. Adams believes that the fact that it was now possible was "unquestionably due to Bryant's success in getting a charter for his smaller enterprise, which, having a distinct object in view, both practical and patriotic, had not aroused conservative apprehension."

Toward dusk on July 4, while all New England was burning powder, picnicking and listening to patriotic orations, grand old John Adams, one of the Fathers of the Republic, now in his ninety-first year, closed his eyes in his final sleep at Quincy. A number of members of the Legislature, among them Dr. Phelps, went down to Quincy to attend the national patriarch's funeral. On the way back to Boston, Dr. Phelps, who had become such an enthusiast for railroads that he was regarded in the light of a nuisance even by friends, induced some of the party to turn aside at Milton to visit Bryant's unfinished railroad. Daniel Webster, then a Congressman, was in the group, and Phelps was eager to hear his opinion of this project and of railroads in general. When asked the question, the great orator pursed his lips, while the smoldering dark eyes searched infinity from their cavernous sockets, and finally replied oracularly, "Well, it is certainly a subject for grave consideration whether roads for general travel cannot be made as you propose"—a fine example of the politician's knack of uttering many and ponderous words and saying nothing. But Phelps, who had been suffering a deal of ridicule from others, was so ready to grab at a straw, so hypnotized by the massive orotundity of the sage, that the pronunciamento, as he afterward declared in a letter, gave him "great encouragement and satisfaction."

Webster, by the way, for a long time feared that frost on the rails in winter would prove an insuperable obstacle to the success of railroads.

There are some differences among historians as to the measurements of this railroad. Some early commentators say that it had a six-foot gauge—one which should then and there have been made standard for railroads, but unfortunately was not—while A. K. Teele's *History of Milton* gives it as five feet. Hale described the car or wagon wheels as being six feet in diameter; Teele says they were "nearly or quite eight feet." To make it easier to handle large granite blocks, the load was carried on a platform hung below the axle, near the ground, and the axles were arched to give room for it. The platform lay on the ground between the rails until the blocks of granite were rolled on it with crowbars; then it was lifted into position by chain hoists which were a part of the car.

Bryant, that now forgotten genius, designed not only this car but the railroad and other appliances which prove his remarkable ingenuity, and all afterward came into general use. These included the switch, the turntable, the portable derrick and a movable truck for the eight-wheeled railway car. He seems to have taken no steps to patent any of his devices, but when someone else patented the movable truck in 1834, he sprang to the defense of his own. The litigation lingered in the courts for five years and cost, it is said, rather more than $50,000. Bryant's claim as the inventor was sustained, but curiously enough he could gain no legal right to any royalty on it, nor did he ever receive a cent. Isn't the law quaint?

The first train of cars passed over the road on October 7, 1826—a milestone in the history of New England railroading. Hale did not fail to give the event plenty of space in his *Advertiser*. He said that, in a test, "three cars, weighing 30 to 35 hundredweight each, loaded with upwards of 16 tons of stone, besides about 20 workmen who got upon the loaded cars, were drawn the whole length of the rail road by a single horse, and the empty cars were drawn back with ease." Hale added, "We learn from a gentleman who has visited the principal rail roads in England that in point of solidity and skill in construction, this is not exceeded by any one there."

For some reason or other, this railroad excited more interest and enthusiasm throughout the United States than any of the small tramways hitherto built: perhaps in part because it was longer and better built and because it was incorporated, just like any transcontinental railway; but also, one fancies, because Bryant's appearance was timed like that of the "inventor" who comes along at the moment we call psychological—when the sluggish public mind has become prepared for his achievement—and who wins success by combining and improving the ideas of others, perhaps also doing a good job of promotion, as Fulton did; whereupon, the idea is thereafter believed by the world to have sprung full grown from his brain. Bryant, as we have shown, made no claim to the title of inventor, and though he actually invented other things than the railroad, he did not profit by them. But his railroad stirred an interest and an amazed admiration which it is difficult for us to comprehend now. To this day some writers speak of it as America's first railroad.

The Baltimore & Ohio Railroad, then just organizing, sent a committee up to look over the Granite Line, and they returned with high praise of it. In Gideon Miner Davison's *The Fashionable Tour: an Excursion to the Springs, Niagara, Quebec and through the New England States*, the 1828 edition begins recommending the Granite Railway as one of the sights. "It will be an object of interest to those who have never seen a rail road to visit this; from whence an excursion may be continued to the residence of the late President Adams, a short distance further." Even the home of a President and one of the Founding Fathers had become, as an attraction, secondary in interest to the Railroad. *The Northern Traveller* compiled by Timothy Dwight—an early annual travel guide book—also mentioned the Granite Railway as an objective for the sightseer. *The American Traveller* said in June, 1827, "This first work of the kind in the Union, is now in full tide of successful operation, and is daily visited by many persons, both from the city and abroad." The road from Boston through Dorchester to Quincy crossed the railroad, and so many stopped to see the wonder and found themselves in need of refreshment "that a citizen living near the point of intersection has been induced to convert his little dwelling into a house of entertainment."

John Quincy Adams, then President, visited the road that summer, escorted by another railroad enthusiast, Josiah

Quincy, and thought he saw already some wear and tear "on the iron tire of the way, and still more on the pine-wood rail beneath it. Colonel Perkins and Mr. Quincy think not, but the Colonel has made an experiment for a small space, of substituting a granite rail in the place of the pine-wood"—which, opined the President, would be more desirable, but would wear out the iron faster. To his journal Mr. Adams confided his doubts that the line would be profitable. "Col. Perkins has great means, ardent public spirit and pertinaceous enterprise," and he was "liberal even to profusion" in keeping up the railroad. "It has already been of great advantage to the town of Quincy," wrote the old statesman, "and promises to be still more. But the danger that the rail-way may prove a bill of expense to its owners casts a shade over the whole enterprise."

Apparently he need not have worried. The line continued to operate profitably for decades thereafter; in fact, it ran, always by horsepower, for forty years. At last, around 1870, having been for some time in disuse, its franchise was bought by the Old Colony Railroad, the track was torn up and a modern one built along most of the right of way. This was formally opened for traffic, as a part of the line to the old Pilgrim port of Plymouth, on October 9, 1871, forty-five years and two days after the original opening in 1826. "There is a certain historical fitness," muses C. F. Adams, "in the fact that through the incorporation of the Granite Railway into the Old Colony, the line connecting Plymouth with Boston has become the original railroad line in America."

But not so long ago there was still a granite railway descending an incline at the quarry, and it was said to run for a very short distance over the old right of way. Some of the stone sleepers of the original road could have been seen embedded in the earth near by, and old-timers tell us that some of them served for many years as curbstones. Two pillars commemorating the pioneer railway have been erected on the two sides of what was the foot of the incline.

Bryant? Oh, he died poor in 1867.

# 3

# The Dawn of Private Enterprise

WHY give so much space to a comparatively insignificant horse railway? Because of its tremendous significance in its day, the vast interest it aroused, and the fact that it marked the turn of the tide, the beginning of an epoch in New England. To pile metaphor upon metaphor, it was the hair that turned the scale, the straw that broke the canal camel's back. After its advent, the canal project no longer had a future, though its advocates long refused to acknowledge this. The railroad to the Hudson was now inevitable, but four years of bickering and education were necessary to induce the majority to believe it, and years more to start the road to Albany humming with the whir of car-wheels.

With the appointment of the Phelps Committee, however, the primary-education phase of the railroad era in New England began. An example of the slow impregnation of the public mind with the new idea is found in the series of articles on internal improvements written by Emory Washburn of the Phelps Committee and signed "Agricola," which appeared in the *Worcester Ægis* in the autumn and early winter of 1829. He favored a canal from Boston to the Hudson, but in his fourth article said, fairly enough, "We are aware that the claims of Rail-ways upon public attention are but little known here." He agreed that they should be considered, for the reason that someone had asserted that one horse could draw as much on rails as eight horses on a highway. He believed a railroad practicable between Boston and the Hudson, and thought that "by proper engineering," even a steam line might be constructed over the route. He quoted a story that from La Guayra to Caracas in Venezuela a railroad was about to be built which would ascend 4000 feet. Although engineers opined that the original cost and upkeep of a canal would be higher than that of a railroad, Agricola considered that the fact that farmers in Worcester County could get their products to the Boston market by rail at eighty cents a ton was worth considering. When one town in that county transported 500 tons annually, if only five dollars per ton were saved, there would be an advantage of $2500 in cold cash right there.

Berkshire County, "beleaguered by nature" in the hills of Western Massachusetts but intent on getting its marble, iron ore, butter and other products to market, had now become a rip-roaring railroad partisan, most vociferous in all New England in favor of the new transportation. There were some brilliant and enterprising citizens out there, too, and one of the more scientific, R. F. Morgan of Stockbridge, partly on his own and partly aided by local funds, had surveyed a railroad route from Albany to Springfield, via Kinderhook, Chatham and Canaan—almost precisely the route over which the Boston & Albany now runs. He reported his findings to a citizen's mass meeting at Stockbridge on December 21, 1826.

He believed that the county's merchandise could be delivered at Albany for a dollar a ton, exclusive of tolls. One horse could draw ten tons on a level, and one man could attend four horses, with a total maximum expense for man and horses of $3.50 a day. The road would have to climb to a height of 1300 feet above the Hudson River at one place, but he thought it could be built for $15,000 a mile. He favored the division of the line into "a succession of levels, rising one above another," with inclined planes between, where the trains would be operated by either water power or oxen; six yoke of oxen would be enough for a plane. Either of these he thought preferable on principles of economy to steam power. By such measures he believed that the "mere mechanical expense" of transportation could be held to one cent per ton-mile.

Mr. Morgan's neighbors were all for the Legislature's busying itself with the job immediately. "An astonishing degree of anxiety," said the *Stockbridge Star* in January, "now pervades all classes of our citizens in this region, to see the beginning of this great work. . . . Even the most faithless may be brought out of the labyrinths of ignorance into a full conviction of the truth of that, which but yesterday, they condemned as visionary and futile." But other parts of the state were as yet immobile.

During the winter session of the Legislature, in January, 1827, the Phelps Committee presented its report. For the benefit of the unsophisticated, it explained: "A Rail Way is a carriage road, so formed that the wheels move upon Rails of any hard, smooth surface, such as iron, wood or stone, instead of forming ruts or tracks." The committee had been somewhat intrigued by and spent much unnecessary wordage in describing a monorail idea, "invented many years ago by our ingenious fellow-citizen, Col. Henry Sargent of Boston, and since claimed by Mr. Palmer in England, but without any just reasons whatsoever." As the report described it, a "single Rail Way" was to be elevated a few feet above the earth on stringers supported by stout posts. The carriage had two bodies, one on each side, hanging down like saddle-bags, so that "the balance and weight are below the Rail." But there were so many objections to this type of road that the "parallel Rail Way"—by which was meant one with two rails, "either of wood, iron or stone"—seemed best. There were long specifications for track-building, for the felloes, flanges, etc., on the wheels. "The question often occurs, why a wheel moves more easily upon a Rail Way than upon the common road," and this was explained at length. The committee had considered nothing but horse traction for the road, and the members were still so bemused by canal practice that they planned graveled paths for the driver on each side of the track, although he might just as well ride on the car and would undoubtedly prefer to do so, save possibly on some crisp winter days.

In rebuttal of a favorite argument of the anti-railroad forces that snow in winter would stop all operations, the committee asserted that "for many years previous to the present season, the *snows* of our winters in Massachusetts have been gradually diminished." How often have we heard old-timers declare that "winters ain't as cold as they used to be," or conversely, that "the winters are a sight colder'n they was when I was a boy"! But here we see signs of progress: the committee veered away from the notion that hills would have to be ascended by means of inclined planes. "Your committee suggest whether great elevations may not be easily surmounted by roads proceeding and returning alternately for given distances, like those adopted in England, and there denominated zig-zags; whereby, though distance may be increased, the ascent of each mile may be lessened."

The report filled three columns of the *Advertiser*, for Hale did not fail to print it there. But meanwhile, through January and into February, he was running in the paper a series of articles of his own—later published in pamphlet form under the title, *Remarks on the Practicability and Expediency of establishing a Rail-Road on one or more Routes from Boston to the Connecticut River*. Despite the wordy title, he wrote well and soundly.[1] Like the legislative committee, he had not yet progressed to the point of contemplating steam locomotion. He disagreed with the committee on its idea of making the railroad a double-track affair, "one for travelling in one direction, and the other for returning, with occasional tracks diverging from one to the other, for the purpose of permitting a fast-travelling team to pass one that travels slowly." He thought the expense of a double-track road should not be risked "until the experiment of a single one is tried. The delay incurred in passing will be trifling."

[1] He had at that time a little son not yet five years old, whom he had named in honor of his friend Edward Everett, politician and orator, and who was destined to write more ably than his father.

He gave much space to costs of construction, the pulling power of horses on rails, and the probable tonnage and freight revenues from all localities. In Worcester County, for example, he reported, prominent citizens had made surveys and called meetings to estimate tonnages and their value. That county's exports to Boston were beef, pork, butter, cheese, oats, chairs and a great variety of manufactured and other articles. From Boston they brought back salt, iron, flour, rum, sugar, molasses, fish, nails, dyestuffs, cotton, plaster, English and domestic goods. It must be evident, said Hale, that the facilitated transportation "will be not merely a convenience, but will produce an entire revolution in the business of this part of the country. . . ."

He figured the cost of a single-track railroad from Boston to the Connecticut River at $1,059,000. One of the important items of expense was the iron rail. America as yet manufactured very little in that line, and Hale said that domestic malleable iron in rail shapes could not be bought for less than $150 per ton. Imported from England it would cost only £12, or $53.28 per ton, plus 15 per cent for freight, exchange, etc., bringing the cost up to $61.26; but when you added the import duty of $30 per ton, your final figure was $91.26. "If the duty on iron rails was taken off for five years," suggested Hale, "until the experiment was fairly made, at the expiration of that time, it is the belief of the writer that more rail of our own make would be wanted than could be produced by our forges and furnaces"—and by that time, we could be producing it more cheaply.

Surprisingly enough, the House of Representatives ordered the purchase and distribution of 300 copies of Hale's pamphlet.

There was a mass meeting of railroad proponents, sponsored of course by Hale, Phelps and a few other supporters, in the Supreme Court Room in Boston on January 12, where resolutions were passed in the hope of swaying the Legislature. But that body was unmoved. As C. F. Adams, whom we must frequently quote, says:

The sentiment of the State moved slowly. On all questions concerning property, especially land, the Massachusetts Legislature was always a singularly conservative body. . . . It was in fact, then a regular squirearchy. The large manufacturing towns of the interior were just coming into life, and had not yet begun to exert much political influence. The State as a whole was still agricultural and commercial. The representatives of commercial towns were few in number, and opposed to them was the country gentry—a colonial type . . . which in 1826 continued to be the traditional power in the General Court. They were leaders of the landed interests, and the landed interest was the dominant interest. These men had many sterling qualities, but for mental receptiveness, they were not remarkable. Moving them was a slow process. . . .

A disgusted Massachusetts promoter remarked that every improvement in transportation was fought by New Englanders: good wagon roads because of the cost and the evils attendant upon facility of traffic; "canals were objected to as endeavors to improve upon the natural waterways provided by the Almighty; turnpikes because the builders charged money for their use, and because they competed with the canals; railroads because they competed with both the canal and the highway, and probably were of the Devil, anyway." This is a somewhat exaggerated picture sketched by a tired and irritated man, though it did represent the attitude of not a few people.

But the time was coming. Among the straws in the winter winds of the day, one is seen in the advertisement, nearly a column in length, in the Boston papers for January, of a work on civil engineering, translated from the French, in which railroads were taken up as a major subject. The science of civil engineering had only just begun to function in America. The Erie Canal was surveyed and built by two village lawyers whose only engineering experience had been some elementary use of a transit in doing a little land surveying for clients. Yet the job they did in creating the great canal was the wonder of two hemispheres—they and certain younger geniuses whose talents were developed as the canal was being built. But now the military engineers began to appear, trained either at West Point or in the Army's hard school of experience. As we continue with this story, we shall find most of the railroad surveying in New England done by "Colonel," "Major" or "Captain" This or That, and usually done exceedingly well, despite the fact that almost none of them had ever seen a railroad.

A modern president of the American Society of Civil Engineers has said of those pioneer engineers, "What they did not understand, they conquered by diligent study, unwearied zeal and sound common sense." And another president of the same society adds that some of the methods which they developed are still practiced. "They were not scientific men, but knew by intuition what other men knew by calculation. . . . What science they had, they knew well how to apply to the best advantage. Few men have ever accomplished so much with so little means."

Late in May of 1827, just before the summer session of the Legislature convened, Andrew J. Allen, a Boston merchant, opened a "Railway Exhibition" in a large upstairs room over No. 70 State Street. Railway models, pictures, plans and books on the subject were on display, and Allen invited everybody who had anything of the sort to exhibit it. It was a pitifully scanty array, God wot, but many went to see it and were impressed, for what they saw was entirely new to most of them.

Mr. Allen also kept in his store a petition begging the state's lawmakers to build the western railroad, and citizens were invited to step in and sign it if they were favorable to the idea. There were 2800 names on the petition when it was presented to the Legislature in June; there would have been more than 3000, but sheets containing about 400 names somehow became misplaced. This and other petitions were laid before the lawmakers by a delegation of citizens of Boston and vicinity and Berkshire County—perhaps fired at them would be a better term, for vigorous old Mayor Josiah

Quincy headed the delegation. Anyhow, they at last succeeded in planting a little dynamite under the legislators, who proceeded to appoint two commissioners and an engineer to make plans and surveys for the railroad. Best of all, they backed their action with an appropriation of $10,000.

As soon as the act had been passed, Governor Lincoln wrote to Secretary of War Barbour, asking whether the federal government could not aid in the survey and also put up a little cash to help the cause along. Mr. Barbour's reply was a firm "No" to both queries.

Action began at once, amid some discordant jeers and protests from the opposition. Editor Buckingham of the *Boston Courier* wrote on June 27:

> Alcibiades or some other great man of antiquity, it is said, cut off his dog's tail, that *quidnuncs* might not become extinct from want of excitement. Some such notion, we doubt not, moved one or two of our experimental philosophers to get up the project of a railroad from Boston to Albany—a project which every one knows, who knows the simplest rule in arithmetic, to be impracticable, but at an expense little less than the market value of the whole territory of Massachusetts, and which, if practicable, every person of common sense knows, would be as useless as a railroad from Boston to the moon.

Others deplored the itch for speed which was laying hold of Americans (it has been a national disease ever since) and threatening madness. When, in July, 1827, the steamer *Connecticut* after a fast run reached Providence at 9 A.M. on a Sunday and her through passengers were set down in Boston at 2 P.M., making the time from New York to Providence eighteen hours and to Boston twenty-three hours, there was quite a piece in the papers about it. Editorials were written on the tendency. The *New York Daily Advertiser* satirized "the mania of steamboat passengers to make the trip. . . *a few minutes* quicker than any others have ever done," and said that "an old gentleman in New England conveyed a just idea of the character of those who are so fond of travelling at such a wondrous rate, when he said he believed that if his son John was riding on a streak of lightning, *he would whip up!*"

Loammi Baldwin was wanted for the railroad survey, but he was busy with other tasks and so passed the billet on to his brother, James F. Baldwin, who did an excellent piece of work. Through the summer and fall he and his staff worked like beavers, while the railroad commissioners sent a circular to all towns through which the tracks might pass, requesting information as to the quantity of goods shipped in and out during the year and the present cost of transport, the cost of land and whether citizens would be willing to donate rights of way for the railroad in exchange for benefits to be received.

They had little trouble in getting a right of way through the Berkshire Hills. The people out there were terribly in earnest. They told the world that their marble had walled the New York City Hall and Girard College in Philadelphia, but now it was too expensive a process to get it to market by wagon, and something must be done. They held meetings at Lenox and Pittsfield in the fall and winter, and Theodore Sedgwick was made chairman of a committee of boosters; he had for some time been active in the cause, and here enters another important name in New England railroad history.[2]

But an English traveler passed through the region that autumn, and in answer to the customary foolish question, threw his cup of cold water on the idea. Captain Basil Hall, who traveled widely and wrote extensively on America, spent an early October night at Stockbridge and journeyed toward Boston next day. He was charmed with the scenery and the lovely villages of the Berkshire country, whose flower gardens and tree-shaded streets reminded him of England, while the rocks, mountains and waterfalls just east of them seemed to him to have something of the Alpine about them. But—

[2] Scion of a fine Berkshire Hills family which gave a noted general, John Sedgwick, to the Civil War, Theodore was a son of an eminent Congressman and judge whose political differences with John Adams attained such a degree of warmth that he called the crusty old President a maniac. Theodore's sister, Catherina Anna Sedgwick, was one of the popular novelists of her day.

In the course of this agreeable day's journey, we traversed a considerable portion of the route over which, it has been seriously proposed, I was assured, to carry a rail-road between the cities of Boston and Albany. . . . In answer to the appeals frequently made to my admiration of this scheme, I was compelled to admit, that there was much boldness in the conception; but I took the liberty of adding, that I conceived the boldness lay in the conception alone; for, if it were executed, its character would be changed to madness.

"What would you carry on your railroad if you had it?" asked Hall of Sedgwick, speaking of what he called "this visionary project." Try to fancy Sedgwick's explosive reply! How sad are the humiliations ambushed in the paths of people who persist in predicting the future!

Meanwhile, the inventors were busy. R. F. Morgan, the Berkshire genius, designed and exhibited in Boston a car with such free wheeling that he claimed friction was almost entirely eliminated. A pound weight hanging by a string over a pulley was sufficient to move it at a mere finger-touch. The Russian minister was said to have asked for a model of it to show to the Czar. John L. Sullivan (not the Boston Strong Boy of later years, of course) invented a railroad which was almost a monorail, though it had two tracks and sets of wheels set close together instead of one, with the weight hanging on each side. And "an old Gentleman," whose name was mercifully withheld from the public, proposed to reverse the positions of rail and wheels, fastening the rail on the bottom of the car and having it pass over rollers on the ground.

The states to northward of Massachusetts were now becoming aroused. In Maine, where meetings looking toward the promotion of internal improvements—this phrase then meaning canals—had been held as far back as 1825, a naïve theorizer advocated the construction of railroads with wooden rails. In his state, where timber was plentiful, he was sure that railroads could be built for $500 a mile. "I believe," he added, "that less than $1,000 per mile would keep a railroad of the above description in complete order forever."

Maine's attention was somewhat distracted at the time,

however, by the acrid dispute over the boundary between her Aroostook County and Canada, which then and for some years afterward was as pent-up dynamite, an actual threat to the peace of the continent. "Incidents" occurred which in Europe would have precipitated war. In fact, in the so-called Aroostook War of 1839, thousands were under arms on both sides, fortunately without a serious clash. Our national government took serious cognizance of the situation, but the men of good will on both sides kept their heads, nothing serious happened, and the dispute was eventually settled amicably.

In November, 1827, the *Concord* (N.H.) *Register* gave publicity to a letter from Mr. Sullivan, the car inventor, and Elkanah Watson, who advocated the building of a railroad from Concord to Lake Ontario as the most feasible connection between Boston and the west. They said that Boston was now connected with Concord by water; all right, now just run a railroad northwest, across the Connecticut, up the White River valley to Montpelier and down the Onion River to Lake Champlain (rails were eventually laid over all this course); ferry across Champlain and continue the railroad on to Lake Ontario at or near Ogdensburg. This was the first of many efforts to get a northwest line across New Hampshire and Vermont to Canada or the Great Lakes; most of the later surveys began at Boston.

When the General Court assembled on January 2, 1828, Governor Lincoln announced that the committee was ready with its study and surveys of railway routes from Boston to the Hudson and to Providence; but he also revealed that some of the best minds among the diehard water-dogs were still toying with the idea of a canal from the Charles River near Boston to Worcester (to offset the Blackstone Canal from Worcester to Providence), and another beyond Worcester, to connect with a proposed canal from Norwich, Connecticut, by which they would reach the Thames River and the Sound. These proved to be but vain imaginings; nothing more was ever heard of them.

The committee's report showed that two routes for the railroad had been surveyed: a southern one through Natick,

Hopkinton, Grafton, Worcester, Palmer, Springfield, Westfield, Chester, Pittsfield, West Stockbridge and Canaan, N. Y., to Castleton on the Hudson, and thence up that stream to Albany; the northern one, coming east "from Troy, N. Y., by the waters of the Poestenkill to the Drowned Land in Pittstown; thence by Shingle Hollow to the Hoosick River near the [Hoosac] Four Corners," and on from Williamstown through Adams and over a course never realized to a crossing of the Connecticut River at Northampton; and so via Palmer, Ware, Belchertown, Rutland, Holden, Berlin, Sudbury and Waltham to Cambridge. (The course from Palmer eastward was built on in later years for local purposes.)

The report said: "The exploration and surveys have been conducted exclusively with reference to the use of animal power, [as] better adapted to the transportation of the endless variety of loading, which a dense and industrious population requires." It was still the belief here that a locomotive could not pull as great a load upgrade as a horse; that its usefulness faded out at a grade of twenty-five or thirty feet to the mile. It is true that the tiny engines at first employed could not get a very firm grip on the track because of their light weight, which decreased their power—a fault overcome as the machines grew heavier. Great surprises were in store for American railroad proponents and opponents in the next year or so.

As to costs of building the road, the commissioners declared that the best canals in this country had cost less than half as much to construct as English canals, the figures being around $20,000 per mile here and $40,000 to $45,000 in England. The average cost of railroads in England had been $25,000 per mile. Was there any reason why railroads could not be built in America for far less than their cost in England—perhaps only half as much?

Many paragraphs of the report were given to the probable tonnage that would be carried in and out of various places. It was said that Springfield already "imported" (from other parts of the country) 700 tons annually, and exported 5000 tons, mostly via the Connecticut River. Lee, in Berkshire County (the railroad survey passed not through but near it), exported every year 400 tons of paper, 75 tons of iron, 100 tons of iron castings, 4 tons of cloth, 25 tons of powder, 10 tons of wagons and wheel hubs and 30 tons of gravestones, nearly all of this being hauled by wagon to the Hudson River. No wonder Berkshire wanted the railroad!

The commissioners had now begun to see possibilities in passenger traffic, too. On the Stockton & Darlington Railroad, in England, they said, "Coaches are constantly plying, which carry six passengers inside and fifteen or twenty outside, with luggage, and run at the rate of ten miles an hour ... which seems an enormous load for one horse, and yet the animal scarcely appears to make any exertion." But they could not resist one small shiver as they quoted the *Quarterly Review* article of 1825, whose author wittily compared train travel at twenty miles an hour to being shot across the zenith on a Congreve rocket. Nevertheless, the report revealed, in a single month corporations had been formed in Great Britain to build 3000 miles of these "iron roads," at "an expense of £20,000,000 sterling." Here, as Adams reminds us, state officials for the first time and all unintentionally pointed to the businessmen of Boston the course they were eventually to pursue. "The time had not yet come, however, when they would stop trying to educate the farmers and help themselves." [3]

At first the report seemed likely to get nowhere in the Legislature. It was referred to a committee, who, after due deliberation, committed themselves to the extent of conceding that "rail-road construction has assumed a new and greater importance." But it was noticeable that the canal idea had

[3] The bill of expenses for the surveyors, embodied in the report, is an amusing document to present-day eyes. We find that Baldwin, as the chief engineer, drew $10 a day salary, which was not at all bad for those times. The hotel and other expenses at every stop are meticulously itemized: "Root's, Middlefield, $5, boy 6 cents = $5.06." Boys were cheap in those days, and what service this one performed for six cents we do not know. Another boy at Westfield earned as much as twenty cents. Another item, "Squire's, Kinderhook Township, $6.85, wagon 41 cents, sugar 13 cents = $7.39."

now dropped out of sight entirely and forever; and in March the solons got around to creating a Board of Directors of Internal Improvements which was to study the subject further and make another report the following winter. The members of the Board were chosen by the Legislature, Governor Lincoln, now a convert to railroads, being one, while Nathan Hale, whose prodding had done much to bring about the existence of the Board, was another. Royal Makepeace of Cambridge, a member of the House, and two other railroad enthusiasts, were among the remaining six members.

The State of New York was in highly co-operative mood at the moment. Its Legislature appointed commissioners to study the subject, and pledged itself that, "if the State of Massachusetts shall construct a rail-road from Boston to the eastern boundary of this State, either directly or through the medium of an incorporated Company, the Legislature of this State, will continue it from thence to the Hudson River, or grant to the State of Massachusetts or some authorized Company the right of so doing." The trouble was that New York too quickly forgot its good intentions.

Some of the Berkshire County people lost patience with all this surveying and reporting, and that summer they induced the Legislature to charter a road of their own—the first real railroad charter issued in New England, the Granite being nothing but a quarry tramway. This railroad, known as the Berkshire & Hudson, was a funny little scenario which began and ended nowhere in particular. Some librarians and others have become confused and called it the Hudson & Berkshire, perhaps because a railroad of that name was chartered and actually built shortly afterward, just over the line in New York, and was to be a part of the Berkshire plan.

The Berkshire & Hudson was chartered at from $350,000 to $500,000 and authorized to build from the state line in West Stockbridge Town, through the villages of West Stockbridge, Stockbridge and Lee, to "the furnace in Lenox." Another, less immediately probable line, was to run from West Stockbridge to "the village of Pittsfield." The map of the whole would look like a gigantic fishhook, with Lenox Furnace at the point. It almost encircled the Lee-Lenox valley, the busiest and most wide-awake portion of the Berkshire country and an area where the problems of grading were not great.

The charter stated that the object of the road was the "transporting, taking and carrying of property and persons . . . by the power and force of steam, of animals or of any mechanical or other power, or of any combination of them." The legislators recognized the value of a railroad to the community by authorizing the company to condemn a right of way and to take stone, earth and timber from property contiguous to its line, paying for the same, of course, and doing as little damage to the property as possible.

The odd thing about this first charter is that it frankly recognized the railway as a public highway. Tolls were to be fixed, and "all persons paying the Toll aforesaid may, with suitable and proper carriages, use and travel upon the said Rail Road, subject to such rules and regulations as the said corporation is, by this act, authorized to make."

The road might later, if it chose, extend to Hudson, N. Y., on the river of that name, though of course in that case it would have to procure a New York charter also. The final section warned that "nothing contained in this Act shall be construed to impair the right of this Commonwealth to construct a Rail Road from the City of Boston to the boundary line between this Commonwealth and New York."

Lieutenant Colonel Perrault, who had made the survey, estimated the cost of construction at $10,937 per mile. He priced the iron—Berkshire iron, no doubt—at $120 a ton, "on the supposition that it would be manufactured in this country by hammering, instead of being imported, rolled, as it may be, at a cost of $70, delivered." (This figure was too low.) Of course he expected that Berkshire stone ties would be used.

There was one prominent citizen of the region, however, who evidently didn't think much of this project. Theodore Sedgwick's eyes were fixed upon the larger conception. That year he published under the pseudonym, "Berkshire," a sprightly pamphlet urging the accomplishment of the great east-west line. The state, he said, was only fifty miles wide, and a rail line lengthwise through it—or better still, one over each of the two surveys—would "almost put the railroad at every man's door." No other states then building internal improvements had the advantage of Massachusetts—"their great territory and sparse population" were against them.

It is the simplicity, the plainness of the work, the talent of the people of New England in making roads, that recommends the Rail Road to us. They have made not only their own roads, but half the roads of the middle States. To this day, a good road is hardly built there without a gang of New England turnpikers. . . .

The improvements in other countries and in the adjacent States have put us upon our self-defence; it is not a question of more or less, but of self-preservation. The old machinery for carrying great burthens is worn out, we must take the new or give up business; the whole system of business is changing, and we must change with it. . . . If England carried Coal now, as she did within the memory of Man, on Asses' backs, Congress would be saved a world of trouble in making tariffs. Will Massachusetts therefore consent to take the head or the tail, in the career of public improvements, or does she prefer no place at all?

. . . It is prudent and safe, to make our calculations upon the basis of present business, but are we a set of Chinese, where the same tools and clothes answer for half a dozen generations? Do not things alter and increase here, is not the country growing like an ox in the stalls, so that when he comes in and when he goes out, you do not know him for the same animal? It is enough for the friends of the railroad to prove that the thing will answer now; all beyond that is clear again.

He believed that passenger traffic would be a large item, and he surprises us by adding, "this at a time when no man, woman or child stops at home throughout the year." One argument against railroads was that the state had no money with which to build them. Governor Lincoln had just told the Legislature: "A sense of duty impels me to throw myself upon your indulgence in earnestly directing your attention to the state of the Treasury"—there being only a little more than $20,000 on hand. But did New York, Pennsylvania and Ohio have full coffers, demanded Sedgwick, when they began their canals? No; the work was made possible by borrowing. Massachusetts was rich by comparison with them. "Our neighbors accuse us of one kind of poverty, that is, of spirit." No public improvement of magnitude had ever been proposed in the state. With the greatest per capita wealth in the Union, with more improvement in the past five years than in any equal period of her history, "does any man suppose that we shall have another Shay's rebellion" about raising a sum that would only be enough to set up a small-town bank?

Sedgwick was all for public ownership. Individuals had no right to rivers, arms of the sea, canals, roads which everybody must pass over. Of course, the state should not monopolize such things as coal mines, the steam engine or the magnet; individuals made the best use of these. "Roads, however, belong to the community, and the Rail Road, so far as public use is designed by it, is a gift of the arts to the States. It is among the few improvements that a State can most successfully manage." Poor Sedgwick of course had not had the opportunity of seeing the United States Government almost ruin the railroad system of the nation during the First World War.

He assailed the "popular cant, very current and very foolish," that the state did nothing so economically as private enterprise. The financial affairs of Massachusetts, he said, were managed with "exemplary economy and fidelity. The reason is obvious"—and the next two sentences are sound enough. "It is a small community, very compact, the government of it, from long habit, is a personal concern of every citizen. . . . It is quite otherwise in an empire as large as that of the United States." It is quite possible to agree with Sedgwick here, even if not to share his horror at the thought of "the people of Massachusetts tenants of their own roads, paying rent at every six miles' distance!! The very proposition is disgraceful!"

He compared the stagnation of his own county with the

progress of Worcester. For twenty years, he declared, Berkshire's population had been stationary. (Hale insisted that it had even declined.) "At present we have little more communication with Boston," said Sedgwick, "than with the capital of Vermont. Our trade is with New York and will in a great degree continue there." He was severe with his indifferent neighbors. "There are men here who will not lift their hands to raise our Lime, Marble and Iron out of the earth." He begged these men to awake, "infuse new life into New England, keep our children at home, save ourselves from sleep and dotage. When a State once makes up its mind that it can do nothing and will attempt nothing, it becomes weaker and weaker, death is at the door."

But there were dissenting voices in the hinterlands. It was objected by many, not only in the northeast and southeast corners of the state, which would not be reached by either railroad, but even by towns along the line of survey, that the whole thing was a Boston plutocratic plot: it would "involve the State in an immense debt, entirely for the advantage of Boston." Sedgwick, in a letter to the *Berkshire Journal*, deplored "the unfounded jealousy that exists between the City and the Country. They are but members of one body. They grow poor or they flourish together."

Again, it was argued by some that facilities for transportation would glut the market with country produce, while the sale would be limited to the present consumption. "What is more easy," retorted a writer in the *Patriot*, "than to foresee this simple example. Open a communication between the counties at fifty or a hundred miles distant from Cape Cod; large quantities of Cider, for instance, will be carried there at a reduced price. Will not so much more fish be caught or Salt made by the inhabitants of that section, as will pay for all this increase of Cider?"

Harrison Gray Otis was elected Mayor of Boston that year, and the principal recommendation in his opening address to the Council was that the city aid in the furtherance of railroads. When the Legislature convened in January, 1829, Governor Lincoln warned it of the necessity for action.

"Every passing day bears witness that for want of facilities to intercommunity between the interior and the Capital of the State, the most serious diversions of trade are taking place to other markets." He was referring to the Blackstone Canal, which had begun business between Providence and Worcester. Not only was that canal carrying New York cargoes, but even timber from Maine was coming by sea to Providence and thence up the canal to interior Massachusetts.

On January 17, a few days after the session opened, William Jackson, in later years an able railway official, delivered a lecture before the Massachusetts Charitable Mechanics' Association, in which he advocated the building of railroads, and under state ownership. He predicted that if Boston and Albany were connected by rail, New York would be forced to build a railroad alongside the Hudson to Albany, "to secure for herself a successful competition with Boston for the inland commerce of the largest and richest part of her own State. Visionary! Merely visionary, methinks I hear some one whispering. . . ."

He, as well as others, called attention to the necessity for such a road in case of a foreign war. He attacked local selfishness, reminding them how, when the old Charlestown bridge was first being promoted, the inhabitants of Dorchester, Roxbury and Brookline protested, their narrow selfishness "blinding and blunting their otherwise acute and penetrating minds to the discernment of their own best interest. We blush for our fathers. Time, however, has been rolling on until it has placed us in their shoes. Shall we give our children the same occasion to blush for us?"

He envied no man that disposition which wouldn't allow him to take a single step in a public cause "until he can clearly see that his own interest, or comfort, or gratification, is to be thereby increased. Nevertheless, 'tis true, too true, that the miserable effects of this disposition are more or less felt throughout every portion of our prosperous Republic, constituting one of the greatest stumbling blocks in the way of improvements."

The report of the Board of Directors of Internal Improvements, presented to the Legislature on January 23, was a well-written, businesslike document prepared mostly by Nathan Hale and read to the joint session by Sedgwick, who was a member of the House. Among the fundamentals for the two railroads in contemplation—to the Hudson River and to Providence—were still mentioned stone ties, strap-iron rails on wooden stringers, a five-foot gauge and horses for power: those were things upon which the Board felt sure of their footing. The Rainhill trials of steam locomotives in England, which were destined to put the horse out of countenance forever, were nine months in the future, and the best-informed men in New England still lacked full confidence in steam. But though the report again based its thesis on state ownership, here for the first time came a hint of private enterprise. England had given the Board something to think about. It admitted that such improvements had usually been obtained through a private company. But such was the magnitude of the project here proposed that it seemed doubtful that individuals would be willing to venture unless they could see ample assurance of safety and a return on their capital; and, "It would be difficult," thought the Board, "to afford an adequate security for this object without the pledge of more exclusive privileges than it would be expedient for the Legislature to grant." But they considered it likely that enterprising citizens might be led to invest if the state, in addition to granting reasonable tolls, would take one-third or two-fifths of the stock. At present there was no application before the Legislature for the formation of such a corporation, but they recommended it. The political mind was veering from the cult of state toward private control.[4]

[4] There is a delightfully homy flavor about Engineer Hayward's survey for the Boston to Providence line, which is embodied in the report: "It was proposed to leave the neighborhood of the meadow near Mr. Shanley's, and pass up a ravine nearly in the direction of the Rev. Mr. Hontoon's church. . . . The distance from Sharon Factory to Mr. Comey's is 5 miles, 17 chains, 50 links. . . . If the line could be carried straight from Mr. Clark's to Mr. Timothy Morse's, the distance would be 5 or 6 chains less. . . . It passes near Jabez Kingsbury's, over what is called High Plain, on the west side of Moose Hill; near Zeba Plympton's and Thomas Clap's. . . ."

Within a few days a petition signed by many prominent citizens asked the Legislature to form such a corporation. About the same time there was some talk of the City of Boston's subscribing to the stock, whereupon "Civis" and other alarmed taxpayers wrote letters to the papers, protesting against it. But the net result of the report was the issuance of two charters: one to the Massachusetts Rail Road Corporation, with a capital of $3,300,000 (33,000 shares), one third of which was to be taken by the state, the remainder by individuals or corporations, to build the railroad from Boston to the western state line, and if New York did not act, from there on to Albany. Of the twelve directors, four were to be named by the state. Payments on the state's stock were to be made from time to time, to the extent of half as much as had been paid on individual subscriptions. No assessments on the state's stock were to be any higher than on those privately owned. The directors might fix the "tolls," but if, after two years, the tolls amounted to more than 10 per cent per annum upon the cost of the road, the Legislature might reduce tolls so as to take off the overplus. Finally, the state reserved the right to buy out the other stockholders at any time after ten years.

Simultaneously, a charter was authorized for the Second Massachusetts Rail-Road Corporation, capital $360,000, one third to be owned by the state, to build from Boston to Providence, "or to such point on the navigable waters of Taunton River as they may deem the most eligible and the most condusive [sic] to the interests of the Commonwealth." The stipulations were the same in this case as in that of the Albany project, and they were apparently too drastic for the taste of men of means, who emphatically refused to have any part of such a concern.

But that was an eventful year in the development of the railroad idea, in New England and in America. R. F. Morgan came to Boston with another conception which has not received from historians the attention that it deserves—namely, the first suggestion of a sleeping car. You may find it written up, pictured and planned in the *American Traveller* of April

14, 1829. The trouble was that Morgan was ahead of his time. His car was far too big for the first railroads. In fact, said the *Traveller*, it might be called a Land Barge, "and to the traveller will furnish an idea of all the conveniences and comfort which belong to the best Steam Boats."

The car was to be two stories high, the upper level being a promenade deck with seats, and covered by an awning. In the lower story was a cabin with five "Births" (so spelled repeatedly) on each side, and so far was the marine atmosphere carried that there was even a captain's office. Through the decades that followed, the American railway conductor never had an office, as those who have seen him counting and classifying his tickets on a vacant coach seat or in the baggage car can testify. Not only was Morgan's car too large for the primitive conception of the first railroad builders, but he must needs picture it with a cupola atop, surmounted by a flagpole!—wholly ignoring the possible limitations of bridges and tunnels. This affords just another hint as to America's blissful ignorance of all that pertained to the railroad.

That spring the "friends of internal improvements" organized themselves as boosters in the Massachusetts Rail-Way Association, with Mayor Harrison G. Otis as president and such men as Hale, Phelps and Makepeace as ardent members. Whenever the Association had a lecture on railroads, it invited the members of the Legislature to be present. It promptly began a debate upon the merits of single- and double-track railroads; committees were appointed to study the subject from each side, and their arguments were published. Present-day readers will find it difficult to believe that so many words were expended in such a discussion, especially by those in favor of a single track, or that intelligent men would be willing to make public pleadings which reveal such ignorance of facts that are commonplaces to us now.

The single-trackers of course had a strong point in the great additional cost of construction and maintenance of the extra track. To them the only possible real advantage of a double track would be that of enabling teams going in opposite directions to pass each other. The double-trackers, however, pointed out that fast or passenger teams should also be able to pass the slow freight wagons going in the same direction. To accomplish this, they proposed crossovers from one track to another at frequent intervals—one theorist even said every eighth of a mile. To this the single-trackers retorted that at that rate there would be 1584 such nuisances on the line between New York and Albany.

To the single-trackers, the problem of meeting teams appeared ridiculously simple. It cited the *Journal of the Franklin Institute* (Vol. IV, p. 278), which resolved the problem in its customary professorial manner. Suppose, it said, a railway 100 miles long, on which coaches traveling at nine miles per hour and freight wagons at three miles, "enter upon their journeys at both ends of the railway after intervals of 12 hours only. The wagon in one direction must meet those of an opposite direction at the distance of 16 2/3, 33 1/3, 50, 66 2/3 and 83 1/3 miles from either end of the railway, after allowing 26 minutes for rest, feeding and changing horses at each interval."

The passenger coaches would meet the returning coaches midway, and they would meet trains of wagons at distances of 25 and 75 miles from either end. "There would then be eight points of meeting on the 100 miles; at each of which a sideling or passing place must be provided; and it must be evident that if the carriages arrived within the prescribed times, the passing would be effected without the least difficulty. Should a team of carriages arrive at a passing place before the prescribed time, it would only be necessary that they should wait for the opposite train to arrive. . . ."

As to lateral branches from the road, "the time of entering from these upon the main tracks should coincide with the arrival of the regular trains of the same velocity, at the junction with the main tracks. This arrangement would be very simple, and could occasion neither confusion nor delay."

The double-trackers, in reply, sneered that "there is such a thing as theory which cannot always be reduced to practice." They then assumed the other fellows' thesis:

The stages, we will suppose, are first paraded in Boston at 6 o'clock A.M. to enter upon the rails. Next to them the carriages which are partly loaded, and last, the heavy loaded cars. The arrangement of these suppose the most perfect submission and obedience of all persons of whatever condition, age or disposition; the feeble and the strong, the halt and the lame must be ready. No accident must prevent every driver and package of goods, as well as every person who is to leave the city for the next twelve hours, from being in their proper place and carriage. Those who arrive too early "have only to wait" until the time of starting; while those who arrive a minute too late must "only wait" until the next 12 hours. . . .

And what would be the picture there at 6 A.M.? They believed that after the railroad was well launched, there would be hundreds, there might be a thousand passengers every morning. Fancy the "confusion and danger," with a thousand people, "strangers, females," and what not, milling around there at once. "How many officers and servants would it require to direct each one to the proper carriage and adjust his or her baggage, short of two hours?" They figured that the procession of 60 to 100 carriages and freight wagons, with their teams, strung end to end in Charles Street, might cover a space of two miles. The committee now suppose that:

The signal is made for the whole line going west to start. The stages pass over the bridge and the cars follow. At Cambridgeport passengers are to be taken in and others let out. And suppose seven minutes from the time of starting, they are met by three or four trains of heavy loaded cars from the County of Worcester, Franklin or some where else, consisting of potatoes, cider, granite, and perhaps barrels of soap grease, to the amount of 50 tons! These may have entered the main line from a branch, say at Watertown. When they meet the stages, it is found, perhaps that Boston time is 27 or 30 minutes faster than in the country. It would appear that under these circumstances . . . more passing places than one in 16 2-3 miles would be somewhat necessary.

Some miscue like this, the double-trackers believed, would be apt to happen almost every day in the year. They also pointed out that the "sidelings" for such a caravan would have to be enormously long. The singlers, in rebuttal, airily dismissed the opposition arguments with statements which, for naïvete and fallacy, very nearly attained an all-time high; certainly they topped all others in this discussion. First:

The committee would observe that there is no mode of transportation known, perhaps none to be discovered, in which the certainty of passing a given distance within a given time is so complete as that procured by means of a railway. With the exception of a very small portion of the year, when it may be covered with deep snow, the structure is altogether beyond the reach of those changes which affect common roads, canals and rivers. The resistance to the moving of loads over it is at all times alike; so that the load which an animal can draw upon it one day, may be drawn on all other days; and this being once known, may forever be relied upon.

Such optimism is practically never met with elsewhere. Any ordinary accident to a single carriage, they said, could be easily remedied. One carriage of every train could carry such machinery parts and tools as might be required to repair either the track or the cars. Should a car be broken beyond repair, "its removal from the railway would, by the united labor of all the conductors, be immediately effected. The disabling of a horse would be of no serious consequence, as his load might be easily distributed amongst the other horses of the team."

As to passengers having to wait twelve hours for the next carriages, that was a mere nothing; the inconvenience was all in their imagination. The single-track committee cited as an example the two passenger lines between New York and Philadelphia, which left both cities by water and each ran two trips a day. "If the public required that they should start at four different hours, they would surely do so." Instead, each company's boats departed at the same time, "thus furnishing

a striking evidence that passengers can, with perfect convenience, commence a journey at one hour as well as another; or
at least, that a suitable and well-appointed hour, being convenient for one, will likewise be convenient for all."

An over-committee headed by Royal Makepeace gravely
weighed the evidence and decided in favor of the double
track.

The stagecoach was supplying railroad propagandists with
some excellent material in those days. The demand for higher
speed was taking its toll. Coaches rocking crazily behind gal-
loping horses were upset in the night by fallen trees or wash-
outs, crashed through flimsy bridges, were occasionally
wrecked by half-drunken drivers, locked wheels with other
coaches while racing and went to smash, or their brakes failed
on steep grades and they piled up in the ditch; always with
casualties, not infrequently with loss of life. It was asserted
that upon the smooth, almost level track of a railroad, this sort
of thing would never happen. "Melancholy accident,"
"Shocking recklessness," said the headlines, with daily references to the rising menace of the craze for speed. Whereas,
upon a railroad, you could have your velocity without hazard.

But at this point, steam came in to complicate the problem.
In the summer of '29, the Delaware & Hudson Canal Company imported three locomotives from England, for use on
the short railroad in Pennsylvania between its anthracite mines
and its canal. One of these, the "Stourbridge Lion," was
tested on August 8, being thus the first real locomotive to operate on a track in America. But because the company feared
that it hadn't built its trestles strongly enough to sustain an
eight-ton machine, they never used it. Nevertheless, its trial
trip showed that it was workable.

Just two months later, on October 6, the Rainhill competition took place on the partly completed Liverpool & Manchester Railroad in England; the test which forever banished
the notion of horsepower from the rails of both continents.
The directors of the road had been pondering the question
whether they should use stationary or movable engines.
They offered a prize of £500 for the best idea, and in the

test George Stephenson's Rocket won, hands down.  On the first day it whirled a coach containing thirty passengers along at a speed of twenty-six to thirty miles per hour, and next day it drew thirteen tons at twenty-nine miles per hour.  As soon as the slow-paced Atlantic steamers brought reports of the trials across the ocean, Hale flung them at full length into print in his newspaper, and some others followed suit.  Hale quoted the *Liverpool Chronicle:* "At this rate of going, Liverpool and Manchester, which are at present, near half a day's journey distant, will be brought within an hour's travel of each other."

Hale now became as flamingly enthusiastic on the subject of steam as he had formerly been regarding horse railroads; so much so that he was looked upon as a fanatic by many people—not crazy enough to be locked up, perhaps, but he would bear watching. When he declared, in a speech at Faneuil Hall, his belief that if people could travel from Springfield to Boston in five hours, an average of nine persons would come over every day, the statement was denounced as preposterous.  But fifty years later, after he was dead, New Englanders were calling him the Father of the American Railroad.  Among his ideas was one which in principle is being used today, though upon a twentieth-century pattern.  Answering the objection that the railway freight car could not go to the warehouse door, and an intermediate haul was thereby made necessary, he suggested shoes to fit over the flanged wheels of the light cars then in use, so that they might be taken off the tracks and hauled about town.  Cars soon became too heavy for any such service, but today the huge less-than-carload boxes of merchandise which are swung from car to truck and carried to warehouse or factory are in effect a fulfillment of Hale's idea.

Many influences combined to keep the word "railroad" before the public that summer and fall. The *Salem Observer* ran a series of articles favoring it.  Vermont aided it by loftily declaring independence of Boston.  The *Castleton Statesman* said that Boston was complaining of hard times—many stores to let, etc.  The Erie Canal and the tightening of the money market, opined the editor, were the reasons. By the Champlain Canal and the Hudson, and also through the Connecticut River, now being improved, Vermont would soon have two fine waterways to New York and would do most of her business there. This spurred the budding scheme of a 112-mile railroad to run from Boston to Brattleboro and to be known as the Franklin Railway. Mass meetings were held in towns along the route during the summer. At a meeting in Boston in September, many signed a pledge to donate five dollars each to get the thing started. But a million dollars was needed to complete the job, so the promoters said, and people were not yet sufficiently courageous to embark on so vast an adventure. This suggestion, however, of a corporation instead of a state-owned line was another passing straw in the wind.

The report that capital in New York was building a railroad was another goad. Here are those New Yorkers getting ahead of us again, said Massachusetts progressives mournfully. But truth to tell, this railroad, the Mohawk & Hudson, was only a little seventeen-mile affair between Albany and Schenectady, which had been chartered three years before and had only just now raised the necessary funds. New York City was not involved in it at all. That metropolis, still complacent in her prosperity from the Erie Canal, was dignifiedly ignoring the current railroad fad and actually had no rails of her own until long after Boston, Baltimore and Philadelphia. As a matter of fact, she was another area beleaguered by nature, a terrific problem to early railroad engineers, for she was surrounded on all sides by water, some of it so wide and deep that to this day there are fewer railroads running into Manhattan than into many a smaller city in the nation, and most of the lines have to land their passengers and freight in the city itself by ferry. The *American Railroad Journal*, our first periodical on the subject—which began so early, when there were so few railroads in the country, that most of its space had to be filled with general news, including murders, suicides and European political gossip—was published in New York, and its first number, January 2, 1832, apologized, saying that this issue was not a fair specimen of what the *Journal* would be when it had more subscribers, "and when we are accommodated with railroads in this vicinity, that our supply of paper may not be detained on the way by ice."

Even music aided the cause in 1829. A Baltimore composer, one C. Meinike, gave much thought to railroad pieces. There were the "Carrollton March," the "Railroad March" and "The Railroad"—"a characteristic divertimento for the piano forte; in which is introduced a variety of national and popular airs," that were picked out by feminine fingers upon ivory keys, even in New England. Some even sang that lively ballad, "The Steam Coach," introduced by "the veteran comedian of the Southern theatres, Mr. Jefferson" (father of Joseph Jefferson), in a "National Operetta" entitled *The Rail Road*, written by G. W. P. Custis and produced first in Baltimore, "to unprecedented applause." Two stanzas of it run thus:

### THE STEAM COACH

Of each wonderful plan
E'er invented by man,
That which nearest perfection approaches,
Is a road made of iron,
Which horses ne'er tire on,
And travelled by steam, in steam coaches.

#### Chorus

And we've no longer gee up and gee ho,
But fiz, fiz, fiz, off we go,
Nine miles to the hour,
With thirty horse power
By day time and night time,
Arrive at the right time,
Without rumble or jumble
Or chance of a tumble,
As in chaise, gig or whiskey
When horses are frisky.
Oh! The merry Rail Road for me, Oh! The merry Rail Road for me!

At the inns on our route,
No hostler comes out
To give water to Spanker or Smiler;
But loll'd at our ease,
We ask landlord to please
Put a little more water in the b'iler.

CHORUS

And we've no longer gee up, etc.

As winter and the meeting of the General Court drew on again, the discussion of railroad plans rose in crescendo. There was now a definite trend in Boston—and in a few other quarters, too—toward private ownership, which greatly alarmed the anti-monopolists. Their feelings on the subject may be understood from an article in the *Haverhill Essex Gazette* in December, in which non-state control is spoken of as a "pecuniary calamity." If this speculation is so certainly profitable, asked the writer, why do not capitalists come forward and offer to build the railroad? Yet almost in the same breath he asserted his belief that if the state undertook it, the income would pay the cost of the whole thing within twenty years. He shuddered at the specter of monopoly: rates would be raised sky-high and "bystanders" crushed.

When the Legislature met, one more effort was made to have the road built by the Commonwealth; but now the opposition came not only from those who didn't favor the railroad at all or were against it if it didn't pass through their town, but from those who had begun to favor corporate ownership. Governor Lincoln, during the preceding year, had suggested a stock system guaranteed by the state, but that didn't seem to suit, either.

Now that steam had pushed its way into the muddled situation, new opponents of railroads arose. The stage-line companies and the turnpike companies had already been in opposition; now they were joined by horse owners, stablemen, horse breeders, wagon and harness makers. Hundreds, maybe thousands of horses would be out of jobs and would have to be shot, as it wouldn't pay to feed them; horse breeding would decline. The farmers who had been producing horse feed tuned in on the anvil chorus. Innkeepers along the stage routes threatened by the rails also saw their business going to pot. Sparks from the locomotives would set fire to buildings, haystacks, wheat shocks, even the wool on the backs of sheep. Hens would be so frightened by the noise that they wouldn't lay eggs. . . . Legislators were under heavy fire from all sides.

The debate in the House on the railroad bill raged for two solid weeks. Theodore Sedgwick, still an uncompromising advocate of state ownership, opened it with a resounding speech. One phase of opposition is typified by Mr. Brooks of Bernardstown. He proved by figures given the House that the saving by rail of freight charges would be only five cents on a barrel of flour from Albany to Boston; and for this small object, we were called upon to spend three million dollars! In no other place, he contended, had such a costly work been undertaken for so inadequate a motive. He said the cost of the railroad would run above the estimate; it always did. Produce must be loaded on wagons and carried ten, twenty, thirty miles to reach the railroad. People wouldn't easily change their habits of business; once under the necessity of loading their produce on their wagons and hitching up their teams, they would carry it to its ultimate destination. Of course, Boston's old customers in Vermont and the Connecticut Valley would have to pay more freight by rail than they now paid by water; therefore, their business would be lost, it would go to New York. He would stand as firm as possible against the delirious project of a railway to Albany but would do all in his power in favor of a road to Vermont.

Among the proponents, Mr. Green of Marblehead, said that in debate on a former occasion, gentlemen had made professions of their sympathy for the fishermen. If they wished to give some proof of that sympathy, he only asked them to give them the railroad. A few years ago the fishermen had brought in 800,000 quintals of codfish in a year; now they brought but 150,000. Give them the railroad, and they would have 1000 men employed in the fishery from the town of Marblehead alone. Give them the railroad to Albany, and the fish might be swimming in the ocean one day and found 200 miles distant in the country on the next day; and it was not unlikely that they might be able to deliver fresh cod in Ohio. Cape Cod had sent a delegation to oppose the railroad. Mr. Green called them short-sighted: the road would help not only their fisheries but their salt works.

Mr. Cogswell of Ipswich was opposed to the whole project. It was premature, it would cost an enormous sum of money, and it would be worth little or nothing. He begged the House to pause, to have mercy on the people, to have some compassion. In the winter the snow would be in some places ten feet deep, and so make the railroad useless. Taking into view the difference in the value of labor in England and in this country, the railroad would cost twenty-three million dollars. We might borrow the money for a time for 5 per cent, but when that time was out, we should have to pay 6 per cent. How would "turkies," butter and eggs, etc., look after coming over a railroad, at thirty miles an hour? Would they have pigs and passengers travel together in the same car? There was nothing else to bring. He called upon the House to wait, before they began the work, till they saw a reasonable chance of getting their money's worth. If they must have a magnificent project, he would go the whole length and would try to bring Heaven down to Earth, or Earth up to Heaven. "Rail-ways, Mr. Speaker," he shouted, "may be well enough in old countries, but will never be the thing for so young a country as this. When you can make the rivers run backward, it will be time enough to make a railway!"

One of the hottest points was the question of the merits of the two routes surveyed, northern and southern. Some (mostly living in the northern part of the state) said that the southern route by Worcester and Springfield would be an absolute injury to Boston and the state: it would "hasten the completion of works already begun, to draw our trade to New York"—referring to the southbound canals and the Connecticut River improvement. But Mr. Perkins of Becket was broad-minded: he would vote for the railroad on either route. The southern route would pass within eight miles of his home, but he would vote for the northern rather than lose the railroad. He had no opinion of the legislation which said, "If the Rail-road don't *go to my house,* it shall not *go at all.*"

"Much has been said of another survey," grumbled Mr. Strong of Pittsfield. "We have had surveys enough already; is the plague never to be stayed? Are we to go on expending money without limit? The people want the southern route; in imagination they already see the bright waves of the Hudson laving the streets of Boston. I would not disappoint them. . . ."

Mr. Russell of Princeton represented the new trend. He was firm in saying that the state should not invest; it ought to be done by private capital. He believed that if the state said now, once and for all, that it would not undertake the project, it would be taken up immediately by a private corporation.

There was one assertion that railroads in England had cost up to $100,000 per mile. Others combated this, and there were some peppery exchanges. Mr. Baylies of Taunton considered the views of the gentleman from Cambridge (Mr. Makepeace) to be wild and fanciful. The debate at times became so acrimonious that several members were declared out of order.

At last the wordy tournament was over, and on January 30 the House rejected the railroad bill by a sound majority of 130 votes. Hale said in the *Advertiser* that many vague, inconclusive and contradictory objections had been made to the measure, and that many members admitted they would have voted for it if the route proposed had been definitely set to pass their own towns. This brought forth a clever satirical poem which the *Advertiser* published two or three days later:

## DEBATE ON THE RAIL-ROAD

I rise, Mr. Speaker, though I very well know
That most of the Members are wanting to go,
But I don't care for that, Sir, I'm as hungry as they,
And I shan't stir a peg, Sir, till I've had out my say.

I've set down so long, Sir, that I'm really quite sore,
And I shan't set no longer, now I've once got the floor.
I've been in my seat, Sir, now more than a week,
And I'm tired to death, hearing other folks speak.
And here I might sit, Sir, from June to December,
And when I go home, be called Sitting Member.
But this, Sir, won't do with one from our town,
And I guess as how, Sir, you can't put me down.
We are told, Mr. Speaker, that we'll travel this road
Twenty miles an hour, with twenty tons load.
And all this to be done, Sir, with a gallon of Steam;
By jinks, Mr. Speaker, 'tis a pretty smart team.
The wheels turn so fast, we are told ('tis no joke),
They say, Sir, you can't for your soul, see a spoke.
'Tis what I call, Mr. Speaker, a pretty good jog,
And as folks now say, it goes the whole hog.
But Sir, I'm no flat, and I knows what I knows,
And I shan't give my vote till I know *where* it goes.
But from what I can hear, Sir, I guess I could tell
Why the route now named suits Mr. A. B. so well.
He lives in blank town, Sir, and as I can l'arn,
The route afore named passes close by his Barn.
Mr. C. D., Sir, wants it to go t'other way,
Because it will help him in carting his hay.
So does Mr. S., Sir, I mean Mr. Scott,
Because it runs near to his ten-acre lot.
That is all very well, Sir, but what will folks say,
Who have ten-acre lots and barns up our way,
When they see other folks go to market by Steam,
While they drag along through the mud with a team?
And that ain't the worst, for there's no use in wailing,
While others have all the advantage in railing.
But, Sir, up in our parts, we are all wide awake,
And when we can see which route you will take,
I can then tell you better whether I'll vote yea or nay,
But I reckon 'twill be for the route our way.
But now, Sir, I'm done, and as Members are dodging,
I won't be the last to get to our lodging.

The rejection of the railroad bill ended the long battle between public and private ownership, ended the first semester of New England's education in the science of railroading; for the five neighboring states were all watching the trend of events in Massachusetts and profiting by it.  To change the metaphor, the rejection of the bill may be likened to the breaking of a dam which held back the flood of private enterprise.  No sooner had the vote been taken than applications were presented for the chartering of four railroad corporations: the Franklin, to build to the Vermont or New Hampshire line, in the direction of Brattleboro; another to Lowell, another to Providence, and another to the western boundary of the state, heading for Albany or Troy.

## The First Charters

WITH something of the wrong-headedness so often manifested by politician-lawmakers when dealing with business matters, the only railroad charters granted at that winter session (which was prorogued on March 13, 1830) were for corporations which never came to life: namely, the Franklin; the Boston, Providence & Taunton; and the Massachusetts Railroad Corporation, which hoped to build to Albany.

The Lowell railroad had failed to obtain a charter of the sort it desired. Its promoters, big business men of Lowell, were canny: they wanted protection against competition. When the bill was presented to the Legislature, it carried a provision to the effect that within ten years no other parallel road might be chartered, "from Boston to Lowell or from Boston to any place within five miles of the northern termination of the Rail Road hereby authorized." That section stank so strongly of monopoly that a motion to strike it out was easily carried. At that, the member who had introduced the bill moved to lay it on the table, saying that the promoters did not believe funds could be raised without such protection. And so the session ended.

During the recess, debate as to the merits of various proposed lines raged hotly in the newspapers and in public gatherings. In Faneuil Hall on March 31, a large meeting was held in behalf of the Franklin Railroad, which now was not expected to stop at Brattleboro, but was to continue on to Lake Champlain, even to Lake Ontario (ferrying across

Champlain from Burlington, Vt.) or to the Canada line. Montpelier and other Vermont towns held meetings, as did Ogdensburg, N. Y., which was spoken of as the northwestern terminus, and Concord, N. H., which hoped to bring the road up its valley. In fact, James Hayward was in the field that summer, making surveys for a rival line via New Hampshire, which, according to a prospectus published in the following year, was to be called the Boston & Ontario. Meanwhile, a meeting of southern Vermonters was held at Windsor to boost the Boston & Whitehall, which was to run up through Lowell and Nashua, then swing westward through Weare, Newport and Cornish, N. H., cross the Connecticut, and by way of Windsor, Plymouth, Shrewsbury and Rutland, reach Lake Champlain at or near Whitehall. The promoters said that because of ice the St. Lawrence was impassable for six months and the Champlain Canal to Albany for four months in the year; and as transportation would at all times be cheaper and faster by rail to Boston than by water to New York, "a great proportion of the trade of the Canadas and that of the valley of the lake, including the immense iron factories of that region, would be secured to Boston."

In April, Royal Makepeace sought to stem this northern tide with a series of newspaper articles in favor of the railroad to Albany. He scoffed at the fears of some that the line to the Hudson would merely enable New York City to swallow up the commerce of Massachusetts and do it more harm than good. As for the proposed northwestern line, Canada was sparsely settled and Ogdensburg a petty village; what Massachusetts needed was a road that was going somewhere. He favored state ownership and called the recent Legislature illiberal and impolitic in refusing to back the railroad. "A Yankee" retorted in favor of the Vermont route, in a letter more than a column long.

In the meantime, a discordant note was sounded against the Lowell line. The Middlesex Canal connecting Boston and Lowell, a Boston project of a previous generation which had many stockholders in that city, saw its feeble existence threatened by the proposed railroad and raised its voice in protest.

In February it laid before the Legislature a remonstrance against the granting of a charter to the railroad. The directors set forth the great trouble and expense which the building of the canal had cost them, and said that if better navigation were extended to Concord, N. H., they could draw all the commerce of New Hampshire and some of Vermont to Boston. They had merely been "awaiting the ripening of public opinion as to the best modes of facilitating an intercourse with the interior." The document proceeded:

> In this state of things, the remonstrants have been surprised by a petition for a railroad from Boston to Lowell, and are much embarrassed to decide what course it may become them to adopt. . . . They are exceedingly reluctant to present any objections to any theories of public improvement, especially at a time when the best minds in the country seem to be intent on effecting something; but on the other hand, they respectfully venture to intimate that there must be some limit, in point of rational principle, to the making of new adventures under public sanction, to the serious injury of those undertaken in the favor of similar auspices. . . . No *mere substitute* for the established accommodation should be allowed without an obvious necessity. If this be not so, it would seem that the patrons of the public welfare and of private and expensive enterprise conducted under this patronage will discourage all efforts of private persons to adventure for the public good.

They informed the General Court that the tolls paid to the canal by the proprietors of the Lowell mills who were now demanding a railroad were only about $4000 yearly. What inducement therefore could they allege for the creation of a railroad?

> It is believed that no safer or cheaper mode of conveyance can ever be established [than the canal], nor any so well adapted for bulky articles. To establish therefore, a *substitute* for the canal alongside of it, and for the whole distance, and in many places within a few rods of it, and to do that which the canal was made to do, seems to be a measure not called for by any exigency, nor one which the Legislature

can permit without implicitly declaring, that all investments of money in public enterprises must be subjected to the will of any applicants who think that they may justly benefit themselves, and that they may do it without regard to older enterprises which have a claim to protection from public authority. With regard, then, to transportation of tonnage goods, the means exist for all but the winter months, as effectually as any that can be provided. There is a supposed source of revenue to a Rail-Road *from carrying passengers.* As to this, the Remonstrants venture no opinion, except to say that passengers are now carried at all hours, as rapidly and safely as they are anywhere else in the world; and if the usual time consumed in passing from one place to another be three hours—there seems not to be any such exigency to make that space of time half what it now is, as to justify the establishment of a rail-road for that purpose merely. . . . To this, the Remonstrants would add, that the use of a rail-road *for passengers only,* has been tested by experience, nowhere, hitherto; and that it remains to be known whether this is a mode which will command general confidence and approbation. . . .

The Remonstrants would also add, that so far as they know and believe, *there can never be a sufficient inducement to extend a rail-road from Lowell westwardly, and north-westwardly to the Connecticut, so as to make it the great avenue to and from the interior, but that its termination must be at Lowell, and consequently . . . cannot deserve patronage from the supposition that it is to be more extensively useful.*

They said that more than two thirds of all the freight that passed between Boston and Concord, N. H., was still carried on wagons, despite the lower cost on canal and river. "In a country such as ours, the habit of teaming cannot be broken up." The horses were there, and they must and would be used. As for passengers, could it be expected that all the stages running from the north through Lowell to Boston would stop at Lowell, and the passengers go the rest of the way by the cars? No! "The projectors will probably find that stage owners will carry passengers between Boston and Lowell gratis, rather than lose the carrying north and west of that place." Even then, the competition was such that one might ride from Boston to Concord for a dollar and to Hanover for two dollars.

The remonstrants' conclusion was that there was no such exigency as to warrant the granting of a railroad charter; but if it was granted, the canal company should be indemnified for the loss thereby occasioned to it. There was more than a touch of pathos in the appeal, which revealed the old canal's fear that it was fighting a losing battle. It was in effect trying to withstand Boreas with a hand bellows. That peculiar itch for speed which was even then becoming an American characteristic was already beginning to outmode the canal as a means of transportation, though the Erie and some others did not feel it for years afterward. England and other European countries are wise enough still to use canals and rivers for freight which need not be delivered overnight, but your highstrung twentieth-century American can hardly wait for that dreamed-of day when he will be shipping carloads of coal and iron ore by air.

The Middlesex Canal protest awakened little sympathetic response in the legislative bosom. The railroad star was now rising. The Lowell promoters girded themselves for another attack in the summer session, and this time they enlisted the powerful aid of Daniel Webster. They themselves were men of means and influence, socially, industrially and politically, which aided them in winning their wish: namely, a charter which guaranteed that no other parallel road would be built "from Boston to Lowell, or from Boston to any place within five miles of the northern termination of the Rail Road hereby authorized," within thirty years from the date of their charter. (They had at first asked for forty.) But the state reserved the right, at any time after ten years from the opening of the road, to buy it back from the corporation, paying all costs of construction, repairs and other expenses, with interest at 10 per cent per annum, *"deducting all sums received by the Corporation from tolls or any other source of profit and interest at the rate of ten per centum thereon."*

A right of way four rods wide might be taken, and settlement for it, if not by voluntary agreement, was to be made "in the manner provided by law for the recovery of damages happening by the laying out of highways." Whenever crossing any private or public way, the Corporation must not obstruct it; but it was given the power to raise or lower such road, if it chose, so that the railroad might "conveniently pass under or over the same." But such grade separation must be satisfactory to the turnpike company or to the selectmen of the town. There was, by the way, much worry then over the question of how wagons and carriages were to cross railroad tracks without jolting themselves to pieces. All doubters were urged to visit the Granite Railway and see how the thing had been worked out, exactly as in the practice of today. The question of how to make "sidelings" was another which even at that late date fretted the railroad-building novices. Mr. Sargent, the monorail inventor, even proposed a switch by which the train would always keep to the right, but a movable tongue was the solution decided upon.

A study of the charter reveals the fact that, under a strict interpretation, it did not empower the grantees to operate a railroad at all!—only to build it and charge for its use, not to run trains upon it. The document was artfully drawn so that it might be interpreted either way. The corporation was given the right to collect "tolls" on passengers and freight, which was the only way they knew of describing the income. But notice this: "The transportation of persons and property, the construction of wheels, the form of cars and carriages, the weight of loads and all other matters and things in relation to the use of said Road shall be in conformity to such rules and regulations and provisions as the Directors shall, from time to time, prescribe and direct"; and finally and significantly: "Said Road may be used by any person who shall comply with such rules and regulations." On the surface, it looked as if they were chartering a mere turnpike, but actually, if the directors chose to prescribe that the public should use only cars and motive power belonging to the corporation, that, under the charter, was what the public would have to do.

The Boston & Lowell charter, dated June 5, 1830, is a milestone in railroad history, being the first granted in New England for a steam railway which was actually built and became a reality. It is interesting to observe also that it did not specify the use of steam: the promoters, still cautious, reserved the right to use horses if steam failed to make good. The company was capitalized at $1,200,000, in shares of $500 each—the only railroad in the country, so far as we can discover, with a share par value of more than $100.

The Worcester and Providence projects had to wait another year for their charters. True, the Boston, Providence & Taunton was authorized in 1830, but its promoters decided, after all, not to try to spread over so much territory, but to leave Taunton out of the calculation and ask for a new charter for a direct line to Providence. Meanwhile, at least one citizen of Boston grew impatient with all these postponements and delays, and he wrote to the *Advertiser* about it. He cited "your Festina Lentes among the Latins; your Piano e Sanos among the Italians; your Poco a Pocos among the Spaniards, your Hâte-toi-Lentements among the French; your make-haste-slowlys among the English." Americans had not, for a century or so, manifested any such leisureliness. But "now, all at once, the good people of Boston and Massachusetts have taken to crawling on their hands and knees, to set an example of prudence, I suppose, to the Flying Dutchmen of New York and Pennsylvania."

It was the state politicians and the public who were at fault, not the promoters, for these were now all in a lather of eagerness to get something going. Even the city government of Boston asked the January legislative session of 1831 for permission to invest in a railroad corporation, but there was so much public opposition to this that the request was denied. The Providence promoters now came forward, asking for a charter for a direct line to that city. The folk who had hoped to throw out a line to Albany had found that with so many projects in the air, the proposal to build a road so long, so difficult in engineering and therefore so costly as theirs, was too frightening to possible investors, so they decided to lower their sights a little and ask for a right to Worcester only, a mere quarter of what they hoped to accomplish later. Furthermore, a railroad to Worcester would to a considerable degree nullify the ill effects of that Blackstone Canal which was draining so much central Massachusetts business down to Providence and New York. Both groups sought action in the winter session, but again it was put over. That was the last delay, however. On June 22, 1831, the act of incorporation of the Boston & Providence was passed, and that of the Boston & Worcester on the following day. One is pleasantly surprised to find that the enacted bills were signed by Leverett Saltonstall as President of the House of Representatives—a name which has become eminently familiar to us again in the twentieth century.

These corporations also obtained thirty-year monopolies. As the Worcester's charter stated, no other line might be built within that time from Boston, Roxbury, Brookline, Cambridge or Charlestown to Worcester. The recapture clause was likewise in these, as in the other early Massachusetts railroad charters, though the time allowed came to be twenty years, instead of ten, as in the first Lowell charter. Josiah Quincy, Jr., who had become a prominent railroad figure (later on, he was one of the leading promoters of the Western Railway and for a number of years President of the Boston & Providence), wrote in his *Figures of the Past* (1883) that the early Massachusetts railroads were "built by patriotic men for the public benefit." Nevertheless, he lauded the "protective clause" which, even when he wrote, fifty years after, "still permits the people to foreclose on any one of the old railroads whenever they choose to do so. . . . It is not the actual use of such reserved rights," he explains, "but their existence *in terrorem* which protects the interests of society against the greed of some small minority of its members."

Opposition smoldered, even after the passing of the incorporation acts. "Common Sense," writing to the *Columbian Centinel* on July 20, gave warning: "I would advise no individual or Corporation to suppose that they have in their possession any circumstances which can control absolutely the location of these roads." Local antagonisms caused many changes in the early railroad routes, as we shall see.

The Troy & Vermont Railroad was chartered in New York that year, and its stock was on the market in New York City—little or none in Boston, as may be imagined. On the other hand, when in March the New York papers remarked that "the demand for Rail Road stocks in this city appears to be unprecedented," it didn't necessarily mean that New Yorkers were buying any stock in the new Massachusetts lines. Vermonters also became a bit excited over a proposed Rutland and Whitehall Railroad in 1831. In the same year, Massachusetts chartered one of the Boston-to-Ogdensburg projects, under the name Boston & Ontario Railroad; and the *American Traveller* spoke of it as "that route, in comparison with which, those which are at present engaging the most attention must be insignificant in their influence on the prosperity of our city."

# 5

## Massachusetts Produces Triplets

THE Boston & Lowell Railroad was the product of an early nineteenth-century boom town. In 1821 Lowell was a village of only twelve houses, known as East Chelmsford. But there were falls, or rather, rapids in the Merrimac River there, and a little canal had been dug around them, years before. In 1822 a group headed by Nathan Appleton—who had begun to build a fortune on his investment in Francis C. Lowell's power-loom business at Waltham—organized the "Locks and Canal Company," to utilize the water power at those Merrimac Falls, and thus founded the city which they christened Lowell. Textile mills were established, and in 1826 the place was incorporated. By 1830 it had a population of 6474, which was not to be sneered at in the New England of that day, when you consider that Providence then had only 16,000, New Haven 10,600, Hartford 4700, Springfield 6700 and Portland 12,600.

The Middlesex Canal gave Lowell slow freight service to Boston, but few people ever traveled on it, preferring the much swifter stagecoaches. By 1829, Patrick T. Jackson, Kirk Boott (whose name still survives in that of a great textile mill), the Appletons and others of the Lowell manufacturers agreed that Lowell must have better transportation facilities, especially with Boston, a scant twenty-six miles away. At that time it was said that twenty-four tons of freight passed daily between the two cities, as well as 100 to 120 passengers in "six fast coaches, drawn by four to six horses each." Jackson, who was the leader in the promotion, suggested early in

1830 a meeting of the directors of the Locks and Canal Company, "to draw the attention of the proprietors of that stock to the project of building a rail-road from this place [Boston] to Lowell." Jackson then lived at 22 Winter Street, Boston, and there, in his parlor, on January 27, the meeting was held which launched New England's first railroad project.

When the charter was authorized in June, the company was soon organized, with Jackson as president and "agent," or general manager, undertaking to oversee the construction. Books were opened for subscriptions to the stock, and Jackson himself led the way by taking 124 shares, par value $62,000. Five others, with such significant names as Munroe, Lowell, Lyman, Pratt and Appleton, signed for 390 more shares, bringing the total subscription for the six to $259,000, more than a fifth of the entire capital stock. But thereafter, the stock-selling was not quite so easy. The project was regarded by many as "Quixotical." Building a line between two big cities like Liverpool and Manchester was logical enough, they admitted, but not to so small a place as Lowell. Daniel Webster remarked during a trial fifteen years later, that "there was no alacrity in filling up its subscription list, and there was great difficulty in procuring funds as the work went on"—in which he overdrew the picture just a little for purposes of argument. The last mile was, as always, the hardest, but the well-to-do men who promoted the road could put up enough money to send it off to a flying start and build it expensively, and that was far better fortune than the other two pioneer roads out of Boston enjoyed. Its capital, $1,200,-000, it will be noted, was larger than that of either of the other two lines, $1,000,000 each, though each of them was about 75 per cent longer, the Lowell measuring only 25¾ miles, the Providence 41 and the Worcester 44.

A route had already been surveyed for the state a couple of years earlier by James Hayward, but now a new survey was made by James F. Baldwin. Jackson was determined from the start that the road should be the best that money could buy. Hence the survey was made for a double track, though it was intended that only one track should be built before the road opened for business. But it is significant to observe how short-sighted even these excellent businessmen were in some respects, just as the wisest of men are still when venturing upon unexplored ground. To Jackson and the others the road was primarily and most importantly a freight carrier between their mills and Boston; all other interests were secondary. Through passenger business came next in consequence. As for local business along the line, to heck with it! The villagers didn't want the railroad, and Jackson was quite acquiescent in that; he preferred to buy a right of way through the country, where land was cheaper.

A peculiar quirk had become manifest: the farmers wanted the railroad, most of the villages didn't. To them it was just smoke, sparks, noise, a menace to life and limb in their streets, a disturbance of their old placid way of life. Jackson suited them to a T when he ordered the survey to bypass the thriving villages of Medford, Woburn, Billerica and Wilmington, and run through open country nearly all the way. Both sides very shortly began to regret their error. The villages found that they wanted the railroad service, and some of them, as they grew, grew toward the tracks. New villages sprang up there, and the railroad in turn found to its surprise that local passenger and freight business was worth thinking about. Medford was so close to the line that Charles Brooks, historian of the town, wrote in 1855 that the railroad had doubled the value of property there, and "for the small fare of fifteen cents, it presents each day a dozen opportunities for going to Boston and as many for return, and occupies about fifteen minutes in the passage." The village was not satisfied, however, with a station so far out of town, and in 1845–46 built the Medford Branch Railroad to Boston, which need not have existed had the B. & L. penetrated the village itself.

Despite Sedgwick's boast of the ubiquity and efficiency of "New England Turnpikers," Irish laborers physically created the Boston & Lowell, as they did nearly all our early railroads and canals. The entire right of way was graded, even bridges and culverts built, before any track was laid. So level is the country that there was no grade anywhere of more than ten

*Courtesy Sidney Withington, Boston & Maine R. R. Warren Jacobs, etc.*

OLD RAILROAD STATIONS
1. Bridgeport, Conn., 1850.
2. 18th century building, Thomaston, Maine.
3. Wolcottville, Conn., 1880.
4. Fall River, Mass., 1850.
5. Union Station at New Haven, built 1848.

SOME OLD BOSTON RAILWAY STATIONS

1. Haymarket Square, Boston & Maine, 1847; 2. Park Square, Boston & Providence, 1875-99; 3. Fitchburg, 1848-94; 4. Kneeland Street, Boston & Albany, 1881-99.

Photos from Boston Public Library, Walter A. Lucas and Chas. E. Fisher

## NEW HAMPSHIRE LOCOMOTIVES
1. Mount Washington Railway in the 1870's.
2. Portland & Ogdenburg R. R. in Crawford Notch.
3. Boston, Lowell & Nashua Engine with "Saxaphone" spark-arrester stack.
4. Concord R. R.'s "Amoskeag".

*Above, courtesy C. B. Curr; Below, New Haven R. R.*

*Above*—First vestibule cars, Naugatuck R. R., 1854.
*Below*—First observation car: it ran between New York and the
White Mountains in the 1870's.

*Above*—A Fall River R. R. train, about 1846.

*Below*—The New York & New England's White train, with Gene Potter and his 167 in the van.

*Courtesy Warren Jacobs, Charles E. Fisher and C. B. Burt*

1. Boston & Maine double-header emerging from east portal of Hoosac Tunnel.
Note original abandoned bore at left.
2. Troy & Boston Engine, 1852.
3. Boston, Concord & Montreal's "Franconia," 1870.

OLD BRASS BAGGAGE CHECKS — SAVE THAT THE NORWICH &
WORCESTER CHECK IN LOWER RIGHT-HAND CORNER IS OF LEAD.

A MILE OF OIL COMING DOWN MILLER'S RIVER IN WESTERN MASSACHUSETTS

feet to the mile. Even after they began work, the directors questioned each other whether the middle of the track should be earthed for a horse-path, or "do we determine to use Loco-Motive Engines?" Someone even timidly mentioned a horse on a car, working a treadmill, as had been tried elsewhere. It was suggested that if the cars were drawn by horses, parties of persons could hire cars and come and go in them at their pleasure, thus to a certain extent carrying out the free-for-all, turnpike-and-livery-stable idea. But the successful opening, with great fanfare, of the steam-operated Liverpool & Manchester Railroad in November, 1830—which Hale took pains to publicize in the *Advertiser*—turned the scale. The Lowell directors decided to use the Loco-Motive Engine, and ordered one from Stephenson, completely equipped, including engineer to run it. The other two new railroads did the same; and as Stephenson had built the first English railroad tracks 4 feet, 8½ inches wide, and—having no orders to the contrary—made the first locomotives ordered from him by America to the same gauge, it came about that all the railroads of Massachusetts and eventually of America unfortunately became fixed at that figure. At the June session of the General Court in 1831, the Committee on Railways and Canals was directed to consider the expediency of fixing by law the gauges of railways in the state, but this proved to be unnecessary: Stephenson's locomotives did the job.

The builders of the B. & L. erred in another respect also. In their zeal to create a railroad which would stand through the ages, as well as in their aping of English procedure, they built it too well: they decided to use stone sleepers, and worse still, supported those ties on parallel stone walls, built deep in the roadbed under the rails. Colonel Baldwin, years before, had satisfied himself that not only would no other type of track withstand the winter freezes, but none other would sustain the trains; on any softer track the locomotive, when in motion, would always be overcoming an ascent caused by the sinking of the rails under its weight. Finally, England was laying her first tracks on stone, and that clinched the argument.

But within a few months Jackson was destined to learn a bitter lesson. That stone-silled, unyielding track caused rough riding on trains and jolted the rolling stock apart at an alarming rate. The little locomotives were so shaken up that sometimes mechanics worked all night putting one into condition to run next day. They were lucky if a collapse occurred on Saturday and they had a whole day for repairs.

*The Fish-Belly Rail Originally Used by the Boston & Lowell*

The Worcester and Providence companies had laid their rails on wood and were proving the superiority of the flexible foundation. It was an embarrassing lesson for the aristocrat of New England railroads and its hard-headed president, but they had to take out the stone ties and walls and substitute wood laid on rubble. Half a century later, an occasional one of those old stone sleepers might still have been seen lying along the right of way.

A much happier imitation of British practice was the grade separation of the Lowell. On the whole line only three grade crossings were permitted, and one of them, by the way, has been a bone of contention off and on for 111 years as these lines are being written. At the hamlet which had been variously called Waterfield, Black Horse Village and South Woburn, the railroad passed directly through the intersection of two roads which are now Church and Main Streets in the little city of Winchester. The company immediately erected gates on either side of the track, but employed no gateman, and the gates were or were not closed by anybody who happened to be near by when the train whistle was heard. So

remarkable an innovation was this that the village was popularly known for a long time as Woburn Gates.[1]

The rails were supported at each sleeper by "chairs" which
gripped the rail-base and were bolted to the tie. The first
rails laid were of the "fish-belly" type, an English design, the
under side of which curved downward between the chairs,
theoretically giving greater strength. A committee report in
1831 said:

> We have a rail from England precisely like that used on
> the Liverpool and Manchester Rail-Road—it is 15 feet long
> and weighs 172 pounds.
> We also have chairs, weighing 12½ pounds each.
> Pins for do., four of them, 27 ounces.
> Keys for do., ½ pound each.

The rails were heated and bent for the curves, not drawn
into place by spikes as in later practice. Jackson, who was
always on the job but whose only knowledge of railroads was
gained by reading and correspondence, was responsible for
some odd doings. For example, as Louis P. Loring, a de-
scendant of one of the first directors, tells us,[2] as fast as the
rails were joined, machinists from the Locks and Canal shop
would lay a steel straight-edge along each joint, and if the rail-
ends failed of a perfect junction by so much as the thickness
of a sheet of paper, they would file the projecting rail down
for a foot back from the junction. If the variance was equal
to the thickness of cardboard, the cold chisel might be used,

[1] In 1834, before the railroad began operation, the county commissioners
ordered the town to elevate the two roads so as to bridge over the tracks,
but this was never done. Many persons were killed at the crossing, and as
the twentieth century dawned, the town declared that something must be
done. It asked the railroad to depress its tracks, but Winchester is only
twelve feet above sea-level, and the earth is so permeated with water there
that this was not practicable. Next, the town demanded that the tracks be
elevated, but the Boston & Maine, by that time the proprietor of the Lowell
road, honestly answered that it couldn't afford the job; and so, after more
than a century, the matter still stood in 1936, at the time of publication of
Henry Smith Chapman's fine *History of Winchester*, from which I have
culled these facts, and so it stands to this day.

[2] In an article, "Early Railroads of Boston," in *The Bostonian* (magazine),
for December, 1894, pp. 299-309, which is frequently quoted herein.

followed by the file. The rail-smoothness of the Lowell was therefore exceptional. The rails were of iron, by the way, and broke easily. They began laying track from both ends simultaneously, and Loring declares that they absent-mindedly started from each end on the right-hand side, so that when they met in the middle, they had to make a reverse curve to join the two.

In November, 1832, the ship *Choctaw* arrived from Liverpool with the Stephenson engine—in knocked-down condition—and "2000 bars of railroad iron." The locomotive, one of the three or four named "John Bull," was built in Stephenson's plant at Newcastle-on-Tyne and was a high-pressure, thirty-horsepower machine with four large wheels and weighed seven tons. The plates on the sides of its firebox were welded instead of riveted, and the boiler was surrounded by wooden lagging or strips of timber. It was shipped from Boston by the Middlesex Canal—fancy how the canal management must have loved that chore!—to the Locks and Canal shop in Lowell, where it was to be assembled. This job was handed over a few months later to two men who were skilled mechanics but who had never seen a locomotive before. They had no working drawings, nothing to go by but their own horse sense and some cabalistic numbers in red paint on the various parts. After puttering with them for a while and making little progress, they decided to go down to Boston and see a Stephenson locomotive which had been bought by the Boston & Worcester and assembled under the eye of a British engineer, who expected to begin using it shortly. But at Boston they were forbidden to come near the new engine, and an explanation of their reason for wishing to examine it only "made the prohibition more positive." They could only go back to Lowell and slowly, by trial and error, work out the problem, which they finally succeeded in doing.

Major George W. Whistler became superintendent of the shops in 1834, his principal job at the start being the construction of two more engines like Stephenson's—with improvements, if possible—on which he at once proceeded to work.

And here we are introduced to two names which bulk

large in early New England railroad history—those of the two young engineers, Whistler and William Gibbs McNeill. As youngsters of twenty-eight and twenty-seven years respectively, they had worked together on the B. & O. survey in 1828 and had been sent to Europe together to study the railroads there. They became fast friends—nay, more: Whistler married McNeill's sister Anna, and some forty years later she sat as a model to her artist son for America's best-beloved modern portrait.[3] As chief or consulting engineers the two chums, either individually or collectively, had much to do with the building of several of New England's earliest and most important railroads.

Had Whistler come to the Lowell road earlier, he might have succeeded in averting that folly of building the track on a stone foundation. As it was, he made its shops the first locomotive-building plant in New England.

On May 27, 1835, the track being completed and an Englishman having arrived to drive the Stephenson locomotive, it sped over the rails for the first time from Lowell to Boston, with Jackson, Whistler and Baldwin aboard a car, in the amazing time of one hour and seventeen minutes—something like twenty miles an hour. It returned to Lowell with directors and friends to the number of twenty-four, just to let them see what it could do, then took them back to Boston again, where it remained for four weeks, awaiting the com-

[3] Whistler's father had come to America as a British soldier under Burgoyne. After the latter's surrender, John Whistler, paroled, returned to England, but came back to America after the peace and enlisted in the United States Army, serving as an engineer officer. He built Fort Dearborn, on the site of Chicago. His son, born in the military post at Fort Wayne in 1800, he named in honor of his late Commander-in-Chief, George Washington. The son followed in his father's footsteps, going through West Point and rising to the position of major of engineers before resigning from the army.

It was while he was living at Lowell that the Major's famous son, James Abbott McNeill Whistler, was born on July 10, 1834. Another son, named in honor of the brother-in-law, William Gibbs McNeill Whistler, became a prominent physician in London. A third son was christened Kirk Boott. It was the whim of the eccentric artist Whistler to deny his Lowell birth and to claim sometimes Baltimore, sometimes St. Petersburg as his native city. But the actual house of his birth is now preserved in Lowell as a shrine to his memory.

pletion of the other two engines, so that regular service might be installed. There were no such numerous and delirious joy rides as had been taking place on the partly completed Worcester road during the past year; the Lowell was too dignified for that. But at last, on June 23, the following announcement appeared in the Boston papers:

June 23d, 1835

To-morrow, 24th, the cars will commence running between Boston and Lowell. Leave at 6 and 9½ A.M. Leave Boston at 3½ and 5½ P.M. The Company expects to run another Engine next week. Additional trains will be put on as fast as the public require; due notice will be given when the merchandise train will be put on. Fare, $1.00, tickets at corner Leverett and Brighton Streets, Boston.

George M. Dexter, Agent

On the following day the first train went out of Boston with directors and many invited guests aboard. Of course it created great excitement throughout the countryside as it sped grandly by: the rich, dark-green locomotive with black striping, the British engineer in his plug hat and kid gloves, and his fireman in full view of the gaping multitude as they balanced precariously on the narrow platforms between the cabless locomotive and its tender; the cars like large, three-compartment stagecoach bodies on flanged wheels, each car with six cross-seats full of cheering excursionists. It was not until several trips later that the conductor sat on what would be the driver's seat of the first coach, enduring the showering hot cinders as stoically as he could, blowing a penny whistle as a starting signal and as a call for down brakes—though the engineer probably could not hear this above the noise of the train, and the brakeman, a car or two behind him, must have had to get the signal by the eye. The brakes, by the way, were exactly like those of a stagecoach, applied by pressing a long foot-lever. The engine had no whistle, and its little bell was rung by a cord about a foot and a half long.

The couplings between cars were three loose iron links, and when the engine started, passengers' necks in one car after another were almost dislocated by the shock; men were jerked out from under their tall beaver hats, and roof-riders sometimes lost theirs. It was quickly evident that the couplings would have to be improved, and more rigid ones were presently devised. Also, it began to be apparent that seats on top of the cars were impracticable (the Lowell never had them), for sparks burned the clothing of outside passengers to shreds. They even flew inside the cars in warm weather when the windows were open, and did much damage.

There was much to be endured on those first train trips, on all three of the railroads, but when this first train neared Lowell, the yelling, hat-waving throng on the hillside at the outskirts (the remainder of the population being at the station), the fireworks, the banquet that followed, the heady stimulus of the wines and flowery speeches made the discomforts seem worth while, even though one's best clothing was flecked with spark-holes.

The complete innocence of the railway's possibilities on the part of the population is illustrated in an anecdote related by Warren Teel decades later in the *Winchester Record*. He was a small boy when the first train came through, and had the curiosity which generations of youngsters have had since, to see what the cars would do to a copper penny laid on the rail. A certain Colonel White saw him, rebuked him and ordered him to remove the coin lest it derail the train! But the colonel himself was now smitten by curiosity and decided to try a silver sixpence, which, being thinner, might be risked. Little Warren placed it for him, but when the train appeared and drew nearer and nearer, both were seized with panic lest they throw the mighty organism off the track, and they both sprang to remove the obstruction. As the cars thundered away, however, the colonel gazed after them and muttered, "Sho! Might have put a silver dollar on the rail and no harm done."

That English engine-driver, William Robinson, who had come over to show Americans how to handle a locomotive, was a dandy and a sport, and lost no opportunity to impress the unsophisticated Yankees. He even brought a fast horse with him and raced it on the Lowell track—for that young factory town had already taken up vain diversions. Legend coagulates thickly about Robinson. He did not trouble himself to be at the station in time to take his train out strictly on schedule; gossip even has him at times an hour late, but we cannot believe that. When he arrived, he would mount to his post, slowly draw on his kid gloves, give a supercilious look around, and start at his pleasure, giving the impression that it was he, not the conductor, who was master of the train. One of his stunts was to stop the train at some hamlet where there were plenty of onlookers, get down, peer under the engine, tinker with some gadget for a few minutes, perhaps take a nut off and put it back again, while some of the passengers would come forward to gaze respectfully, and finally they would start again. Then the report would be—it might even get into some of the papers—that the engine had broken down, but that Mr. Robinson, with his superior skill, had quickly righted it again.

On June 30 and July 1, the two new locomotives built by Whistler were ready for service, and there was much pother over the naming of them. Among others, "Double Speeder" and "David Crockett" were suggested, and one report has it that these names were actually used, but this appears to be erroneous. The directors thought the first one completed should be named "Jackson," in honor of the tireless builder who had for four years given up most of his time and no little of his sleep to the job. But Andrew Jackson was then in the White House, and the overwhelming Whiggish majority in the directorate saw that the name wouldn't do, for political reasons, so they compromised on their president's given name and christened the engine "Patrick." The one which received its finishing touches on the following day was named "Lowell." Both of these, as well as the "Boston," built a little later, had brass driving wheels. Then on one named "Merrimac," they went to the opposite extreme and used wooden drivers—iron-tired, of course.

All these early Massachusetts locomotives were wood-burners. New England still had vast areas of forest, but no coal, and that commodity had to be brought from Pennsylvania by sea. Worcester became excited early in the century over a low-grade deposit of coal found near by; but its heating quality proved to be poor, and firemen who used it were inclined to swear that more residue came out of the firebox than coal went in, so it was soon neglected. Lower Rhode Island also has a small coal vein, but it is too poor to be used.

Mr. Robinson tested the two new machines and shook his head over them. Under his guidance they broke down immediately; they hadn't been properly constructed, he said. But one story that comes down to us is that after a couple of days of this, an employee hid in the engine-house at night and saw Robinson steal in and damage some part or other, which insured another breakdown next day. With that, Major Whistler sent Robinson packing back to England. Some mechanics trained in the shops took over the engineer's duties and did very well with them. To prove his confidence in his own work, Whistler set the Stephenson engine to pulling the "burthen train" when it began operating on July 5, while his own two machines handled the passengers. Two ex-stage drivers were the first two passenger conductors and remained on the job until old age incapacitated them.

As the importance of the railroad grew on the consciousness of Boston, a warmer interest and desire for co-operation became manifest. When Jackson—instead of condemning a right of way across the city's tidal flats, as his company had legal authority to do, so that its trains might enter the city instead of stopping in Charlestown—petitioned the municipality for the right, Mayor Otis and the Council unanimously granted it, assuming that a satisfactory payment for the property could be agreed upon. The track would cut off water access to the City Prison and the House of Correction, but the Council voted to remove the latter to the city's lands in South Boston. Earth and gravel from cuttings on the line were brought in to fill the marshes. This filling and bridge were not quite ready when the road began operation, and the trains for a time stopped at East Cambridge. The first station in Boston was a small, one-story brick building.

At first conception, the vision of the promoters extended no farther than their own termini, but even before the line was completed, they were making arrangements for through business, as witness an advertisement of late June:

Lowell Rail-Road and Steam-Boat Lines for New-Hampshire and Vermont.

The Cars for these lines will leave the Depot in Boston at 9 o'clock A.M., on and after Monday, June 29th. On the arrival at Lowell, carriages will take the passengers free of charge immediately on board the Steamer, which will convey them to Nashua, N.H., where stages in connection with the Concord, N.H., and Amherst and Francestown lines will be in readiness to take them forward. The passengers will dine on board the Steamer while she is passing up the River.

THOMAS LEWIS
Captain of the Steam-Boat "Herald."

Lowell, June 27th, 1835.

Passenger business leaped quickly into importance, and super-service was supplied. Those wise Lowell directors didn't mind admitting it when they had made a bad guess. The *Merchants' and Traders' Guide* for 1836 said, "Before the starting of the cars, stages leave Nos. 9 and 11 Elm-street, and City Tavern, Brattle-street, and call at almost any part of the city for passengers, and take them to the depot, free of charge."

Country business, too, bobbed up as unexpectedly important. At first, the only scheduled stop for the passenger trains was at Woodburn—appropriate name, for the halt there was not to serve passengers but to take on water and fuel for the wood-burning steed. But within six months, the "agent" (manager) was telling the company: "We are requested to stop at six places, and I think it will require five minutes for each stop. If we add twenty minutes to the time that it now takes our regular trains . . . my opinion is that it would injure our reputation for speed. . . . But I would try the experiment." The problem was solved by building a fourth locomotive and putting on a purely local train, which promptly began to do a good business. There was at first no provision for passengers at South Woburn (Winchester), and the first station—not used until 1837—was a former cobbler's shop about fifteen feet square which stood near the tracks.

The growth in all departments astounded everyone. When they began construction, it was guessed that three locomotives and less than a score of cars would serve all purposes for years. Now there seemed no limit to the possibilities. The second track (on wooden ties) was begun as soon as possible and pushed forward as funds would permit. The *Merchants' and Traders' Guide* for 1836 said that five miles of it had already been laid.

Now that we have launched the Lowell, let us glance at the other two lines which were building simultaneously.

The Boston & Worcester had no such group of wealthy "angels" as the Lowell to give it a sendoff. It was created through great tribulation. It had an even smaller village than Lowell as its western terminus; for Worcester, by the census of 1830, could boast of no more than 4172 inhabitants, though it had some small factories and, as many believed, a bright future. However, it had become somewhat alienated from Boston by reason of the Blackstone Canal and its resulting trade with Providence, and little or no investment in the railroad could be expected from its citizens.

In March, 1831, four months before the B. & W.'s charter was granted, a legislative committee recommended that the state subscribe for one third of its capital stock. The shares of the Lowell road had then been practically all sold, and some were regretting that they had not got in on its ground floor. The General Court, however, refused to consider buying any Worcester stock, which was not considered to be as gilt-edged as that of the Lowell. Nevertheless, when its Incorporation Act was passing through the House and a doubter sneered, "It'll never be built," Mr. Bond of Boston, one of the promoters, calmly replied, "I have no more doubt of its being built than I have of my own existence"—in which he differed from certain eminent philosophers, who even questioned the probability of their own existence. Mr. Bond may have had his doubts later.

Henry Williams, one of the directors, spoke in after years of the difficulties which beset the project at the outset, without the aid of the capitalists, who feared to embark on so perilous an adventure. "The work," said he, "was commenced and has been completed by the middling class in the community." This was not strictly true, for the wealthy did invest, though only in small amounts, and the rest had to be placed by hard labor among the "middling class." And as Adams remarks, the science of railroad financiering was as little understood in America then as that of railroad building; but the New England merchants, editors, bankers, doctors and artisans who went in for it learned it admirably, though indeed by the hard way. Their amateur status in railroading is seen in the roster of officials and directors of the Boston & Worcester, elected when it was organized in August, 1831. Nathan Hale, journalist, was its first president, and he had given the subject such intensive study for five years past that he did a creditable job.

But the corporation was handicapped by lack of funds at the start, for subscriptions to its stock were paid off only in small installments. Its first track was cheaply built and some of its equipment was inferior. Construction began in August, 1832. The B. & W. had no such charmingly flat terrain to deal with as the Lowell had; there was some high, rough country between its termini. Within 44 miles the road had to ascend 556 feet going westward, and then drop 100 feet to reach Worcester. James M. Fessenden had surveyed the route, and after much agonizing it was decided to avoid the use of inclined planes. Sharp curves were introduced, not only to keep the maximum gradient to 30 feet to the mile but to avoid deep cutting wherever possible. There was one ledge, however, in the town of Wellesley which had to be gashed—and extensively, too. The broken rock from it was dumped into Back Bay, thus beginning the foundation for Boston's most fashionable residence quarter in later years.

Stone sleepers were at first contemplated and had actually begun to be laid; but the officials learned, as the report of February 5, 1834, says, that "experiments made on the Rail-Roads in the Middle States" had proved their undesirability. Hale, too, alert to all ideas that were in the breeze, doubtless knew that Engineer McNeill had begun laying wooden ties on the Boston & Providence, and his reasons therefor. So the ties used, as officially stated, were chestnut and swamp cedar, though a correspondent of the *Maine Farmer*, seeing the line in 1834, spoke of the rails as being "laid on cross-sticks of oak, chestnut, etc." Whatever they were, wood was a great saving over granite at seven cents per cubic foot.

For reasons of economy, a very narrow roadbed was graded and a light edge-rail was used, the sort that was apt to come loose at the end and curl up as a train went over it, making so-called "snake-heads," which might even pierce the floors of cars and injure passengers. In Boston the terminal arrangements were at first small and shabby. A one-story building, "barely large enough to receive two cars at once, sufficed for indoor freight." Bales of cotton were handled in the open, often exposed to bad weather.

The company quickly began to encounter the hostility of villages and interested parties against its obtaining a right of way. Its cautious president had divined what the Vermont & Massachusetts later had to learn *post facto*, as we guess from the V. & M. directors' report of 1850, in which they say:

These suits for land damages have given us much trouble; and we are fully satisfied that, in the construction of a railroad, it is best to settle such matters before a spade is put into the ground. Men who would freely give their lands to induce you to locate your road through their premises, will afterwards maintain that they are greatly injured by it, and seek to obtain enormous damages. In some cases, however, we ought to say that owners of land have deported themselves like honest men.

The B. & W. had intended entering Wellesley Township through Newton Lower Falls and Wellesley Hills, but it was so strongly opposed by those communities that it avoided them and established the Wellesley Farms station, "merely a place to flag a train," in the open country. The line had been surveyed through Watertown and Waltham, but neither village wanted it, and said it so emphatically that the road kept to southward of them, through the plains of Newton. In Framingham, the course through Framingham Center was most feasible, but there the leading stockholders in a turnpike fought it so strenuously that it took an alternate course to the southward. Even there, the selectmen were directed by a town meeting in April, 1834, to look into "the Incrochments made on the Town roads by the Boston and Worcester Rail-Road." The directors now began to learn of the oppugnancies of railroad creation, and to fight back in self-defense. In Westborough: "The location of the road seriously interfered with the usefulness of the old meeting-house. The society demanded $1,000 damages for the land taken and other disadvantages, but were unable to get so much." [4]

So timorous were the small stockholders, so perturbed were they by these and other early troubles, that in January, 1833, only five months after construction had begun, one of them procured the signatures of the holders of a thousand shares of stock to a call for a stockholders' meeting, to consider the question of stopping all work, calling the whole thing a mistake and losing the money they had put into it, rather than throw more after it. This attack of panic was countered with difficulty.

This was the first of the New England railroads on which trains were operated. Curiously unlike the Lowell's, its promoters had, from its inception, counted more on passenger than on freight traffic. Three Stephenson locomotives were

---

[4] There was one instance when the management was too cautious. An old farmer opposed their crossing his property, save at an enormous price, and to avoid legal measures, they just ran the line around him, thinking that the best and most punishing *riposte*. But the business of the road increased so rapidly, there were such bad curves and so much additional mileage around the old chap's farm that they finally had to buy his land at an exorbitant figure, which, after all, seemed the easiest way out of the difficulty.

ordered—light-weights, as it was feared that the track would not endure heavier ones. With this in mind, the theory was that short and numerous trains would be preferable to long, heavy ones. When the line was completed as far as Newton, nine miles out of Boston, in the spring of 1834, it was planned to begin operations. President Hale announced in the *Advertiser* late in March that it was proposed to run the passenger cars to Newton, "as soon as two locomotives shall be in readiness, so as to insure regularity. One locomotive, called the 'Meteor,' has been partially tried, and will probably be in readiness in a few days; the second, called the 'Rocket,' is waiting the arrival of the builder for subjecting it to a trial, and the third, it is hoped, will be ready by the first of May." [5]

On April 4, the first locomotive moved upon the rails, drawing a gravel train. It caused enormous excitement. The editor of the *Transcript* wrote:

> Crowds of people were assembled yesterday at the Tremont-street terminus of the Worcester Rail-road, to witness the operation of the Locomotive Engine. It was the first time we ever saw one in motion, and we candidly confess that we cannot describe the singular sensation we experienced, except by comparing it to that which one feels when anticipation is fulfilled and hope realized. We noted

[5] There is, in the early story of these Boston & Worcester engines, a dark, unsolved mystery which even Charles E. Fisher of Boston, President of the Railway & Locomotive Historical Society and America's leading authority on locomotive history, cannot quite penetrate. Hale here speaks of the "Rocket," though the records show that the company's real "Rocket" did not come from the Stephenson shops until the following spring; it went into service in May, 1835. Why, then, is Hale speaking of a "Rocket" in March, 1834? Mr. Fisher has found that the B. & W. tried out a locomotive built by Norris of Philadelphia, did not like it, and turned it over to the Boston & Providence. My own theory, given for what it is worth, is that—although this engine was later known as the "Philadelphia"—Hale at first entertained the romantic notion of christening it "Rocket," in honor of George Stephenson's first famous creation. This seems to be bolstered by Hale's remark that "the builder" was coming to test it. Norris, a beginner in locomotive building, would be apt to go to Boston to see his job well launched, whereas Stephenson would not cross the ocean in person but would send an expert to oversee the setting up and testing. The third engine of which Hale speaks in this passage was the "Yankee," an imitation of the Stephenson pattern, then being built at the Mill Dam Foundry in South Boston: this was the first locomotive produced in New England.

it as marking the accomplishment of one of the mighty projects of the age, and the mind, casting its eye backwards upon the past, as it was borne irresistibly onward, lost itself in contemplation of the probable future.

The more prosaic reporter of the *Patriot* noticed the engine was "blowing off waste steam a great part of the time, and evidently capable of carrying a much greater load or moving with greater rapidity." The *Advertiser* reported that "the engine worked with ease, was perfectly manageable, and showed power enough to work at any desirable speed."

Three days later, on April 7, a party of directors and friends, sixty or seventy in number, went for a trial trip as far as Davis's Tavern at Newton, nine miles out. Said the *Advertiser*, "They returned in thirty-nine minutes, including a stop of about six minutes, for the purpose of attaching five cars loaded with earth." Next day a larger party went over the ground, about 130 being invited. Hale strongly believed in giving away samples of the goods. But this trip was not so successful, for "after proceeding a short distance, their progress was interrupted by the breaking of a connecting rod between two of the cars." This caused a considerable delay, and worse still, it happened at least three times more on the trip, which was very depressing.

During the following week another jaunt to Newton was staged, and this, too, turned out badly. The train was drawn by "the rail-road engine constructed at Philadelphia" (Norris's), and "owing to some impediment in the action of the engine, their progress was unusually slow." On the return, they had traversed only one third of the way when the locomotive failed entirely, "in consequence," reported the *Transcript*, "of a great waste of steam, occasioned, as was found upon examination afterwards, by a board nail much bent and lodged immediately under the safety valve, in such a manner that the escape of steam could not be prevented. The nail must have been left in the valve chamber beneath the valve seat at the time of its construction," and been pushed up into the valve by the steam pressure. "Much inconvenience was unfortunately occasioned to the passengers." This was probably the contretemps that finally disgraced the Norris engine and caused its rejection. One would think that these breakdowns would be bad publicity for the railroad, but apparently the public accepted them as an inevitable part of the process of getting a new enterprise started.

On May 12, the home-built "Yankee" having been completed, the first railroad advertising to be seen in a Boston newspaper announced the opening of passenger service. It did not actually begin, however, until four days later. On May 16 another party was given, six cars—carrying about twenty persons each—making the trip without untoward incident. It was considered remarkable that the return journey was made in less than an hour. The cars they used were the same sort of slight enlargements of a stagecoach body—some say in two compartments, some three—that we have mentioned as operating on the Boston & Lowell. The Worcester's had running-boards along the side, upon which the conductor walked to collect the fares, clinging to an iron rod above and reaching through the window. Between times, he sat on a perch on the foremost car like that of the driver's seat on a stagecoach. The brakeman sat facing the other way on a similar seat farther back. The cars were the product of Osgood Bradley & Company of Worcester—who built many railroad cars thereafter—and were hauled to Boston on big wagons, probably drawn by oxen.

As the road opened its farther extensions—to Needham in July and to Hopkinton in September—more excursions and celebrations took place, always with a spread at some hotel and much speechmaking. It is said that 200 guests went to Hopkinton on a train of seven of "the company's largest passenger cars," which would indicate that the first coach bodies were already being superseded. Governor Davis and former Governor Lincoln were among the guests that day, and according to the *Advertiser*, "the weather was unusually fine, and the sweetness of the atmosphere, the rapidity of the motion and the beauty and novelty of the scenery which was successively presented to view, appeared to produce in all the

party an agreeable exhilaration of spirits." It certainly did in
Mr. Hale's bosom, at any rate.

The usual whoop-it-up excursion to the opening at Westborough in November suffered another of those annoying
setbacks, this time from high wind. Leaving Boston at
11 A.M., the excursion was to meet another train eastbound at
Needham, but the latter, drawn by the "Meteor"(!), had
been delayed by "a strong head-wind." The excursionists
waited at Needham in the unheated cars until they lost patience and decided to go ahead, which they did cautiously,
almost at a snail's pace. Four miles out they met the delayed
"Meteor," close-hauled, beating up before the gale from the
Atlantic. Then the excursion had to back-track to Needham
and didn't reach Westborough until 2 P.M. There they had
dinner, and Hale led the speechmaking.

When that train, drawn by the "Yankee," passed through
Framingham, an old-timer recalled that it stopped at the Farm
Pond for water, which was passed up to the engine in pails
by the trainmen. A Westborough chronicler spoke in later
years of the road's "two fussy little engines of English manufacture, or at any rate, in the English style." But Chris-
topher Columbus Baldwin, librarian of the American Antiquarian Society at Worcester, was more awed by them. "I
saw today for the first time a railway car," he wrote in his
diary. "What an object of wonder! How marvelous it is in
every particular! It appears like a thing of life. . . ."

Two more Stephenson locomotives arrived early in 1835,
the "Comet" in January and the "Rocket" in May. Not until
July 3 was the track ready to Worcester. On that afternoon,
two six-car trains carried a party of guests to that city. After
a stay of an hour they started back, but again disaster overtook them: one engine broke an axle at Newton and had to
be retired. The other engine brought all the twelve cars into
the city, but they did not arrive until 10 P.M. Mechanics
doubtless worked all night to repair the damage, for the next
day was to be the great occasion when the road was really
opened to the public. The fractured axle must have been
repaired or replaced, for on July 4, the four engines each

made four round trips, a total of 176 miles, two eleven-car trains leaving each end of the road at the same time. About 1500 passengers were carried during the day without accident or detention. It was a real triumph.

When the railroad first began to operate to Framingham, it was decided to charge 75 cents fare to Boston in summer and $1.00 in winter, because of the greater cost of operation during the stormy months. Later, however, year-round fares were fixed at 30 cents to Newton (9 miles, 30 minutes running time), 40 cents to West Needham, 60 cents to Natick, 70 cents to Framingham, $1.50 to Worcester. This shows a rate of 3 1/3 to 3½ cents per mile. A little later, the fare to Worcester was raised to $2, or about 4½ cents per mile. But that was too high, and in 1839 it came back to $1.50. Then, under pressure from the Western Railroad, it was reduced to $1.25. Of that, more hereafter.

The vicissitudes of early railroading can be only faintly appreciated by a study of the record book of the Boston & Worcester's engine performances during the first three years' history of the road.[6] We have space for but a few selections from it here. In winter the commonest trouble was the freezing of the hose by which water passed from tank to boiler; at these times, water was often taken in through the valves. Derailings were common. There was a stiff broom fastened to the pilot over each rail to sweep the snow off, but it was of no avail when the snow was deep, and sometimes when it wasn't deep. On February 7, a note says, "Snow on rails, wheels revolve, but do not go ahead." When an axle or journal broke on a car, they just derailed that car and went on, picking it up later. Once when a wheel under the tender broke, they took a pair of wheels from under a passenger car—perhaps jamming that car's passengers into other cars— and went ahead.

The poor devils who traveled then suffered untold harassments. "Hose froze, and passengers sent on by horses."

[6] The indefatigable Charles E. Fisher found this book somewhere and published a digest of it in the *Railway and Locomotive Historical Society Bulletin* for November, 1930. I quote therefrom.

"Crank shaft broke, passengers brought in by horses." Once, in a snowstorm, the westbound train struggled into Westborough by 6 P.M., put the passengers into stagecoaches and sent them on to Worcester. The favorite sneer at the pioneer automobilist in trouble, "Git a horse!" was probably tossed by more than one grinning rustic at the railroad in the 1830's. Even crippled locomotives were ignominiously brought in by horses.

Night running was avoided whenever possible, but trains were frequently stalled overnight by accident or snowstorm. Once in 1836 a belated train ran into some cattle at 9 P.M. and killed two of them. "It was so dark, could not see," and of course there was no headlight. Neither were there any bumpers at the ends of the tracks in the Boston station, and trains coming in too rapidly and badly braked sometimes just went right on, perhaps through the wall of the depot.

Characteristic bits, sometimes oft-repeated, from this old book, are: "Engine would not steam"; "Opposite the poor house at Newton, derailed by ice on the track"; "Ashpan came off at Hopkinton"; "Forty-four ton train, steam failed several times"; "Cross-head bolts broke, and obliged to back in with one engine"—presumably meaning one cylinder; "Found bridge burned down over Charles River, and took the passenger train back to Worcester"; "Pumps would not supply boiler. Found dirt and small piece of bagging in tender valve"; after cleaning out, "engine went well. Strainers to be placed over all tender valves."

A few of the livelier days of that first winter are these:

Feb. 23, 1835. "Yankee." When coming around Parker's Hill, forward shaft of engine came apart in center, where it had been attempted to be welded by Mr. Tufts, but was not. Passengers brought in by horses, and the "Comet" brought the "Yankee" in.

Feb. 27. "Meteor." On eastward trip, about 300 yards from Westborough, broom scraper standard caught on rail, broke standard and derailed engine and tender down a 6-foot embankment and bent forward shaft of engine. Five pairs of oxen got the engine on the rails again, and the down trip was made the day following.

Same day. "Comet." Snowing, could not go fast for wheels sliding on the snow. At Natick, ran out of wood; went to Needham and took wood; backed to the Ledge and took water. Passengers sent on by horses. About 2½ miles from Framingham, hose froze, and at Framingham the hose and pipes were thawed out. About ¼ mile beyond Framingham, tubes burst in the boiler, and engine was hauled back to Framingham by horses.

But the most astounding performance, as the book records it, was this:

April 17. "Meteor." On return trip to Boston, about ½ mile below Westborough, the engine and tender were derailed. One of the Air spring drawbars on the Whitmore Car was broken, and engineman went one mile before he found that he had left his cars. [QUERY: Had the engine and tender been put back on the track before they lost their train, or were they just cutting across country?]

A merry, merry life the train crews led in those days! But like our other pioneer ancestors, they took it all as an inevitable part of the game. Remember, the same things were befalling the Lowell and Providence roads, too, and the public, likewise accepting the inescapable and optimistic as to the future, continued to patronize the roads and to build up their business beyond expectations. It is true that the Worcester freight business for some time was nothing to boast of; that town, somewhat alienated commercially from Boston, still clung to its Blackstone Canal and New York connections. So little did the railroad's directors esteem the freight business that one of them—that same Mr. Bond—actually proposed that they let it to a concessionaire for little more than a nominal return. Fortunately, his suggestion was ignored, and after a few incidents like that of the Worcester manufacturer who ordered from Philadelphia in late summer a cargo of coal which was to be shipped by Blackstone Canal, but which, upon reaching Providence, found the canal too nearly dry to carry it, there came a change of attitude toward the railroad. This manufacturer then ordered another cargo of coal, to be shipped via Boston and the railroad, and it was delivered at his door within ten hours after it had reached the Boston wharf.

A notice in the *Boston Advertiser* in the autumn of 1836 announces that "on and after Nov. 7th, the Passenger cars will start from the new brick building at the corner of Beach and Lincoln-streets, at the usual hours, viz., 7 A.M. and 3 P.M., and proceed without stopping at the old depot on Washington-street." This was the new South Cove station, the result of a promotion of 1833, known as the South Cove Association, which provided a better terminal and yard space for the B. & W. The story of the numerous railroad stations in Boston would be a history in itself. Terminus, the Roman god of boundaries and landmarks, was represented without feet or arms, to indicate that he never moved from the position he assumed at the beginning of the world; but his name-sakes in American cities—and particularly in Boston—have had no such static permanence.

Turning to the Boston & Providence, we find that it had its full share of troubles, too. When state ownership was in prospect in 1828, the Directors of Internal Improvements had asked Rhode Island for permission to make surveys in that state and to build the line; both these requests were granted. At most, there would not be more than a mile of track in Rhode Island, for Providence was then on the eastern border of the state: a small slice of land across the Seekonk River from the city, then in Massachusetts, was later annexed to Rhode Island, though it didn't increase her stature greatly.

But many of the original subscribers to the stock of the B. & P. didn't pay up promptly, and in 1832 the franchise was sold at auction. This instability of the corporation was to some Rhode Island politicians a valid reason for withholding the right of the company to enter the state. Providence was none too keen about the project, anyhow, foreseeing that the importance of her canal to Worcester would be diminished and that she might become more definitely a mere way station

on the road from New York to Boston. The B. & P. promoters nevertheless went ahead with their plans. They could
if necessary terminate their road across the river from Providence, say at India Point, and ferry passengers across; furthermore, they could make arrangements with the New York
steamboats to land at India Point for a direct transfer of
passengers, thus by-passing Providence entirely. There was
nothing that Rhode Island could do about it, and it decided at
last to accept the situation. In 1834 the General Assembly
therefore authorized the entry of the railroad, chartering it
as the Providence and Boston Railroad and Transportation
Company, thus salving local feelings by naming Providence
first, even as Dogberry ordered that the name of God be
placed ahead of those of the malefactors in the indictment.

Thomas B. Wales, another of Boston's great early railroad
builders (he lived at 24 Winter Street, next door to Patrick
Jackson), was the first president of the road, and one finds
among the first directors the names of Jackson and John F.
Loring, two of the Lowell promoters. A fourth director who
signed the report of 1835, when the road was completed,
arouses our interest—Joseph W. Revere, grandson of Paul
Revere. The Herald of the Revolution was not only a silver-
smith but a copper and brass founder, and he established a
small plant at Canton, southwest of Boston, in 1785, where,
in greatly enlarged form, it functions yet. The Boston &
Providence skirted the environs of that village, and it was
natural that Revere should become a large stockholder.

The B. & P.'s engineer, Captain William Gibbs McNeill,
surveyed, all told, eleven slightly varying routes for it.
There was comparatively little climbing or descending between the termini. The final survey made it almost an air
line; in fact, there was one stretch of 16 miles absolutely
straight, and no curve sharper than a 6000-foot radius. From
Boston for nearly 15 miles the track is almost continuously
level, and no grade on the road exceeds 37 feet to the mile.
Near Canton the vale of the Neponset River was considered
so deep that inclined planes on each slope were at first contemplated. But before the building of them was begun, a

party of businessmen went sight-seeing on the near-by Granite Railway one day and started down its short incline on a car. The rope broke and the car ran away, killing a Mr. Gibson, a well-known man, and injuring all the rest of the party more or less seriously. That ended all thought of inclines on the B. & P.; it was decided to build a stone viaduct across the ravine. Thus by trial and error the early builders learned much of their trade; and every accident, as Adams says, "taught men something, brought about some great advance in railroad construction, or appliances for safety."

McNeill was not only the surveyor but the builder of the road (assisted by General William Raymond Lee), and he built that Canton viaduct for eternity. Though only a single track was being laid at first, the viaduct was wisely made wide enough for two tracks. So well constructed was it that it needed no repairs for half a century, and it is still there today, doing business at the old stand. Built in the days when they could conceive of no locomotive weighing more than eight or ten tons, the vast traffic of the New Haven Road thunders continuously over it, sometimes drawn by locomotives weighing 300 tons! How happy McNeill would be if he could see how his work has endured for more than a century, and how nonchalantly it bears a far greater and more continuous burden than he ever dreamed of as possible on rails.

Here again stone sleepers were considered, but McNeill, who had studied British railroads at first hand, had shrewdly diagnosed the reason why stone was being used there: namely, because timber was so scarce in England that they dreaded trying to find enough of it for ties. He also saw the bad effect that stone was having on the rolling stock, and so the Boston & Providence was laid on what would be considered today a luxurious foundation of pure cedar. But cedar was cheap then, and the substitution of it for stone resulted in a saving of $3443 per mile, or more than $140,000 for the whole route. Had it not been for that Canton viaduct and a bog in Mansfield where the earth and stone filling at first sank forty feet into the muck, the B. & P. would have been built at a cost per mile far less than that of the other two.

It is a curious and inexplicable circumstance that, although in engineers' and directors' reports, distances were always figured in miles, when they came to set "mileposts" along the line, through somebody's whim they measured the distances in kilometers.[7]

At Attleborough—they spelled it with twelve letters instead of nine in those less hurried days—the builders ran into a hornet's nest. The desire for straightness carried the line directly through a parish cemetery known as the Old Kirk-Yard, consecrated in 1744. The town rose in high indignation, quoting the state statute for the protection of the sepulchers of the dead. But this railroad, unlike the Worcester, was adamant: its resolve for directness had become an obsession. The parish carried its protest to the Legislature, which confessed itself powerless under the law giving the railroad authority to condemn a right of way. The railroad paid liberally for the footage it used, and bought a tract on the other side of the church which it donated as an addition to the cemetery, but much ill-feeling remained. The remains of about 150 persons were removed from the right of way itself; in the small triangle cut off from the churchyard by the track, some of the kinsmen stubbornly refused to remove their dead, leaving the old stones standing for decades thereafter, until they finally fell and disappeared.

"Is there no spot in this wide world where the bones of the dead can rest in peace?" asked John Daggett, a prominent citizen who wrote two pamphlets on the subject. "Can they spare us no space of earth where we can feel an assurance that the hand of violence or cupidity will not disturb the ashes of our kindred? . . . This is not the worst. A few of our own neighbors have been concerned in the transaction. Will it be believed by succeeding generations that men (hitherto regarded as men of feeling) could be found in this town,

[7] This has been doubted by some, but that eminent railroad antiquarian, Warren Jacobs, and others still alive have seen the posts.

who, from selfish or worse motives, were willing to lend their influence, and combine with a *foreign* corporation to disturb the repose of the dead? Yet such is the fact."

This incident is mentioned as one of the first signs of an inexorability which became necessary to the railroads and was followed by an increasing resignation to the inevitable on the part of the public. Less than five years later, we find Pittsfield readily agreeing to a right of way for the Western Railroad through a cemetery.

The B. & P., like the Worcester, began operating trains before its completion. The *Transcript* announced on May 29, 1834, that the line "is nearly ready for the cars as far as the Low Plain in Dedham. It is expected they will be put on for an experiment on Wednesday next." The records of the road show that on June 4, "Rail-road opened this morning for ten miles from Boston, rate of travelling exceeded 23 miles an hour—part of the distance nearly 30 miles an hour." The terminus was temporarily in the country in Dedham Township, where a large old farm mansion house had been taken over to serve as a depot. Fare for the round trip was set at 75 cents, "private cars holding twenty passengers, $15." [8] Such cars were undoubtedly of a different type from the early B. & P. car preserved in the New Haven shops at New York, which is simply a small stagecoach body and would come nowhere near holding twenty people. As already suggested, the passenger car had begun to evolve even before the railroads were completed.

McNeill christened the first engine in honor of his brother-

---

[8] Here we read the first suggestion of a privately chartered car, which of course was only for a very brief trip. The origin of the true private car has so far eluded search. It is said by various authorities to have originated in New England, with a private carriage rolled bodily up on a flat car and the owner's family riding in snobbish state therein. It certainly began that way among the nobility in England, who hadn't been accustomed to riding with *hoi polloi* in public stagecoaches and couldn't be expected to rub elbows with them in railway cars. Others did it, too. R. S. Surtees—an English author who is too little read nowadays—in his novel *Handley Cross*, published in 1845, pictures Jorrocks, his cockney grocer-sport, going to the country for his annual fox-hunting season, he and his family in their carriage (with two hams and a warming-pan slung underneath) on a flat car. Moreton Frewen enjoyed a journey thus as late as 1856.

in-law. On August 20 the newspapers announced that until further notice the passenger cars, with the locomotive "Whistler," would be dispatched daily except Sunday to the Sprague Mansion House from the depot "at the south-west corner of the Common, in Pleasant Street"—where it remained until 1874, though a much larger station had meanwhile been built.

On the twelfth of September, the road was open for 15 miles, to a point "in the Township of Canton" where it connected with coaches for Providence and the New York boats. The stages, by the way, were at first very contemptuous of the railroad. "Just let the train run off the track when going thirty miles an hour and kill two or three hundred people a few times," said a coach-line proprietor in Providence, "and people will be ready to stick to the stages." But as the railroad steadily invaded their territory, the stages co-operated by bridging the intervening spaces. There was nothing else they could do.

Dedham, a village which really wanted the railroad, was deeply grieved at being left a couple of miles off it in the final air-line survey. E. B. Grant in his pamphlet, *Boston Railways*, published in 1856, was sharply critical of this unswerving policy of the railroad. "Built mainly with a view to securing the New York travel, its line was run in the most direct practicable line . . . and as time has shown, injudiciously avoiding towns whose large traffic it has since been thought necessary to secure by the construction of expensive branches." Mr. Grant sounds rather funny today. Generations of later executives have risen up to call those B. & P. builders blessed for that straight track.

The Dedham Branch was one of those which Grant had in mind. Already there were some Boston businessmen who lived out there and went into the city each day, a matter of ten miles, by stage or private conveyance. But the Dedham Hotel, with its stable of sixty horses, burned in 1832, and the stable of the Phoenix Hotel, with fifty-three horses, in January, 1834, and the town began to wonder whether the less combustible iron horse might not be necessary to its existence.

McNeill, the builder, and his associate, General Lee, both lived in Dedham and were ready to lend aid.[9]  So when the village asked the Boston & Providence to give it a branch, the directors agreed, provided Dedham would contribute a right of way and land for a station.  This was promptly done, and the branch from Dedham to the main line at Readville was opened in December, 1834, before the main line was completed to Providence.  Until that completion, the cars were drawn all the way between Dedham and Boston by horses.  With the opening of the main line in the summer of '35, horses were used only to Readville, where the cars were hooked on to the steam trains.  Eventually the Dedham Branch had locomotives of its own.

Season tickets immediately began to be sold.  With the opening of this and the Worcester lines, railroad commuting began.  There were some sybaritic conservatives, however, who still preferred the stages, because those vehicles would pick them up and deliver them at their homes; and so—although the railroad tried to meet competition in Dedham by installing a carriage to call for passengers—a long, four-horse bus continued to operate into Boston until 1841.

In the city, the distribution of passengers was not gratis.  An official notice told the public that "Mr. McIntire, the conductor of the cars, will have in readiness on the arrival of the cars at the depot in Boston, a carriage to convey Passengers to any part of the city they may desire to go, at 12½ cents each."

The road was open as far as Canton by September 12, 1834, coaches running from there to Providence. Construction was begun from the south end, and by early June, 1835, the line was complete, save for the Canton Viaduct and the bridge from India Point into the city of Providence.  On the first of June, a party from Providence and New York made the first trip to Boston over the new road.  On the previous day, the

[9] General Lee continued to reside there, and old-timers recall how, in his old age, when he wished to visit Boston, he never troubled himself to go to the depot, though it was not far off; he just walked down through his garden to the railroad track, which was back of it, held up his hand, and any train would stop for him.

fine new Sound steamer *Lexington*, built by Commodore Vanderbilt for the New York–Providence run but doomed to a short life and a dreadful death, had had her trial trip, and soon went into service in connection with the new railroad. Some New York editors and reporters came up on her to enjoy the first jaunt over the new railroad.

The plan was that the visitors should ride grandly behind "the new engine that arrived from Philadelphia only the day before, but some of her pipes were not in order," [10] so they set off rather ignominiously behind horses; but it was consoling to reflect that "the application of horses afforded us a most fortunate opportunity for inspecting the grand structure over which we passed." They had to transfer around the still uncompleted viaduct at Canton, but they viewed it with awe as "a stupendous work," testifying, with its embankments, "in strong language, to man's dominion over nature, and his ability to overcome any obstacle to any undertaking that is not morally or physically absurd." The *New York Journal of Commerce* man spoke of it as a work "which in days of yore might have done honor to the enterprise of an Emperor." From Canton the party dashed into Boston by steam power, and enjoyed "with keen appetites and grateful hearts the overflowing hospitality" of the Directors at the Tremont House, being entertained for the rest of the evening at President Wales's home on Winter Street. The eminent J. Watson Webb, of the *New York Courier and Enquirer*, was one of the party, and wrote in amazed italics of his rapid journey back, "We yesterday *breakfasted at Boston, left there at 2* A.M. [how is that for an early breakfast?] *and arrived in this city off Dry Dock in eleven hours and fifty-nine minutes from Providence*—performing the entire distance in less than sixteen hours, and bringing with us the Boston daily papers of yesterday morning."

[10] Poor William Norris certainly had bad luck with those first locomotives which he sent to New England railroads. The Providence took over that one which the Worcester rejected, and ordered four more from Norris, none of which proved satisfactory. But he so improved his product that he later sold locomotives abroad, and by 1855 his plant at Philadelphia was spoken of as the largest locomotive works in the world.

For several months, through traffic was carried on, passengers being transferred across the Neponset ravine by buses. But on July 28, 1835, the viaduct was opened, steam trains began to run through, and thus the last of the three pioneer lines out of Boston came into full operation. It was an interesting thing that they were all opened throughout their full length within a month of each other.

Fast service to New York began immediately. It was considered a wonderful thing to eat an early dinner in Boston, take the train, change to the boat at Providence, leave there at 4 P.M. and reach New York before business hours next morning. The trains ran in close synchronization with the boats. The railroad made a contract with the New York and Boston Transportation Company, boat owners, by which certain trains were to connect with the New York boats and "shall at all times proceed to and from the steamboats at a rate more rapid, so as to effect the passage in less time than ordinary passenger trains of equal burden, and without stopping more than three times on the route." This favoring of plutocratic boat passengers over common local jog-trotters was dwelt upon by politicians as having a flavor of the scandalous. It was charged later in the Massachusetts Legislature that the railroad and boat company owned blocks of each other's stock.

For several months the Boston & Providence trains did not enter Providence; passengers were transferred by buses across a wagon bridge over the Seekonk River and into the city. But a bridge across the river was begun that summer and was ready for use by the following December. One span was a covered wooden bridge just like those which carried horse vehicles across streams all over the country then, and in some cases, do yet; and it might be added that they also carried railroads over streams all over the country then, and that a few of them survive in northern New England to this day. Another span was a draw, which was operated by manpower. The harbor inlet still remained between the B. & P. and the business part of the city, and a ferry across it was established to connect this road with the New York, Provi-

dence & Boston Railroad, then building down to Stonington.
In 1848, when a union station was built in Providence, the
B. & P. entered the city by a new route, coming in via Paw-
tucket, the way that is still used.

In 1840 an interesting comparison was made of the original
construction costs of the three pioneer roads, and their income
for 1839. These are the figures:

| Railroad | Length | Cost | Per Mile | Receipts for 1839 | Net Profits | Dividend |
|---|---|---|---|---|---|---|
| Lowell | 25¾ mi. | $1,608,476 | $62,465 | $241,220 | $149,069 | 8% |
| Providence | 41 " | 1,782,000 | 43,460 | 313,907 | 220,345 | 8% |
| Worcester | 44½ " | 1,799,255 | 40,433 | 231,807 | 105,413 | 6½% |

The enormously greater cost of the Lowell per mile was of
course mostly chargeable to those granite sleepers and stone
walls under the track. The cost per mile of the Providence
over that level terrain would have been very low had not the
expensive Canton viaduct pulled it up. The low income and
net profit of the Worcester may be accounted for by its lack
of freight business. Freight then, as now, was far more profitable than passengers. But the Providence, with its monopoly
of the New York trade, made even passenger business pay by
charging about five cents a mile for several years.

The men and boys who delivered newspapers in those days
used to have someone concoct a "New Year's address" for
them, usually in rhyme, which was printed on a sheet with a
fancy border and handed around to patrons, in the hope of a
tip. The address of the carriers of the *Hingham Gazette* for
January 1, 1835, was a survey of the times, and read in part:

> Who would have hazarded the thought
> That time itself would bring about,
> That *vapor* e'en should aid a man
> The great Atlantic thus to span.
> This hour shake hands in Hingham Street,
> The next, his friend in Boston greet.

Which was something of an imaginative flight, since Hingham had no railroad as yet.

But that year 1835 left folk dazed with the immensity of its changes and their possibilities. Charles Francis Adams, II, epitomizes it beautifully in his railroad chapter in the Winsor history. Remember that he was writing in 1880:

The year 1835 marked an historical dividing line. The world we now live in came into existence then, and humanly speaking, it is in almost every essential respect a different world from that lived in by the preceding six generations. Down to 1835 Boston was still the provincial New England capital. So far as intercourse with Europe or with the exterior was concerned, the motive power in use was the same that had been in use when in 1632, Winthrop first visited Plymouth. In 1835, except on interior waters, the sail and the horse were still the only agencies of commerce and travel. As respects population, Boston, it is true, had since the Revolution very considerably increased. . . . In all essential respects, however, the place was still only a large town. Territorially, it was still confined to the old natural limits, within which dwelt, not the residents of the city alone, but those also who were regularly engaged in business in it. The range even of country abode and summer resort was limited to neighboring towns, such as Roxbury, Brookline, Dorchester, Cambridge and Watertown—now suburban, though then rural enough—within the distance of an easy noon day drive. . . . The home had to be near the place of business. The office or the counting room, it is true, was no longer in the dwelling house, but it was in some street conveniently near. Every one, too, had some calling by which he was at least supposed to earn a living; and to have none was looked upon as scarcely respectable. No generation had yet grown up accustomed to wealth from its birth; there was no class of men of leisure.

The railroad changed all this. It brought to Boston the full current of modern city life,—turning the large New England town into a metropolis, if a provincial one. Of the rapid increase, both in wealth and population, which then ensued, the census figures tell the story. . . . There is, however, another story. . . . In a quarter of a century after the three initial railroads were opened, both the ancient city limits and the modes of life traditionally pursued within them had disappeared. Boston had become the counting-house, as it were, the daily business exchange of a vast concourse of active men having their homes in every neighboring town within a limit of thirty miles. The ancient municipalities immediately adjoining the city had been absorbed into it; Salem, Lynn, Lowell, Lawrence and Worcester became its suburbs. Meanwhile, business vocations not only diversified themselves, but increased in volume so as to lose all proportion with what they had been. New branches of industry came into existence, and their rapid growth soon caused them to overshadow the traditional callings which were inseparably associated in the New England mind with the idea of accumulation. . . . All the large fortunes, as they were then, had had their origin in the fisheries, in the [sea] carrying trade and in foreign commerce. Thenceforth, these were to become of minor importance.

. . . A wholly new America was meanwhile shaping itself; an America with which the relations of Boston and New England were yet to be established. New York remained the financial center of the whole; but Chicago, in 1835 a mere frontier out-post town, was transformed into the chief distributing point of an interior, compared with which that region which the foreign trade of Boston once supplied was lost in insignificance. Boston meanwhile developed into a local center of a busy manufacturing population . . . in all eastern New England. . . . It had not become nearly as considerable a railroad center as it might at one time have been made. In this respect, opportunities were lost. . . .

# 6

# Over the Hills to the Hudson

THE Boston & Worcester had only got its construction well under way when some of its directors decided to launch the extension to Albany that had been the objective from the start. But the present company had authority to build only to Worcester. Either its charter must be altered and its name changed, or there must be a new company. The latter course was decided upon; and so began a tragedy of errors which was a great detriment to both companies and, in the end, to Boston itself.

On March 15, 1833, the men who were then directors of the Boston & Worcester Railway were individually incorporated as the Western Railroad Corporation, with a capital stock to be not less than ten nor more than twenty thousand shares at $100 per share, and with authority to build a line from Worcester to the western boundary of the state. Thus the B. & W. was the mother of the Western, and at the start, before any stock was sold, would appear to have control of its destinies. It is interesting to observe how this relationship faded and the two companies became estranged in the decades that followed.

The directors promptly decided to go the limit and set the capital at $2,000,000, which was well enough, save that for a year or two it was practically impossible to sell any of the stock, or to collect anything on it even when it was subscribed for. The New York Legislature sought to give aid in 1834 by chartering the Castleton & West Stockbridge Railroad, authorized to build from Castleton, nine miles down the Hudson from Albany, to the Massachusetts line. Two years later this still shadowy company was metamorphosed into the Albany & West Stockbridge; but meanwhile, another company, the Hudson & Berkshire, had been chartered in 1835 to construct a line from the town of Hudson, some thirty miles below Albany, to the same point on the state line at which all parties were aiming. Hudson was a prosperous little city, and though more than a hundred miles up the river of that name, had, oddly enough, made its fortune mostly out of whaling.

Adams remarks that, in view of the fact that the three railroads then nearing completion or completed were more than fulfilling expectations, and that a railroad-building mania had laid hold of the nation, the want of confidence in the Albany project is hard to understand. But a survey of the national picture and of the state of mind of Massachusetts at the time gives us a key, we think, to the story. The thing that had most to do with it was President Jackson's personal war with Nicholas Biddle, head of the United States Bank. The removal of government deposits from the bank in October, 1833, and Jackson's threat to kill the Biddle institution created intense excitement and no little distrust throughout the country. In New England, business was depressed, money was scarce and panic seemed imminent. A great meeting in Faneuil Hall drew up a protest which was signed by 6600 persons and sent to Washington in deprecation of what was considered the Administration's perilous financial policy. The businessmen of Boston did something then unheard of; they combined themselves for their own protection and "for the mutual benefit of creditor and debtor." If any had to sue to collect a debt, it was to be done for the benefit of all creditors; they were to confer with each other and act in concert. In such pessimistic times, money was naturally tight.

It was during this period of suspended animation that secret overtures were made by New York parties, supposed to be in the Stock Exchange, with a view to their taking over the whole capital issue; but this offer was rejected by Hale in behalf of the incorporators, who did not choose to "throw the whole enterprise into the vortex of the stock gambling operations of Wall-street." They shrewdly saw that if this were done, the project on which years of travail had been spent for the sake of Boston and Massachusetts would, in the words of George Bliss, an early president and the historian of the Western, "be in hands interested to defeat this object and divert the business to the city of New-York."

In March, 1835, a convention of delegates from various towns on or near the proposed route was called at Worcester. More than a hundred of them gathered to meet the promoters and engineers. But Rejoice Newton of Worcester—who, in the estimation of the promoters, belied his name—threw a whole barrel of cold water on the gathering by telling them flatly but courteously that the citizens of Worcester "believed the extension of the road would be injurious to them, and they must not be expected to contribute . . . but they would throw no obstacles in the way of it." Incidentally, three years later, when the road was well under way, only six persons in Worcester held any stock, and they only 27 shares; while in Springfield 343 persons owned 1834 shares.

Other towns had not this dog-in-the-manger attitude but asked the projectors to organize as soon as possible and make a survey. James M. Fessenden, the B. & M. engineer, was accordingly put on the job, and quickly resurveyed the line from Worcester to Springfield, fifty-four miles, and thence down the Connecticut River to Hartford, twenty-three miles farther. The reason for this latter diversion lay in a slick move on the part of Hartford to steal the Boston-Albany line bodily. It began as a seemingly harmless Worcester-Hartford project, which would be a link in the Boston–New York route; for the Hartford & New Haven Railroad dream was already nearing the boiling point. On the twenty-eighth of that same March a railroad convention was held in Hartford, where were assembled "delegates from all the towns between New-Haven and Boston interested in connecting New-Haven with the Boston and Worcester Rail-Road *in the most direct*

*route practicable.*" Resolutions were passed, and a committee
applied to the Connecticut Legislature for a charter. That
body responded in May by authorizing the petitioners to
build from the terminus of the Hartford and New Haven
Rail-Road in Hartford to the northern boundary of the state
in the most direct line toward Worcester. Surveys were
made by Alexander Twining, and then it leaked out that
there was talk in Hartford of a road from there to Albany,
too. The mask was now stricken from the foul plot, as the
Western promoters put it, and the whole thing was seen in
all its naked chicanery as an attempt to wangle a Boston-
Albany line in a long detour via Hartford. Something must
be done to block this end run, and the Western directors set
about it.

The Hartford crowd, with consummate nerve, staged a
two-day meeting at Worcester in July, with twenty towns
and villages in Connecticut and fifteen in Massachusetts represented. Former Governor Lincoln unsuspectingly presided.
Of course the Hartford-Albany scheme was not mentioned:
the meeting was given over to boosting the Boston–New York
direct route. Former Senator Nathan Smith of New Haven
said, "We can promise this: Boston to Worcester in two
hours; to Hartford, four hours; to New Haven two hours,
and by boat to New York five hours; in all, thirteen hours."
But the dryly satirical comment of the *Worcester Palladium
and Spy* after the meeting did not indicate much support in
that city.

The Western directors, now highly alarmed, put on a ten-
day stock-selling campaign in August, with books open in
Boston, New York, Springfield, Albany, Hudson (N.Y.),
Pittsfield and Lee. But though they strained every nerve, at
the end of the ten days only 8500 shares had been subscribed
for in Boston and vicinity, and 4500 elsewhere, leaving 7000
still unsold. There had been some large subscriptions in Boston—200 shares by one banking concern, 150 each by two
others, 100 each by four companies and three individuals, 50
each by some twenty-five more. But as C. F. Adams says,

"Many well-known Boston names are not found at all," and worse still, "A number of the subscriptions, including some of the larger ones, suggest grave doubts as to the faith in which they were made. Nothing was paid on them." New York had been a great disappointment. Stock-selling there had been far below expectations, because, as one of her capitalists wrote, the proposed railroad would divert the trade of Albany and the West from New York to Boston, and New York "would not let Boston people come Yankee over them" —a very natural reaction.

On October 7 the promoters called a booster mass-meeting at Faneuil Hall, with Abbot Lawrence presiding and Edward Everett showering golden eloquence over it, not to mention the presence of a delegation from Albany headed by the fine old Dutch name of Harmanus Bleecker. Lawrence declared that Boston and vicinity were destined to be improved far more by the railroads than New York City had been by the Erie Canal. The canal, said he, had advanced the price of real estate in New York by 50 per cent, whereas in Boston much real estate had already doubled in value, even with the railroads uncompleted. "What will be the effect," he demanded, "of a railroad to connect this city with the great West? I forbear to estimate. If I expressed my feelings, I should be called latitudinarian."

Yet money was still reluctant. Josiah Quincy, going about Boston with Edmund Dwight, the great textile builder of Chicopee, trying to sell stock, confided to his diary: "Some think the city is large enough, and do not want to increase it. Some have no faith in legislative grants of charters since the fate of the Charlestown bridge. . . . It is the most unpleasant business I ever engaged in." And when such an optimist as Quincy spoke thus, it must have been pretty bad. Another mass meeting was held in November, and finally, by December, 1835, the stock issue was fully subscribed. Collecting the cash on the subscriptions was quite another matter.

Meanwhile, the Hartford committee had gone before the Massachusetts Legislature in an effort to procure a charter for a company to build the Massachusets end of the Worcester & Hartford Railroad. Here Twining [1] exhibited his plans and estimates. The committee wanted directness, and he gave it to them, regardless of expense. His prints showed one tunnel more than a mile in length; one bridge 1000 feet long and 45 feet high; a viaduct 800 feet long by 80 feet high; a rock cut 800 feet long and 40 feet deep and an embankment 1600 feet long and 45 feet high—all lush extravagances for a railroad of those days. Twining's estimate of the cost of the sixty-seven-mile line—including a horse-path, for Connecticut was still a bit skeptical of the efficiency of locomotives—was $4,000,000, or nearly $60,000 per mile; which, considering the costly items named above, was much too low. But that didn't matter, for the General Court, unwilling to embarrass the Western Railroad, refused to grant the charter, and that railway was never built.

At the first meeting of the Western directors, in December, 1835, Thomas B. Wales, already president of the Boston & Providence, was elected president of the new corporation, Ellis Gray Loring, clerk, and Josiah Quincy, Jr., treasurer. Some of the same names persist, it will be observed, all through the early acts of the New England railroad drama. As to the engineers, it is difficult from the records of those earlier years to determine what each man's job was, but Captain William H. Swift, another West Pointer, is at first spoken of as resident engineer, with William Gibbs McNeill as sometimes "chief," sometimes "consulting" engineer. Then brother-in-law George Whistler was called from Stonington—where he had been surveying the New York, Providence & Boston—to become another consulting engineer and, a little later, chief engineer and superintendent.

[1] Alexander Catlin Twining, another of the early engineering geniuses of New England, was preparing for the ministry at Andover when he found that engineering had the stronger hold on his imagination, and went to Yale to study it. He was only thirty-three when he was surveying the Hartford & New Haven Railroad. After five years of this work and ten years as a college professor, he settled down to civil engineering in New Haven. He invented the first known ice-making machine in 1849, but though he spent many years in trying to promote it, he never succeeded in getting it used commercially.

The resurveys began in April, 1836. It was the opinion of some of the directors that for economy's sake only a single track should be planned, and to save grading, the road should follow the contour of the land pretty closely, with many curves. But Whistler argued that although only one track might be laid now, the grades and bridges should be made wide enough for two, and that more grading and fewer curves would be the better policy. He so convinced President Wales that the executive declared he would have nothing to do with any such damned tuppenny cowpath as the conservatives wanted, and ordered the engineers to go ahead. On the large thin-paper maps in their elaborate, 120-page report to the directors, we may trace the long scrambles of McNeill and Whistler through the rocky glens, laurel thickets and brawling streams of the Berkshires; the main recommended route, and in dotted lines the half-dozen—sometimes more—alternates. The route chosen ran west of the Connecticut course up the gulch of the Westfield River and so through Pittsfield—whereupon all subscribers in Stockbridge and Lee, left off the line, repudiated their subscriptions, on which they had made only one or two payments of five dollars each. Quincy eventually took over their stock on behalf of the company.

Before beginning the grading, it was necessary to make an "assessment"—as the effort to collect a partial payment was then called—of ten dollars per share on stock subscriptions. This proved to be no easy task. Some subscribers had moved away, others had gone broke and could not pay, and some claimed that when they subscribed they were told that upon paying five dollars per share they could surrender the stock, and this they were willing to do, but no more. By reselling such stock and by other expedients, enough money was raised to begin the grading in the winter of 1836-37, on the easier stretch east of Springfield.

For all New York's fair words, she was doing little to aid the project. The Legislature authorized the city of Albany to buy $250,000 worth of stock of the Albany & West Stockbridge Railroad in 1836, but though the subscription and surveys were made, nothing was paid on the stock. The Hudson & Berkshire, chartered in 1835, opened its line in 1837 from Hudson to West Stockbridge. It was a flimsy track, a flat iron rail on timber stringers. But nothing was done toward building the important Albany link, though Western directors made personal trips to Albany to plead for action.

The little money collected on stock subscriptions did not go very far, and somebody worked out a new idea, that of a Western Railroad Bank, with a capital of $5,000,000 or $10,000,000, through which the corporation could borrow cash. The Legislature would not agree to this, but it lent the company $1,000,000 on consideration that the state should appoint three members to the Board of Directors. Then the panic of 1837 broke over the land, to deal another heavy blow. Assessments of $900,000 laid on stock brought in only $600,000; and it was now figured that the road was going to cost $4,000,000, not including engineering, depots and general expenses, whereas the company was capitalized at only $3,000,000! In November of that year the directors decided to ask the state for another loan of 80 per cent of the face value of the stock in state scrip having thirty years to run, at 5 per cent interest, payable in London, with warrants for the interest.

This petition was presented to the Legislature at the January session of '38 by Emory Washburn of Worcester, stockholder as well as member of the assembly. He pointed out that the panic had destroyed the ability of subscribers—merchants, farmers, and so on—to pay. The company believed it could scrape up 20 per cent of the sum needed, but no more. Already the work was being impeded by lack of funds, and unless help was given, it must be suspended. Washburn fought the measure through a committee which tried to reduce the loan, then battled manfully on the floor of the House against another attempt to cut it, or, if it was granted, to increase the state's membership on the Board to four or five. He succeeded pretty well at all points, and in February the bill was passed, granting the company a loan of $2,100,000 in scrip, which was perhaps as much as they had hoped for.

This gave a fresh impetus to the work, though when the scrip reached Baring Brothers in London, who were expected to take care of it, the cold reply came back that "owing to the repudiation of Pennsylvania, there is no sale of American stocks at any price." How the directors cursed those wild-eyed Pennsylvania featherheads! But that first letter somewhat overstated the case, perhaps to pave the way for a heavy discount. Quincy took up the battle, and as he was probably the world's best salesman—never acknowledging defeat—he finally succeeded in placing the bonds in London, but at a discount which made the directors groan. He had abandoned his law practice to give all his time to the Western's financial affairs, the whole burden of which fell upon him. There was not even a committee of directors on finance. Through that depression, whose effects were felt until 1843, Quincy always succeeded in borrowing money somewhere: from banks, institutions for saving—which should never have lent it to him—and elsewhere, to keep the work going. Now and then he squeezed a little more out of the embarrassed subscribers. He had an able collaborator in George Bliss of Springfield, who had the enormous task of physically creating the road and who finally became president in 1842.

New construction gangs were at work both east and west of the Connecticut, but still the Albany & West Stockbridge project slumbered, and Messrs. Quincy, Bliss and Lemuel Pomeroy went to Albany to stir things up. The Western was much afraid that A. & W. S. stock, which was quoted at a very low figure, might be bought up by New York parties interested in blocking Boston's effort to get a Western outlet. The visiting committee found many "respectable" Albany citizens opposed to the Boston-Albany line, on the ground that it would work an injury to the projected New York and Albany Railroad, diverting "the western trade from our commercial metropolis to Boston." So nothing could be done there at the moment. Trying again in May, 1839, the Western emissaries induced the New York

Legislature to authorize Albany to borrow $400,000 and use it in buying stock of the A. & W. S. But though the bill passed in due form, nothing more happened. There was one resident of Albany who tried in vain to move his fellow townsmen. In an anonymous broadside, he urged the citizens to step up and buy stock in the company, pointing out that

Should the New York and Albany road be made, it unites with this road fourteen miles from Albany; so that from Stockbridge this road will have the business of two roads, to-wit, the Boston road, passing through the whole state of Massachusetts, and the Bridgeport road, passing through the whole state of Connecticut, and for fourteen miles, the New-York and Albany road, if made; and if not made, then the whole New-York and Albany travel will come by Bridgeport and Stockbridge over this road.

By the "Bridgeport Road," he meant the Housatonic, whose grade was then pushing northward toward Stockbridge.

By the first of January, 1839, the Western directors had decided that the road was going to cost fully $4,200,000, and there was only $3,010,000 in sight, even through rose-tinted glasses. They could think of nothing but another appeal to the state. The usual paring took place, but finally $1,000,000 in scrip came out of the hopper. The work was now pushed vigorously, and on October 1, 1839, the road was opened for passenger traffic from Worcester to Springfield. J. S. Buckingham, an English traveler, after quoting several pages of Governor Everett's eloquent address at the Springfield celebration, marveled, "With such a population, such governors and such enterprises as these, what may not the United States, led on by those of New-England, achieve?" [2]

By the first schedule, the trains—two a day each way—made seventeen stops and took six hours to make the 54 2/3-mile run between Worcester and Springfield. "Burthen trains" began to operate three weeks later. During the

[2] *The Eastern and Western States of America*, London, 1842.

following summer, the Boston & Worcester increased its passenger service to three trains a day each way, though these required two hours to cover the 44-mile distance. The B. & W. now had eight locomotives, of which only one of the original English group survived. The sturdy little "Yankee" was still around, but was usable only for light trains. Despite the early unpleasant experience with Norris's engines, there were now five of his jobs in service on the B. & W., and one from the Locks and Canal Shop at Lowell. In 1840 the B. & W. tried on its track a Western engine weighing 11½ tons, heavier than any it had ever had before, and with, "consequently, a greater power of adhesion." It was found that it could draw over the B. & W. track, "under the most favorable circumstances," 30 cars or 90 tons of freight, and "under ordinary circumstances of the state of the road *and the wind*," 25 loaded cars or 75 tons of freight. But the officials were afraid of the tractive weight of so heavy a machine on a single pair of drivers on their light track. Perhaps if there were two pairs of drivers, the track might stand it.

In January, 1840, the Western directors thought the funds in hand might be sufficient to complete the road within Massachusetts, and still not a sound was heard from neighboring New York. Bliss, Pomeroy and P. P. F. Degrand went to Albany to find whether the ectoplasmic Albany & West Stockbridge could not be materialized. The Western wanted to control the road all the way to Albany, but the committee dared not broach this idea at first. It was known that there was uneasiness in New York City over the westward push of the Yankee railhead and there was still danger that Wall Street might get control of the A. & W. S. As usual when the Massachusetts men came over, Albany awoke and effervesced with hospitality. The city agreed to subscribe for $650,000 worth of the stock of the A. & W. S., or take over that already subscribed by individuals, and pay for it in city scrip or bonds at thirty years. Now the important question was brought up, and Albany agreed to let the Western build the A. & W. S., which it undertook to do as quickly as possible. The Western further promised that after completion, it would not run its locomotives north of Greenbush (East Albany). New York wanted no Yankee octopus growing within its borders.

It was agreed, however, that the Western might, if it could, get possession of the Hudson & Berkshire. From Chatham Four-Corners to West Stockbridge the track of that road coincided fairly closely with the proposed route of the A. & W. S. So a deal was made for the use of this portion of the road for two years after the completion of other portions of the line to Albany. The H. & B.'s defects included not only the cheap strap rail but some terrific grades and a course as crooked as the way of a serpent through a copse. Whistler, who had begun resurveying toward Albany, wanted to relocate it between the state line and Chatham, but the H. & B. refused permission.

Now that the Western had assumed the building of the Albany link, a new financial problem arose. It was solved in part by persuading Albany to take another $350,000 in stock, increasing that city's investment to a million. Meanwhile, storm clouds were rising. The enormous state loans to the company, with only mortgages of doubtful value on the uncompleted plant as security, were a focus of attack by the Democratic Party. At its state convention in 1839, the party "Resolved, that we protest against the system adopted by our Whig Legislature, of loaning the credit of the State to Corporations under such circumstances that the profits, if any, will enure to the Corporations, and the losses, if any, fall solely on the State." In campaign propaganda, they told the people that every farm in the state must be said to be mortgaged, because of the Western Railroad. It cited figures to show that on one farm in Worcester County, the private and public mortgages amounted to seventy-two dollars per acre.

The year 1840 was a turbulent one. The different stockholder ownership and the changing directorates of the Western and its parent road were beginning to have their effect.

The question of passenger fares came up. It seemed to have been understood from the start that—contrary to common practice in those beginning days when, as a rule, you had to buy a fresh ticket and change cars every time you encountered a new, independent railroad, even though it might be only fifteen miles long—through tickets should be sold from Boston to Springfield and other points on the Western. The B. &. W., still dependent mostly on passenger business, had at first charged $1.50 for its 44-mile ride, then had raised the rate to $2, and finding that wouldn't do, had dropped to $1.50 again. The Western, after opening its line to Springfield, had persuaded the B. & W. to join in setting the through fare to that place at $3.75, the Western taking $2.50 for its 55 miles, the B. & W. $1.25 for its 44½. Some of the Western folk thought the fares still too high and wanted the rate to Springfield cut to $3. The B. & W. refused to slash its rate further, so the Western fixed the through fare at $3 anyhow and took only $1.75 of the amount. When the line was opened to Albany, the Western officials seemed obsessed with the notion that the price was still too high, and argued that the passenger fare from Boston to Albany might be "safely fixed at $3, and the rate on flour at 50 cents a barrel." The Worcester would not listen to talk of any further reduction, and the Western eventually announced the $3 rate, taking only $1.75 as its share for a 155-mile trip, or about 1⅛ cents per mile. But there wasn't any money in this, and the two lines wrangled for years over the subject, the Western directors sometimes quarreling almost as volubly among themselves.

The Worcester was having troubles of its own in 1840— notably on June 17, when the worst accident that had yet occurred in New England befell it. A great popular gathering in Worcester that day brought thousands from hither and yon, and the road had difficulty in handling the traffic. All eight engines were out, and men wholly new to the job were in some cases put on as trainmen. There was of course no telegraph, and as might have been expected, the meeting orders of two trains were violated or misunderstood, and

they came together, smashing both engines to junk and partly
wrecking some of the cars.  But though no one was killed,
and not more than twenty injured—since they were probably
not running more than twenty miles an hour—the incident
was regarded with horror, and a stockholders' investigation
was presently set on foot, to discover, not only why such
a thing could occur, but why the company was paying no
more than 6 per cent dividends when the Providence and
Lowell were paying 8 per cent.

No serious mismanagement was discovered.  But in that
same year, the State Senate, feeling a proprietary interest
in the Western, investigated its affairs.  These interminable
legislative investigations of anything and everything began,
you see, long, long ago.  There were charges that officers'
salaries were too high, that officials were absent from their
posts for long periods, attending to other business, that too
much was being paid for timber, firewood, etc.  As to the
last item, General Agent Bliss was able to show that there
was clearly a combination of forest owners along the line
to mulct the railroad by selling timber to it at high figures,
and he had therefore been forced to buy tracts of forest off
the line, up the Connecticut River.  Amasa Walker, one of
the directors, agreed with some of the "solons."  He thought
"consulting engineers were superfluous. . . .  The building
of railroads was a very simple affair.  Common business men
and mechanics are abundantly able to carry on those works,
requiring only skill in surveying and civil engineering—
services which might be performed by active young men in
all our towns at salaries of $500 or $600."  Fortunately,
few of the legislators were as naïve as Mr. Walker, and the
hearings ended in complete vindication for the officials.

This triumph encouraged the directors to ask for more
money.  Floods in the mountain gorges had warned the
engineers that some stretches of track would have to be
relocated at higher levels.  Perhaps that is why at one place
the grade is now as much as 87 feet to the mile, although
it was originally believed that 83 would be the steepest necessary.  By contrast, there was an 1100-foot embankment in

a spot which sank 80 or 85 feet below the level of a swamp, and there were other unexpected costs; railroad building was still a youthful science. So the directors asked the state for another million, and had the usual battle. A legislative committee opined that in view of the state's large investment, it should appoint five of the nine directors; some even thought the state should take over and own the road. Senator Emory Washburn, now critical, said that the needed cash should be supplied by the stockholders and the city of Boston. But in the end, through the able advocacy of Quincy, Bliss and Wales, the company got $700,000 and averted any increased state representation on the Board of Directors.

Work went on more rapidly in 1841. The bridge across the Connecticut at Springfield was ready on July 4, and the line up the Westfield River was completed speedily thereafter. When it was opened to Chester in the autumn, Editor Porter of the *Westfield News-Letter*, who went on the celebration excursion, said, "It is the last route in the world where we should ever dream of making a railroad." Nevertheless, it appeared to him to be "one of the safest and best that we ever passed over. . . . In all our railroad travels [vast, no doubt] we never felt more perfectly at home than under the guardian care of Major Whistler, the chief engineer." As for the celebration, he says that "nothing short of an entire basket of champagne was drank on the occasion."

In December, 1841, the road was completed through to Albany—though for several miles between Chatham and the state line they had to use for nearly a year the poor, strap-rail track of the Hudson & Berkshire, while the new and better line of the A. & W. S., which involved a 600-foot tunnel, was being completed. The celebration, from December 27 to 30, dwarfed all previous affairs of the kind. The directors, "the Boston City Government in a body," and other guests from there and neighboring places, left Boston two days after Christmas and with a brief pause at Springfield reached Greenbush "at seven and a half P.M.," where they were formally received by the city authorities of Albany and escorted by them and the militia to their lodgings. Next day they were received at the City Hall by the Mayor and at the Capitol by Governor William H. Seward, after which they visited the Court of Errors, a singularly appropriate place for early-day railroad men. At the grand banquet that evening, Josiah Quincy was the scintillating star. "On such an occasion," Governor Seward wrote, "Quincy was inimitable." The flashes of repartee between him and the Albany men kept the table in a roar.

"In order to lend point to the astonishing fact that, leaving their homes in the morning, they would in fifteen hours be in Albany," the New Bedford contingent, "during the small hours of the day"—they must have been very small indeed—caused some candles to be molded from New Bedford whale spermaceti, and they illuminated the banquet tables in Albany on the evening of the same day. But the New Yorkers were not to be outdone. A large party of them shuttled back to Boston with the Massachusetts men for another celebration and dinner—at which Judge Van Bergen spoke in Dutch, so near were the Patroon days to the railroad era—and the tables held not only candles molded in Albany that morning but salt which, it was declared, only thirty-six hours before had been 300 feet underground at Syracuse. Moreover, a barrel of flour came along, of which "the flour had been in the sheaf and the barrel in the tree" two days before, either at Rochester or Canandaigua—the chroniclers differ on that point. The phenomenon of speed, even though it was no more than twenty miles an hour, still struck men's minds breathless.

The editor of the *Utica* (N. Y.) *Daily News* considered that "a new era commences" with the opening of the Western. He continued:

New England, the birthplace of many of us, and the home of many of our Fathers, which we have been accustomed to regard as far removed from us, has, by this magical operation, approximated to our border. The influence of the road upon New England and upon New York can hardly be estimated. We have hitherto been strangers to the people of Boston and they to us. . . . But the Capitals of the Bay and the Empire State now lie cheek by jowl. Visiting and trading calls will frequently interchange. . . . Boston will be our sister depot. Throughout the year now, we stand upon the very seaboard. Yankee travel and notions will pass through our city for western New York and for westward of New York. Boston may now double her importations and her manufacture of wooden nutmegs and basswood cucumber seeds and all other knick-knacks that render life agreeable. Bring them on, gentlemen, bring them on. Here is a western world now, open to Yankees, which all your ingenuity and industry cannot fill.

The *New York Standard* copied this, calling attention to the readiness of central and western New York to take advantage of the new accessibility of Boston, and warning its own city of "that huge bunghole in the Hudson River at Greenbush, through which—(unless New York taps Lake Erie at Dunkirk) all the trade, freight, travel and opulence of the West will pour into the 'Queen City of the East.' . . . What admirable tapsters those Yankees are!"

It is amusing to observe how the tune has changed. Only a few years ago Bostonians were berating each other because they were letting New York get all the Western business. Now the shoe was on the other foot, and New Yorkers were indulging in intramural recriminations because the New York & Albany Railroad, which had been talked of for seven or eight years, hadn't even been begun. Pamphlets, essays, editorials—all had failed to move the Gothamites, who thought the Erie Canal was all they needed. When they finally broke ground for the railroad in 1842, a committee of the New York Board of Aldermen who participated in the ceremony said in its report:

Heretofore, we have been accustomed to consider the Erie Canal as the property of our own State, and we have looked upon it as a proud monument of our enterprise, and as one of the richest sources of our wealth; but while we have been sleeping in our supposed security and dreaming of golden harvests, we have been surprised by the stealthy march of our rivals, who have extended their Western Railroad, by dint of effort hardly equalled by the citizens of any State, to the depot of our supplies, and thereby turned the channel of our trade into a new direction, by adopting the better improvement of the age.   Boston and not New-York, is now reaping the great advantages of our internal improvements and this, too, at a cost of nine millions of dollars—a cost greater than that of both our Erie and Champlain Canals.   This feat has been achieved by the private enterprize of a people numbering less than one-fourth of the State of New-York.

Who has not seen our newspapers teeming with reports of the receipts upon the Western Rail-road, uniting the cities of Boston and Albany?   This trade legitimately belongs to our city. . . .   When it is known that for freight and passage, about thirteen to fifteen thousand dollars are the weekly receipts of the Western Railroad, exclusive of receipts over the Boston and Worcester Rail-road, some idea may be formed of the amount of produce that is weekly diverted from us to *another* market. . . .

But that was not all.   Governor Seward, when the Western was opened, wrote:

December was signalized by several evidences of railway progress.   A new winter route was opened to New York. This was from Albany to West-Stockbridge by rail; then 22 miles by stage to West-Canaan; then by rail down the Housatonic Valley to Bridgeport; thence by steamboat to New York—a total distance of 194 miles, but an improvement, in point of time, upon the tedious stage ride down the post road along the bank of the Hudson.

But it appeared that some travelers went even farther. The *Boston Atlas* remarked:  "By a singular coincidence, the Hudson River closed just as the line was completed, and travelers are now carried for $6 each between Albany and New York, via Springfield and New Haven.   The trains are well filled, and the receipts highly encouraging."   Here was a 102-mile railroad journey to Springfield, 26 miles of staging to Hartford, another 36-mile rail trip over the new railroad thence to New Haven, and finally, about 60 miles by water to New York, a total of some 225 miles. That some travelers went so far is probably explained by the better boat service from New Haven than from Bridge-port. [3]

The Western was the longest railroad yet constructed in America by a single corporation, and the most expensive; a section near the Berkshire summit had cost $134,000 a mile. Adams, in his impressive way, sums up this great achievement by saying that the 155-mile line, including that "painfully built through the Berkshire Hills at an average rate of twenty miles a year," might seem a small affair, but it "was the most considerable enterprise of its kind which had then been undertaken in America; and taking all the circumstances of time, novelty and financial disturbance into account, it may well be questioned whether anything equal to it has been accomplished since."

But he was highly critical of its dependence upon the state; it should have worked out its destiny in obedience to business laws:

> Palsied by State aid, the Western road never got firmly rooted in the private enterprise and capital of Boston. For years it remained in the air, as it were. It was separated from its natural base; and this fact very sensibly affected the course of subsequent events. The railroad to Albany should, in the development of those events have been to Boston what the Pennsylvania was to Philadelphia and the Baltimore & Ohio to Baltimore—the nucleus about which the ability, enterprise and capital of the city crystallized, until it enlarged and strengthened into the basis of what was to prove an expansive internal development. This did not take place. Instead of it, the two segments of what should have been a single property wasted twenty years in bickering over the

[3] When the New York & Harlem Railroad completed its line to Chatham in 1852, it began running cars through from New York to Albany, using the Western from Chatham, competing for the Albany business with the Hudson River Railroad, which had been opened the year before. Thus another feeder contributed to the Western's prosperity.

division of a joint business, while the private wealth and individual enterprise of Boston sought and found their field in a system of railroads which made Chicago its base.

When the Western was completed, says J. E. A. Smith, the historian of Pittsfield, there were two freight locomotives on the mountain section, "but even the most sanguine friends of the road doubted whether freight enough would ever be offered to test their full capacity." Wood was plentiful and the popular fuel, and "of coal, not a pound was brought to Pittsfield for several years; the first being a small quantity which, sent to Mr. Levi Goodrich as an experiment, and after lying a long while near the depot, was finally carted away by some unknown persons."

Through freight, however, soon began flowing freely. On May 6, 1842, the *Springfield Gazette* noted that a train of sixty-eight cars had just passed eastward, "the longest and heaviest, it is believed, on the road so far." Among other things it carried 1330 swine, 40 cattle, 40 bales of wool, 350 barrels of flour, and 20 tons of shingles, the whole weight of engine, tender and loaded cars being about 712,000 pounds. "The average daily freight from Boston is forty cars." But in the following winter the road suffered one of the old-time humiliations, which sounds like early days on the Worcester. A train was stuck in the snow near Washington Summit, and "after a detention of 19 hours, the engine was hauled out by oxen and horses collected from the surrounding neighborhood, and another engine was procured, which hauled the train towards Boston."

Whistler had found by 1840 that a ten-ton locomotive could draw over the steepest grades between Boston and Springfield fifty-nine tons of merchandise, while a fourteen-tonner could draw eighty-five tons. For the Berkshire grades he needed engines which were heavier still, and therefore had a better grip on the track. He found in the shop of Ross Winans at Baltimore two twenty-ton machines—later derisively called "crabs"—which must have appeared already obsolete, since they had upright boilers; but when tested, they proved to be good pullers. The difficulty was that the stacks of those pickle-bottle boilers were so tall that they wouldn't pass under the occasional covered bridge on the Western; and when the stacks were shortened, they didn't steam properly. Whistler liked them so well, however, that Winans built several more for him (nicknamed "mud-diggers"), which aroused some criticism among the directors. But Whistler didn't stay to fight out the controversy. The Czar had invited him to come over and build Russia's state railways, and in 1842 he departed with his family for that country, where unfortunately he fell a victim to a cholera epidemic seven years later.

When Whistler left, the directors piled his duties upon the shoulders of George Bliss, who had just been elected president and now combined the duties of president, general agent, engineer and superintendent at the princely salary of $500 per annum.

The Western soon became fairly prosperous. The newspapers reported with awe that in 1844, amongst other freight, it carried 300,000 barrels of flour eastward. It soon began to be haunted by the inevitable specters of competition. A Pittsfield & North Adams company was chartered in 1842, intended to form a part of a line from New York to Rutland, Vermont, the Housatonic being its connection to the south. But when an east-and-west railroad through Greenfield, connecting Boston with Troy, was talked of, the Western feared that the P. & N. A. might become a link in a competing line from New York to Albany and so took a thirty-year lease of the little project—which so far couldn't get hold of any money—promising to build the line itself, which it did in 1845-46. The branch was always an incubus, but at least it eliminated a threat.

The Western was soaring high at that time. Its net earnings in 1846 were $541,738. In the following year it increased its capital stock by $1,600,000, to enable it to double-track the road and buy new equipment. That year its net earnings were $648,646, and its stock was selling at from 98 to 114. During the year it bought twenty ten-ton engines and ordered twenty-eight twenty-ton engines and five hundred freight cars. In 1848 it obtained permission to add another million to its capital stock. It was now laying seventy-pound rail on the new second track. (But that double-tracking through to Albany was not completed until twenty years later.)

In 1848 the Troy & Greenfield Railroad petitioned the Legislature for a charter. Its line, together with the Vermont & Massachusetts and the Fitchburg (both today a part of the Boston & Maine), would complete a route from Boston to the Hudson River, actually a little shorter than the Western and with easier grades—a highly disturbing prospect. The Western presented a "long and able" remonstrance to the lawmakers against this unfair competition, but in vain; the charter was granted. However, in 1853, when the Troy & Greenfield applied to the state for a grant-in-aid for building the tunnel through Hoosac Mountain, a necessary part of its route, the Western again protested, and for one reason and another, the loan was not made. This was a lifesaver for the remonstrant. That little matter of boring the tunnel kept the T. & G. busy for another quarter-century, and by that time the Western, which had become the rich and powerful Boston & Albany, didn't much care.

In 1851–52 the receipts, which had been steadily climbing ever since the road's completion, showed a slight decline; due, it was said, to competition on its south side, where the new Connecticut railroads, Sound steamers and Erie Railroad were now getting considerable western business, and on its northerly side, where the lines through New Hampshire and Vermont toward Ogdensburg and the Great Lakes were also beginning to make themselves felt. In an effort to cope with the situation, the passenger service was improved and freight rates were cut. The annual dividend, which had long been 8 per cent, was pared to 6½ that year.

In 1854, the Hudson & Berkshire, unable to pay either principal or interest on a loan by the State of New York, was sold at a foreclosure sale to its lessor, the Western, which had found Hudson a valuable river terminal, particularly for the handling of Pennsylvania coal.

In 1848 the New York & New Haven Railroad finally effected its entrance into New York over the tracks of the Harlem Railroad, thus completing a pretty direct connection between Boston and New York via Springfield. In 1849 through passenger service began, via Boston & Worcester, Western to Springfield, Hartford & New Haven from Springfield to New Haven, and New York & New Haven the rest of the way. For decades this was the main Boston–New York rail line, and as it is only eight miles longer than the New Haven's shore line, it has its patrons yet.

Bliss resigned as president in 1850 and went to other executive positions with lines in the Middle West. He was succeeded by Addison Gilmore, who died in 1850; General William H. Swift served from 1851 to 1854, and then came Chester W. Chapin,[4] the greatest of the road's executives. It was Chapin who built the fine stone office building of the Western in Springfield, adjoining the brick depot and the Massasoit House, whose food was famous among travelers. Into that station came also the Hartford & New Haven's Springfield extension and the Connecticut River Railroad to Northampton, which was completed in 1845 and of which Chapin was president from 1850 to 1853. It became a bustling junction point as rail lines were extended northward into Vermont and New Hampshire and via New Haven to New York.

Chapin quickly became involved in one of the recurrent squabbles with the Boston & Worcester. In 1845 the Western, still chafing under inequities of compensation, had appealed to the state for a commission to determine the division of income between itself and the B. & W. The latter

[4] As a young countryman of twenty, Chapin had driven an ox-team supplying material for the building of the Dwight Mills at Chicopee. Later he had become a stage-line proprietor, and then an operator of steamboats on the Connecticut River and part owner of the boat lines from Hartford and New Haven to New York. When the Springfield extension of the Hartford & New Haven was opened in 1844, he disposed of his Connecticut River boats.

promulgated a long reply, not entirely frank, claiming, among other things, that the Western was overcapitalized—which was painfully true, but inapposite. No arbitrator was appointed by the state, and officials of the two roads tried their hands at the job. Long conferences were held and compromises offered, but the Worcester road was still difficult, and nothing came of the effort. Friends thereupon suggested a union of the two companies. Stockholders in both appointed commit- tees, and these decided—the Western the more heartily of the two—to recommend the amalgamation. Boston and Worcester citizens were all for it; Worcester in particular was always a sort of wrestling-mat for the bouts of the two concerns, and constantly complaining of it. But here Nathan Hale of the B. & W., usually wise and progressive, was reactionary. He and others talked ominously of monopoly, and he fought the suggestion so strenuously that when the committee report was submitted to a large meeting of his stockholders, they voted to postpone it indefinitely.

The two companies did, however, come together in a sort of compromise in 1846—though the Western had to yield most—and for nine years got along without further serious contention. Then in 1855 it was discovered that the freight clerks of the two lines had through all that time been mis- construing the agreement of 1846 and giving the B. & W. more than its share. As might be expected, the B. & W. promptly claimed that the clerks' interpretation had been correct. A referee was appointed, and on technicalities, gave an award mostly in favor of the B. & W. The con- tract was therefore terminated, and wrangling began again and continued year after year, to the great detriment of service.

In 1862 the Boston Board of Trade begged for peace and *"Union, early perpetual Union"* of the two companies. "Our regret, our deep regret," said the Board, "is that the Presidents —Ginery Twitchell and Chester W. Chapin, who are gentle- men of marked ability—are so much devoted to rules of dividing the receipts of the joint business, that a considerable portion of their intellectual power is absolutely lost to the public." But as Patrick Henry said, "Gentlemen cry Peace, Peace, but there is no peace."

In 1863 the "monopoly" clause in the B. & W.'s charter, the one which forbade the building of a parallel railroad, expired. The Western now had a powerful weapon in sight, if they could get permission to forge it—namely, the thrusting of a competing line from Worcester into Boston, permission for which was immediately asked of the Legislature. The B. & W., now alarmed—and high time, too—asked for conferences on the subject of consolidation, and the Western did not press its petition. The Legislature thought the idea a good one. Not only were we in the midst of the Civil War, but England's complicity in the *Alabama* raids, and Ambassador Charles Francis Adams the Elder's threatening remark to the British Foreign Minister, "It would be superfluous for me to point out to you, my Lord, that this is war," had made thinking Americans shudder at the thought of a possible conflict with Great Britain. Hence, legislators thought it best for military reasons that this important but broken east-west rail line be united. Yet when a joint committee of the two companies drew up a plan for consolidation, again a bare majority of the B. & W. stockholders, still with a Hitlerian belief in their own invincibility, defeated it. Peleg W. Chandler, politician and stockholder in both companies, warned them that "the public will at length get thoroughly roused, and will knock your two heads into one and so end the mischief." But they would not listen.

Chapin now girded his loins for battle. In 1866 he asked the Legislature for permission to increase the Western's capital stock by $3,850,000 and to build a line from Worcester to Boston. Josiah Quincy, Jr., long since resigned as treasurer of the Western, read a long paper, "The Railway System of Massachusetts," to the Board of Aldermen—it became Boston City Document No. 109—in which he revealed that in the past ten years the Western had added 212 freight cars to its equipment, the Worcester none. He showed that the tonnage of the Western was greater in 1847 than in 1865, and attributed this to the recalcitrance of the Worcester. But his idea of a solution differed vastly from that of Chapin. He wanted the state to buy both roads, the B. & W. stock at $160 a share and the Western at "an equitable price," issuing $20,000,000 in bonds for the purpose, and using a part of it to buy new rolling stock and provide new deep-water depots in Boston.

But Quincy, though now cynical about private ownership of railroads, was equally so with respect to state management. "The great objection to my proposition," he admitted, "is the ownership of the railroad by the State. The people have justly a want of confidence in the administrative ability of public officials. They demur at the vast increase of patronage which would thus be given to the Government. . . . Of course, management by Government would never be permitted." To obviate this objection, he suggested that the state, once in possession, should hand over the management to a board of seven directors, four to be chosen by Boston and one each by Worcester, Springfield and Pittsfield; one director to go out of office annually, none ever to receive any compensation, while the manager must never be a member of the board. He had a number of other ideas, including a considerable reduction of fares; in fact, his paper had a very noticeable Utopian aroma. The Aldermen listened politely; then: "The thanks of the Board were voted to Mr. Quincy and he was requested to furnish a copy of his communication for publication." And that was that.

Chapin paid no attention to Quincy's proposal but pressed his petition, and on May 24, 1867, the Legislature passed "An Act to Authorize the Extension of the Western Railroad to the City of Boston and for other Purposes." The Boston & Worcester was licked. Its stockholders came to their gruel, not without some wry faces, and after long discussions, the two companies consolidated as the Boston & Albany Railroad. On October 23 a board of directors was chosen for the new corporation, Chapin being elected president. The B. & W. by that time had several short branches, from 1¼ to 15 miles in length—to Millbury, to

Newton Lower Falls, to Brookline, to Framingham Center, to Saxonville and to Milford, while the so-called Agricultural Branch Railroad, from Framingham to Northborough, built in 1852–55, was under lease. The B. & W. owned, all told, 142½ miles of track and 30 locomotives.

Quincy, still unsatisfied, read another paper, "Public Interest and Private Monopoly," to the patient aldermen, recommending that the state now buy the Boston & Albany. Railroads were in rather bad odor at the moment. The Hoosac Tunnel imbroglio had kept Massachusetts in a stew for years; in New York the Wall Street brawl over the Erie was in progress, and there were other unfavorable symptoms elsewhere. Quincy, whose own record was not entirely flawless, was now highly critical. Years later, in 1883, he wrote:

> To the older railroad men of Massachusetts, her iron thoroughfares are consecrated ground—consecrated by the labor, the anxieties, the sacrifices which they cost. They are monuments to the public spirit of the dead, not vulgar instruments for extracting a maximum of money for a minimum of service. . . . The railroads have come to hold a power which should only be committed to the State, unless, indeed, some way can be devised of holding their management to strict accountability. . . .

# 7

## The Birth of the Boston & Maine

JUST as you cannot tell the story of Thor without telling that of the giants who were his favorite enemies, so the first half-century's story of the Boston & Maine is necessarily a dual one: you can't relate its biography without also telling that of its rival, the Eastern Railroad. Come to think of it, there is a third late-entering contestant which must be included—though perhaps it would be nearer accuracy to call the Maine Central the innocent bystander, for it could not hold its own against the other two but was alternately punching bag and puppet.

The building of the Boston & Lowell was scarcely begun when the citizens of Andover, no more than eight miles off the line, began to wish among themselves that they might have a connection with it. Early in 1833 a petition went up to the General Court for the right to connect the town with Wilmington, on the B. & L. The charter for the Andover & Wilmington Railroad was approved on March 15, 1833, and the corporation was organized in June. A survey was made, followed by a study of the passenger and freight traffic of horse vehicles between Andover and Boston, which as usual proved highly encouraging. Meanwhile, the objective had expanded far beyond the little eight-mile neighborhood line. The very first and primly worded report of the directors to the stockholders in 1834 reveals this: "It is believed that this is to be the first section from the Lowell Rail Road of a Rail Road to be extended over the Merrimac River to Haverhill, and so on through New-hampshire to Maine." Therefore, in constructing the road-bed, it would be wise to "have reference to another set of Tracks, to be laid at a future period." For the present, however, "it is thought that one set of Tracks, with one or more Turnouts, will be sufficient, provided locomotive power is used, which is now considered the cheapest and most expeditious mode of propelling Cars on Rail Roads."

They planned to run trains through from Boston over the Boston & Lowell. As to the latter's charge for this service, "Your Directors have no means of stating what this may be." They had heard that the usual rates were "one cent per mile for each Passenger, and one-half cent per mile per Ton of Goods. This item may be more, and it may be less." But they were sure, from what they knew of the liberal views of the Lowell management, that the charges would not be unreasonable.

The financing and building were not easy, and more than three years elapsed before the midget road was in opera-tion. In their report to the state, early in 1836, the direc-tors said that their plans had been ready in January, 1834, but "Rail-road stock in general was so depressed at this time, that it was considered inexpedient to incur any further ex-pense during the year." (This was the "Andrew Jackson Panic," already mentioned.) Of the $100,000 capital stock, a considerable portion was subscribed by the Andover Academy and Theological Seminary, a curious risk for such an institution.

The directors profited quickly by the experience of others. They did not use the fishbelly rail of their connecting road, the Lowell, but bought rail in England like that being laid on the Boston & Providence, "which is said to be the best rail now in use." Also, the track was laid on cedar ties. When the line was opened, on August 2, 1836, it had two locomotives, the "Andover" and "Haverhill," built in the near-by Locks and Canal Shop in Lowell; another engine, the "Rockingham," came from the same factory in the following year.

That locomotive name, "Haverhill," was significant. The

people of that village on the Merrimac, northeast of Andover, had begun to yearn for a railroad as soon as the Boston & Lowell company was born. At a meeting at the Eagle Tavern in January, 1834, a committee was appointed to further the idea, and as a result, early in the following year, permission was obtained to extend the track to "the Central Village in Haverhill," the name of the corporation being changed at the same time to Andover & Haverhill. The nine-mile addition was completed to Bradford, across the river from Haverhill, by October 26, 1837, and early future extension to Portsmouth, N. H., and to the Maine boundary was talked of to connect with the Portland, Saco & Portsmouth, which had just been chartered in Maine. Unfortunately, by this time the drive to the unproductive village of Haverhill had left the company financially flat, its credit gone and its directors either putting up cash or signing notes to keep it going. But it had done one memorable thing, for the separate company which it was necessary to incorporate in New Hampshire on June 27, 1835, for the proposed Maine extension had been chartered under the now historic name of Boston & Maine. It next procured a Maine charter as the Maine, New Hampshire & Massachusetts Railroad.

All it needed now was money and management. It found the latter in 1838 in the person of Thomas West, an able and far-seeing businessman of Haverhill, who became first a director and shortly afterward its president. He was the man who put the company on the road to greatness. Bond issues to pay debts were not legalized in Massachusetts until 1854, so West used other methods. He caused new stock to be issued and sold to stockholders and others at the bargain price of sixty dollars a share, which brought some relief. Another issue was auctioned in Boston, and surprisingly enough, brought seventy-two to seventy-five dollars per share. Two loans by the state, of $100,000 and $50,000 respectively, enabled the company to bridge the Merrimac at Haverhill, and push on to New Hampshire. It was now aware of a serious rival, the Eastern Railroad, on its right hand; one which was, in fact, ahead of it and had won the race to Portsmouth. The Boston & Maine might have gone on to Portsmouth, anyhow, but it was now more willing to be deflected. When it was surveyed to Exeter, the town of Dover, a few miles farther on, began to wish for it. In October, 1838, Dover held a mass meeting to lay plans for bringing the railroad that way, instead of through Portsmouth, and as a bait, it was decided to buy a block of stock. In town meeting in December, the selectmen were instructed by the people to subscribe for 140 shares, to be paid for "out of the surplus revenue." And so the railroad grade, passing northwest of Portsmouth, came toward Dover. But when, in the autumn of the following year, the railroad asked Dover to pay an installment on the stock, another town meeting was called, to ascertain whether the citizens would instruct the selectmen to do this, and the "mutable many" voted against such authorization by 220 to 117. It was all right to subscribe for the stock, but paying for it was another matter—which proves that Demos may repudiate a pledge quite as nonchalantly as any soulless plutocrat or corporation.

The railhead reached Exeter in June, 1840. By that time the original Massachusetts corporation had become the Boston & Portland, while the proposed Maine extension had been rechristened Boston & Maine. The parent company made one of those amusing corporation contracts with its child in New Hampshire, promising to pay the latter $12,000 a year for the use of its track; in reality, for its support. Of course, peculiar state laws as to corporations forced this "let's-play-like" course upon the railroad companies. The line finally reached its junction point with the Portland, Saco & Portsmouth at South Berwick, Maine, at the end of 1842, though the connection was not physically ready for use until the following February 2.

The Boston & Maine was one of the best constructed of the pioneer railroads in New England. It was surveyed and built by James Hayward, who had done some of the earliest surveying in Massachusetts. One of his assistants was a mere youngster named John W. Brooks, of whom we shall hear again in these annals. In all its early history the road had only one accident that might be called serious.

From the first it had begun running trains out of Boston to its northern terminus, using the Boston & Lowell tracks to Wilmington. This went on year after year, with what appeared to be amicability; but naturally the Lowell, always self-centered, was interested first of all in its own business and was not inclined to favor a mere renter, so that the B. & M. and its patrons were at times subjected to much inconvenience and annoyance. In 1844 the B. & M. therefore asked the Legislature for permission to build its own track from Wilmington into Boston. The Lowell made quite a hullaballoo, claiming that this would be a violation of its (the B. & L.'s) charter rights; but as the B. & M. did not reach Lowell, and therefore was not a competing line, the Legislature ignored the complaint.

The B. & M.'s new track into a temporary station in the city was ready for use early in 1845. In October of that year it began using its new brick station at Haymarket Square, a building which did service until 1894, when the present big North Station was completed. The company wisely built the station larger than was immediately necessary, and for several years let the second floor for business purposes. When the station was first put in service, there was a city ordinance forbidding steam trains to cross Causeway Street, so the passenger cars were drawn for the last quarter-mile by oxen, ringbolts being fastened to the ends of the cars for that purpose.

When the Andover & Wilmington was first built, Lawrence, a mile or so to westward of the line, was a mere crossroads hamlet of two or three houses. Then the great Lowell mill-owners, Nathan Appleton among the rest, who were looking about for new industrial sites, chose Lawrence and Amoskeag, New Hampshire (which they rechristened Manchester), and overnight, those villages began to grow like mushrooms. The Boston & Maine, seeing that Lawrence was destined for future greatness, relocated its track to pass through that new city in 1847-48—necessitating the building of a new bridge across the Merrimac—and as a final gesture of confidence, removed its repair and car shops there; for it had begun building its own cars, the directors maintaining that not only economy but safety of operation were promoted if a railroad produced its own "running furniture."

The company next began throwing out branches: the one to Medford, for example, which brought it some valuable suburban business, and the one from Lawrence to Methuen, on the New Hampshire state line, completed in 1849. This was a part of a branch to the other booming cotton-mill town, Manchester, and the portion in New Hampshire had to be separately incorporated, under the clumsy laws of those days, as the Manchester & Lawrence. Here, however, the B. & M. made a serious mistake. It leased the small Methuen end of the line to the Manchester & Lawrence. The latter, by changes in stock ownership, became estranged; and the distance from Concord to Boston by this route being shorter than via Lowell, the Manchester & Lawrence was leased by the Concord Railroad. Twenty-eight years later, when the Concord itself was taken under lease by the Boston & Maine, the Manchester & Lawrence paid a cash dividend of 50 per cent.

The story of the rival line, the Eastern Railroad, began soberly enough with the desire of the dignified old port of Salem for rail connection with Boston. It had excellent stage service to the capital, not only in coaches starting from Salem, but in others coming through from Newburyport, Portsmouth and Portland. But that was not enough: the maritime plutocracy of Salem wanted the best and latest. A few Boston promoters were interested, and when the first petition for a charter came into the General Court in 1833, it bore among the rest the familiar name of Colonel Thomas H. Perkins.

The promoters did not see how they could enter Boston proper without a long detour through Charlestown, so suggested two possible terminals, at Chelsea and at East Boston.

Promptly the Salem Turnpike Company, the Chelsea Bridge
Company and the Chelsea shipowners arose in opposition, the
latter fearing that navigation would be interfered with.
There was another outcry from the mill-owners at Lynn, because the road proposed to cross the Saugus River there by a
drawbridge, which would slow up water traffic to their
plants. The whaling industry of Lynn (three vessels) joined
in the chorus of protest, and the charter was refused. The
Senate committee thought that with thirty coaches a day to
Boston, Salem ought to be able to get along, especially as
"persons owning fine horses and carriages would certainly
not give them up to ride in the dirty steam cars."

The petitioners regarded this as only a temporary setback.
In 1835 they appointed a committee to further the cause and
make another bid for a charter. In the meantime, they had
chosen their southern terminal. Noddle's Island, a partly
marshy tract lying just across a narrow but deep arm of the
harbor from the city proper, had been taken over by a group
of promoters, and the suburb of East Boston founded on it.
By filling with stone and earth, they made it a part of the
mainland and increased its area. They would have done anything to further its cause. To attract visitors, they even let
Colonel Sargent set up a section of his monorail railway there
and trundle cars to and fro, without any visible effect upon
the course of human events. They had talked of a railroad
to Salem as far back as 1831 and had employed an army officer to make a survey of the island for that purpose. They
intended promoting a steam ferry to the city—under another
charter—and, as they announced in a broadside, "The locomotive would then run itself into rails on the steamboat dock,
corresponding with those on the road, and land its goods and
passengers in Commercial-street in Boston with scarcely a
moment's interruption." Another little promotion near by,
the Winnisimmet Company, also made a bid for the terminal,
but Noddle's Island was the better location.

The railroad promoters were now told that they would be
more apt to get a charter if they planned to go on beyond
Salem, through Beverly·and Ipswich to Newburyport, with

perhaps a branch to Gloucester. Fessenden accordingly surveyed all the way to Newburyport, and when books were
opened for stock subscriptions, the citizens of those coast
towns signed up for 8300 shares at $100 each, "without the
asking of a dollar from Boston," unless you count the East
Boston Company, which alone subscribed for 3250 shares.
Another plea to the Legislature in 1835 was met with a postponement, but when they went into the Capitol early in 1836
with a petition signed by 1200 citizens of the northeast coast,
the lawmakers succumbed and on April 11 granted the desired charter for the Eastern Railroad, against another storm
of determined opposition.

The Eastern made its contract with the East Boston Company and promised to buy into the ferry company, though
there was still some worry over the ferry terminal on the
Boston side. Under the agreement, the railroad built a pile
wharf, upon which it erected a "commodious and expensive"
depot.

Ground was broken only three months after the granting
of the charter. This was another corporation that didn't
want to antagonize anybody. In the General Committee's
first report to the stockholders—signed, incidentally, by its
first president, George Peabody, the businessman who became
one of America's greatest philanthropists—it was explained
that the projectors had "a conviction that no route should
be attempted in opposition to the wishes of the owners of
estates, as long as a line could be found where the inhabitants
would willingly dispose of their property at a fair value."
The committee reported that a survey had been carried to
the New Hampshire line, and "little doubt can exist of its final
continuation to Maine."

But the company now found itself at a standstill in the
matter of getting new stock subscriptions or collecting payments on those already made. Borrowing from the state
therefore began, at the very outset—$500,000 in scrip in 1837
and $90,000 more in the following year. The panic year,
1837, was a tough one, and that construction went on at all
was considered amazing. Three eleven-ton locomotives,

named "Essex," "Suffolk" and "Merrimack," with a single driver on each side, were built for the company in the Locks and Canal shop at Lowell, and sixteen fine four-wheeled passenger cars were turned out by Davenport of Cambridgeport. These cars seated twenty-four each, and "differed from those of other railroads in this vicinity, particularly in having doors at the ends, by which a passage is afforded from one end of the train to the other." Again we are reminded how quickly the old stagecoach body disappeared.

On August 27, 1838, the grand opening of the line to Salem took place. That morning the stockholders of Salem and vicinity filled two trains, luxuriating on the fine haircloth-covered seats—the sort that you slid off of almost as fast as you could right yourself—and went down to East Boston, where a trainload of Boston stockholders and friends joined them, and the three trains jogged back to Salem at a leisurely gait, half a mile apart, giving everybody a chance to see the sights. The grievous contretemps of the day was that there was no room on the trains for the Lynn stockholders who thronged the station expecting to get aboard; and though "an explanation was made by the superintendent," explanations were phooey to Lynn, and an appalling delinquency, even repudiation of subscriptions in that city, resulted; but we must not intimate that this had anything to do with those timbers placed on the track near Lynn on the following day, with intent to derail a train. It was said that a thousand passengers went over the road on that second day of operation. There were six daily trains, and the fare between Salem and Boston—only fifty cents, just half the stage fare—was very attractive.

The directors' ideas were now expanding too rapidly: it occurred to them that they might as well house the hinterland folk after bringing them into town, so the company went into the hotel business. They erected a handsome granite structure at the Boston landing of the ferry—which, unfortunately, was a failure, because the guests could not endure the sewer-fetid stench of the harbor water. That was the first of the costly errors of the concern, which were piled like Pelion upon Ossa as the years went by.  Another was the building of the pier station, just across the ferry, with a roof so low that it promptly caught fire from an engine stack and burned both the depot and a part of the pier.

In Salem there was at first no station; just a space rented in a warehouse across the street from the track, with some seats and a ticket office in it.  Salem found it difficult to get accustomed to the wonder of the thing.  A week after the opening, the *Register* reported that "on every occasion of the arrival and departure of the cars, the grounds in the neighborhood of the depot and on the eastern bank of the mill pond are covered with delighted spectators of the bustling scene, while the new faces in our streets, and the hurrying to and fro of carriages for the accommodation of passengers, have given to our city a busy appearance to which it has long been a stranger. . . .  The ground around the depot is hardly extensive enough to accommodate the vehicles which congregate there."

Five months elapsed after the opening of the road before the first freight train ran over it.  Meanwhile, the line was being extended beyond Salem, and the Eastern Railroad of New Hampshire had been chartered, with two gentlemen of the picturesque names of Ichabod Goodwin and Daniel Drown as its first president and clerk.  The ultimate destination of the road was Portsmouth, N. H., where it was to connect with the Portland, Saco & Portsmouth.

The bells from three impoverished old churches or convents in Spain had been sold in some European market for junk and sent by the buyer to New York for resale, where they were spied and bought by Fessenden for the belfries of the Eastern Railroad depots at East Boston, Salem and Newburyport; since it was the custom then to warn townspeople in this manner of the imminent departure—or at a way station, of the coming—of a train.

No less a person than Nathaniel Hawthorne wrote the carriers' address to patrons of the *Salem Gazette* on New Year's Day, 1839.  It took the form of a conversation between the Old and the New Year:

"Have you done so much for the improvement of the city," asked the New Year. "Judging from what little I have seen, it appears to be ancient and time-worn."

"I have opened a Railroad," said the elder Year, "and half a dozen times a day, you will hear the bell (which once summoned the monks of a Spanish convent to their devotions), announcing the arrival or departure of the cars. Old Salem wears a much livelier expression than when I first beheld her. Strangers rumble down from Boston by hundreds at a time. New faces throng in Essex-street. Rail-road hacks and omnibuses rumble over the pavements. There is a perceptible increase of oyster-shops and other establishments for the accommodation of a transitory diurnal multitude. But a more important change awaits the venerable town. An immense accumulation of musty prejudices will be carried off by the free circulation of society. A peculiarity of character of which the inhabitants themselves are hardly sensible, will be rubbed down and worn away by the attrition of foreign substances. . . . Whether for better or for worse, there will probably be a diminution of the moral influence of wealth and the sway of an aristocratic class, which, from an era far beyond my memory, has held firmer dominion here than in any other New England town."

Many other optimists besides Hawthorne were cheered by the probable broadening and uplifting influence of the railroad. Alonzo Lewis, the chronicler of Lynn, thought that "it may be regarded not merely as a civil convenience, but as a work of great moral influence, tending to break down the barriers of sectional prejudice, and to promote feelings of benevolence and refinement, by bringing persons of both sexes into habits of social and daily intercourse."

All of which appears to have been refuted by the discovery of a more modern philosopher, the late Will Rogers, that the more closely men and nations make contact with each other, the more they fight.

The railroad reached Newburyport on August 28, 1840. There they had contracted in the spring with the owners of a wagon bridge across the Merrimac to build a new double-deck bridge upon their piers, paying therefor the sum of

$5000. The bridge company at their own cost removed the superstructure, whereupon the railroad corporation built the two-story affair, the upper level carrying the railroad track, the lower the wagon-way, which the railroad was to keep in repair. This was a phenomenon seen in a number of places in New England thereafter.

The track reached the state line on November 9. In New Hampshire the road was already under construction, and drove into Portsmouth on December 31. The fare from East Boston to Newburyport, 33 miles, was fixed at $1.25, and to Portsmouth, 54 miles, $2, or nearly four cents a mile. A three-mile branch was built from Salem to Marblehead in 1839, and a funny little teakettle of an engine and one car made three round trips daily: fare 12½ cents, or what America used to call a "bit." At Portsmouth the road connected with steamers that ran to Portland. This continued until the Portland, Saco & Portsmouth Railroad was completed in 1842.

Relations between the Eastern and the Boston & Maine were still amicable, and early in 1843 the two of them concluded a joint lease of the Portland, Saco & Portsmouth, at a 6 per cent annual rental. But the Eastern was always closest to the P., S. & P., as is indicated by the fact that David A. Neal of Salem, who succeeded Peabody as president of the Eastern, was also the first president of the P., S. & P. It was Neal, by the way, who built Salem's first railway station in imitation of an English medieval castle and placed in the waiting room a small replica of an English cathedral with which he had fallen in love while on a European tour.

The Portland, Saco & Portsmouth had been a quick job for the time: its 52 miles from the Maine metropolis—through Kennebunk, North and South Berwick and Kittery—to Portsmouth, had been constructed in about a year and a half, and at a cost some $280,000 less than its capital stock issue—which constituted a record for the times. Its president, D. A. Neal, in the directors' report for 1843, spoke of the contract with the other roads as eliminating "that ruinous competition that is alike dangerous to the public and fatal to their own interests. By this arrangement the Railroad travel between

Maine and the South and West is left to its own course over
the other Roads, but is wholly secured to this—which is the
only outlet of this description that does or probably ever can
exist." The optimism of early days was at times well-nigh
boundless.

The inevitable stockholders' investigating committee of the
Eastern Railroad had found in 1840 that subscribers to stock
had been so remiss in paying for it that the directors had
taken over 641 of their shares, of which they succeeded in
placing two hundred with the contractors as part payment
for their work in building the road. President Peabody never
received any salary (Neal amended that), and the treasurer
was paid $2500, out of which he had to employ a $900 clerk;
but he also received a commission on all iron bought for the
company, which was a temptation to chicancry.

And now began a merry guerrilla war in northeastern
Massachusetts which continued until late in the 1850's, then
smoldered a while, and broke out again after 1870. Every
small city or town in that area pined for a railroad to every
other place; and with rival and parallel lines of some importance on both sides of them, the rural promoters shrewdly
saw here their opportunity to obtain help or shelter by playing one big cousin against the other.

Only a few men in the city of Lowell were stockholders
in the Boston & Lowell Railroad, and others had begun to feel
the hand of that concern as rather heavy upon them. In
1845, the year when the Boston & Maine was building its own
track into the capital, two projects appeared in which Lowell
was particularly interested, both planning short lines which
would top the B. & M. and thus give competition with the B. &
L. into Boston. One was a company which at first intended
connecting Lowell and Andover, but changed its mind and
built from Lowell to the new boom town of Lawrence. The
original purpose was accomplished by the Salem & Lowell
Railroad, which ran from Salem to Tewksbury on the Lowell
& Lawrence, crossing the B. & M. and thus affording that road
the line it desired; in fact, it began running through trains
from Lowell via Tewksbury and Wilmington Junction into

Boston. On the ground that this was a violation of the thirty-year monopoly clause in its charter, the Boston & Lowell promptly employed counsel no less eminent than Daniel Webster, and fought the case up to the State Supreme Court, where it won. The court's ban on the B. & M.'s through trains from Lowell to Boston was undoubtedly justifiable under the law, but popular sentiment was against the plaintiff.

In 1846 a group received a charter for the building of what was called the Essex Railroad, to run from Salem through Danvers to Lawrence, twenty-one miles. The Eastern favored this line from the beginning, even sponsored it by lending it $90,000, expecting to get Danvers business over it and also to invade the B. & M.'s bailiwick at Lawrence. When the road was opened, first to Danvers and then to Lawrence in 1847–48, the Eastern operated it. Simultaneously, the Eastern threw out branches to Gloucester and Salisbury.

What appeared to be a retort to the Essex appeared in 1848 in the form of a charter for the South Reading Branch Railroad, which began business in 1850. Only eight miles long, it ran from South Danvers, now Peabody, where it touched the Salem & Lowell, to the Boston & Maine at South Reading. Thus its trains were enabled to operate between Salem & Boston, and as somebody had supplied it with enough money to buy very fine equipment, it began slashing rates and cutting into the Eastern's business most annoyingly. Using dummy agents, the directors of the Eastern began picking up South Reading stock, even paying as high as 110 for it. It would have been illegal for the Eastern as a corporation to own stock of the other road, so the directors kept the shares in their own names, fired the S. R. B. directors and management at the next stockholders' meeting, sold the fine equipment, replacing it with rattletrap stuff, hoisted fares and disarranged the timetable, thus eliminating the menace. The minority stockholders uttered outcries, but though they succeeded in forcing the new owners to run four trains each way daily, this availed little.

Scarcely had the Eastern squashed this nuisance when another appeared, the Saugus Branch, which ran from the Boston & Maine at Malden to Lynn. The Eastern gained possession of a majority of the stock of this road, too, and was given permission to take it over. It then severed the connection with the B. & M. at Malden and extended that end to a junction with the Eastern's own main line again at South Malden (Everett) Junction, thus making a loop practically parallel to its own main line.

These projects sometimes came out just as the promoters had hoped they would, sometimes not quite so. Dozens of petty rails like this were created in New England (and elsewhere), often in part with cash begged from a bigger corporation, built with the double purpose of giving a rural area rail service and either selling out or leasing to the larger connecting line. The latter was fondly expected. A little later we find the Cochero Railroad in New Hampshire growing peevish because the Boston & Maine did not take it over. It was thus that the larger corporations, in many cases against their wish, became burdened with fringes and tatters of small branches which for decades they were not permitted to abandon, but many of which have been in the red since the day they were born, while others have finally been dismantled.

Four other little "pumpkin vines" next showed their cotyledons above the soil—the Danvers Railroad, intended to connect South Reading and Danvers; the second from Danvers to Georgetown; the third from Georgetown to Newburyport, and the fourth from Georgetown to Bradford, opposite Haverhill. The Boston & Maine, either believing or claiming to believe that the Georgetown-Danvers idea was backed by the Eastern, sought to block it by leasing the Danvers–South Reading project when it was still a mere germ—this was like entering a boy for Dartmouth before you even know whether it is going to be a boy or not. The B. & M. called its action defensive, the Eastern declared it offensive, even putrid. Said the Eastern President in 1853:

We understand that the Directors of the Boston & Maine Railroad have taken a lease of the Danvers Railroad, for the purpose, as we suppose, of opening another avenue to Salem, and also to Newburyport, not regarding any rights we may have connected with that business.  This arrangement we consider a direct breach of faith, as at the request of the President of the Boston & Maine Road, an understanding was had with him, that neither of us would directly or indirectly aid or assist in the building of that or the continuous road to Georgetown, without the knowledge or consent of the other.

The Boston & Maine denied this, saying that the agreement between them covered only the lines to Haverhill and Newburyport.  As to the prenatal lease of the Danvers, the B. & M. directors said in a public statement, "Unless the Boston & Maine had consented to hire the road, it is certain from the letters of Mr. Northend [its president] that it would never have been built or even begun."  And they would not have "hired" it, they declared, if they had not been reliably informed that the Eastern was preparing to back the building of the Danvers & Georgetown.

The complaints of the rivals against each other in those years are highly entertaining now.  They were just two concerns with considerable investments at stake, forced by (originally unintentional) parallelism into rivalry, fighting for life and dividends sufficient to justify existence, and likewise nudged by the scheming of local promoters into backing or taking over small neighborhood lines, often in self-defense.  But the directors' reports and pamphleteering each represent the undersigned as the long-suffering and innocent victim, imposed upon by the craft and chicanery of the other outfit.  They did not call each other crooks—they were too gentlemanly for that—but seeping through their verbiage one detects the conviction that the opposition is composed of a parcel of fellows with low ethical standards.

The four little roads were built, and in 1854 advertising appeared of the new routes from Salem and Newburyport to Boston, part way over the B. & M., at rates lower than those of the Eastern.  The route from Salem was too roundabout to get much business, but passengers from Boston to Danvers learned the trick of buying tickets through to Salem and selling the remainder of the ticket to expressmen and others, who resold at a profit. The later notorious business of "scalping" was very quickly learned. Finally, the two railroads made a peace treaty which held good up to 1864, when war broke out again, and for a time—until another treaty was signed— the Eastern was selling tickets between Newburyport and Boston for fifty cents, about half the regular rate.

In 1851 a new Eastern president had forced through the cherished idea of some directors to eliminate the ferry passage into Boston and enter the city proper by building a six-mile detour from Revere through Chelsea, Everett, Somerville and Charlestown to a station site on Causeway Street, between the depots of the Boston & Lowell and the Fitchburg, forming a veritable "Railroad Row." The cost was $791,600, not to mention the lawsuits with the Boston & Maine and Fitchburg, whose tracks were crossed at grade. A minority of stockholders fought bitterly against the expense, one sneering that the diversion "seemed to have been planned to enable the traveller to gaze upon all four sides of Bunker Hill Monument." The trains first entered the Causeway Street station April 10, 1854. It was a temporary wooden shack so small that locomotives didn't venture into it but detached themselves and made a flying switch outside it, letting the cars roll in on their own momentum; this required some careful hand braking to prevent their going right on through the depot wall into the city traffic. This building burned in 1862 and was replaced by a new one of brick. All these Causeway Street stations were eliminated in 1893–94, when the present great union North Station was erected.

Maine had begun to open up rapidly as a field for travel, and we presently find those semi-hostile corporations, the Boston & Maine, the Eastern and the P., S. & P., combining to build jointly a fine side-wheel steamer, the *Daniel Webster*, to run from Portland to Rockland and up the Penobscot to Bangor, competing with the Maine railroads. In 1857 the Eastern raced the B. & M. for the mail-carrying contract between Boston and Portland, a favorite stunt of those days.

The Eastern's engine, "City of Lynn," bested the B. & M.'s "Massachusetts," and won the contract.

The Eastern began branching out in other directions in the early 1850's, guaranteeing $160,000 in bonds of two small, struggling concerns which connected South Berwick with North Conway, N. H., and also $131,000 in bonds of the Grand Junction Railroad, a belt line uniting the wharves and station in East Boston with the railroads entering from the West and South. In 1865 the Portsmouth, Great Falls & Conway Railroad was incorporated in New Hampshire under the aegis of the Eastern, which took over two smaller lines and gradually crept through to North Conway in 1874, giving the Eastern two lines—one more than necessary—to the White Mountains, which were then becoming a highly popular summer resort. The Boston & Maine had also saddled itself with some incubi, such as the Cocheco, from Dover to Alton, N. H., and those little lines up in the corner of Massachusetts.

Despite its errors, the Eastern had been fairly prosperous in the early fifties, but a $250,000 defalcation by its treasurer, along with other troubles, topped by the panic of 1857, put the company in a critical condition. The twenty-year-old state scrip fell due that year, and the company simply couldn't pay. The state granted a stay until 1863, after which the debt was to be paid off at the rate of $75,000 a year. When the time arrived, the country was in the midst of the Civil War, gold was at a great premium and Congress had passed an act making paper legal tender. The Eastern accordingly proffered payment in greenbacks rather than in gold, which would have cost it far more than the face value of the scrip. As Massachusetts was still scrupulously paying principal and interest on its bonds in gold, there was great indignation under the Sacred Codfish, and the state treasurer refused to accept anything but specie. But after a wrangle, the attorney-general opined that under the Legal Tender Act he didn't see how the company could be forced to pay in gold, so it proceeded to pay not only its state debt but its bond redemptions and interest in paper. This caused much criticism, and some people even insinuated that the Eastern directors were "Copperheads," interested in furthering the rebel cause.

During and after the Civil War, the Eastern again prospered. In 1869 it even approached the Maine Central with a view to obtaining control of that growing system, but it was not successful. The Maine Central, however, now made the shrewd move of offering the Portland, Saco & Portsmouth 5 per cent in gold for a lease, a better figure than the 6 per cent in depreciated paper which, much to its stockholders' dissatisfaction, it was receiving from the Eastern. The P., S. & P. therefore annulled its lease, as it had a right to do under the agreement, by proffering $100,000 in cash to each of the lessors, and threw itself upon the market, the other three roads all bidding for it. When they had all—though with moans of anguish bid up to 10 per cent, the Eastern, through its interlocking ownership with the P., S. & P., won the lease.

Thereafter, the Eastern refused to take on the Boston & Maine trains at South Berwick, as it had always done, and haul them to Portland, or even to wait for its passengers. Orders to conductors were: "If the B. & M. train has already arrived when you reach there, take on the passengers; if it isn't in sight or sound, don't wait for it—go ahead and let 'em get along as best they can." The result was that frequently a flock of angry B. & M. wayfarers would be marooned for hours at the drab village of South Berwick. Indignant sufferers wrote letters to the directors and to the papers, and Edmund Vance Cook, a popular poet of the day, who was one of them, penned a rhyming satire on that

> Slow and woeful Junction Town,
> Where devils laugh and angels frown
> To see a passenger set down;
> Where trains run only with a view
> To help a restaurant or two;
> Where rusty rails and barren boards
> Are all the point of view affords.
> But O, the barren board of all

Is that within that eating stall!
Yes, stall I said, and well-deserved
The name! where beastly feed is served.
And so I say without compunction,
My curses on this Railroad Junction.

This procedure forced the Boston & Maine to extend its track from South Berwick into Portland, which it reached in 1873.

The Eastern now began reaching out covetous fingers toward the Maine Central. In 1871 it succeeded in putting over a contract by which it handled all the Central's western business. Through passenger trains, including a night train, now ran between Boston and Bangor, and Pullman cars were seen for the first time in Maine. They were smaller than the Pullmans of today, but still so much larger than the ordinary coaches that a tunnel had to be enlarged and the projecting eaves of several stations on the Eastern cut off to let them pass. The Negro porters on these Pullmans had to twist the brakes on their own cars when nearing a stop.

In June, 1871, a series of fatal accidents began which injured the Eastern seriously in both purse and reputation. In the worst of these, at Revere—mentioned elsewhere in this volume—thirty persons were killed and sixty injured. This disaster—due to the almost criminally antiquarian habit of thought of Superintendent Jeremiah Prescott, who had no signaling system, refused to use the telegraph in dispatching trains and was unbelievably muddle-headed and careless—cost the company half a million dollars in damages. Under Prescott the road hadn't even a wrecking train, and there were no air brakes, though Westinghouse's patent was then two years old and there was a vacuum brake still older. The Old Colony had begun using air a year before. After the accident it was brought out that Conductor Goodhue of the Bangor Express had more than once complained to Prescott and to President Browne that it was impossible to make a quick stop with hand brakes. To this the answer always was, "Do the best you can."

The Revere disaster forced the retirement of Browne, and a young man named Thornton K. Lothrop—son-in-law of Samuel Hooper of Salem, the leading stockholder in the company—was elected president. Prescott, who seemed to have some mysterious sort of "pull," remained on the job until 1874, when he was made superintendent of the Hoosac Tunnel. But Lothrop put a man over Prescott—Charles F. Hatch, brought over from the Lake Shore & Michigan Southern and installed as general manager. Hatch had been accustomed to telegraph operation of trains, and he brought with him a good dispatcher, so that Eastern trains were thereafter handled in a more careful manner.

The company had been wasting money with appalling prodigality. For several years a manufacturing group in Lynn had been wanting a second station built in their neighborhood. They were of course opposed by neighbors of the old depot, and a feud known as the "depot war" raged, even influencing city elections. President Browne, after wavering a while, bought for $216,000 a tract satisfactory to the first-named faction (it had been assessed for taxation purposes at $4500) and built a new station on it, meanwhile remodeling the old one at a cost of $130,000. Two stations in a town like Lynn were of course absurd, and when Lothrop came in he demolished the new one. Thus the Eastern had spent half a million dollars, most of it unnecessarily, in Lynn, and aroused animosities which presently resulted in the building of the Boston, Revere Beach & Lynn narrow-gauge railroad, opened in 1875. This was a well-managed line which throve and heavily sapped the business of the Eastern in its territory. And there were other drains: horse cars had begun operating from East Saugus to Boston in 1860 and from Lynn to Boston in 1861.

Lothrop sought to end the war between his own road and the Boston & Maine by combining the two systems, and even succeeded in getting before the Legislature a bill to authorize such a move. But the B. & M. management, who had no intention of being saddled with the other company's enormous debt, fought the measure strenuously and defeated it.

The Eastern also lost heavily on badly managed rail purchases and on demurrage on Maine Central cars, under a contract of 1871. Lothrop and his father-in-law Hooper therefore decided—just like that!—to take over the Maine Central. Early in 1873, these two bought $533,000 worth of M. C. stock at prices above the market—even paying par for some shares quoted at 30—enough to give them voting control in the election of M. C. directors in March, 1873. To accomplish this, they used cash from Eastern Railroad coffers, placing the stock in the name of the company's treasurer, John B. Parker, as "trustee." Lothrop and Hooper then pledged the stock at various banks as collateral for loans with which to buy more Maine Central stock. By the end of 1874 they were in complete control, owning 15,274 shares, which had cost them, including interest, $1,220,538. And still the Eastern stockholders and most of the directors didn't know what was going on. But then they began to find out, and in the resulting flare-up, Lothrop resigned and went to Europe "for his health." John Wooldredge, a Lynn shoe manufacturer with no experience in railroading, was elected in his stead, but refused to serve unless he received a salary of $20,000 a year, instead of the $8000 on which Lothrop had subsisted. Being an insider, he had his way, though such a salary, considering the times and the strength of the corporation, was fantastic.

Other extravagances were under way when he came into office. The Maine Central people, though in a minority, had demanded better terminal facilities at Boston, and the Eastern bought land (some of it, as later proved, at inflated prices) and erected buildings thereon which brought the total cost to more than $1,600,000. They also bought a controlling interest in the Portland, Bangor and Machias Steamboat Company, which served, among other places, the increasingly popular Mount Desert Island. Rumors that the Boston & Maine might run an opposition boat to Mount Desert caused the Eastern to buy a rotting old wharf, the only available landing at Bar Harbor, for an exorbitant sum, which included a grafting "agent's" fee; and then it turned out that they could not even obtain a sound deed to the property. Meanwhile the road was still building new track here and there and still having some costly wrecks.

The Panic of 1873 caught the Eastern with a funded debt nearly twice its capitalization. The situation of the company was critical. They tried to cut expenses by welding two trains into one and having some of the Portland expresses make local stops, but gave it up after a few weeks. Charles W. Felt, one of the most persistent pamphleteers of that period when such things were the rage, rubbed salt into the Eastern's wounds in 1873–74 with two pamphlets which he called *The Eastern Railroad of Massachusetts, Its Blunders, Mismanagement and Corruption, Numbers 1 and 2*. Felt, a scion of an old Salem family, was a lecturer for the Massachusetts State Grange; and those moderns who may have forgotten the Granger movement of the 1870's are reminded that it was a nation-wide farmers' organization, among whose chief foci of attack were the growing power and misdeeds of the railroads.

Felt started out with the object of vindicating the conductor of the express train who had been blamed unjustly for the Revere disaster, but his little booklets were also scathingly frank exposures of the skeletons in the Eastern closet. He charged: "The Eastern Railroad has been for many years managed by two rings, the prime object of both of which is to hold their power, and the two have long worked together with this single aim. The chief ring is the Hooper family, and the minor ring is made up of a few of the officials," who "simply ask to be let alone." The Revere holocaust, he said, had caused some friction: "The chief ring charged the minor ring with leading them into difficulty, but they salved the scratch" by making a scapegoat of Conductor Nowland. Felt followed up these excoriations with three pamphlets on "dead-heads," persons who rode the rails on free passes.

His exposures and stockholder-awakenings had their effect, and President Wooldredge, who had devoted most of his time to endeavors to borrow more money, found the job too hot for him, resigned because of "ill-health" in October, 1875, after only a few months' incumbency, and hurried away to

California.  It was evident that the time had now come for economy.  Samuel C. Lawrence, who was the new president, slashed his own salary to $5000, and the superintendent's from $5000 to $3500.  The $10,000 general manager's job was abolished, the Portland, Saco & Portsmouth was induced to accept a 6 per cent annual rental instead of 10 per cent, and many other savings were effected.  But Lawrence made one grave error in trying to fight the Boston, Revere Beach & Lynn by building a parallel line through Revere Beach and meeting the narrow-gauge's fare of a dime from Lynn and a nickel from the Beach to Boston.  It was too costly a battle; rates were presently restored, the new line was abandoned, and the narrow-gauge remained triumphant and prosperous.

There was another disappointment.  The Portland & Ogdensburg Railroad, which was intended to connect Portland with the Great Lakes, had succeeded in building a line partly across northern New Hampshire and Vermont but had never got into Portland; it finally agreed with the Eastern to use its Great Falls & Conway branch to reach the Maine metropolis.  There were high hopes in Eastern councils for this through traffic, but the Vermont portion of the P. & O. went bankrupt in the year when it was opened, 1877; a hoped-for extension into Canada was never built, and the whole scheme failed to work out.

Here it may be interjected that the great railroad strike of 1877, which reached such a bitter and destructive pitch in states farther west, touched New England scarcely at all.  Its only manifestation there occurred on the Boston & Maine, where engineers whose wages the company proposed to reduce—only temporarily, it was claimed—from $3.75 to $3.40 per day, left their posts, and were promptly discharged and replaced by engineers from other parts of the country, who were out of work because of the business depression.  The expelled men were forced to find jobs as firemen with the Eastern Railroad at about half their former salary.

Felt had continued his nagging with two pamphlets issued in 1876 and 1879, both entitled *Nuts for Butler to Crack;* for the sinister hand of the notorious lawyer-politician, General

Benjamin F. Butler, had been pulling strings in Eastern Railroad history for some years. These pamphlets consisted of pointed questions addressed to Butler. As the author says in an opening paragraph:

> Benjamin F. Butler will now take the stand. There is no need of administering the oath; for we shall not call upon him to make answers, because if he did answer, we should have to exercise our judgment about believing him.

Among the questions were:

27. John Sanborn was one of your unscrupulous Cape Ann neighbors, was he?

30. John was a lobbyist at Boston and Washington, was he?

31 John took $125,000 of Eastern Railroad money, did he?

33. That money was supposed to be used in lobbying the legislatures of Maine, New Hampshire and Massachusetts, was it?

35. Was any of the money used to help your election to Congress?

37. John Sanborn had the means of getting an almost unlimited number of free passes on the Eastern Railroad, annual and trip, for parties and individuals, did he?

38. And those passes were used to promote your election, were they?

66. By the way, Benjamin, didn't you attempt to ride on the Boston & Maine Railroad in 1874 as if you had a free pass, but was compelled to pay your fare?

14. Now, Benjamin, having got the nomination in 1866, will you tell us whether in 1868, 1870 and 1872, you were elected by the people or by the Eastern Railroad, with a station in nearly every town in the district?

Felt aired the $200,000 land purchase for a depot in Lynn and revealed that Butler was counsel for the seller, receiving a $10,000 fee for his services. "In other words, you helped to swindle the Eastern Railroad, and took a share of the gross proceeds, did you?" He charged that Wooldredge was "the high cock-a-lorum in all matters pertaining to the Lynn depot, the $200,000 land purchase and other iniquities." He reviewed the misdoings of Lothrop and hinted that Sanborn, Lothrop, Parker and Wooldredge all ought to be in Concord prison at that moment. He wound up by glancing at Butler's unlovely Civil War record.

The Railroad Committee of the Massachusetts Legislature took a hand in 1876, condemned the recklessness and chicanery of past regimes and the directors' negligence in not keeping themselves informed of what was going on. Even current directors called before the committee were found to be reprehensibly ignorant of the company's functionings. The general ticket agent of the road confessed to the committee that free passes were still costing the company $500 a day; the superintendent, who signed the passes, actually had to have a special clerk to do this work for him.

Upon the recommendation of the committee, "A Bill for the Relief of the Eastern Railroad Company," meaning for the relief of the people whose money was invested in it, was passed by the Legislature, putting the concern in the hands of the bondholders—the largest being good old Baring Brothers of London—who were to elect a board of trustees to represent them. Among Felt's questions to Butler were:

> 92. Will you tell us how Baring Brothers of London came to make large loans to the railroad when it was in such a critical condition?
> 93. They were cheated into the belief that the road was in a sound condition, were they not?

One wonders how Barings ever survived their numerous bad investments in America.

The stock of the company which had been quoted at 65 in 1875 had declined to 3½ in 1876, and reached 2½, its all-time low, in 1877. Under the trustees it slowly recovered, creeping up to 51 in 1883. The directors and bondholders now thought it best for all parties concerned that the company be united in some fashion with its better-managed and more prosperous rival, the Boston & Maine. Accordingly, in

1884, the Eastern was leased to the B. & M. for fifty-four years, with financial provisions too complicated to be listed here. Actual amalgamation of the two companies, to be brought about as soon as possible, was in the minds of both parties but was angrily contested by some Eastern stockholders who believed that their road was just about to enter upon its inheritance, its real career of prosperity. There were suits to set aside the lease and prevent the consolidation, but they failed, and the roads were welded into one in 1890.

The Boston & Maine had thereby practically doubled its mileage, had insured to itself all traffic west and southwest of Portland, and with its controlled Maine Central tracks had vicariously reached the boundary of New Brunswick. But this was only the start of its era of expansion.

# 8

# New Haven Becomes a Railroad Center

CONNECTICUT, with the coast of a quiet sea and good harbors fringing its longest boundary, with a navigable river crossing it in the opposite direction and another penetrating deeply into it, and with one of the finest systems of turnpike roads in the country, had been slow to become excited over railroads. She needed no better connection with New York; she was right next door. President Timothy Dwight of Yale noted in his memoirs in 1821 that six good turnpikes sprayed out from New Haven, and the coach service was considered superb. But the agitation in Boston over a desired railroad to the Hudson River naturally stirred comment in Connecticut, at first somewhat jocular, as if the project were something in which Connecticut could be only academically interested. A New Haven editorial of 1830 treated the railroad as a public highway:

> Gentlemen will keep their own steam coaches, and find it cheap, pleasant and convenient to travel, and not at the slow rate of twenty miles the day, in their private vehicles. Stables will cease to be an annoyance; steam carriages will be patient animals, never kicking for flies, nor whisking their tails in men's mouths, nor sending out noisome odors. When a gentleman would take a ride, he has only to direct
>
> > John to put the kettle on, and
> > Whisk away in a jiffy.

When Massachusetts chartered and launched the construction of three railroads, some people in the Wooden Nutmeg area began to take the business more seriously. In 1832 an enthusiast signing himself "Clinton" wrote frequent letters to the *Connecticut Herald and Journal* of New Haven, urging the prosecution of a railroad between Hartford and New Haven, via Middletown. The Boston & Worcester was then building, and with real prophetic vision, "Clinton" saw the Hartford–New Haven line as a link in a through route between Boston & New York. He pondered the effect upon the uncompleted canal from New Haven to Northampton—about which Connecticut was very touchy, though it had been a money-loser from the start—and thought the railroad would not divert a dollar's worth of freight from it. As to passengers, "there have never been many passengers on the canal." He next went off the deep end and declared that the turnpikes "have been of comparatively little importance to the public or the stockholders." Another correspondent denied this: he saw railroads as inevitable but said the pikes had been useful public servants and should not be turned out in the cold, unpensioned. He thought they might be quieted for a few thousand dollars. "Clinton's" imagination soared. "It is evident," he guessed, "that about 18 per cent annually can be made on passengers alone." He proposed for the small city of New Haven three stations in different parts of town, to accommodate all classes of passengers. "Construct the railroad between Hartford and New Haven," he trumpeted, "and soon THE FULL-ORBED SPLENDORS OF A NOONDAY BUSINESS ON IT will crown all efforts with abundant success."

An alarmed publicist in Hartford ridiculed the idea and revealed his true feelings when he argued that "it may even be injurious to Hartford; and that the interests of Hartford would be against shortening the distance to New York, if there was any chance of preserving the then existing relations of country and town." Hartford (population 4789) then had to share the honor and profit of being the state capital with New Haven, more than twice its size, and may have feared that it would lose even its half-loaf.

For New Haven, even more alarming portents appeared on the horizon. Not only the railroad from Boston to Providence but another from Worcester to Norwich and a third from Providence to Stonington were to be built, perhaps even an extension to New London; and from all these ports, boat lines were planned to New York. New Haven saw herself being by-passed. Her citizens agreed that something must be done, and in 1833, a petition, backed largely by men of that city, went to the Legislature, asking for a charter.

Despite protests from high authority that the investment of widows, orphans and persons of moderate circumstances in turnpikes and steamboat lines "and many other of the vested interests of our citizens would be utterly destroyed" by the railroad, the charter was granted in 1833, authorizing the petitioners to construct a "single, double or treble line of track"—which became a stock phrase in Connecticut charters—between New Haven and Hartford. Prominent among the New Haven incorporators was the man who was elected as the first president of the new company, James Brewster, manufacturer of horse vehicles. For Mr. Brewster this investment may be said to have represented a climbing on the bandwagon, for he had made many a gentleman's traveling carriage, an article now to be superseded by the new transportation. Nevertheless, until the automobile came, the name of Brewster, as manufacturer of carriages and other vehicles, continued to be perhaps the most famous in America.

The young engineer, Alexander C. Twining, of whom we have heard before, was engaged to make the survey, and to figure on a horse-path, too, for emergencies. After he had run a line according to his orders, via Middletown, it was decided that that route was indirect and required too heavy cutting and grades; the track must be located farther west. But this conclusion was not reached without an argument with the director from Middletown, Mr. Hubbard. Director Seth North of New Britain wanted it to come through his village, but Director Elisha Cowles of Meriden and others thought that too far west. So Mr. Cowles induced the two New Haven directors to join him in persuading Messrs. Hubbard and North to let the line pass *between* their two villages;

which—they agreeing—it did, but went right spang through Mr. Cowles's village of Meriden!

There was one village, however—in fact, a whole township—which didn't want the railroad, and said so. The *New Haven Herald* reported in 1836:

> The Newington folks, we are told, hearing that it was proposed to run a railroad through their town, presented a remonstrance to the directors, representing that they were a peaceable, orderly people (which, in truth, they are), and begged that their quiet might not be interrupted by steamcars and the influx of strangers. As good luck would have it, there is no occasion to contravene their wishes. . . .

In New Haven the charter unequivocally stated that the terminus was to be "at some point between the Canal Basin and the west end of Tomlinson's bridge, so called." A little later, local critics were asking: Why was the terminal point so carefully specified in the charter? Why wasn't it left to be worked out after more extended investigation, as in other cases? Simply because Somebody's property—You Know Who—was to be benefited: that's why! A depot elsewhere would have been more convenient and useful to both railroad and citizens, these captious ones said.

That, however, was a closed chapter; the next had to do with the usual problem, that of getting money. Construction began modestly in 1836, and then came the panic year, 1837, when payments on stock almost entirely ceased.[1] The state seemed the last and only hope. Not only this company, but the Housatonic and the Norwich & Worcester went, hat in hand, to the Capitol, but met with a stunning rebuff. Connecticut solons, for some reason, had ideas differing widely from those of Massachusetts. As the Hartford & New Haven directors delicately phrased it:

[1] It was on April 17 of that year that a Mr. and Mrs. J. S. Morgan of Hartford announced the birth of a son whom they christened John Pierpont. It seems almost symbolical that the greatest of railroad bankers, the man who became depression-proof, should have been born in Hartford just as Connecticut's first three railways—whose destiny he is said to have influenced so greatly seventy years later—were in the throes of nativity.

Encouraged by the success of the Western Rail-road of Massachusetts, before the liberal and patriotic legislature of that State, it was determined to present the claims of this Company to our legislature, and ask the aid of this State to be granted in the safe, liberal and enriching manner which Massachusetts had adopted. This was zealously and urgently, but unsuccessfully attempted. This refusal of the State to avail itself of an opportunity to increase its wealth and power, and at the same time, confer a lasting benefit upon the Company, will always be deeply regretted. Failing in this resource, the Directors turned their attention to capitalists, who lend as a matter of business, and not from benevolence or patriotism, and from them succeeded in borrowing money. . . .

And so the railroads had to stand on their own legs, and were all the better for it. (It may be mentioned that Connecticut legislatures became more generous in later years.) On the other hand, those plutocrats who lent money for sordid reasons—and charged 7 per cent for it—evidently had a larger vision, more confidence in the new invention or a greater willingness than the lawmakers to risk their money for the general good of business or the state. Anyhow, by borrowing from these moneyed men and by wringing a few more dollars out of subscribers, the company slowly drove the road through.

For economy's sake, they decided to lay a strap rail, though Engineer-Professor Twining gently objected that the wisdom of this course was "very questionable." However, they managed to get along with it for eight years. Spencer Fullerton Baird, the zoologist, traveling over it in 1846, noted in his journal with a scientist's attention to detail that the track was "wooden, with iron bar rails 13/16ths inches thick, laid on Southern pine six inches square, and about 20 feet long. Costs about $25.00 per thousand feet. The wood is replaced about every three years. Road very good. Few or no accidents." The strap was replaced by a T-rail soon after his visit.

In November, 1838, an engine and some cars having been

procured, the agent and directors, "with a small party of gentlemen," according to the *New Haven Herald*, made a short excursion, "to try the quality of the materials and test the susceptibility of motion." They went out about seven miles, and made the return trip—downgrade, it was explained—in nineteen minutes, "without any effort at extra speed. Everything worked kindly and happily, showing that the parts of the machinery were properly adjusted to the purposes for which they were designed." The smooth track and the elegant and commodious cars were complimented, "and there was none of that jerking and jarring motion in starting and stopping, that we have observed on other roads."

Late in the following month the railhead reached Meriden, eighteen miles up country. But the financial difficulties of the company compelled another year to elapse before the first train passed over the remaining eighteen miles, into the "engine-house in Hartford," on December 14, 1839. Scarcely had the road begun operation through its full length before a blizzard piled snowdrifts over the track, which it required a day and a half to remove.

That month in directors' meeting it was voted by five to two to run a train each way on Sunday solely for the purpose of carrying the mails. When the question arose of whether passengers should be permitted on these trains, it was voted down by four to three. There was criticism even of the Sunday mail trains, and the opposition to traveling on the Sabbath finally crystallized into a state law against Sunday trains save for mail-carrying, and this law stood for decades. Toward the end of the century, however, passengers were finally permitted to ride on the Sunday mail trains.

Even when the road was in operation only from New Haven to Meriden, it was, if the reader will believe it, declared by New Haven papers to be "decidedly the best and most popular route in the winter season between New York and Albany." The traveler came up to New Haven by boat; took the train which departed upon the boat's arrival, about 1:00 P.M.; went from Meriden by post coach to Hartford, arriving about 4:00 P.M.; had to wait there until 10:00 at night for another coach, and was scheduled to arrive at Albany at 3:00 P.M. next day. With good luck, it required only about thirty-two hours.

To further this through service, the railroad had made an early agreement with the New Haven Steamboat Company to run its trains in connection with that company's New York boats, and no others; in return, the Steamboat Company was to pay the H. & N. H. $500 per year until the line reached Hartford, when the annual stipend would be increased to $1200. When the secret of this agreement leaked out—although today we cannot see any great culpability in it—it caused much criticism, and was the subject of an anonymous pamphlet, *Secret Monopoly*.

The arrangement was particularly damaging to the Connecticut River Line, which operated boats from Hartford to New York, and it threatened to make a way-stop at New Haven, which it had not hitherto done. Alarmed by this, the New Haven Steamboat Company sold out to the Connecticut River concern, which thereupon began evading the contract with the railroad. The latter retaliated by obtaining state permission to operate steamboats of its own from New Haven to New York. Its service was no sooner installed than another, a privately owned boat, entered the field, and as might be expected, a rate war broke out, the fare to New York being cut to twenty-five cents and finally to "one bit." After this folly had faded, the railroad continued to run boats to New York for ten years, finally selling them to Chester W. Chapin.

The road was no sooner completed than promotion work began for an extension from Hartford to Springfield, and under a separate charter, work on this was begun in 1842 and completed in 1844. It crossed the Connecticut by a 1500-foot wooden bridge at Warehouse Point, and the legislators, intent on proving that they never overlook a trifle, specified a draw in it, though any of the little boats on the upper river (Dickens spoke of the one on which he rode as of "about the thickness of a warm sandwich") could have passed under the bridge with no trouble, and did. Incidentally, that bridge was blown clean off its piers by an October gale in 1846, and was replaced by a new one in forty-five days.

Thus another step toward the all-rail line from Boston to New York was taken. The next may seem to us to have been slow in coming, but the fact is that the boat service between New Haven and New York was so good—and especially attractive when rates were cut to the bone—that the need for a railroad was not keenly felt; furthermore, it was believed that the deeply indented shore line would make construction difficult. Vague gestures in that direction, however, had been made; and here we shall have to pause to mention two contributory projects which played minor parts in the drama.

The citizens of Danbury, the hat town, bestirred themselves in 1835 and procured a charter for the Fairfield County Railroad, to run from their village to tidewater, either in the town of Norwalk or in Fairfield. Their actual objective was Wilson's Point, just below Norwalk, which had the best year-round harbor in the vicinity and from which they foresaw a boat line to New York only 40 miles away. A local booster of the day might well have said, "Keep your eye on Wilson's Point." The promoters' vision expanded northward, too, up the Housatonic River beyond Danbury. They took their pencils and figured, New York to Wilson's Point, 40 miles; to Danbury, 26 miles; to West Stockbridge 74 miles; thence by that about-to-be-built railroad to Albany, 30 miles; total, 164 miles and the Best Possible Route between New York and Albany. They were thus in the field—in imagination, at least—before the Housatonic Railroad.

The queer thing was that they at first planned it as a horse railroad! Alexander Twining, who surveyed the line, included in his estimate as to equipment needed, six passenger carriages, fifteen wagons for burdens and thirty horses, with stables, harness, etc. They quickly gave up that idea when the locomotives around Boston began to demonstrate that they would actually run and pull trains.

But when, before the end of 1835, Twining began to prowl north of Danbury along the river, Bridgeport, the next waterside city east of Norwalk, became alarmed. Promoters there had already been talking of a railroad up the Housatonic into Massachusetts, and now these chaps at Danbury seemed about to snatch the idea away from them. In behalf of Bridgeport, Alfred Bishop visited Danbury and offered to take the job of building their Wilson's Point line off their hands if Danbury would put up $100,000. The village flatly refused, so Bridgeport promoters bent their efforts to the task of promoting the Housatonic Railroad themselves; and since Bridgeport was much larger than Norwalk, they succeeded, though by rather desperate measures. Another decade passed before Danbury obtained her railroad, but it was at last built in 1850–52 as the Danbury & Norwalk.

The Housatonic Railroad was chartered in 1836—somebody at the State House wasn't strong on spelling, for it was chartered as the Ousatonic, and so you will find it in a number of old documents—to build up along the valley of that river to the Massachusetts state line. New Haven, less than sixteen miles east of Bridgeport, was berated by its publicists in later years for having made no effort to get the southern terminus of the road. Bridgeport would have put up a fight, however, for she was determined to have it, and she paid well for it. The city subscribed for $50,000 worth of the stock, and citizens individually for $50,000 more. The city likewise agreed to give the company $150,000 worth of its bonds, to be paid in installments as the work progressed.

Construction began, despite the panic, in 1837, and so did the unhappiness of Bridgeport citizens. With money scarce, taxpayers objected to their additional burden resulting from gifts to the railroad. East Bridgeport seceded from the city government, though it remained in the town. Some taxpayers moved out of the city to get out from under the incubus. There was a popular demand for repudiation of the city's pledge, but the courts declared the contract valid, and the city had to pay.

Meanwhile the Housatonic directors, coasting along comfortably, began to talk of extending the railroad to New York. R. B. Mason, the company's engineer, made a survey in 1838 from Bridgeport through Norwalk to Sawpits Village

*Courtesy New York Central Railroad*

*Above*—Where Whistler surveyed the Line: a Boston & Albany (N.Y.C.) giant toiling up along Westfield River in the Berkshires. *Below*—One of many such scenes along the same line after the great flood of 1927.

## YANKEE-BORN BUILDERS OF WESTERN RAILROADS

A. A. Robinson (Vt.)  Thos. Nickerson (Mass.)  E. P. Ripley (Mass.)
Santa Fe, Mex. Central  Santa Fe, Mex. Central  Santa Fe.

W. B. Strong (Vt.)  Fredk. Billings (Vt.)  Josiah Perham (Me.)
Santa Fe  Northern Pacific  Northern Pacific

## CRACK TRAINS OF TODAY
*Top*—Flying Yankee, Boston & Maine-Maine Central.
*Middle*—Yankee Clipper, New Haven.
*Bottom*—The Ambassador, Central Vermont (Canadian National)

*Courtesy Charles E. Fisher and Boston Public Library*

### MAINE LOCOMOTIVES
*Top*—Maine Central's "Penobscot", 1871
*Middle*—First locomotive in Maine: Bangor & Piscataquis, built by
Stephenson, 1836.
*Bottom*—An early job of the Portland Locomotive works.

## NEW ENGLAND-BORN BUILDERS AND EXECUTIVES

John W. Brooks (Mass.)    James F. Joy (N. H.)    Henry B. Plant (Conn.)
Mich. Central    Mich. Central, Wabash, etc.    Plant System, Sou. Exp. Co.
Austin Corbin (N. H.)    Daniel Willard (Vt.)    M. E. Ingalls (Me.)
Reading, Long Island    Balto. & Ohio    Big Four, Ches. & Ohio, etc.

NEW ENGLANDERS WHO FIRST SPANNED THE CONTINENT

Oliver Ames       Collis P. Huntington       Oakes Ames
Grenville M. Dodge                     Thomas C. Durant

*Courtesy Chas. E. Fisher, New Haven and Canadian National Railways*

## MODERN LOCOMOTIVES

1.—A Fitchburg Beauty of 1900. 2.—A New Haven electric giant of today.
3.—One of the Central Vermont 700 series, largest locomotives in New England.
4.—One of the New Haven's 1400 Series

## DISTINGUISHED NEW ENGLAND RAIL MEN

| | | |
|---|---|---|
| Onslow Stearns | Ginery Twitchell | John A. Poor |
| Charles P. Clark | Charles F. Adams, Jr. | Charles S. Mellen |

(now the thriving manufacturing city of Port Chester, N. Y.), and reported that while one stony place "at first presented a very forbidding appearance," he had found a way around it, and believed a connection with the Harlem Railroad to be feasible. The proposition then languished, though stirring feebly from time to time. As late as 1844, Stamford held an enthusiastic town meeting to back the petition of the Ousatonic Railroad for the right to build track from Bridgeport along the Sound shore to Byram River. But by that time the task was passing to other hands.

In the meantime, the doings in Bridgeport took on what now seems the aspect of comic opera, though they were anything but funny to Bridgeport. It was apparently to be a question whether the property of the city or its citizens must go by the board. The mayor adopted the curious expedient of deeding or assigning municipal holdings to individuals: for example, for $15 cash he assigned the fire houses to George Kippen, his heirs and assigns, "to have and to hold for twelve months." In that same year an agent was authorized to convey to another man all the city's property, real and personal, for the benefit of creditors. Apparently this didn't go through, for we next find the city selling its engines and fire houses for $1249.09 and leasing them from the buyer for $75 a year. The courts refused to sanction these goings-on, and in 1845 the city returned the money and took its property back. Slowly it began to pay interest and pay off the bonds, while the Legislature passed a law forbidding cities to lend their credit to build railroads.

By December, 1841, as we have seen, the Governor of New York was speaking warmly of the excellent rail-stage-boat route—partly via the Housatonic—between Albany and New York. The road's northern rail-end was then at West Canaan; it reached the state line in the spring, and almost simultaneously a continuation of it, the Berkshire Railroad, was opened from the state line to West Stockbridge, thus completing a continuous line of rails from Albany to Bridgeport and a shorter Albany–New York route than the one via Springfield and Hartford. Later on, the Housatonic built an extension to Pittsfield, and continued to be a prosperous concern for many years thereafter. It is interesting to note that this was one of the first railroads to ship milk in large quantities into New York City. The directors reported in 1868 that 100,000 quarts a day were going down the valley, from as far north as Pittsfield; and the Housatonic Valley Milk Association triumphantly said that (even in those pre-pasteurizing days) the old dictum that milk could not be successfully shipped more than a hundred miles had been disproved.

Despite the excellence of the boat service between New Haven and New York, a rail line between the two cities was an inevitability, as the importance of railroads loomed larger in the national economy. After much simmering, the pot boiled, and in 1844 a group of Connecticut and New York bankers and businessmen obtained a Connecticut charter for the New York & New Haven Railroad, with an authorized capital of $2,000,000, which might be raised to $3,000,000. Two of the most prominent promoters, presaging alliances, were Joseph E. Sheffield, president of the money-losing Farmington Canal, which ran up to Northampton, Mass., and Samuel J. Hitchcock, then president of the Hartford & New Haven Railroad. The first president of the new company was Robert Schuyler of New York, grandson of a general of the Revolution; with his brother, he composed the highly-regarded brokerage firm of R. and G. L. Schuyler. Sheffield procured the charter, subscribed for the biggest block of stock and had the survey made by Alexander Twining, paying most of the bills for it himself.

In 1845 an application to the New York Legislature for a charter was successfully opposed by the New York & Harlem Railroad and the Westchester Turnpike Company. To overcome the first obstacle, the N. Y. & N. H. had to agree to use the Harlem's tracks into New York City, almost on the latter's own terms, and an arrangement was made for a junction with the Harlem at or near Williams Bridge, now in the upper edge of the Borough of the Bronx. The Turnpike Company had to be bought off, too, and then the charter was granted in 1846.

A contract was made with Alfred Bishop, builder of the Housatonic, to construct the line for $2,250,000. Whether Bishop estimated too low or not, we do not know; but because of the numerous estuaries, it was an expensive road to build—there were more than a mile and a half of bridges, with six draw spans, in Connecticut alone; it was afterward charged by the *American Railroad Journal* that the line was poorly constructed, Bishop mostly doing his own engineering, and that a sharp curve at the Norwalk River bridge, put in to save expense, was a contributing cause to the fatal wreck there several years later. The road underwent a constant process of reconstruction for years after it opened.

Late in December, 1848, the track was laid to the connecting point with the Harlem at Williams Bridge. In a comedy of errors, a triumphal trainload of folk from New Haven who set out on Christmas Day for a joyous opening junket to New York found upon reaching Williams Bridge that the connection with the Harlem track had not been quite completed, and so were compelled to return ingloriously to New Haven and wait a few days. The Harlem's station in New York was then on Fourth Avenue, between 26th and 27th Streets, whence a track continued southward to Canal Street, some cars being brought up by horses from there to the main station.

Competitive threats arose, to be fought off or laughed off, or to collapse of their own weakness: for example, a proposed railroad from the New York & Harlem at White Plains to Hartford, whose pretty prospectus appeared in 1845, was never built; its dreamers could not conjure money from the air. Then came another problem. Joseph E. Sheffield had been elected president of the unprofitable Farmington Canal in 1843, while Henry Farnam, a lifelong *fidus Achates* to Sheffield, was superintendent. In 1845, having sold most of his stock, Sheffield resigned, and the other directors, casting about desperately for a life-belt, thought of building a railroad over the canal's right of way, from New Haven to Northampton, Mass. At that, the mercurial Sheffield bought quantities of the canal stock held by parties in New York, and in 1846 he obtained permission from the Legislature to metamorphose the canal company into a railroad company. Twining made a survey; work began in 1847, and the line was completed to Plainville by the end of the year. On January 17, 1848, the opening celebration took place, when all the New Haven city and town officials, the faculty and officers of Yale College and "the members of the law and medical professions" were invited to ride on the railroad in (as usual) "four as splendid cars as were ever placed upon an American railroad." Entire populations greeted the train as it moved northward, and Messrs. Sheffield and Farnam were evidently considered to be the *dei ex machina*, for at Plainville one of the demonstrations was a big banner inscribed "Success to Sheffield and Farnam"; while upon the return to New Haven that evening, the crowd, before dispersing—we quote the *New Haven Palladium*—"gave three hearty cheers for Mr. Sheffield, the chief proprietor [he was president of the company] and Mr. Farnam, his assistant and also a proprietor."

But the railroad had now used up its cash, and the next move was one which Sheffield may have had in mind all along: it was leased for twenty years at a $45,000 annual rental to the N. Y. & N. H., with the understanding that its construction was to be continued northward to a terminus at either Northampton or Springfield. Those shrewd chaps, Sheffield and Farnam, took the contract to do the building, their payment to be in stock.

The new road thus became a deadly parallel competitor for the Hartford & New Haven and its Springfield extension; and as might be expected, the next scene in the drama shows that concern moving to block the competition. Forgathering with the New York & New Haven directors, it promised, for a modest annual compensation over a term of five years, to withdraw its day boats from the New York and New Haven service, and on the less popular night boats to fix a fare only fifty cents less than that by rail. Both parties were to make all efforts to operate the best possible through rail line—in conjunction with the Western—between New York and Bos-

ton. And finally, the canal railroad construction was to be
halted at Avon, not far north of Plainville, unless the Legislature insisted upon its being continued. There was much
more.

But the Hartford & New Haven and the New York & New
Haven could never get along. Between moments of pseudo-
amicable agreement about steamboats, and promises not to
poach on each other's preserves, they were usually suing each
other about something. As a result, the compact to halt the
canal railroad could not continue long. In 1849 that unwanted child was trying to enter Massachusetts, but a charter
was refused there through the machinations of the Western
Railroad, perhaps instigated by the H. & N. H. Again in
1850 it was blocked, but in 1852 persistence was rewarded;
the Northampton & Westfield was incorporated in Massachusetts, and the line was opened through to Northampton in
1855. It was handed back to its owners in a dilapidated condition at the expiration of the lease in 1869.

During these mutations, another north-and-south line had
sprung into existence and was to become another future
branch of the great New Haven system: namely, the Naugatuck Railroad, following the river of that name from the
Sound up to Winsted. It was a product of the busy brain
of Alfred Bishop of Bridgeport, who obtained a charter for it
in 1845. He had some strenuous days, however, when it
came to raising the necessary money. He traveled up and
down the valley through the towns to be served—Winsted,
Wolcottville (Torrington), Plymouth, Waterbury, Naugatuck, Ansonia and Birmingham (Derby), but found many
skeptical of there ever being any dividends. Some men of
means were so contemptuous that they preferred to make out-
right donations. Seth Thomas, the clockmaker of Thomaston, gave $15,000, and Anson G. Phelps of Ansonia, a promi-
nent stockholder of the New York & New Haven, was another large donor. The money was finally raised, and Bishop,
as contractor, completed the road to Winsted in September,

1849.[2] Bishop offered to make New Haven the southern terminus if it would buy $75,000 worth of stock, but it refused, and so he ended the road at a junction with the New York & New Haven only five miles east of Bridgeport. This was for many years a well-managed and profitable railroad.

While we are on the subject, we may as well remark that New Haven, regretting its error with regard to the Naugatuck, promoted the New Haven & Derby Railroad, built in 1868–71, to tap that line at Derby, the city putting into it half a million in stock, bonds and cash loans; but it was then too late; business was not diverted as expected, and the thing proved a costly adventure.

That decade of the 1840's was a busy one for railroads in Connecticut. New promotions blossomed at every change of the moon. The next that we have to notice was the one which forged the last link in the shore line between New York and Boston, as the great New York, New Haven & Hartford Company operates it now. The New York, Providence & Boston Railroad, from Providence to Stonington, had been completed and in operation more than a decade, in connection with boats which ran from Stonington to New York. Now promoters began asking: Why not a rail line all the way, cutting the time between New York and Boston, and eliminating the boats entirely? Accordingly, in New York, New Haven and to the east, men joined in organizing the New Haven & New London Railroad, chartered in 1848, with an authorized capital of $500,000 to $1,000,000. It was not given permission to bridge the Connecticut River, its navigation being considered too important to be interfered with. The company had no intention of bridging it, anyhow; the estuary of the great stream was too big.

Twining, as usual, made the surveys; the work was soon begun, and in 1852 the road was open to New London. Its

[2] A quaint instance of industrial specialization is found in the prospectus of the road, where we read that in the town of Colebrook, just north of Winsted, the principal businesses are five large tanneries and eleven mills for sawing clock cases, coffee-mill boards and hemlock stuff. Go and look at Colebrook now, and think on Shelley's epigram, "Naught may endure but Mutability."

extension or sister road, the eleven-mile New London & Stonington, began at Groton, across the Thames from New London—for the Thames was another deep, wide river which for years daunted bridge builders. In 1856 the Legislature authorized the amalgamation of the two roads. In an effort to make the route popular, large ferryboats were provided at Lyme and New London to take whole passenger trains across the two big rivers. The State Railroad Commission, in its report for 1853, tried to make it appear that the Connecticut River ferry was no inconvenience at all. It claimed that "about five minutes more would be lost in supplying the engine with wood and water at this place, and passing over the river on a bridge. The boat is of ample dimensions, and arranged with many conveniences. The ferry is found in practice rather of an accommodation than otherwise to the passengers of the road." Charles Dickens, however, was inclined to disagree with them. On his second visit to America in 1867, he traveled over the shore line, and wrote of it:

Two rivers have to be crossed, and each time the whole train is banged aboard a big steamer. The steamer rises and falls with the river, which the railroad don't do; and the train is either banged up hill or banged down hill. In coming off the steamer at one of these crossings yesterday, we were banged up such a height that the rope broke, and our carriage rushed back with a run down hill into the boat again. I whisked out in a moment, and two or three others after me, but nobody else seemed to care about it.

Others must have disliked the ferries, too, for the twin roads, before and after they became one, were frequently in process of reorganization. As the anonymous historian of Middlesex County says, acridly but aptly, "In accordance with the usual custom in such cases, and with the usual result to stockholders, the road passed into the hands of the bondholders by the foreclosure of the first mortgage." In 1864, when the bondholders took over once more, they reorganized under the name of the Shore Line Railway, and in 1870 they leased the road to the New York & New Haven. The latter company bridged the Connecticut in 1870 and the Thames in 1889, finally completing a through, no-ferry route between New York and Boston, via Providence.

It is now time to go back to the New York & New Haven and glance at the crisis in its existence. The Norwalk disaster in 1853, which cost the company nearly half a million dollars in damages, was a severe jolt, but in the following year came one which threatened the very existence of the company. On July 1, 1854, Editor Henry V. Poor, of the *American Railroad Journal*, speaking of the depression of N. Y. & N. H. stock (it had dropped from 128 to 105 after the Norwalk accident), said that the road "probably occupies the best line for business in the United States." The State Railroad Commission report for 1854 showed that nearly twice as many passengers were carried over it as over any other line in the state. But, said Poor, "it has had the life-blood squeezed out of it in the same manner as have the Erie and the Central. It has cost at least fifty percent more than it should." The managers of the lines between New York and Philadelphia, he added, "make their money out of the *earnings* of their roads." In the case of the N. Y. & N. H., "there has been altogether too much money made out of *construction* to allow much for dividends."

These words were scarcely off the press when the revelation came which shook financial New York to its foundations. The Board of Directors, in a report to stockholders a few days later, admitted that "large sales of the company's stock had attracted the attention of one or two of the Directors as early as the twenty-ninth of June." (The director chiefly concerned over the matter is said to have been Anson G. Phelps.) But, continued the report, "no suspicions were entertained by anyone" (error: Mr. Phelps had tried to see the stock-books of the company, and failed) until the morning of the third of July, when a director met President Robert Schuyler's attorney on the street, bearing a letter to another director. The lawyer intimated that the letter referred to an overissue of stock. This director took immediate possession of the stock ledger, and in company with several others, spent the Fourth of July in examining it. Meanwhile, Schuyler's letter had been delivered, in which he resigned as president, director and transfer agent (for the directors had placed full control of transfers of stock in his hands). He said, "Your attention to the stock ledger of the company is essential, as you will find much there that is wrong." Evidently, Phelps' suspicious sniffings had convinced him that his long dereliction was in its last inning.

It was found that he had issued and either sold or hypothecated for loans 19,580 shares of the company's stock, a face value of $1,958,000, all the money going into his own pocket. In addition to this, he had embezzled thousands more by other means. He had had three sets of books kept by different clerks in different rooms. One contained only entries relating to construction; the second, income and expenses resulting from transportation by the company; while the third contained only entries of the receipts and disbursements of the treasurer. By artfully juggling figures from these three sets of books, Schuyler was able to draw up a balance sheet which made it appear that the large floating debt resulted from construction alone. But though he could fool the stockholders, it seems that he feared the State of New York, for the annual report required of each railroad corporation by the state had never been turned in for 1853.

The city was stunned. That a man of such high standing and fine family should be guilty of felony was unthinkable. He had been a ruling spirit not only in the N. Y. & N. H., but in the Harlem, the Illinois Central, the Vermont Valley and other roads. He had at one time been president of four roads and treasurer of four others. The *American Railroad Journal* now revealed that he had been one of the contractors for the building and rebuilding of the N. Y. & N. H. It was a notorious racket by which railroad and telegraph officials all too often bled their own companies in those days. "No concern in the country," declared Poor, "has been so victimized and plundered by its managers from the start." The lease of the New Haven & Northampton, he said, meant a dead loss to the company of $40,000 a year. The annual reports proved that the road had never earned the dividends it paid; the construction account in stock and bonds was regularly increased from year to year to an amount much greater than the dividends. "If it has ever really earned anything over its expenses and interest," the fearless editor went on, "which is very doubtful, it has been regularly squandered and stolen by the managers." And he added a sweeping criticism: "The tone of railroad management in New York City has been very low."

Why was it, demanded Poor, that the directors permitted Schuyler "to issue unlimited amounts of the stock *without the check of any other signature except his own* —they well knowing all the time that he was a Wall-street speculator on an enormous scale and constantly borrowing large sums of money at high rates of interest. . . . The imputation of the most gross and culpable negligence, to say the least, must rest upon them." They resigned, and the infuriated stockholders elected another board, who tried to repudiate the Schuyler stock but did not succeed.

Schuyler, in his letter of confession, had declared that his brother was not implicated in the frauds; but the brother was dragged down with him, and their brokerage house closed its doors. The culprit himself disappeared from view, but he was said to be still in New York three months later, though Poor was asking why he had not been arrested. Such was his business and family prestige, however, that no agency of the law laid hands on him: no one wanted to arrest the nephew of Alexander Hamilton. He finally slipped away to Europe—no one knows just when—and was reported to have died in Italy, unwept and unhonored, in 1856.

Meanwhile, the railroad company was plunged into a morass of litigation from which it did not extricate itself for years. Persons who had bought the spurious stock fought for their rights. The courts held that—as the corporation itself had no right to increase its stock issue—*a fortiori*, its agent, unauthorized, certainly could not, and therefore the Schuyler certificates were void. Nevertheless, it was held that the company was liable for its negligence in permitting its operations to be so carelessly managed, and was under obligation to pay the amounts in which the stock had been issued, by way of damages. The company fought the issue into higher courts, and many of the claimants were finally wearied into settling on a basis of one good share for two of the bogus shares. Others battled through to the end and obtained full recovery from the corporation.

That disaster kept the company in bondage for years. A complete reorganization took place, and in 1855 the company was empowered to issue $3,000,000 in mortgage bonds and to add $2,000,000 to its capital stock, which would aid it in paying the claims against it. Such was the earning power of the road that, once put upon an honest basis, it recovered rapidly.

It is a curious fact that through his unwitting involvement in the Schuyler imbroglio, Cornelius Vanderbilt finally became the great magnate of New York Central. He had been elected a director of Hartford & New Haven in 1846 and bought his first New York & New Haven stock in 1849. He met Schuyler during negotiations over steamboat and railroad traffic along the Sound. Later, Schuyler handed 2210 of his fake shares over to the Commodore as collateral for a large loan. When the crash came, Vanderbilt brought suit but finally compromised. But for a time he was the largest stockholder in N. Y. & N. H. He had been inveigled by the Schuyler brothers, the two highest officials and largest stockholders in New York & Harlem, into buying $1,000,000 of that company's bonds, and it wasn't many years before he was a Harlem director and presently its dominant figure; and from there it was but two steps to New York Central.

A committee of the Connecticut Legislature, appointed in 1852, "to inquire whether any railroad companies have combined to prevent the construction of any other railroad, and whether any railroad company has leased the road of another company, to the injury of the public interest," found that the New York & New Haven lease of the Canal Rail-

road enabled the lessee to plot with the New Haven, Hartford & Springfield to prevent extension of the Canal Railroad
(then halted at the state line) to Springfield or to a connection with the Western. Railroad executives "confessed,"
the committee said, that it would be a violation of the contract between them to "ticket through from New York to
Boston over the New Haven & New London Railroad or
over the Air Line Railroad, when the said roads are built."
The executives justified such contracts as preventing ruinous
competition and being really in the public interest. "Your
committee, however, cannot regard the matter in this light."
They considered it "an unwarrantable exercise of the power
granted" the railroads, for them thus to "defeat the intention
of the Legislature to afford Rail-road facilities whenever and
wherever it might please the Legislature to grant them."

There was perhaps some ground for complaint on some
of these counts. In a memoir, published anonymously in
1880, of Edwin Ferry Johnson, civil engineer, who was one
of the promoters and the builder of the Air Line, it is said
that his efforts in its behalf "provoked the narrow-minded
spite of the managers of the Hartford & New Haven Road,"
and "for years a persistent and unscrupulous war was carried on against the Air-Line Road, both in and out of the
Legislature." The writer even charges that "by false
representation, the maps and profiles of his survey were
obtained from his office by parties employed for the purpose."

But that legislative lobbying worked both ways. It long
prevented the consolidation of the Hartford & New Haven
and the New York & New Haven. They were in the
Capitol, asking for it time and again, but for years the opposition of other railroads in the state defeated them. In 1867,
William D. Bishop was elected president of the N. Y. &
N. H., and he began a vigorous campaign for the union,
though he would seem to have had enough to do elsewise
—with one hand fighting off one of the numerous threats
of a parallel road from New York to New Haven, with the
other leasing the Shore Line Railroad and building its bridge

across the Connecticut River. His son was president of the Naugatuck Railroad, and no crystal-gazer was needed to foretell the destiny of that line. But at last the Hartford & New Haven and the New York & New Haven entered into an agreement which was ratified unanimously by the stockholders of the former and almost unanimously by those of the latter. This had its effect upon the Legislature, and consent was finally given for the consolidation. And so, on August 6, 1872, the New York, New Haven & Hartford Railroad was born.

To northward the astute Chapin, head of the Boston & Albany, watched these movements with concern. For some years there had been good traffic between New York and Boston over his road and the two which had just combined. They had even put on a night train, the Owl, leaving each city shortly after 8:00 P.M. One of the early sleeping cars, Hopgood's—the name is quite forgotten now—ran on this train; and a little later, when Webster Wagner entered the sleeping-car business, the N. Y., N. H. & H. put one of his cars on its shore line, but the ferry at New London was still an objectionable feature of that route. Chapin and his successor, William Bliss, who assumed the B. & A. presidency in 1877, knew, however, that it would not be many years before the New Haven bridged the Thames, and then it would have a New York–Boston line a little shorter than that via Springfield. As a desperate measure to controvert this threat, the B. & A. directors actually discussed the possibility of trying to lease the whole New Haven system on a 9 per cent rental basis. But that idea was too extravagant to be actually attempted.

All this time the two roads continued to operate their New York–Boston through line in apparently perfect harmony. Fine new passenger cars and locomotives were built for it, in which the two companies shared a pro rata proprietorship. Some parlor cars produced in 1880 were so "elegant and refined" that the *Railroad Gazette* indulged in gentle sarcasm regarding them. They glided over the rails on the new pressed paper wheels, and each seated thirty-two in the "main room" and four more in the smoking room. They had unusually large windows, and there was so much mahogany that the *Gazette* editor was reminded of a coffin. "With no other color to relieve it," said he, "the decoration has a sort of Egyptian solemnity." The chandeliers, on the other hand, were so fussy and titivated with perpetually jingling glass prisms that they seemed "as if they would flutter away out of pure exuberance."

But all the neighbors knew that, behind this joint operation, the two companies were not in close harmony. The B. & A. suspected the New Haven of flirting with the New York & New England (whose history we shall tell in the next chapter), which would have given it another entrance into Boston. Bliss next had an idea of taking over the New Haven & Northampton and building a line across from it to the New York & Harlem Railroad at White Plains. William H. Vanderbilt, then head of the family and the New York Central, was said to have pledged $1,000,000 of the $5,000,-000 necessary to build the new track. But the New Haven, whose constant danger from enemies had bred in it a feral watchfulness, was aware of the plan and was buying New Haven & Northampton stock even before the B. & A. had put its first scouting parties along the proposed right of way in 1881. The market also sensed something doing in Northampton, and the price of the shares shot up from almost nothing to 80; so that old Joseph E. Sheffield, who seemed to have been born lucky and who had been holding a bale of that seemingly trifling stuff for decades, now gathered in a million or so on it and had some more cash to hand over to Yale's scientific school, which had been given his name when he endowed it so generously twenty years before.

And so, with stock control of the canal railroad, the New Haven took a 99-year lease of it and, like Monte Cristo, marked another menace off its list. The Northampton had been pushed northward to a connection with the Fitchburg near Greenfield, so that the New Haven now had a line up the Connecticut Valley almost to Vermont. Why the

B. & A. had let this trick slip from its hands can be explained
only by saying that President Bliss was not the master strate-
gist that Chapin had been.   But it did not yet yield its desire to have a line of its own from Springfield to the Harlem
Railroad, or anything else to worry the New Haven.   There
was a little road known as the Connecticut Valley, built in
1869–71, which followed the Connecticut River from Hartford down to the Sound at Saybrook.   It reorganized in
1881 as the Hartford & Connecticut Valley, brushed up,
put on its best pinafore and began looking for buyers.   To
give itself a nuisance value, it talked of extending north to
Springfield to hook up with the strong Connecticut River
Railroad, of taking over the Springfield & New London, etc.
It had the Boston & Albany "interested."   It even went so
far as to let a contract—with a string to it—for building the
extension northward.   At that, the New Haven capitulated
and bought a controlling interest in 1882.

The New Haven was constantly menaced by those "parallel" schemes along the Sound.   It had scorched one years
before, the Harlem & Port Chester, which was chartered
in New York and was about to get a Connecticut charter
when the New Haven took it over, and seeing some possible utility in it, built track over a part of its right of way,
from New Rochelle down through the present Borough of
the Bronx to the Harlem River, and leased it at 7 per cent
of its cost.   Now, in 1882, the B. & A. was bending a sympathetic ear to other threatening projects.   One was the Hartford & Harlem, which was to run from New Britain southwest toward the shore and then to parallel the New Haven
into New York.   It was to have connection with New
Haven by absorbing the New Haven & Derby, a little road
which had been a great disappointment to its backers.   But
the H. & H. was opposed by another corporation still in
the blueprint stage, the New York & Connecticut Air Lines,
popularly known as the Olmstead Road—"Olmstead Plan"
would have been more appropriate—and the two fought each
other fiercely in the courts, legislatures and elsewhere until
the H. & H. died of anemia, while the other was drawn into

a plot (to be described in the next chapter) in which the New York & New England and the Housatonic were involved, but which finally faded out. And the Boston & Albany never did get that Springfield–New York cut-off.

Charles P. Clark, one of the shrewdest of New England railroad men, became president of the New Haven in 1887 and set out with the definite determination to put his company in control of all southern New England trackage. The prosperous little Naugatuck was leased that year, and the Stamford & New Canaan three years later, giving the New Haven a branch over which plutocrats now commute daily in club-car trains to New York, playing bridge all the way. In 1892 the New Haven obtained stock control of the Housatonic and likewise leased the New York, Providence & Boston. In the following year it completed its entrance into Boston by swallowing the entire Old Colony system in order to get the coveted 44-mile Boston & Providence. In that Columbian year, 1893, Clark was also trying for possession of the Connecticut River Railroad, which would have put the New Haven far up into New Hampshire and Vermont. But a strange and artificial situation existed at that time. One A. A. McLeod, ambitious president of the Reading Railroad, had invaded New England via the Poughkeepsie bridge over the Hudson, and had momentarily got stock control of the New York & New England and the Boston & Maine. The New Haven and Connecticut River presidents had signed a lease of the latter to the former, and awaited only ratification by the stockholders. McLeod meanwhile stealthily bought Connecticut River stock until he had control, then repudiated the lease to the New Haven and demanded a lease to the Boston & Maine. The Massachusetts Railroad Commission declared that "no more unconscionable transaction has occurred in the railroad history of the State."

The bankruptcy of the Reading, the collapse of McLeod's tinsel "empire," and his disappearance from the scene all followed within a few months. But before his exodus, the New Haven and the Boston & Maine had signed a peace treaty,

dividing New England into two zones of interest, north and
south, each promising not to trespass on the other's pasture.
The New Haven had at last gathered in that major annoyance, the New York & New England, as well as the little
Shepaug (Bethel to Litchfield) and some other odds and
ends; .and with 10 per cent dividends rolling in regularly,
with its feet firmly planted in New York and Boston, with
Connecticut, Rhode Island and southeastern Massachusetts
pretty completely covered by its tracks—the only exception
being that Central Vermont thrust down through Connecticut to New London—it had reason to be content.

# 9

# Ghost Train and Ghost Road

THE wildest, weirdest story in all New England's lore is not the legend of Chocorua's curse but the true narrative of the career of the railroad known in its later years as the New York & New England—the strangest, most loose-jointed, shambling, anomalous congeries of rails, with the most melodious name in all the six states.  It was a system built on a hodgepodge of some two dozen smaller lines, the majority of which had no sound reason for existence —though, after all, that was also true of many others which kept their heads above water for years.  The N. Y. & N. E. and its preliminary incarnation, the Boston, Hartford & Erie, managed to make a terrific noise and keep competitors around it worried for thirty years by sheer nerve and bluff.  Its history has something of the fantastic about it.

Throughout its entire career, it was living not only on borrowed money—all railroads did and do that—but on borrowed time; for it was born with the seeds of death in its blood-stream.  Looted by pirates in infancy, with a main line as crooked and hilly as a snake-trail, unable to obtain any sound outlet to west or southwest, menaced by so well-entrenched an antagonist as the New Haven, its eventual demise was as certain as the sunset.  Nevertheless, it was determined to plow a way for itself through the national railroad field, and for more than three decades its various managements fought sturdily, often bitterly, toward that unattainable end, using every device in the book and some theretofore undreamed of.  It did some of the most spectacular railroading in our history; and how it managed to put on so brave a show, to do so much with so little, is still a matter for wonder.

Chronologically, the story of the New York & New England may be said to begin with the chartering by Connecticut in 1833 of the Manchester Railroad, which was to extend from Hartford "to a notch in the mountains in the town of Bolton, or somewhere near the stone pits in Bolton and Vernon"—all east of Hartford. This was one of those little ectoplasms which never materialized. In 1846 a group of Providence capitalists procured a Rhode Island charter for the Providence & Plainfield Railroad, to connect their city with smaller industrial towns in western Rhode Island and eastern Connecticut. Rapidly their idea expanded. It should extend to Willimantic—then, taking over that old Manchester charter, it would continue as the Hartford & Providence into the Connecticut capital. And then, in less time than it takes to tell it, the Connecticut portion became the Hartford, Providence & Fishkill Railroad, capital $3,000,000, with its ultimate destination Fishkill Landing on the Hudson—or, as we now call it, Beacon, for Fishkill proper is some four or five miles back from the river—whence its traffic was to cross by ferry to Newburgh and continue westward on the newly created New York & Erie Railway.

The road between Hartford and Willimantic was open in 1849. In 1851 formal permission was given by the two states to unite the Rhode Island and Connecticut corporations. But the raising of funds to carry on the work proved to be an onerous job. Since private means were so difficult to coax from pockets, the cities of Providence and Hartford, in 1850–51, were permitted by their legislatures to exchange their bonds for those of the railroad, in the sum of $500,000 apiece, each city taking a first mortgage on the track in its own state and a second on that in the other state. With this aid, trains began running between Providence and Hartford in 1854 and between Hartford and Waterbury three months later.

In 1855, Governor William Sprague of Connecticut was

elected president, and while he lived, kept the company on its feet by lending it money out of his own pocket and from the coffers of A. & W. Sprague, the banking firm of which he was the surviving partner. But he soon died, and when the panic of '57 came and the railroad begged for more money, A. & W. Sprague hesitated, refused and then brought suit to collect what they had already lent. Since the road was unable to meet its obligations, the trustees under the mortgages took it over and were destined to operate it for more than twenty years.

Now we turn the pages back a few years to notice the Norfolk County Railroad, which was created to split the wedge-shaped area between the Boston & Worcester and the Boston & Providence. Though heartily opposed by both of those corporations, it obtained its charter, anyhow. It ran from Boston past Dedham and Walpole to Blackstone, near Woonsocket, where it connected with the Providence & Worcester. The first train, on May 18, 1849, was greeted with the usual joyous antics and salvos of artillery from the villages en route, and at Blackstone the celebrants "were greeted by Welcome Farnum, Esq. [and who could be more appropriate?], who had provided a handsome colla- tion at the Blackstone House," after which they returned to Dedham and had another snack.

A few miles to the north, two smaller concerns, the Charles River Branch and Charles River Railroad, now came into being. The original purpose of the Charles River Branch, opened in 1852, was the hauling of stone and gravel from the barren hills in Needham to fill the marshlands of Bos- ton and greatly increase that city's area; also to carry ice from two large ponds in Newton. As a sideline, it did a casual commuter business, but its passengers complained acrimoniously of being sidetracked for gravel trains; for years those who lived near by were kept awake at night by forty-car trains clattering past, for they rushed by at the rate of one every forty-five minutes through the whole twenty-four hours. Yet the directors of the Charles River Railroad, which continued the line on to the newly developed mill village of Woonsocket, R. I., boasted of its "passing through a country possessing every variety of scenery, hill, valley and plain, with an excellent soil and every local advantage and convenience which makes a country residence desirable."

It is not strictly accurate to say that it built its track to Woonsocket, which was less than a mile from the Massachusetts frontier. Of course, under its charter, it could build no farther than the boundary; from there into Woonsocket, a railroad slightly longer than your middle finger was chartered under Rhode Island law as the New York & Boston —a portent of things to come. Promoters were working behind the scenes, and in 1856–58, the State Legislatures sanctioned the union of the Charles River and its Woonsocket connection, another little road projected from Woonsocket to the Connecticut line, and yet another in Connecticut, all into a new New York & Boston, whose aim was now admitted to be an air-line route from Boston to New York via Willimantic, Middletown and New Haven. It managed to build a few miles of track west of Woonsocket, and that was all.

For close alongside it was a rampageous rival. The modest little Norfolk County Railroad had now fallen into the hands of promoters with large aims and had become the Boston & New York Central. Its ambition likewise was to build to Willimantic, but there to connect with the Hartford, Providence & Fishkill, and thus become a part of a through line from Boston via the Erie to the West. It took over a small road, the Southbridge & Blackstone, and by 1860 had built an extension from Southbridge to Mechanicsville, on the Worcester & Norwich. From there it had to content itself with taking over the charter of the Thompson & Willimantic, which was as yet a mere blueprint, but which, when completed, would carry it well on toward its goal.

In the course of a dozen years this road was known variously as the Boston & New York Central, Midland Railroad, Midland Land Damage Company (Investor Damage Company would have been a more fitting title), Southern

Midland Railroad, and, eventually, the Boston, Hartford &
Erie. That last name finally struck its keynote. In 1864
its promoters were busy men indeed. They had bought the
franchises of the Hartford, Providence & Fishkill, and on
December 16 they absorbed their rival, the New York &
Boston, thus having two closely parallel lines from Boston
to Blackstone and Woonsocket. Now, when or if they
completed their connection between Mechanicsville and
Willimantic, they would really begin to have a railroad
system. The Hartford, Providence & Fishkill carried them
as far west as Waterbury. From there their aspirations
extended not only to the Hudson and a link with the Erie,
but into New York City. So far, whether via Hartford or
via the Naugatuck from Waterbury, any possible entry into
New York would finally have to depend upon the New
Haven and the New Haven's good will—which might not
endure, for the B. H. & E. was now becoming a rival. But
if, from Waterbury, they threw a line westward through
Danbury to Brewster, N. Y., they would touch two parallel
roads, the Harlem and the New York City & Northern,
both leading into the metropolis.

From Brewster their line would have to wriggle westward
over the hills to Fishkill-Beacon. Here was seen one great
drawback to this project—the rough country through which
it must pass. From Rhode Island to the Hudson, the ridges
and river valleys all run from north to south, and a railroad
crossing that terrain from east to west must be crooked,
full of heavy grades, costly to construct and operate. A
considerable part of such territory was inevitably rural, and
remained so. Yet the promoters . . . but before we go any
farther, who were they?

At this late date we cannot attempt to characterize them.
Let us rather turn to Charles F. Adams's *Chapters of Erie*,
written in 1870, while the subject was still hot and these
men very much alive, yet delicately reluctant to sue Mr.
Adams for his trenchant words. He is speaking of the three
interests striving for control of the Erie Railroad: first,
Cornelius Vanderbilt; second, a group headed by Daniel

Drew, which group he refers to collectively as the Scarlet Woman of Wall Street. And third:

A faction made its appearance composed of some shrewd and ambitious Wall Street operators, and certain persons from Boston who maintained for the occasion the novel character of railroad reformers. This party, it is needless to say, was as unscrupulous, and as the result proved, as able as either of the others; it represented nothing but a raid made upon the Erie treasury in the interest of a thoroughly bankrupt New England corporation, of which its membership had the control. The history of this corporation . . . would be one curious to read, though very difficult to write. Its name was synonymous with bankruptcy, litigation, fraud and failure. If the Erie was of doubtful repute in Wall Street, the Boston, Hartford & Erie had long been of worse than doubtful repute in State Street. . . .

These daring blades went right on accumulating property. In 1866 they leased the Dutchess & Columbia (later Newburgh, Dutchess & Connecticut), which was chartered to build from Fishkill-Beacon northeast through an iron-mining region to the northwest corner of Connecticut, where it was to meet the Connecticut Western, building out of Hartford. The Connecticut Western promoters had hoped to lease the Dutchess & Columbia, but the B. H. & E. had forestalled them; had, in effect, bottled them up.

The clique had already made a move in 1865 toward getting a coveted foothold in Erie—or saddling itself upon the neck of Erie. Adams puts it in another way: they "looked abroad for a victim and fixed their eyes upon the Erie." For the moment, they had Vanderbilt on their side. Robert Schell, the Commodore's chief agent in Wall Street, suggested to the Erie directors that it would be a good thing if some of them were on the B. H. & E. board. That concern, said he, was on the way to becoming a great property, an enormously valuable feeder to the Erie; the two were destined to form a mighty super-highway from Boston toward the West. There should be a closer entente. The

Erie topsawyers were impressed, a committee formally took a ride over what there was of the New England line, and formal notice was given of their willingness for a sort of marriage of convenience. And thus it came to pass in December, 1865, that the B. H. & E. directors, who had no doubt instigated the whole thing, saw seven Erie directors—including Erie President Robert H. Berdell and Daniel Drew—elected to their own board.

The next move was a historic one. Three months later, on March 19, 1866, President Berdell and two other Erie directors agreed to sponsor as trustees a $20,000,000 bond issue by the B. H. & E., which it hoped to sell for at least $17,000,000 in cash, so that it might pay off $8,200,000 of the old mortgages and have $9,000,000 with which to complete the projected lines. There was no great rush to buy the bonds, and the company then took a step which was characteristic of its nerve. It asked the Erie to guarantee the payment of interest on $6,000,000 of B. H. & E. bonds on the promise of the latter to set aside a certain amount of the receipts from its coal traffic to secure the Erie in its guaranty. It must be remembered that these coal-carrying revenues could not materialize until the road was completed to the Hudson; and even then, they depended on how much coal the Erie itself succeded in bringing from Pennsylvania. It was not only a when, but an if proposition. The Erie would not go so far, but after much chaffering it was induced to take $5,000,000 of the Berdell bonds—as they were ever afterward called—in exchange for $4,000,000 of its own acceptances, which the B. H. & E. discounted as promptly as possible.

Even with that mecd, the company hadn't enough to pay its debts, let alone build track. We are therefore not surprised to see the directors, in 1867, under the Golden Dome on Beacon Hill, begging the State of Massachusetts for a loan. They pointed out that some 2,000,000 tons of Pennsylvania anthracite per year would be coming through Newburgh and Fishkill—if they got this loan—to the great advantage of New England. Lumber, cattle, hematite and magnetic iron ores, now with difficulty finding markets, would add to the revenue.  Boston would have a great new passenger and freight line to the West.  The arguments sounded well, but it seems incredible that the legislators should be beguiled by a company in such condition.  Its directors' report for that year admitted that the 245-mile road had already cost $20,000,000 (they didn't mention the graft included in this amount), the same as its capital stock; that there were ten mortgages on it, and its funded and floating debt was $10,326,406; but with all this investment, its income for 1867 was only $369,577, and for rolling stock it had only twelve locomotives, twelve passenger cars and sixty freight cars.  Finally, its stocks and bonds were never even within shouting distance of par.  But the oily eloquence of the emissaries and the amazing nerve and agility with which the B. H. & E. had been leaping like a lumberjack from one rolling, sinking foothold to another seemed to dazzle the solons, and they agreed to lend the company $3,000,000 in scrip—$100,000 at a time as it was needed; but at each hand-out of this sort, the company must deposit $133,333 worth of its bonds in the state treasury—those Berdell bonds, of course.

The next device to tie the road more closely to the Erie was that of transferring President Eldridge of the B. H. & E. to the headship of the bigger road.  Vanderbilt favored this, and though the incumbent Erie president, Berdell, naturally opposed it, it went through, and Berdell thereupon resigned as a trustee of the B. H. & E. bond issue.  The other two original trustees resigned in the following year and a whole new set came in.

But this is going too fast.  It was in 1867 that the B. H. & E. people decided to get rid of Daniel Drew.  Posing as reformers, Adams says, they found Drew too odoriferous for them. They thought they had Vanderbilt with them, for he and Drew had been antagonistic, Drew depressing the market, while Vanderbilt was on the bull side.  But shrewd old Dan'l, scenting what was toward, got to the Commodore first and promised to aid him in giving the market an upward trend. In his whining and wheedling way, Drew had a knack of

getting around Corneel, as he called him, and the result was
that Vanderbilt bluntly told the B. H. & E. directors that
he had decided to keep Drew on the board. This was carrying it with a high hand, and they were furious. Vanderbilt
was not the dominant stockholder in the company, *but*—he
had just taken over New York Central and he had reached
a pitch of power where he was not lightly to be defied.
When they rebelled, he threatened a coup by which they
would all be thrown out, and they yielded.

Still the B. H. & E. couldn't sell enough bonds and
Massachusetts scrip to pay all its debts and complete its
projected lines. But though groggy with creeping bankruptcy, it continued to give an impersonation of a winner
by leasing the Norwich & Worcester in 1869 at the inordinately high rate of 10 per cent on the stock, plus the fixed
charges. This road, which ran down to Allyn's Point on
the Thames below Norwich and had a connecting boat
line from there to New York, was of some value, giving
the B. H. & E. a rail-water line between Boston and New
York.

The company was in the State House at Boston again in
1870, begging for a loan, but this time the Attorney-General
denounced it in no measured terms, charging that $7,000,000
had been misappropriated, more than half a million of it
being used for bribery and corruption. There was no loan,
and the company could not even pay the interest on its bonds
that year. A receiver was appointed, and in August, 1871,
the trustees under the Berdell bond mortgage foreclosed
and took possession, the title to the property thereafter being
absolutely vested in them. On April 17, 1873, a meeting
of bondholders was held and a new corporation organized,
which was christened the New York & New England Railroad. The capital stock, $20,000,000, was issued only in
exchange for the Berdell bonds—so that not nearly all of
it was issued. The trustees transferred the property they
held to the new company in July, 1875.

With that, the Boston, Hartford & Erie and its ribald crew
for the most part passed from the scene and became skele-

tons in the closet: the new company was on the way to becoming respectable, though still necessarily adventurous. William T. Hart was elected president, and efforts at up-building began. There was extended difficulty over get-ting possession of the main stem of the system, the Hartford, Providence & Fishkill, which was still being held by its bondholders, and the legal imbroglio over this was not finally ironed out until 1877. Under Hart's direction, things were being accomplished—a new entrance into Providence and another into Springfield by means of a small road taken over, the Connecticut Central. After the H. P. & F. tangle was eliminated, the extension of the road from Waterbury was pushed through Danbury and Brewster, N. Y., toward the Hudson. It touched its leased line, the Newburgh, Dutchess & Connecticut, at Hopewell Junction, twelve miles from the river, and from there used the other's track down to the landing, which was reached in 1881. Coal and other freight thereupon began moving across the river on the busy fer-ries.

The Air Line, as has been related, had been completed from New Haven to Willimantic in 1876 and had come under New Haven control, but the N. Y. & N. E.'s New York–Boston traffic continued to use its own track as far as possible—that is, via Hartford. In 1876 the road began running its Washington Night Express and Philadelphia or Centennial Day Express from Boston via Hartford to those cities. They followed the New Haven's Harlem River & Port Chester line to the Harlem River, where the cars went bodily aboard the ferry *Maryland*, the property of the New England Transfer Company, which took them around to the Pennsylvania Railroad in Jersey City. Later, in 1880, the N. Y. & N. E. bought a half interest in that transfer company. It was in 1876 that the company began using the Maltese Cross trade-mark, and railroad men nowadays will shake their heads and tell you that no company which used that emblem ever had any luck.

In 1881, the year the railhead reached the Hudson, Presi-dent Hart's incumbency ended and General James H. Wilson came in for two years. That seemed an auspicious year, for the Baltimore & Ohio also began turning freight shipments over to the *Maryland* and the N. Y. & N. E. at Jersey City. General Wilson believed that this through traffic would be the salvation of the company. New "Despatches" and "Fast Freight" lines were planned. Wilson also labored to improve operating standards, with the frankly avowed purpose of selling out to the Erie. The latter did make an offer to lease the road, but on terms which promised little or nothing more than paying the fixed charges and so were not acceptable to the stockholders. Erie officials of course knew as well as anybody that the New England would never be a profitable concern, and they were not going to saddle themselves with another liability: they had enough of their own, Heaven knows.

In 1883, General Wilson gave up his post, and Charles P. Clark, former general manager of the road and one of the shrewdest of New England railroad men, became president. Between that date and 1887, Clark was president twice and receiver for one year. He at once set about abrogating some of Wilson's policies. Instead of the through traffic which had been the general's fetish, Clark sought to develop the local traffic, and he improved relations with connecting roads, which had been impaired by his predecessor. But the stark facts remained that the system was not earning its fixed charges and that on January 1, 1884, $1,700,000 in unfunded debts was due. Clark and the directors therefore arranged a receivership, with Clark as receiver, to protect the company while he brought about his planned economies. The Norwich & Worcester lease made by the B. H. & E. roisterers was canceled—the N. Y. & N. E., being another company, was not obligated by it—and a new one written, reducing the annual rental from 10 to 8 per cent. The Dedham Branch, where twenty-six trains a day had been running, was entirely eliminated. Some miles of the Boston end of the old Charles River Railroad had been sold to the Boston & Albany. Unnecessary service was discontinued wherever possible.

But Clark struck out upon one adventure which gave the road much publicity.  In 1884 he launched a new fast train, the New England Limited—later known by a much more famous name—between New York and Boston, using for the first time the Air Line (the New Haven's road since 1879) between New Haven and Willimantic, and continuing to roll over the N. Y., N. H. & H. between New Haven and New York.  The Limited was an evening train, leaving New York and Boston simultaneously at 3 P.M., stopping only at Bridgeport, New Haven, Middletown and Willimantic, and making the run through in six hours flat.  The eighty-six-mile non-stop run between Boston and Willimantic was an unusually long one for those days; and that the road was now keenly up to date is indicated by the fact that the engines scooped water from track pans near Putnam —then a comparatively novel idea.  The train increased in popularity until it was doing a good business, as is proved by the New Haven directors' report for 1886, which says that the Air Line had never earned enough to keep itself in repair and pay its rental until that year, when it actually showed a $15,000 net profit.  The New England Limited contributed largely to that.

Wall Street influence in the councils of the N. Y. & N. E. had been increasing.  It was an ominous fact that in 1882 the number of New York directors on the board suddenly increased from two to seven, and perhaps worst of all, among them was Jay Gould.  Whenever and wherever that little dark man appeared, it meant trouble for everybody within a considerable radius.  In 1887 there came a complete turnover  At that election nine New Yorkers and only three Bostonians were chosen to the board.  Clark passed out and became president of the New Haven, which spelled bad luck for the New England.  Its new management thrust out wildly in all directions, trying to find new supports for the tottering structure, but its decline from the precarious height which it had reached began from that moment.

The first blow fell when the New Haven forced it to sell its interest in the New England Transfer Company, which

operated the car ferry *Maryland* at New York. The New
Haven held the whip hand, for it gave the N. Y. & N. E. a
precarious passenger entrance to New York. But next the
Monopoly, as it was beginning to be freely called, withdrew
from the N. Y. & N. E. all Pennsylvania Railroad and Union
Line freight to and from points beyond Worcester. The
New Haven had simply decided that the other was a noisy
nuisance which must be eliminated.

The N. Y. & N. E. now strove to find entrance to New
York via Brewster. The Harlem, Vanderbilt-controlled,
refused to co-operate, because of an agreement with the New
Haven not to compete on New York City business. The
little New York & Northern, whose terminus was at Brewster, was willing, but the New England, clutching in all
directions for threads of hope, now concocted yet another
scheme. It formed an alliance with the Housatonic, whose
track crossed it at Danbury and whose own career had for
years been somewhat wild and irrational. It had even—
for a brief period in 1887—got hold of the little Lebanon
Springs Railroad, which led up toward Vermont and
dreamed of itself as a New York–Montreal route, a vision
which was to fade.

The Housatonic now controlled the Danbury & Norwalk,
which, as we have seen, continued southward through Norwalk to Wilson's Point, a good harbor a few miles below
that city. The new allies organized the New England
Terminal Company and with it operated a line of car floats
from Wilson's Point to the East River piers in New York.
Later, they attempted passenger service that way, too, calling the route the Long Island and Eastern States Line,
transferring the cars by ferry to the Long Island Railroad
at Oyster Bay for transmission to New York City—a clumsy
idea which was doomed to failure from the start. It drew
little business. The New Haven detailed spies to watch the
trains and see how the line was prospering, and the other
fellows were well aware of this. It was later asserted by
the New Haven that the N. E., in a desperate effort to give
an appearance of prosperity, had cars on the trains with

stuffed dummies at every window, simulating passengers. We cannot vouch for this story, but we know that the Wilson's Point–Oyster Bay adventure was a dreadful fiasco.

As a last expedient, the New England–Housatonic partnership approached the Legislature, seeking means, artfully camouflaged, of building "branches" of the Housatonic which would turn out to be a parallel of the N. Y., N. H. & H. from New Haven to New York. It required no second sight for the New Haven officials to see right through this trick and to point it out to the Legislature, which very properly blocked the move. Just to make the thing decisive and end the annoyance, the New Haven took over stock control of the Housatonic in 1892, and Wilson's Point as a railroad terminus disappeared from view. A mortgage on the property of the New England Terminal Company was foreclosed, and its sponsors suffered a heavy loss.

The year 1891 saw another straw grasped at—this time an adventure in publicity. The New England Limited, still using New Haven track from Willimantic to New Haven, was painted all white with gilt lettering from stem to stern, with the exception of the locomotive, and became the White Train, a name that lingers in the memories of some who have forgotten all else about the New York & New England —all else, perhaps, save another nickname which presently attached to that train; for as its pale, sinuous length streaked across the Connecticut countryside through the dusk, it had so eerie an effect that it came to be popularly known as the Ghost Train. Its running time was presently reduced from six hours to five hours and forty minutes. Rudyard Kipling, then sojourning in Vermont, was intrigued by it and found in it the idea for a short story which he entitled "007."

And was that train elegant! Well, a contemporary newspaper account of it says:

The parlor cars are furnished with velvet carpets, silk draperies and white silk curtains; the chairs are upholstered in old gold plush, and large glass mirrors set off the car handsomely. Three of them have a state room and 26 seats in the main saloon, and the other four have 30 seats each. The royal buffet smokers which will be run in addition to the ordinary smoking cars are decorated in the same manner as the parlor cars. . . . The Pullman Palace Car Company has designed a special dining car for the train.

Again the harassed management turned to the neglected but still willing little New York & Northern for an entrance into the metropolis which it could depend on. It established a considerable freight business by that route and actually began running some passenger trains which, from the Northern track, passed into Manhattan over one of the city's elevated railroad tracks. It was worrying the New Haven no little, and the latter decided that this leak must be stopped, once and for all. Charles Parsons, who was president of the New York & New England at the moment, was actually consulting his brokers as to the possibility of buying control of the New York & Northern, when the enemy forestalled him. The New Haven had persuaded its ally, the New York Central, to obtain a stock majority of the little road, which it rapidly proceeded to do through J. P. Morgan. The New Haven is said to have paid a part of the purchase price, but ever since, that minor road from the Harlem River to Brewster has been the Putnam division of the New York Central.

The next-to-last chapter in the life story of the N. Y. & N. E. was characteristically bizarre—nothing less than an invasion from Pennsylvania. The Philadelphia & Reading Railroad, under the presidency of A. A. McLeod—another plunger whose vision had not even a horizon—had, by leasing and buying control of small roads, obtained a continuous line from its Schuylkill coal fields up to and across the newly built bridge over the Hudson at Poughkeepsie, and incorporated a group of these roads as the Central New England & Western. This company quickly took over the Hartford & Connecticut Western and then consolidated with the

Poughkeepsie Bridge & Railroad Company as the Philadelphia, Reading & New England—which company in turn startled the world in October of that year by showing control of the New York & New England and Boston & Maine. McLeod's object was to get New England-wide distribution for the Reading's enormous oversupply of anthracite coal. He even made preliminary gestures toward taking over the Old Colony. The man's appetite was insatiable. But like the novice in the cafeteria who heaps too much on his plate, he couldn't swallow it all. For a few months McLeod was president of the New York & New England, and then in 1893, with a resounding crash, the parent company, the Reading, fell into bankruptcy, and with it, on December 27, the New York & New England. The Philadelphia, Reading & New England line was taken over by the Central New England & Western, which still had a corporate existence.

Now, with its weaker rival prostrate, the New Haven had its way. A reorganization plan for the N. Y. & N. E. had a $20 per share assessment as a major feature, and that quickly drove the stock into the market. Although the New Haven management and J. P. Morgan strenuously denied it for a long time, the big banker was buying N. Y. & N. E. stock for his Connecticut clients, and by September, 1895, the New Haven was admittedly in control. The reorganized company, now known simply as the New England Railroad, was being operated by its triumphant rival, and Charles P. Clark was president of both corporations.

From his head office in New Haven, Clark made frequent trips to Boston and liked to travel on the White Train. His favorite engineer was Gene Potter, a daring yet skillful magician of the cab, a big-mustached fellow who could not only do wonders with a locomotive but could go before a boys' school and make a talk that enraptured the youngsters. If the White Train was late, Clark always liked to see Potter overcome the deficit. One evening when Clark was in the parlor car nearing Willimantic, the train was half an hour late, and he overheard two passengers near him grumbling about it. One of them had wanted to catch a train for Maine at Boston and said he could never do it now.

"Maybe they'll make up the time," suggested the other.

His friend jeered. "The New England never makes up any time," he said.

A moment later Clark, who was unknown to the others, saw the brakeman coming through the car. He beckoned to him and said in his ear, "When Potter hooks on at Willimantic, tell him to get us into Boston on time."

The brakeman's eyes widened, he gulped, said, "Yes, sir," and went on. When Potter's sleek 167 was coupled to the train at Willimantic and the brakeman gave him the message, he, too, stared and swore. Making a quick calculation, he saw that to make up the half hour, he would have to do the eighty-six-mile non-stop run to Boston at better than a mile-a-minute rate. But Potter was no man to say, "It can't be done." He opened the throttle, and away they went through the night for a memorable run: swaying through the hill country of northeastern Connecticut but taking the curves so skillfully that the passengers did not realize how fast they were moving; thundering over switches and crossings, through Putnam, Blackstone, the outskirts of Woonsocket and Franklin and Walpole, waking country folk from sleep to mutter, "Them fellers are certainly hittin' it up tonight," and finally, in a little more than eighty minutes, slowing gently to a stop in the old station at the foot of Summer Street at nine o'clock to a split second, precisely on time. The traveler for Maine could scarcely believe it.

Superintendent Allen, a cautious and meticulous fellow, considered that too dangerous a stunt. A couple of days later Potter received a letter from him, saying in effect, "Hereafter under no circumstances are you to make up more than twenty minutes' time between Willimantic and Boston." But as luck would have it, only a few evenings elapsed before Clark was again a passenger, and again the train was late—this time twenty-five minutes. Just as Potter had his hand on the throttle, the brakeman came running to the cab steps and said, "Mr. Clark is aboard and he says to make up the time. He's got an appointment in Boston this evening."

Potter was thrown on his beam-ends by that message. As he said afterward, "For the first few miles, I couldn't decide what to do. Then it came to me that a railroad president is a lot bigger man than a superintendent, and so I turned her loose."

They arrived on time, of course. But the superintendent had his ear to the ground, and promptly next morning Potter received a summons to report to his office. He went, taking the official's letter with him. In the hall he encountered Mr. Clark.

"Nice run you made last night, Gene," said the president.

"Yes, but I'm afraid I'm in trouble about it," replied Potter.

"How so?"

Potter handed him the superintendent's letter. "He's ordered me to come in and see him this morning," he added.

Clark read the letter, noticed the date, twiddled the paper between his fingers and at length looked up with a boyish grin.

"Want me to go in and see the super in your place, Gene?" he asked.

"I'd certainly be glad if you would, sir," replied Potter.

So the president, letter in hand, marched into the superintendent's office—and that was the last Gene ever heard of the ban on making up time.

But very shortly after that, on October 20, 1895, the White Train disappeared: it was too much trouble to keep it clean. Clark still liked the idea, however, of a fast Air Line train between New York and Boston, so the Ghost was immediately replaced by a still faster train, the Air Line Limited, running at the same time of day and making only one stop—at Middletown to change engines. It was the only train that ever ran through New Haven without stopping.

The New Haven was now supreme in southern New England, but somewhat in deference to public opinion, it did not complete its swallowing of the New England until 1898. By that time it owned 129,099 shares of New England common and 11,975 shares of the preferred. The Vanderbilts, who had been buying, too, owned some 54,000 shares and were a potent influence. Thereafter, slowly, certain sections which were less important began to fall into desuetude, as did some others which were once connected with the New England but which the New Haven did not take over. The 124-mile Hartford & Connecticut Western, for example, from Hartford and Springfield to Rhinecliff, N. Y.—once a part of McLeod's Philadelphia, Reading & New England empire—has been dismantled and has vanished from the face of the earth— as has also the Newburgh, Dutchess & Connecticut, except for the twelve miles between Hopewell Junction and Beacon, which was still being used by the New Haven at a recent date. Other small sections are gone. Most startling of all, over the old Air Line course from New Haven through Middletown to Willimantic, where once the Ghost Train flitted through the twilight, the New Haven Railroad now operates only a line of buses; for its almost gradeless shore line through New London and Providence is far preferable from an operating standpoint to the sharp curves and heavy grades of the so-called Air Line. These long stretches of once busy track, the products of so many years of thought and labor, into which so many millions of money were poured, have joined the White Train in the realm of ghosts.

# 10

## "In the Land of the Pine and the Cranberry Bog"

N O VANISHED railroad in all New England seems
to dwell quite so sweetly in the memories of those
who knew it as the Old Colony. Its very name was
a happy conception, a phrase hallowed by centuries of history
and harking back to one of the most celebrated events in the
chronicles of America: it invited the clustering about it of
pleasant associations. Although its life was comparatively
peaceful and unspectacular, it was notable in many ways. It
fostered the most famous boat line that ever navigated our
waters, it ran the longest-lived train in American railroad
history, and the compact little 600-mile empire which it built
in a corner of Massachusetts was one of the best managed and
most definitely gilt-edged railroad properties on the continent.

As all outlanders may not know, the name Old Colony
was long ago applied to that southeastern portion of Massachusetts where the Pilgrims first settled and whose historic
seat is Plymouth. So when Plymouth decided that it
wanted railroad connection with Boston, the name of the line
was right there, ready for use. The road was chartered on
March 16, 1844, and work began on the thirty-eight-mile
line in the autumn. Sir Charles Lyell, who went down to
Plymouth to see The Rock in 1845, while construction was
under way, wrote: "The New Englanders laugh at the people of the Old Colony for remaining in a primitive state, and
are hoping that the railroad from Boston may soon teach them

to go ahead." Sir Charles did not know that it was the people of the Old Colony itself who were going ahead. The new railroad was their own. Of the original incorporators, twelve were from Plymouth, one from Kingston, one from Quincy and only two from Boston.

Not all the intervening territory wanted the innovation. No community in New England was more stubbornly anti-railroad than Dorchester, now engulfed in Greater Boston. When the road was first talked of in 1842, a Dorchester town meeting opined that, in addition to the immense sacrifice of private property involved, the road would be an "incalculable evil to the town generally"; crossing and running contiguous to public highways, it would be "a permanent obstruction to a free intercourse of our citizens," and a "great and enduring danger and hazard to all travel upon the common roads." Their representatives in the Legislature were instructed to fight it, and if the railroad must be built, to demand that it run through the marshes, where it would inconvenience nobody. A citizen's letter to a newspaper asked what better means of travel could be desired than the Neponset River or the adjacent ocean. He saw "beautiful gardens and farms made desolate," enterprising mechanics and merchants ruined, "all sacrificed under a car ten thousand times worse for the public than the car of Juggernaut."

But the railroad came, and though Dorchester grumbled loudly at first, it came to like the new transportation, and traffic on the Neponset River languished. The road was opened November 10, 1845, with the usual excursion to and dinner at Plymouth, and personages no less than John Quincy Adams and Daniel Webster present and making speeches. From the very beginning the Old Colony moved in an aureole of history. Of its first four locomotives, one, the "Comet," was a cheap little affair bought for a thousand dollars in England, but the other three, built by Hinkley & Drury in Boston, were christened "Governor Bradford," "Governor Carver" and "Miles Standish." Immediately following came the "Mayflower," "John Eliot," "John Quincy Adams" and some with historic place-names. The Indian King Philip and Daniel Webster were among those soon honored. On the sides of the tender of the "Pilgrim" a few years later were elaborate paintings representing the landing of the *Mayflower* voyagers on Plymouth Rock.

The company erected what the *Boston Journal* of March 3, 1846, described as "a large and splendid depot" at the corner of Beach and Albany Streets, "with double tracks and all modern improvements. . . . Over the depot there is to be a commodious hall with suitable drawing-rooms connected, the floor being built on the patent car spring, which is to be used for the accommodation of dancing parties and public and private assemblies." This station was used only a little more than a year, however, the company moving into another at South and Kneeland Streets on May 19, 1847—a memorable date in the calendar, for on that day a famous train began running, and a traffic connection was made with another road which within a few years was destined to become a marriage.

That other was the Fall River Railroad, which was being built, from its namesake city toward Boston, at the same time as the Old Colony. Southeastern Massachusetts was indeed awakening. Taunton had become a railroad town a decade before, when the Taunton Branch had been extended from the Boston & Providence; and in 1840 it had got another line, the New Bedford & Taunton. New Bedford's neighbor, Fall River, saw that it must bestir itself. Its leading family, the Bordens, were active in promoting the new company, which was at first the Fall River Branch Railway and ran only from Fall River to Myricks on the New Bedford & Taunton. On the first trip over the line, in June, 1845, the celebrants rode in "three splendid cars," and it is no surprise to learn from the *Fall River Weekly News* that they were "surpassed, we venture to say, by none in the United States for elegance and convenience."

At the same time the Middleborough Railroad Corporation was building from Myricks, through what we now call more briefly Middleboro, to Bridgewater, while yet another little line was being created to extend from Bridgewater to a junction with the Old Colony at South Braintree. These end-to-end fragments were all quickly assembled by the Bordens into a new corporation, the Fall River Railroad.

It was inevitable that a continuous pair of rails from Boston to Fall River should become connected with a boat line to New York. Early in 1846, Captain Thomas Borden and his brother, both stockholders in the Fall River Railroad, had begun operating the little steamer *Eudora* between Fall River and New York. She was only 155 feet long, and they used oxen to warp her into the dock at Fall River, but she carried more than 50,000 passengers that year and earned $10,335. That success made it certain that the new Old Colony–Fall River rails coming down from Boston would soon be hooked up with a boat line to New York. Incidentally, the *Eudora* followed the Gold Rush to California in 1849 and reached there safely, but now nobody hereabouts knows what became of her.

The next idea we hear of seems a curiosity today. The Long Island Railroad had been pushed out to Greenport, on the northern prong of Long Island, solely with the idea of making it a part of a New York–Boston route—the first plan including boats running from Greenport to Stonington or Allyn's Point on the Thames above New London, from which ports railroads led to Boston. The Fall River Railroad spoke of this connection with some enthusiasm at the beginning of 1847. Calling the distance by boat from Fall River to Newport seventeen miles, and thence to Greenport sixty miles, it figured the distance from Boston to New York as 221 miles, mostly by rail, and therefore faster than by boat from Fall River or Providence. Remember that at that time there was as yet no all-rail route between Boston and New York.

But the Long Island scheme quickly passed into the discard in the spring of 1847, when the Fall River and Old Colony put their heads together and agreed to run a train especially to connect with a new line, the Borden-owned Bay State Steamboat Company, which was to operate the *Massachusetts* and *Bay State*, overnight boats between Fall River and New York. The launching of this service was of such importance as to call for the reproduction of its first announcement in the Boston newspapers, on May 19, 1847:

> The new steamer Bay State, Captain J. J. Comstock, will leave Fall River THIS EVENING, on the arrival of the cars from Boston. Train leaves the depot of the Old Colony Railroad, corner of South and Kneeland Streets, Boston, at 5 o'clock P.M. Berths and staterooms secured at 7 State Street, and at Ticket Office of the Old Colony Railroad.

Thus began the famous Boat Train, which continued to run for ninety years thereafter, making it the longest-lived train in American history, though for world records, a London-Edinburgh train may by this time have outdone it. Its leaving time was changed to 5:30 in 1853, and in 1875 to 6 P.M., at which time it left ever afterward, with the exception of some slight variation during the Spanish-American and First World Wars. It even departed at 6 P.M. by Daylight Saving Time when that custom came in. Its route was also varied slightly three times as new lines were built or taken over; but the only changes in its running time were to make it always a little faster. And that train could always be depended upon to have the very latest devices for speed, comfort and safety. For many years the boat "clerks" or pursers went through to Boston and back on the trains, "to give the lady passengers especial attention from the Boat to the Train and from the Train to the Boat."

That May day in 1847 also marked the beginning of what came to be known in later years as the Fall River Line of steamboats, which was always an adjunct of the Old Colony Railroad and its successor. But what bitter rivalry it had in the earlier decades! The competition was terrific. It seems desirable to pause here and glance at the history of some of the other railroads terminating in South Shore ports and striving for connecting water traffic.

To begin with, there was the strongest of them all, the Boston & Providence, whose story we have already told. Then there was the Providence & Worcester, first talked of in 1837 but not chartered by Rhode Island and Massachusetts until 1844. It was put into operation in 1847, and thereafter did a good business. Antedating the P. & W. there was the Norwich & Worcester, first chartered in Massachusetts and Connecticut in 1832 as the Boston, Norwich & New London, changing its name to the shorter and more realistic form in 1836 when the two companies were united. It seemed destined to prosperity, for the directors said in a Statement of Facts that between Worcester and Norwich, within five miles of their track, there were seventy-five cotton mills and twenty-seven woolen mills—mostly small ones, to be sure—and many factories of other sorts beside; and the directors added in their first annual report, "There are no people in the world more locomotive than the manufacturing population of New England"; hence, was the inference, much passenger traffic.

Both companies began borrowing from their states immediately, and in 1840 the line was opened to Norwich. That city is nearly twenty miles up the Thames from the Sound, but the National Government deepened the channel and placed lights at the river mouth, and a line of boats began running between Norwich and New York in connection with the trains. With through rail service from Boston via Worcester, this was no mean competitor. But the upper portion of the river voyage was difficult and sometimes impossible in winter, and so in 1843 the road was extended some ten miles farther downstream to Allyn's Point on salt water, which Sound steamers could easily reach. It was claimed by the N. & W. that the water journey from here was only three miles longer than that via Stonington, but the Stonington competitors found it fourteen miles longer. From here, too, in 1846, the experiment was tried of shuttling boats across to Greenport, to send passengers into New York by Long Island Railroad; but that did not continue long.

Earliest built of all these railroads—for we are listing them backward—was the one always known popularly as the Stonington Railroad. Largely New York owned, the company was chartered as the Providence & Stonington in 1832, but when the Rhode Island and Connecticut companies merged in the following year, it was as the New York, Providence & Boston. Its survey and building were done by William H. Swift and those two noted brothers-in-law, McNeill and Whistler. Work began on the road very soon after it was incorporated. In 1837 Whistler came back from Lowell and lived at Stonington, which became his favorite home; in fact, it was so dear to him that when he died in Russia he was brought back to Stonington to be buried. There in the evenings, while completing the line and putting it into operation, he tootled on the flute, his favorite relaxation, while little Jimmie at the age of four was already drawing pictures which the neighbors regarded as amazingly good for so young a child. After its completion in 1837, Whistler managed the road for a short time before being called to the uncompleted Western job.

The N. Y. P. & B.'s boat connection at first was only with the Boston & New York Transportation Company, which operated from Providence and made Stonington a way stop. It ran only three boats a week and in winter dropped one of the trips. In later years and for many years, there were New York boat lines which terminated at Stonington and gave the connecting railroad prosperity.

Thus by 1840 we see at least four ports, all rail-ends, from which steamers competing for Boston business took off for New York—Fall River, Providence, Stonington and Norwich, later Allyn's Point. We might even add a fifth, Springfield, now served by the Western Railroad, from which little steamboats ran down the Connecticut River and around to New Haven, connecting there with larger boats for New York. Let us hasten to say that we cannot so much as attempt a hint of the history of the innumerable competing boat lines on the Sound, many of them almost as short-lived as the May fly. It requires a whole volume to do that even briefly, and Roger Williams McAdam has written it.[1] But slowly the Fall River Line came to dominate them all.

The talking point of the Stonington and Norwich boats was the absence of that rough trip around Point Judith,

[1] *The Old Fall River Line*, Brattleboro, 1937.

Rhode Island's evil cape, which the Providence and Fall River boats had to pass. In a somewhat milder degree, it might be called the Cape Hatteras of the New England coast. The Fall River and Providence fellows in their informal publicity made many a joke about the early rising that eastbound passengers had to do to change from boat to train at Stonington or Allyn's Point; to which the opposition had a telling riposte in describing the seasickness that overwhelmed Fall River and Providence passengers as they rounded Point Judith, where the comparatively small boats of those days rolled and pitched like a wounded whale.

The Stonington Railroad was in grave financial trouble from the very beginning. The panic of '37 dealt it a heavy blow. One of its first locomotives was for some strange reason christened "Little Rest," and that must have pictured pretty accurately the state of the company's officials as they fought off creditors and attachments and tried to borrow money from banks in New York and Philadelphia, not only to finish building and equipping the road but to pay interest on the bonds and keep the wheels turning. Once, some contractors who had been paid for their work in bonds brought suit and attached some of the company's property in an effort to get cash. The company owed two Rhode Island attorneys $2100 and $650, and it issued bonds with which to pay them. One day Superintendent Phelps, at Stonington, wrote to headquarters that four more attachments had been placed on the company's real and personal property, "being for the balance of the bonds of the company not included in the mortgage." He had somehow rescued enough coal and cars and locomotives so that "the operations of the Road continue."

They offered to lease the railroad to the Transportation Company, but the latter didn't want it. Then they talked of leasing the Transportation Company's boats, but that was absurdly beyond their means. The boat company, however, bought the opposition steamer *Lexington* and held the railroad up for $10,000 as an inducement to them to withdraw that boat from the New York–Providence trade and stop it

at Stonington.  But gradually the popularity of the Stonington Line increased, and one day late in 1838, President Courtlandt Palmer wrote exultantly to a director, "I am very happy
to state that the earnings of our Road for one day last week
was $1,000." [2]  Affairs were on the mend, but years passed
before the company became profitable.

During those years the Old Colony was beginning to reach
out.  It leased the little South Shore Railroad, opened in
1849 and running out to Cohasset, and it had two branches,
one from Whitman to Bridgewater, the other a tiny one, from
Dorchester to Milton.  Among the company's valued sources
of revenue was ice from the many little lakes in that corner
of Massachusetts.  It is interesting to observe how much ice
was shipped and how far, in those days when only natural ice
was available and America was rapidly becoming a cold-
drink-loving nation.  In 1849 the Old Colony directors reported that 7749 tons of ice had been shipped from Plympton
to Boston in the preceding season.  From its Boston wharf,
coastal vessels shipped ice to southern cities in winter, to cool
the lemonades and juleps and toddies of the following
summer.

The Old Colony had an agreement with the Fall River,
which used its tracks from South Braintree to Boston,
whereby neither was to encourage the building of any rival
line or to use such a line if built; but officials on both sides
wondered gloomily whether the other would strictly live up
to the agreement. Receipts were to be divided on a pro rata
basis: the Fall River received a small fixed sum and provided
the cars, while the Old Colony supplied the engines and the
Boston terminal.  The famous Boat Train, which ran north
in the morning after the arrival of the New York boat at Fall
River, and back in the evening, had begun to be a lucrative
feature for both.

The years 1850 and 1851 were the fashionable years for
stockholders' investigations of the affairs of their companies.
If there was a railroad in New England which escaped the

[2] This N. Y. P. & B. correspondence is in the manuscript room, New
York Public Library.

contagion around this time, we haven't noticed it. The Old Colony stockholders' committee put on just about the biggest show of all, its inquisition lasting three months. The committee had President E. H. Derby, one of the leading railroad executives and attorneys of New England, on the stand for three days and hurled 159 carefully prepared questions at him. Derby later pointed out in an able reply which he published that they had spent a deal of the company's money in that long tribunal and in bringing witnesses from hither and yon; he did not mention the cost, which must have been considerable, of printing the report, a sizable book. It was a pretty heavy expense all told for a railroad which didn't control more than sixty miles of track, owned and leased. And after all, the committee didn't find much that was seriously wrong.

But the acrimony that developed between them and Derby made it impossible for him to remain as president; he passed out, and F. B. Crowninshield, another very able man, came in as executive. He found trouble awaiting him. The Fall River Railroad was becoming a bit hoity-toity, feeling that it was doing most of the work between Boston and Fall River and getting too little of the proceeds. In 1852 it formally declared the existing arrangement unfair and said that it could better itself by building its own track over that eleven-and-a-half miles from South Braintree to Boston, and cease using the Old Colony rails. The Old Colony made the obvious retort: it could also extend its Whiteman-Bridgewater branch through Taunton to either Bristol or Newport, R. I., and run its own boat line from there to New York.

The Fall River had other complaints to make. It alleged that the Old Colony treatment of passengers at Boston was bad. "Complaints have been frequent and very general. The feelings and the wishes of passengers apparently there has been no disposition to consult." One grievance was that the Old Colony was carrying passengers to and from the station in Boston and picking up a bit of change thereby. The O. C. retorted that it had taken over much of that work because there had formerly been such a rabble of hackmen around the station, fairly tearing passengers apart, that it became intolerable and had to be abated. Another Fall River grouch was that the Old Colony was charging for the storage of baggage at Boston. And here in 1852 we find the first attempt that this writer has discovered at the modern ten-cents-a-day checkroom or parcel room. The Old Colony directors replied that "to prevent a growing habit of passengers leaving baggage at the Boston station to be stored—often for weeks—and frequently in such quantities as to be beyond the capacity of our baggage room to accommodate," they began making a small charge for the storage of baggage, "of no account as a source of income and not intended for any such purpose." But the Fall River people and the public made such a hullaballoo over the "hold-up" that it had to be abandoned—for many years, at least.

The Fall River now became still more crotchety, and in March, 1853, presented a series of eleven demands, among them that: the Fall River was to determine the number of trains to be run daily over the combined lines; Fall River trains were not to do any local business or stop between South Braintree and Boston; when northbound Fall River and Old Colony trains arrived simultaneously at South Braintree, the Fall River train was to have the preference; a baggage room in the Boston station was to be devoted exclusively to Fall River luggage; carriages for the accommodation of passengers to and from Fall River trains were to be under Fall River management—and there were six more demands.

Crowninshield rejected the whole category so bluntly that President Nathaniel B. Borden of the Fall River was taken aback and assumed a much more moderate tone. A long argument which ensued finally brought from the Old Colony a suggestion that the two companies merge their interests. Borden thought they might unite on the basis of two shares of Old Colony to one of Fall River. What he meant, of course, was that Fall River stock was worth twice as much as Old Colony; but Crowninshield blandly replied that the offer was quite satisfactory and that the Old Colony would thus receive 22,500 shares of the stock of the new company, the

Fall River getting 11,250. Borden complained that this was a gross misinterpretation of his meaning—and so they bickered and sparred for the better part of a year, finally coming together in 1854 on an equitable exchange of stock, to organize the Old Colony and Fall River Railroad Company with a capital of $3,000,000.

An important connection of the new company was the growing Cape Cod system. The Cape Cod Railroad had opened its line from Middleboro to Sandwich in 1848. Much Fall River money had been invested in it, and it expected to be taken over by the Fall River Railroad, but the latter for some reason failed to do so. In 1850 the Cape Cod Branch Railroad was chartered, to continue from Sandwich to Hyannis. But money was hard to come by, and there was much wrangling over the question of whether the line should run directly to Hyannis or detour through Barnstable and Yarmouth. A considerable portion of the Cape—as the whole peninsula is erroneously called, though in truth the actual Cape Cod is at Provincetown—was fuming over the railroad project, because it would take business away from the coasting vessels.

Nantucket was much more active than Hyannis in promoting the railroad. The whaling masters who were the mainstay of that island community wanted fast transportation to Boston, and they invested $50,000 in stock of the new company. It had galled them to be compelled to travel to Boston by way of their rival whaling port, New Bedford. They loaded some hundreds of their townsmen on a boat in 1850 and ran it to South Hyannis (now Hyannisport), to prove to them that it was but little more than half as far to Hyannis as to New Bedford. "The people of Nantucket," said the *Inquirer*, "have for the last twenty-five years apparently taken particular pains to add to the profit and importance of New Bedford." And what thanks did they get for it? The New Bedford folk "patronize us as a vapid city buck does his country cousin. . . . We have made ourselves mere bobbins to the New Bedford kite, and have to pay high for the privileges."

Some discordant voices were heard from the Cape, but the

railroad was finally completed to Hyannis in 1854. It ran via Barnstable and Yarmouth, and everybody was happy but the coasters. At South Hyannis a granite pier was built, to which excellent steamers began running from Nantucket, and the islanders now luxuriated in the convenience of breakfasting at home and eating noon dinner in Boston, making the journey more cheaply than by way of New Bedford and saving hours of time besides. The Hyannis station had a Ladies' Saloon, from the rapturous description of which we can cull only bits: "A large, spacious room, richly carpeted and elegantly furnished . . . luxurious sofa, chairs, rockers . . . table of costly style and structure. . . . Another saloon so richly and luxuriously furnished cannot be found in any depot on the Cape." But the railroad hadn't done it. It had been "freely and generously furnished" by the ladies of Hyannis.

While we are on the subject, it may be as well to add that the road was pushed on from Yarmouth to Orleans in 1865, to Wellfleet in 1870, finally completing the hook around to Provincetown in 1873. President Grant enjoyed a trip out there in the following year.

Long before these dates, the independent Fairhaven Branch Railroad had been built in 1854, leaving the Cape Cod track at Tremont to run down to Fairhaven, whence a boat ran to Martha's Vineyard three times a week.[3] But when the Cape Cod built its own branch from Buzzard's Bay to Woods Hole in 1872, both the Vineyard and the Nantucket ferry businesses were transferred to Woods Hole.[4] Perhaps Hyannis didn't

[3] Henry H. Rogers, the Standard Oil multimillionaire, began life as a brakeman on the Fairhaven Branch. He never forgot his old railroad comrades, and when he went back to Massachusetts on vacation, he always called at station and roundhouse to see them. It is recorded that on one of these occasions, one of the veterans asked, "Henry, what's the best time to buy Standard Oil stock?" "Any time between ten and three," promptly replied Rogers, meaning whenever the Stock Exchange was open.

[4] They tell of a new brakeman on the Cape Cod who was instructed that in announcing Buzzard's Bay station, he must add, "Change for Wenaumet, Pocasset, Cataumet, North Falmouth, West Falmouth, Falmouth and Woods Hole." He strove hard to memorize the list, but like Snug the joiner, he was slow of study. As the train eased toward a stop there on his first trip, he entered a car and bellowed, "Buzzard's Bay; change for Wunaumit—uh—Cataumit—uh—oh, dammit, Woods Hole!"

greatly care, for she was becoming the center of one of the most popular summer resort areas on the coast. The Cape Cod system, though a valuable connection, was not taken into the Old Colony family until 1872.

Meanwhile, the Old Colony was rapidly expanding in other directions, though not without growing pains. One highly controversial move was the extension from Fall River to Newport. This was eagerly desired in Newport and everywhere between there and Fall River, but violently opposed in the latter city, which now saw itself becoming a mere way station. The avowed purpose of the railroad management was to move the steamer terminal to Newport, thus shortening the water run to New York and enabling the boat to make valuable western and southern connections at New York which were now being missed. The Bordens, who had never liked the amalgamation of the roads but who were now a minority, fought the extension bitterly. Josiah G. Abbott, attorney for the Old Colony, in a speech before the State Committee on Railways and Canals in 1861, reported them as saying in effect: "Buy us off! Buy us off! Pay us ten or twelve dollars a share more for our railroad stock than it will bring in the market. Pay us twelve or fifteen hundred dollars a share for our boat stock, which is worth only one thousand dollars in the market. Buy us off, and you will have no trouble with the people of Fall River." But despite every possible obstacle which they and their allies could put in the way, the extension was built, and then—the most unkindest cut of all—the name of the system was once more changed in 1862, from Old Colony & Fall River to Old Colony & Newport!

A menace which sprang up weedlike, the Dighton & Somerset Railroad, was turned into a benefit. This road, mapped to run from Braintree through Randolph, Raynham and Taunton to Fall River, was absorbed and completed by 1866, thus giving the Old Colony an entrance into Taunton and a shorter main line than the one being used via Middleboro. Next, another little nuisance, the Middleboro & Taunton, over which the Cape Cod had been sending some north- and westbound business, was taken into the fold, closely following the absorption of the Cape Cod system in 1872. With that last acquisition, the company changed its name again, back to the original, simple Old Colony, which it ever after remained. The railroad at this period, and until his death in 1878, was under the presidency of Mr. Onslow Stearns, who, with remarkable versatility, served also as president of the Northern (New Hampshire) Railroad from 1852 to 1877, and Governor of New Hampshire in 1869–71—something inconceivable in the present era, but, as will be observed farther along in our narrative, mid-nineteenth century governors of New Hampshire and Vermont appear to have been railroad presidents ex officio, and vice versa.

What merry wars the Sound boat lines were waging in those mid-century days and after! It should be mentioned here that the Old Colony's boat terminal did not remain long at Newport: it was presently moved back permanently to Fall River, though the rail extension to Newport continued functioning. Other lines were prospering: the Stonington had become one of the best, and its connection, the New York, Providence & Boston Railroad, was thriving on it. Thomas Colley Grattan, a British traveler, rode over it in 1858, and wrote enthusiastically, "There were upwards of 300 passengers, and nothing could exceed the order and regularity with which their accommodation was provided for." It was a summer night, and he passed most of it strolling on deck. "I never heard the voice of captain, pilot or boatswain," said he. "I never before, except in military evolutions, saw anything to compare with the good management on board this fine steam-boat; and from ample subsequent experience, I can vouch for its being nothing extraordinary in the United States." [5]

Another port, Bristol, Rhode Island, had come into the field. The Providence & Bristol was incorporated in 1850 in Rhode Island; its name was changed later to Providence, Warren & Bristol, and by 1855 it had linked those three towns. Its first northern terminus was at East Providence,

[5] *Civilized America*, London, 1859.

and there trains were broken up and drawn by horses up Main Street to the Providence & Worcester Depot. In 1860 an appendage, the Fall River, Warren & Providence, was opened, running from Warren to Fall River. Now Bristol really came into its own. In the latter sixties, boat lines were running to New York not only from Stonington but from three ports around Narragansett Bay—Providence, Bristol and Fall River. The rivalry reached a high pitch, and rates at times were cut to the bone. Band concerts were given on the wharves at Providence and Bristol before the departure of the boats, and the Merchants Line at Providence went the others one better by serving tea on the wharf, with the manager in white kid gloves—a fresh pair every day—as host. As the story was told to us—and you may take it or leave it—his stripping off those white gloves, rolling them up and throwing them into the harbor was the signal for the boat to cast off.

The eventual triumph of the Old Colony and its Fall River Line was in the cards, and nothing could change it. The Boat Train and its connecting boats became leading American institutions. Presidents—Fillmore, Grant, Arthur, Cleveland, Harrison, even Franklin D. Roosevelt in his younger days—and many other great ones of the earth were carried by them. The fine steamers *Bristol* and *Providence* of post-bellum days were supplemented and succeeded by the still bigger and finer *Puritan* and *Pilgrim;* and then in the nineties came the *Priscilla,* perhaps the best beloved of all the Fall River boats, though the *Commonwealth,* which was added in the present century, was just a little larger. Electrically lighted, with luxurious lounges and famous cuisine, and steady because of their size, they were really ocean liners on a somewhat smaller scale.

As for the train, it kept pace with the times as each new device came in: air brakes, steam heat, parlor cars, Pintsch gas lighting, then electricity, vestibules, steel cars. When the son of President Holmes of the Old Colony visited England in 1865, he was impressed by the British type of railway carriage and induced his father to have two of them built for the Boat Train. Separated into locked compartments as they were, the conductor had to pass along their sides, winter and summer, to enter and collect the tickets. Americans, with their characteristic weakness for anything European, were greatly intrigued by the cars for a while; then their popularity waned, and in the seventies the Old Colony put on its own modern parlor cars, "Pilgrim" and "Puritan." In 1891 came the first two Pullman parlor cars, "Violet" and "Pansy." Old-timers still shudder at the memory of those names.

The Boat Train, in all its ninety years, had only ten conductors; and one of them, Asa R. Porter, was one of the most famous conductors in America. For thirty-two years, from 1864 until he died in harness in 1896, he shuttled back and forth on that train between Boston and Fall River, save for times when he might be called upon to take charge of a President's special—and he was always the one billeted for such a task. His popularity began with his great kindness to sick and wounded soldiers during the Civil War. A dignified but genial figure in his frock coat, always with a flower in his buttonhole at first a pink, it grew into a carnation in later years—with shaven upper lip and short beard which gradually turned from brown to white, he was not only the master of the train, but the host. Even company officials called him Mr. Porter. Evenings at Fall River, as the passengers moved from the train to the gangplank, he stood, shaking hands with scores of them as they passed—many through frequent trips had become friends or acquaintances—with a smiling word for each: "Good-night, ma'am—and a pleasant journey"; "Good-night, sir; hope to see you again"; "Good-night, Mr. Lyman; take care of yourself"—and all with a sincere heartiness that never seemed to slacken. It used to be said that he had much to do with making the Fall River Line the great success that it was. He was more than once offered a higher post by the company, but preferred to remain where he was.

By the middle seventies the Old Colony was becoming one of the leading summer resort carriers in New England. Scores of beaches and quiet beauty spots, such as Cohasset, Nantasket, Scituate, Duxbury Beach, the dozens of playgrounds of the Cape, Martha's Vineyard, Nantucket and many others—and how pleasant and restful they were in those pre-automobile days before they became overcrowded and noisy!—were being advertised by the road in illustrated booklets as the eighties came on. There are elderly men and women still alive who fondly recall the golden yellow cars of the Old Colony as bearing them to many a halcyon vacation time, long ago. Another famous train was launched in 1884, a three- or four-car private affair for subscribers only—extra high fare, of course—which left Boston on summer afternoons at three o'clock and dashed over the seventy-two miles to Woods Hole in an hour and a half, so that bankers and other "malefactors of great wealth," closing their roll-top desks a little early, might eat supper at the Sea View Hotel on the Vineyard as early as six o'clock, if they liked. It was promptly nicknamed the Dude Train, and so it continued to be known, quite soberly, by railroaders, until the United States Railroad Administration of the First World War abolished it in 1918.

With the year 1879 the Old Colony entered upon its period of greatest expansion. The story of it may begin with the little Agricultural Branch Railroad, which, with the backing of the Boston & Worcester, was completed in 1855 between Framingham and Northboro. It used Boston & Worcester rolling stock and seemed to be a dependency of that road, but it had reserved the right to lease or be leased by any railroad in the vicinity. In 1866 it extended its track northward to North Sterling, where it made connection with the Fitchburg & Worcester. Three years later the Agricultural and the F. & W. united and became the Boston, Clinton & Fitchburg. The managers of this road were good promoters. They engineered the construction of the Mansfield & Framingham, which, completed in 1870, was immediately taken over by the B. C. & F., giving it a connection at Mansfield with the Boston & Providence. The B. & P. had donated $15,000 toward the construction of the new road, seeing it as a northerly outlet for coal brought from the boats at Providence.

The B. C. & F. managers were not yet satisfied. In 1872 a railroad was completed from Framingham to Lowell, and they gathered that in. With dazzling rapidity, this was followed in the succeeding year by the leasing of the New Bedford Railroad, which had just been formed out of the Taunton Branch and the New Bedford & Taunton. Reorganized in 1876 as the Boston, Clinton, Fitchburg & New Bedford, here was now an important-looking northwest and southeast line from Fitchburg (and Lowell) to New Bedford, where it ran out on the docks of the Philadelphia & Reading Coal Company, "one of the largest coal receiving plants on the Atlantic Coast," so the publicity said. From there they expected to send Pennsylvania coal not only to Massachusetts but to Vermont, New Hampshire and Maine. They envisioned New Bedford as a coming great port, to which the grain and flour of the West, coming via Ogdensburg, the Hoosac Tunnel and even over the B. & A. from Albany, would be diverted from Boston, for export to Europe.

That dream did not come true. The B. C. F. & N. B. was soon in financial trouble, and staved off its creditors in 1878 only by persuading them to accept preferred stock in payment of the floating debt. In 1883 the directors were quite willing that their company should be gathered under the sheltering wings of the Old Colony by lease—incidentally making a total for the latter company of a well-managed system of 459 miles of track, the largest under one governance in Massachusetts.

Still, the Old Colony was not entirely happy. There remained one very small fly in the ointment—the Boston & Providence, which, in its own main line, as well as its controlled lines, the Providence, Warren & Bristol and the Fall River, Warren & Providence, was in some degree a competitor and a threat. There were rumors that the New York, Providence & Boston, that very concern which had been so feeble fifty years before, might lease the Boston & Providence, and if that happened, the next step would be the New Haven's taking over the N. Y. P. & B. The New Haven, now a powerful system, was steadily pressing, an irresistible force, toward Boston; soon it would engulf the New York & New England. But to block its best possible entry into Boston, the

Old Colony, having bought stock control of the Boston & Providence, leased that road and its dependencies in 1888, paying through the nose for it—a million dollars cash, a guaranty of its fixed charges, plus 10 per cent per annum on its stock.

Soon after this amalgamation, the New York, Providence & Boston leased the Providence & Worcester, thus obtaining a connection with the New York & New England at Blackstone and a route to Boston which obviated the necessity of its using the Boston & Providence. But the breath of the inexorable Connecticut giant was hot on its neck even then; in 1892, the N. Y. P. & B. became an appurtenance of the New Haven. Now there was just one forty-four-mile step needed to fulfill its ambition, and quietly its brokers were buying stock to complete that. In 1893 the Old Colony, now a 600-mile network, passed under the control of the New Haven by lease, and the present smoothly gliding Shore Line trains between New York and Boston were made possible. As a final move to accomplish this, the big fellow found it necessary to ward off the attempt of A. A. McLeod, the Philadelphia & Reading plunger—who had obtained control of the New England—to seize the Old Colony as well.

Since then the Old Colony, still a living thing, though in a state of suspended animation, has been operated as a part of the New Haven system. With the increasing competition of the automobile and truck, and the depression which began in 1929 and continued until the time when the Second World War brought us a false prosperity, darker days came to the Old Colony domain. The Fall River Line ceased to be profitable, and its fate was balanced on a razor edge when, in 1937, a strike of employees precipitated the end. To the incredulous ears of the nation, the suspension of service was announced. After ninety unbroken years, the Boat Train ceased to leave Boston each evening, and *Priscilla* and *Commonwealth*, those glamorous queens of the Sound about whom Harry von Tilzer had written a popular song only a few years before, "The Old Fall River Line," were towed to a scrap yard, an ignoble fate that saddened many as if beloved friends had died.

Those latter thirties were untoward on land, too. Industries had moved westward from the cities, and though the summer resort country was more popular than ever, the motor vehicle, on paved roads, public-built and operated, was having its way in unfair competition. At one swoop on a summer morning the New Haven struck from the time-table eighty trains on lines running into the Cape Cod area. Some branches have since been abandoned, and villages that once listened for the cheery whistle of the locomotive will never hear it again.

# 11

## The Fitchburg and the Great Bore

A FEW years after the first railroad tracks in Massachusetts were laid, Fitchburg, a manufacturing village of modest size, some forty miles northwest-by-west of Boston as the crow flies, began to feel yearnings for rail communication with the capital. The first meeting to consider the project was held by its citizens in November, 1841. There Alvah Crocker, a local man of means, stood out as the protagonist; from that time on, he was chiefly instrumental in bringing about the consummation. In fact, the Fitchburg Railroad was often spoken of as Crocker's own creation.

But though Crocker was well-to-do, he was not able to build the railroad alone, and for some time the project lagged, even after it was incorporated. E. Hasket Derby, whom we have met as the President of the Old Colony, was later attorney for the Fitchburg, and in a hearing before the Committee on Railways and Canals in 1873, he said, speaking of that corporation's birth-throes:

It began in extreme poverty. For one or two years the subscriptions to the stock stood at $450,000, and there was a clause in the charter that not a blow should be struck until $600,000 was subscribed; and from month to month, as the directors met, as many stockholders died or left as were added to the stock list. The enterprise seemed to be upon its last feet. I recollect very well meeting with the directors one evening in a gloomy room at Earle's Coffee House, when Mr. Crocker rose from his seat and went to the mantelpiece, where two tallow candles were burning, and blew out one of them, suggesting that the road could afford but one candle in its condition at that time. . . . Finally, that prince of contractors, Belknap, came forward and subscribed the remaining $150,000 for the stock, and the road went on.

We shall hear of Mr. Belknap again. Derby and Crocker went to England and bought cheap rails at $18.75 a ton, and when they reached port in Boston, "the duty was more than the cost of the iron." "It was a surface road," said Derby; it wriggled along the banks of the streams to avoid heavy grading. Crocker also employed some cheap foreign labor: he was in Boston when a shipload of Irishmen arrived, bound, as they thought, for the Middle West, but he persuaded them to settle in Fitchburg and build his railroad.

When the road began to be built, starting from Charlestown, opposite Boston, in 1843, it took over the track of a little line which had been built solely to haul ice for Boston consumption from Fresh and Spy Ponds, a few miles distant, to a Charlestown wharf. At its other end, in Fitchburg, an uproar arose in 1844 when the location of the road's terminus was revealed. Fitchburg at that time consisted of two little huddles of population, with centers about half a mile apart. One, called the Old City, considered itself the most distinguished and important, though the other, known as the Village, had more inhabitants, and more business: it was "uptown." When the surveyors ran their final line into the Old City, a storm of indignation arose in the Village. Every means was essayed to induce the officials to change their plans, but in vain. A remonstrance signed by most of the Village citizens called attention to the clause in the charter, "to some point in the village of Fitchburg which shall best accommodate the people," and added (we can quote only briefly from the impassioned pages): "If it had been known that the depot would have been located in the Old City, not one-tenth part of the subscriptions would have been taken, you find in your books. It is not true—it never will be true— that we shall quietly and cheerfully acquiesce in the above designation. Can it be supposed that we shall be disregarded,

neglected, trodden down and some of us seriously injured in
our property without the common feelings of humanity? . . ."

The reason given by the directors, that they could save
from $20,000 to $40,000 by locating the terminus in the Old
City, was jeered at by the *Fitchburg Sentinel*—published in
the Village—which asked, "Why not locate the depot on the
flat at Baker's Pond and save another $40,000?" Many people
in indignation disposed of their stock, and when the road was
completed, there were comparatively few stockholders in
Fitchburg. When the opening celebration was staged in
March, 1845, the Village practically ignored it. Then a petition signed by 310 voters was seriously presented to the Legislature, asking for a charter to connect the village of Fitchburg
with the Fitchburg Railroad!

The road's eastern terminus was for five years at Charlestown, between which and the company's office on Brattle
Street a stage ran for the conveyance of passengers. Late in
1843, when the road was open only to Waltham, we find that
this stage ride added a mere nickel to the fare. But upon
completion of the line to Fitchburg, the public notices read:

> Passengers by applying at No. 11 Elm-street or City
> Tavern, Brattle-st., will be called for at any reasonable dis-
> tance in the city, and conveyed to the Depot for 12½ cents,
> or between the above office and the Depot for 6¼ cents.
> The Freight Train will run daily over the road both ways.

These notices are signed by S. M. Felton, Engineer (shortly
afterward superintendent), a man who in later years became
a noted railroad executive, even outside of New England.

As the rails neared Concord battlefield in their westward
course, they passed close by a famous little body of water—
Walden Pond, on the shore of which the philosopher-
naturalist Thoreau built a shack and lived for more than two
years. One would expect that this rather anarchistic indi-
vidualist and forest-lover would be annoyed by the railroad;
on the contrary, he was delighted with it, and gave several
pages to it in his *Walden* volume. He praised the fortitude of

the snow-plow men at their bitter task; he saw beauty in the golden-tinted smoke-cloud from the locomotive at sunrise; the cargoes clattering by in both directions, mostly raw materials eastward, manufactured goods westward, aroused meditations in him of the coming new economic era, of the closer knitting of society, of the valor of the men who were doing this. "What recommends commerce to me is its enterprise and bravery. It does not clasp its hands and pray to Jupiter. . . . It seems as if the earth had got a race now worthy to inhabit it." Almost the only plaintive touch in the book has to do with the trains: "Now that the cars are gone by and all the restless world with them, and the fishes in the pond no longer feel their rumbling, I am more alone than ever."

Even before the railroad had begun building, President Crocker's vision was expanding westward. He, like so many other Yankee railroad promoters, was allured by the Northwest Passage: he wanted a link with the new railroad systems of Vermont, with Canada and the Great Lakes. He accordingly planned the Vermont & Massachusetts Railroad, to connect Fitchburg and Brattleboro, and in 1842 went to the latter place to sell stock. At the road's opening celebration, seven years later, he told of his experience there, talking his throat dry for two weeks and never getting the scratch of a pen. Then, rather than let him go away empty-handed, two kindly citizens subscribed for two shares apiece. At that, others, embarrassed and wishing to avoid the reproach of so trifling a participation, wrote down their names for larger sums. The snowball had begun to roll. He went away with $8000 in subscriptions and picked up $22,000 more on the way home, enough to bring co-operation from the countryside.

The company was incorporated in Vermont and in Massachusetts in 1843–44, but the going was still hard. Crocker's designs through Fitchburg to the Connecticut River, plus the talk that now began to be heard of realizing Loammi Baldwin's extravaganza—as it had been considered—of a tunnel through the Hoosac Mountain range, made the Western Railroad look upon the V. & M. as a parallel competitor, and aroused its opposition, which never thereafter slackened.

The V. & M. had local troubles. Two towns west of Fitchburg, Templeton and Gardner, became incensed when the survey, at first made through their precincts, was changed, to carry the track through Winchendon, farther north. Both towns appointed committees, appropriated money, employed counsel and made a fight for their "rights" before the county commissioners. "Alvah Crocker of Fitchburg" was denounced as the "ringleader" of the "conspiracy" to cheat Templeton and Gardner. The commissioners decided in favor of the towns. The railroad appealed to the Legislature in 1845 but lost again; so its track, when built, had to make a sharp turn southward from South Ashburnham. But that turn was the making of Gardner, though Templeton did not seem to profit greatly by it.

Crocker's blueprint for the Vermont & Massachusetts carried it westward from Fitchburg to Grout's Corner (now Miller's Falls), eight miles east of Greenfield, then turned it at a right angle northward up the Connecticut River to Brattleboro. A branch was to be extended to Greenfield—a branch which eventually became a part of a busy main line. All this planning aroused Northampton, farther down the Connecticut, which clearly saw itself being left high, dry and railless, halfway between two east-west trunk lines. A mass meeting in Brattleboro in December, 1843, to boost the Vermont & Massachusetts, was followed three weeks later by one in Northampton, where the scheme of a Northampton & Springfield Railroad was given a good start. The town also hailed joyfully the news of a convention in Windsor, Vermont, to plan a railroad up the valley of the Connecticut and Passumpsic Rivers. Northampton citizens attended, and in fact, helped to promote a meeting at Greenfield on January 2, only a few days after their own booster gathering. There they told Greenfield folk that the Fitchburg track to their town would never be anything but a branch, and it was important for them to be located on a great north-and-south line along the Connecticut, extending from Canada to Long Island Sound.

Greenfield for a time held back, waiting to see what the Vermont & Massachusetts would do for them, but when they became convinced that it would give them nothing but a branch, they plumped wholeheartedly for a railroad to Northampton, and its charter was granted in January, 1845. The Northampton & Springfield was already well under way and was open in December of that year; the Greenfield & Northampton was ready eleven months later. Even before completion, it was merged with the Northampton & Springfield to form the Connecticut River Railroad. But the promoters were not yet satisfied: they wanted to reach the Vermont border, for possible contact with that talked of railroad coming down from the Passumpsic. They accordingly raised some more money and laid track to South Vernon, on the edge of Vermont, which was reached on January 1, 1849.

For several years the Fitchburg and the Vermont & Massachusetts had the same president, yet operated quite independently; though, lying end to end as they did, they were logically parts of the same line. The Fitchburg had the usual troubles with little "jerkwater" roads built alongside or connecting with it, which it had to take over (usually just what the promoters wanted): the Watertown Branch, the Waltham & Watertown, the Lexington & West Cambridge, the Lancaster & Sterling—these were some of them. It fostered another, the Peterboro & Shirley, leaving its main line at Groton Junction (now Ayer) and heading northwest toward Peterboro, N. H. But the company soon wished itself well rid of all offshoots. When it passed its dividend in 1854, for the first time in its history, the directors attributed it to "one of the most remarkable years for railroad depression ever known," but listed its branches under the heading, "Business not deemed remunerative"; and in the following year's report, they said peevishly that in their opinion the Boston railroads would all be better off if every branch was discontinued and torn up by the roots.

The two sister railroads also had their troubles with other minor promotions. There was the Fitchburg & Worcester, for example, which, when completed, advertised itself as a through line from Fitchburg to Boston via the Boston & Worcester, though this really meant a pretty considerable detour. It made a strong bid for traffic from the Vermont & Massachusetts, which, however, naturally preferred to give its business to Crocker's other road, the Fitchburg. According to the V. & M. directors in 1856, the Fitchburg & Worcester resorted to "impositions and tricks" to gain its ends, but to no avail. In the case of the Fitchburg, as reported by the directors that same year, its tactics were much rougher. "Certain employees of the Fitchburg & Worcester became insolent, uproarious, and riotous . . . invading the [Fitchburg] cars to persuade the passengers to leave them." Remonstrance with these fellows did no good; they were ordered out, but when they refused to go, "we were obliged to order them removed to the station house, which was done by the gentlest possible means. Finally, a huge porter, who received the name of a 'bully' among the people of the neighborhood, was sent into our passenger house to browbeat and overawe our men, and to shout with his stentorian lungs and call people from our cars to those of the road he represented. These measures made absolutely necessary to direct the riotous individual to be kept off the premises of the Fitchburg Company until he could deport himself accordingly."

It was long before this that the ideas of Crocker and his brother directors had begun to expand. West of them the Troy & Greenfield Railroad had been chartered in 1848, with the idea of connecting Troy, N. Y. (and thereby the New York railroad and canal systems), with Greenfield, Mass., through a tunnel under the Hoosac Mountain range. The charter specified that the road was to be located and completed in seven years—an absurdity, to begin with. Manifestly, such a railroad could not be built without a large stock sale, and that did not materialize. Troy & Greenfield representatives were seen in the State House lobbies in Boston

every few months. In 1849 they obtained permission to relocate the road, and in 1850 the time for changing the location was extended. In 1851 they began grading in a small
way, just to give them an excuse for asking for a state loan.
It was refused, and they tried again two years later with the
same result.

In 1854 the directors, headed by President Hitchcock, were
on Beacon Hill again, begging for state aid. "I do not think
there will be any masonry or arching required," said Hitchcock, speaking of the tunnel. "I do not believe it would require any more masonry for its support than would be necessary for a good, sound stick of timber with an auger-hole
bored through it." Someone had figured for him that the
tunnel could be completed in 1556 days. How calamitously
wrong he was! The truth of the matter is that not a soul
then living had the faintest idea of the magnitude of the task
of boring the tunnel. Every "estimate," every utterance
about it was almost as much of a guess as our own about the
inhabitants (if any) of the planet Mars.

But Mr. Hitchcock's plea softened the legislative heart
slightly, and a $2,000,000 loan was granted, specifically "to
construct the Hoosac Tunnel." The conditions, however,
were hard. The company must sell $600,000 worth of stock
and actually collect 20 per cent of that amount in cash; must
have seven miles of track built and 1000 linear feet of the
tunnel "completed" before the first $100,000 in scrip would
be handed over. And so it must continue, stock collections
keeping pace with payments of scrip, the last $200,000 to be
held up "until the company have opened said railroad for use
through the Hoosac, and laid a continuous railroad from
Greenfield to the line of the State in Williamstown."

In 1855 certain towns were authorized to subscribe for
stock of the company, and a little more money dribbled in.
In the following year, finding that it couldn't raise the required $600,000, the company, with a nerve that had in it
something of the sublime, petitioned the state to subscribe
for $150,000 worth of stock, so that it might be enabled to

draw the first installment of scrip! It was pathetic, too, for of course the move was simply one of desperation—and it, too, met with refusal.

The company had already made a contract with E. W. Serrell & Company to bore the tunnel, but without money Serrell could do nothing, and presently withdrew. A $900,-000 bond issue had found few buyers. The company now began dickering with Herman Haupt, who was destined to become a storm center the like of which New England had never before seen. A West Point graduate, he had been a railroad engineer and a professor in Pennsylvania College at Gettysburg, and in 1856 was employed by the Pennsylvania Railroad. In his *Reminiscences*, published in 1901, is a sketch of his life written by Frank A. Flower, the material for which was undoubtedly supplied by the subject himself. Therein the statement is made regarding his tunnel venture that in 1856 he was asked "to take an interest in the contract for its construction and assist in raising $100,000 as additional capital—a portion of which came from his associates in the Pennsylvania Railroad."

Haupt had every opportunity to know what was public knowledge—the awesome magnitude of the tunnel project and the practically helpless and hopeless condition of the little corporation which had bitten off so much more than it could chew; so he walked into major trouble with his eyes open. How he could induce Pennsylvania Railroad associates to invest in such an enterprise is a mystery. His story goes on to say:

He mortgaged his own large property in Pennsylvania, sold stocks and borrowed money from personal friends, and kept the work going until the financial crash of 1857. At that time, he himself was carrying a floating debt of about $200,000. With the exception of $67,000, he had provided all the capital to carry on the work. Not a dollar had been paid by the company or anybody in Massachusetts.

He adds that three of his partners had failed, and he was forced to take up $20,000 of their discredited paper which had been discounted. "Their failure impaired his hitherto gilt-edge credit."

By 1858 he had obtained a contract with the Troy & Greenfield, under the terms of which he agreed to build the road and tunnel for $4,000,000, guessing that the tunnel would cost $2,100,000, "omitting all considerations of interest." As a reward for taking the load off its shoulders (a most dubious reward!), the company transferred to him the entire property of the corporation, with all subscriptions, present and prospective, and agreed that he should collect all the state loans for drilling the tunnel, and in addition, $2,000,000 for building the road (if he could get it). He now owned nearly four-fifths of the Troy & Greenfield stock issue.

The $4,000,000 included a bonus of $300,000 to Haupt for subscribing to $600,000 worth of stock. Frank W. Bird, an implacable enemy of the tunnel who wrote several pamphlets on it, charged in 1862 that Haupt's subscription was bogus, that he pretended to pay for it in "work," and that by means of it he managed to get two or three hundred thousand in scrip out of the state. Haupt flatly denies this. At this distance in time, it is impossible to assay with certainty all statements made in the twenty years' bickering that went on over this, the most controversial enterprise ever launched in New England, the one which caused the most bitter feeling, name-calling, litigation, political jobbery, pamphleteering—why, for years the air of the state was beclouded with a snowstorm of pamphlets. Bird was accused of being a propagandist for the Western Railroad: he seems to have been the one who first nicknamed the tunnel the "Great Bore." He need not have been a hired agent, for he was a large paper manufacturer at Walpole, and well-to-do. The fact of the matter is that Massachusetts had become divided into two parties, one favoring the tunnel, the other violently opposed to state aid for it, as ruinous to the public credit and a mere pouring of the people's money into a bottomless pit. Naturally, the Western Railroad lost no opportunity of keeping the acrimony of the latter faction at fever heat.

There were both right and wrong on each side. Haupt

was highly vulnerable, and though some of Bird's statements about him have been proved false or exaggerated, others cannot be controverted. He built the eastern section of the railroad, from Greenfield up the Deerfield River to the tunnel entrance, and it cannot be denied that the bridge he erected over the river at Greenfield promptly fell when some loaded cars were pushed out on it for a test, killing one man and injuring two others. It could not be denied that the first bore he started on the east side was abandoned and another hole started a few yards to the right of it. (You may see the old entrance in one of the pictures.) Also, it was revealed that Haupt was cheapening the job. As planned when the original loan was granted, the tunnel was to be 20½ feet high and 22 feet wide at the base, the walls flaring slightly for greater strength until they were 24 feet apart before they curved inward. Haupt was building the walls perpendicularly until the spring of the arch was reached, and he was making the tunnel only 14 feet wide and 18 feet high—this to accommodate a double-track railroad! Under the original plan, 15 cubic yards of rock per lineal foot of tunnel would have been removed; Haupt was taking out only 8½ cubic feet.

Biographer Flower admits that Haupt had much to do with writing the Act of 1860, by which most of the original safeguards were jettisoned. The $600,000 stock subscription and cash-in-hand requirements were abandoned, and so was the provision for a sinking fund; and finally, delivery of scrip was promised at the rate of fifty dollars for every lineal foot of tunnel bored. But Flower says that Haupt could not have pulled through had not a friend in Philadelphia, a Pennsylvania Railroad director, "unsolicited and without security," placed $30,000 to Haupt's credit and enabled him to complete sufficient work to entitle him to $100,000 in scrip. The Executive Council approved the work done so far and ordered delivery of the scrip. But just at that moment, in 1861, Governor N. P. Banks went out of office and John A. Andrew came in. Banks, though favorable to Haupt, so Flower's story goes, through pure inadvertence forgot to sign the order for payment; and when Governor Andrew, who was an anti-tunnel man, at least as far as Haupt was concerned, was seated, he refused to sign it. Haupt thus contradicts Bird's story that he received $200,000 or $300,000 in scrip. Just how much he did receive is a matter of dispute.

Haupt's narrator goes on to say that Andrew expressed a lack of confidence in the State Engineer, asked him to resign and appointed one Whitwell in his place. Flower asserts that the Western Railroad officials had suggested his name and that he spent a day or two at Springfield, getting his orders, before he assumed office. He inspected the work at the tunnel and refused to approve it or sanction further payments. A long hearing was held before a legislative committee, at which several noted experts supported Whitwell; nevertheless, the Legislature voted to make payments to Haupt's company according to the Act of 1860, at fifty dollars per lineal foot.

This brought forth Bird's pamphlet, *The Road to Ruin*, in which he alleged that the actual cost of the work so far had been $768,250 and that Haupt had received $925,389 in scrip, giving him a net profit of $157,139, to say nothing of $125,500 paid by towns along the line. He said the Troy & Greenfield Railroad was practically mythical; it was all Haupt. He showed—and these figures were uncontested— that Alvah Crocker, who now popped up as president of the T. & G., owned only 15 shares; that Haupt owned 5987 shares and all others only 1679 shares. These latter, said Bird, were the only bona fide stockholders, the only ones who had ever paid a dollar on their stock; and in another pamphlet in 1866 he claimed that even they had paid in only $7430, of which $1800 was for "services"—at which he jeered. He wrote a little playlet in which the characters were W. T. Davis, treasurer; H. Haupt, stockholder; H. Haupt, contractor; H. Haupt, engineer; H. Haupt, director; a bank teller and a clerk. The report of Haupt the contractor was OK'd by Haupt the engineer, and Haupt the director then authorized payment to Haupt the contractor, etc.

But though the legislative committee authorized payment of $150,000 to Haupt and a bill was passed by the Legislature to that effect, the governor said he would veto it unless the work was taken out of Haupt's hands. He now suggested that the work be put under state commissioners, and that is what was done, the state actually taking over railroad and tunnel. Andrew, the relentless foe of Haupt, refused to permit the payment of another dollar to him, and for twenty years thereafter Haupt fought for what he claimed was due him. He had left his mark on the job; he had driven the two headings 2400 and 610 feet respectively into the mountain, had sunk the west or minor shaft 325 feet to grade and tunneled 56 feet from it. Leaving Massachusetts, he went directly into the Army of the Potomac, where he made an excellent record as a builder of military railroads and bridges and earned the rank of Brigadier General.

The state was now committed to the building of the tunnel on its own. It promptly (1863) leased that portion of the Troy & Greenfield which lay east of the tunnel to the Vermont & Massachusetts and Fitchburg Railroads at a rental of $30,000 a year—a bald holdup by the state, for the road was not even completed until five years later, and when complete, was worth little to the lessees, save as insurance, until the tunnel was ready. But some talk had been heard of a Massachusetts Central Railroad, an east-west line which would split the territory between the V. & M. and the Western, and though it was wholly unnecessary, a mere nuisance promotion, it must be guarded against.

Meanwhile, three tunnel commissioners had been appointed —John W. Brooks, Samuel M. Felton, eminent engineer and then president of the Philadelphia, Wilmington & Baltimore Railroad, and Alexander Holmes, president of the Old Colony. It was Brooks who did the work; Felton and Holmes were busy men who had no time for the tunnel. We have met Brooks long ago as a youngster working on the Boston & Maine, but he had since distinguished himself as chief promoter and builder of the Michigan Central and other roads. His taking personal charge of the tunnel work meant that something would be doing, for he was a high-pressure executive.

Bird immediately turned his fire on Brooks: he was against anybody who was trying to build the tunnel. "Insolent and domineering," "plausible," "incapable of liberal and comprehensive policies," this was his description of Brooks; to which the pro-tunnel men retorted with still more colorful adjectives about Bird. The sneers about President Crocker's fifteen shares were answered with the assertion that Crocker had put thousands into the work out of his own pocket and said nothing about it.

When the state appointed an engineer, Laurie, to do the technical work, Brooks sent him packing—this is Bird's version. Brooks had his own engineer, Doane, and they soon began driving the great central shaft, 1028 feet deep, and enlarging to the originally specified size the sections already bored. At first they used the crude drilling machine employed by Haupt; but on the Mont Cenis Tunnel, then being constructed under the Alps, compressed air drilling had been introduced, and Brooks and Doane took it up. Here, through ignorance of a new device, they made their most serious mistake by damming the Deerfield River near the tunnel, in the hope that it would supply the power necessary to drive the pneumatic drills, not only in the east entry, but in the central shaft, high up on the mountain. But this was a great disappointment: it did not supply enough power even for the east entry.

A still more disheartening trouble was encountered in the west entry—"demoralized rock," they called it, which, when exposed to air or water, crumbled and flowed like quicksand. That increased costs enormously. But in 1866 George H. Mowbray began supplying his "trinitro-glycerine" as a blasting agent, and in the same year, electric firing of blasts was introduced. Nevertheless, the failure of the Deerfield dam, the ceaseless attacks of the anti-tunnel faction, whose chief mouthpiece was Bird, and the undeniably high costs under Brooks' direction, due to one thing and another, impaired the latter's usefulness. He resigned in 1866, giving ill health as the reason, and a new commission was appointed by the governor, with none other than Alvah Crocker at the head of it. The tunnel was steadily becoming a more important objective to Crocker's railroads.

The new chairman decided to let the work to contractors, and the firm of Dull & Gowan were given the task in the spring of 1867, but within a year he forced the annulment of the contract. James M. Shute, one of the commissioners serving with Crocker, now resigned, and of course published a pamphlet. [1] He characterized Crocker as "blundering, untruthful, covetous," and by implication, even worse. He declared that he had heard Governor Bullock say, in apology for appointing him, "Crocker has built two railroads by lying, and I thought he might lie the tunnel through." Among other things, he charged that two good types of pneumatic drill, one of them developed by the state at a cost of $50,000, had been pushed aside in favor of an inferior patent, bought up by "parties in Fitchburg," and then owned by a corporation, in which Crocker as well as two legislative committeemen were interested. His statements were found hard to contradict.

With that, the state ceased trying to manage the task itself. A little more than 9000 feet of tunnel had been bored, leaving 15,693 feet yet to do. The state now decided to take Engineer Latrobe's advice and let the work by contract, provided it could be completed within seven years and at a cost of no more than $5,000,000. Bird tossed off another pamphlet, *The Last Agony of the Great Bore*, called forth by the fact that the Legislature, at the behest of "the Ring," as the anti-tunnelites called the tunnel advocates, had just appropriated $5,250,000, plus $350,000 for annual interest on past expenditures, "to be sunk in that all-devouring maelstrom." Bird paraphrased Oliver Wendell Holmes:

[1] *Rejected Papers in Relation to the Hoosac Tunnel*, Boston, 1868.

When "lobbyists" no longer steal,
  And pay for what they stole before,
When the first locomotive wheel
  Rolls through the Hoosac Tunnel's bore,

Till then let Cummings blaze away
  And Miller's friends blow up the globe;
But when you see that blessed day,
  Then order your ascension robe.

Whereupon a counterblast called *Death of our Minotaur* ("Bird and his ring" being the Minotaur) came from an anonym calling himself Theseus, apparently because he believed that with that pamphlet he had slain the Minotaur.

Walter and Francis Shanly, Canadians, won the contract to complete the tunnel and proved to be the answer to the whole problem. They systematized everything, installed an elevator (then a novelty: you probably could have counted on the fingers of one hand all the elevators in America) in the big central shaft, and spent $90,000 for a pump to lift water out of that shaft, where it gathered at the rate of 1000 gallons a minute. Among their hard-rock men were Germans, Irish, Danes, French Canadians, Cornishmen and a sprinkling of Piedmontese and Savoyards who had worked on the Mont Cenis Tunnel. Through strikes, political quarrels and jockeying, the Shanlys toiled ahead imperturbably. Professor Mowbray, who had settled down in North Adams, near the west portal, to spend the rest of his life, continued to supply his trinitro-glycerine for blasting (500,000 pounds of it, all told) from a shack which was the terror of the countryside.

And finally, on Thanksgiving Day, November 27, 1874, at a distance of 10,134 feet from the west portal, the headings met in the presence of a large audience of legislators and railroad officials. Presumably Mr. Bird was not among them. It was not until the following February 9 that the first train, a string of work cars, passed through, and not until autumn, October 13, 1875, that the first passenger train bore a few dozen thrilled, half-frightened riders through the dark passage on its way from Boston to Troy. The Great Bore was a completed actuality, and we cannot find that anyone ordered an ascension robe. Somehow, Massachusetts had muddled through to the accomplishment of the greatest engineering feat, the longest tunnel that had been constructed on the American continent up to that time. [2] The "antis" were beaten, but they found a keen relish in pointing to the cost of the job—195 lives, and nobody, living or dead, knows how much money, but somewhere from $17,000,000 to $20,000,000, probably much nearer the latter figure. It was a fearfully expensive achievement—and who was going to use it? The time has come to consider that.

From North Adams, at the west portal, the only feasible railroad route followed the gulch of the Hoosick (Hoosac) River past Williamstown to the Vermont line and crossed a tiny corner of Vermont into New York. The Troy & Boston Railroad, a New York corporation, was opened in 1859 from Troy up the Hoosick to the state line. Of course there must be a separate corporation, the Southern Vermont, for that little stretch of some seven miles across the corner of the state named. The Troy & Boston leased this for $12,000 a year, plus that portion of the Troy & Greenfield from the Vermont line to North Adams, also the Troy & Bennington and the Western Vermont, extending north from Bennington to Rutland through a region rich in iron, marble and other minerals.

The T. & B. had no little trouble with its flock of leases.

[2] The tunnel is 25,081 feet—about 4¾ miles—in length. The mountain under which it passes is a double ridge, the western crest being 1718 feet above the tunnel floor, the eastern 1420 feet. From the bowels of the mountain about 600 gallons of water per minute are discharged at the western entrance, 100 at the eastern. The central shaft between the ridge-crests, a great perpendicular tunnel, 15 by 27 feet in dimensions and 1028 feet deep, was long used for ventilation. As the traffic through the tunnel became heavier during its first quarter-century, smoke and gases in hot weather finally made it impossible for trackmen to work inside, and in 1899 ventilating machinery, including a 16-foot fan, was installed in the building over the shaft. Trains now operate electrically through the tunnel.

The Western Vermont trustees in bankruptcy eventually sold the road to the Bennington & Rutland. There was some difficulty with this concern, and after a time it developed that J. Gregory Smith, mogul of the Vermont Central and the slickest of Vermont railroad manipulators—which is putting it strongly—was to become the lessee of the B. & R. at the expiration of the Troy & Boston's nine-year lease. Smith requested that the T. & B. leave its equipment on the road, as he lacked enough at the moment to operate it. The T. & B. courteously agreed, but were stunned one morning to learn by telegraph that seven locomotives, ten passenger cars and sixty-five freight cars had been seized under attachment for alleged damage to the road—meaning a lack of necessary repairs. It was still more annoying to learn that the T. & B.'s manager for the Vermont division had been in the pay of Smith and had been busy getting as many cars as possible into Vermont to be grabbed. The T. & B. had to settle by giving up its Western Vermont lease immediately.

But it still controlled, by ownership and lease, its line from Troy to the tunnel, and as work on the big bore neared its end, the T. & B. joined with the Vermont & Massachusetts in asking the Massachusetts Legislature for permission to consolidate these two with the Fitchburg and the Troy & Greenfield in a through line from Boston to Troy. (The V. & M. now considered its track from Grout's Corner to Brattleboro—once a main line—a branch, had lost interest in it and turned it over to the Rutland Railroad.) But the Fitchburg directors were unwilling to go into an amalgamation with the "foreign" Troy & Boston, "dilapidated and infirm"—and notoriously unethical, too, though they didn't put that into words.[3] The Fitchburg management for some

---

[3] The Troy & Greenfield, too, was an object of contempt. Colonel John H. George, attorney for the Boston & Lowell, addressing the State Railroad Commission in 1873, called it "the meanest road today within the borders of Massachusetts. . . . A one-horse road—no, sir, not a one-horse road, I have too much respect for the equine race to call it that." He said the road was so crooked that when you rode on it, you frequently had the impression that the engine was about to run into the last car.

time had had in mind a new line from the tunnel northwest
to Oswego, or at least paralleling the New York Central to
the Great Lakes.

The Boston & Lowell was also on Beacon Hill in 1873,
asking for the right to take over the Fitchburg. It was being
blocked, as we shall see, by the New Hampshire Legislature in its ambition to absorb the Concord-Northern route
to Vermont and Canada, and was now seeking an outlet to
westward. But the Fitchburg was rapidly acquiring considerable influence in state councils, and it succeeded in defeating
both petitions, as well as a minority report favoring a state-
owned system. [4] This minority actually wanted a state-
controlled trust with a capital of $54,000,000, to buy and
operate a chain of railroads all the way from Boston to Lake
Ontario. The old specter of state ownership was hard to
down.

The Fitchburg, on June 1, 1874, proceeded to strengthen
its position by leasing for 999 years the Vermont & Massachusetts, which in turn had the Troy & Greenfield east of the
tunnel under lease. It felt some fear of the Massachusetts
Central, which had been incorporated in 1869 and was being
actively promoted westward through the middle of the state.
There was nothing to prevent its building to the Hoosac
and running trains through it, for the state was operating
the tunnel as a toll road. Massachusetts Central salesmen
were using high pressure to induce towns along the line—
Ware, Belchertown, Amherst and others—to subscribe for
blocks of stock. Amherst at a town meeting in 1870 refused to take $100,000 worth, as suggested, and was so ridi-

---

[4] That its influence continued to increase is seen in the speech of Hon.
A. E. Pillsbury before the Railroad Commission twenty-four years later
(1887) in behalf of the revival of the dead charter of a little line projected
in western Massachusetts. Said he: "We are not seeking this charter as a
club with which to beat the Fitchburg Railroad—and by the way, Mr.
Chairman and gentlemen, the humor of that idea is exceedingly rich.
Fancy anybody beating the Fitchburg Road about this State House!
There is not a railroad corporation in Massachusetts that has not felt the
lash of the Fitchburg on its back at some time or other—not one. The
Fitchburg corporation is not in the habit of playing the under dog in any
sort of a fight. . . ."

culed by neighboring towns that some of its embarrassed citizens called another meeting. With the largest attendance ever seen in the town, and with Squire Dickinson, father of the immortal Emily, in the chair, this meeting voted by 369 to 270 to buy the stock. The "antis" claimed that the vote had been juggled, and much acrimony resulted, developing into acute remorse and many I-told-you-so's as time went on.

To conclude the Massachusetts Central's story, construction was begun in a small way in 1872, but after ten years and several millions of dollars had been spent, less than fifty miles had been built, and this was foreclosed on by the bondholders. The Boston & Lowell gave the company some aid, and in 1886, in consideration of $20,000,000 in Massachusetts Central bonds, the B. & L. took a long lease on it, agreeing to complete the tracks to Northampton, which it did in 1887, the same year in which the Boston & Lowell itself passed into the hands of the Boston & Maine.

West of the tunnel another grandiose project, fostered by General William L. Burt, was the Boston, Hoosac Tunnel & Western, which was to run into New York and then fork, one branch going to Oswego, the other to Buffalo and even beyond that; for the general planned to have a line through Canada to Detroit and on to Chicago, beyond which his through cars would continue to the Pacific Coast. But as it turned out, he had all he could do to build a little line from the tunnel to the Mohawk River; beyond that point his survey was later used by the West Shore. The Troy & Boston, whose line he paralleled for most of its course, fought him at every step, but without success. He was less fortunate in 1877 when he went before the Massachusetts Legislature with a plea to let him consolidate a line from Boston to Lake Ontario, beginning with the Fitchburg. He told the legislative committee that, as matters stood, the New York Central controlled the destiny of the tunnel. Said he, "The New York Central can deprive the Troy & Boston of absolutely every pound of freight, just as the Troy & Boston in their turn can deprive the tunnel of every pound of freight and every passenger, just as she is depriving it of a through line today, and you have no redress."

He declared that President Onslow Stearns of the Fitchburg went to William H. Vanderbilt and said, speaking of his road's Pullmans, "You cannot have those cars excluded from running over the Fitchburg Railroad while we are a part of the Hoosac Tunnel Line; the Commonwealth of Massachusetts comes in between."

Whereupon, said Burt, Vanderbilt called in Robinson of the Troy & Boston and asked, "You have got an offer from Pullman & Dixon for a through line to Boston, haven't you?"

"Yes, sir."

"Well, you cannot run their cars over the New York Central, you know."

"Yes, sir, I know that."

"I want you to say to Mr. Pullman, 'You cannot run your cars over the Troy & Boston Railroad, and so you cannot get them to the Tunnel. Now, I want you to contract exclusively with Mr. Wagner for his cars, in which we are interested.' "

So, concluded Burt, the Fitchburg was forced to accept the Central's Wagner sleepers instead of Pullmans.

Thus the Fitchburg, now having arranged both passenger and fast freight service to westward with the New York Central and doing a good business thereby, lost its desire to join hands with the Boston, Hoosac Tunnel & Western, which was a death blow to Burt's hopes. The Legislature rejected his petition, but he built his road on to the Mohawk River, reaching in 1879 a point a few miles northwest of Schenectady at what later came to be Rotterdam Junction; for the tracks of the New York Central's young rival, the New York, West Shore & Buffalo, presently joined it there and continued westward on Burt's old survey.

The Fitchburg now had two connections from the tunnel to the Hudson. But the New York Central turned cold in 1884, discontinued its through passenger and freight lines and forced the Fitchburg to deal with the West Shore. Rather sure of itself now, however, it took over the Boston, Barre & Gardner, giving it a strategic entry into Worcester, and also thrust a tentacle into New Hampshire. And just in case somebody unwanted should barge in, it began making preparations to take over everything west of Greenfield. Burt was scheming with the feeble Central Massachusetts (its name had now been reversed) to form a line from Boston through the tunnel, and while there seemed little danger from that quarter, an unpleasant miracle might happen. Long negotiations with the state were necessary but were finally completed in 1887. In payment for the tunnel and the Troy & Greenfield Railroad, the Fitchburg handed over to the state $5,000,000 in 3 per cent bonds and a new issue of 50,000 shares of common stock—its face value of $100 per share of course making another theoretical total of $5,000,000. But the old stock of the Fitchburg had now all become preferred, with a guaranteed 4 per cent income, and as George Pierce Baker figures it: "With the expectation of a 5 per cent return on the 'preferred' and therefore a 1 per cent return on the common, the common would have been worth hardly more than $1,000,000, making the purchase price of the Hoosac Tunnel and its approaching lines a scant $6,000,000." [5] On the books, the state had suffered a heavy loss, but the tunnel has been worth its cost to the commonwealth.

In that year, 1887, the Fitchburg also gathered in the Troy & Boston and obtained stock control of the Boston, Hoosac Tunnel & Western, although actual absorption of the latter did not take place until 1892. A fear that it would fall into other hands was evident toward the last, for the Fitchburg paid rather dearly for it. Along with it came the Continental Construction Company, which had been created for the purpose of building the Burt lines to Lake

[5] *The Formation of the New England Railroad Systems*, p. 193. Cambridge, 1937.

Ontario and elsewhere. But this concern never meant anything to the buyer: its control was just a somewhat expensive bit of insurance.

The Fitchburg was now running through Pullmans and freight via Rotterdam Junction and the West Shore to Buffalo, and thence via the Nickel Plate and Wabash to Chicago and St. Louis. As the 1890's wore on, it became evident that a union between the New York Central and the Boston & Albany was drawing near. The Vanderbilts would have liked to control the Fitchburg also, but felt sure that the State of Massachusetts would not permit them to take over both competing lines. This approaching consolidation, however, was a threat to the Fitchburg. Its position had weaknesses. Its prosperity leaned heavily on the Boston & Maine, which gave it much business but could just as easily turn most of it over to the B. & A.–New York Central. While they were in conversation on this subject, President Lucius Tuttle of the Boston & Maine suggested to President Codman of the Fitchburg that the latter road be leased to the B. & M.

It seemed to be a good idea, but when submitted to the Fitchburg directors, they voted 7 to 6 against it. They agreed unanimously, however, to leave it to the stockholders, and the latter voted yes. Accordingly, in July, 1900, the Fitchburg passed under the control of the Boston & Maine, and another of the famous names in New England rail history passed out of existence.

A note about the tunnel remains to be added. As locomotives and automobile-carrying freight cars increased in size, the tunnel became too small for some of them, and many freight trains had to be detoured through Vermont, with a loss of several hours' time and with much extra trouble and expense. According, in 1926-27, without interfering with traffic, the bore was enlarged, by dropping the floor in some places and changing the curve of the arch in others, so that today any engine or car in existence may pass through it.

# 12

## The Forty Years' War in Vermont

IF YOU count recharterings, a dozen railroads were born—
some of them still-born—in Vermont before ever a rail
was laid. The Rutland & Whitehall in 1831 was the
pioneer; it was authorized again in 1836, along with a supporting bank, neither of which materialized. A Vermont Railroad chartered in 1832 also got nowhere. Of a proposed
railroad to connect the Connecticut River at Brattleboro
with the Hudson at Troy, a local editor said, "There is now
a capital M'Adam road making from Troy to Bennington,
and this might serve, we should think, to lay rails on, without interfering with the ordinary travel." Of course he was
thinking of horse traction "Then," he added, "with a
stationary [*sic*] power to pass the Green Mountains at
Bennington, the route might, we should think, be found
practicable." [1]

Not to mention several other projects, in 1835 the Vermont Central, the Rutland and the Connecticut & Passumpsic Rivers all received their papers, but couldn't get going
until eight years later. These early efforts were premature.
Wealthy Boston, where most of the money came from, was
only just getting her own first three railroads under way,
and most of New England still regarded the whole business

[1] As an example of the wild dreams of some early promoters, there was
the "Boston & Ogdensburg" scheme, a rhapsody of 1837. It was planned
to make it a covered road all the way across Vermont, and even farther,
so that it would never be stopped by snow. As to Lake Champlain, they
couldn't decide whether to have the trains hauled across the ice by horses
in winter, or to keep a channel cut in the ice and ferry across!

as somewhat of a hazardous experiment. There were few capitalists in Vermont, and Boston would risk no investment in that thinly populated area, where towering mountains would make a railroad a costly undertaking.

And so matters drifted along, with some new project stirring the air at times, until 1843, when the three future greats of Vermont were again chartered. A new force had now entered the lists—native-born Charles Paine (1799–1853), a successful manufacturer who had served in the Legislature and been governor in 1841–42. He, too, cherished the thought of a great northwest-southeast trunk line between Boston and Canada, the Great Lakes and Chicago—the Ogdensburg dream which beset New England promoters through two generations. The course of his railroad was vaguely defined in the charter as "from some point on the eastern shore of Lake Champlain, thence up the valley of the Onion River," to a point on the Connecticut River "most convenient to meet a railroad either from Concord, N. H., or Fitchburg, Massachusetts." The charter didn't mention it, but most important of all, that railroad must pass through Paine's highland village of Northfield, where he owned the woolen mill as well as other property handed over to him by his aging father, Judge Elijah Paine—for judges were very often in business, too.

Simultaneously, another group in Burlington, on the shore of Lake Champlain, launched a rival project. The leader there was Judge Timothy Follett, largely interested in the carrying trade on the lake, which had become a great business since the invention of the steamboat. In October, 1843, the same month in which Paine's road was authorized, a charter was granted for the Champlain & Connecticut River Railroad, which changed its name three years later to Rutland & Burlington. Again the Northwest Passage was the idea—a line from Burlington, veering inland through Rutland and so down to the Connecticut River at Bellows Falls, whence the Cheshire and Fitchburg Railroads would give it entrance to Boston. Burlington was more than half way down the lake toward Canada, and so would not interfere

greatly with the steamboat carrying trade but would be
a logical continuation of the lake route from Canada to
Boston.

And in the same year the Connecticut & Passumpsic Rivers
was chartered again, with the ambitious intent of following
the two streams mentioned in its name from the Massachusetts line to the Canadian border.

Paine, who was not interested in steamboats, had an ace
up his sleeve for his Burlington opponents—that of paralleling
the lower lake with rails all the way to Canada. He said
nothing of that at the moment, but began his promotion work
with a whoop. At a railroad convention held in Montpelier,
January 8, 1844, with Hon. Charles Paine presiding and
several other Hons. and Gens. as vice-presidents and secre-
taries, enthusiasm ran so high that one man, James R. Lang
don of Montpelier, advanced $10,000 for the purpose of
making surveys from lake to river, and they were made that
season by Samuel M. Felton, well-known engineer. But the
stock-selling moved slowly; the company was not organized
until July, 1845, and the first spadeful of earth was turned
in December of that year on the farm of Paine's father. Only
$500,000 worth of the $1,000,000 authorized stock had been
sold in Vermont, with $200,000 of that in Montpelier.

Paine temporarily blocked the Burlington group that year
by making a secret agreement with the Cheshire and Fitchburg directors for an exclusive line to Boston. The Vermont
Central was not to connect with the Northern Railroad
without the consent of the Fitchburg, while the Fitchburg
should not in any manner aid or countenance the construction of the Rutland & Burlington without the consent of
the directors of the Vermont Central. President Follett said
in delicate and mournful reproach that the Rutland Road
had been "neglected and discarded by those who were expected to have nurtured and cherished it." Nevertheless,
there were those in the Fitchburg management who wanted
to see the Rutland line built and did not fully trust Paine
to come down to them with his track, rather than cut across
to a nearer and easier junction with the Northern Railroad

of New Hampshire. This suspicion grew upon the board, until they decided that they had made a mistake. In October, 1846, they annulled the agreement with the Vermont Central, leaving that company free to connect with the Northern, while the Fitchburg now considered itself at liberty to "aid and countenance and subscribe towards the construction of the Rutland Railroad (so called)," if it chose. Paine promptly agreed to the cancellation, seeing that it would be easier, anyhow, finances being what they were, to connect with the Northern at White River Junction on the Connecticut. Fitchburg stockholders now subscribed liberally to the Rutland & Burlington, and its construction began.

Meanwhile, Paine was pursuing his usual smart course. Instead of using a more direct and easier grade farther east, he was carrying the road through his hilltop village of Northfield, where he had already added to his large real estate holdings, so that he might have plenty of land to sell when the railroad boomed the town. From Northfield, the road, coming by steep grades down a narrow gulch, struck the Winooski or Onion River a mile or more west of Montpelier, leaving the capital city to be reached by a short branch. When this dawned upon the population of that place, there was great indignation: Montpelier directors resigned and many citizens there repudiated their stock subscriptions. But Paine's course was unchanged. He installed the repair shops of the railroad at Northfield—on land which he sold to the company at a good price, and with water power supplied by him—and he made Northfield a division point and overnight stopping-place for trains.

On June 20, 1849, his road was complete from White River Junction to Burlington, and the first train to operate in the State of Vermont, drawn by one of the gorgeous, green-and-gold, brass-hooped, red-wheeled locomotives which the V. C. thereafter affected, trundled gingerly over it to the lake shore—although even after that, the superintendent reported that much of the track was not yet at final grade but would have to be raised from six inches to two feet, and that even more of it was not yet ballasted. In 1853 the directors admitted that the ties had "depreciated with great rapidity," and that the bridges were "originally weak in their truss arrangements," but had been repaired and strengthened. Notwithstanding this, Paine, several months before the road's opening, had written to Matthias Baldwin, the locomotive builder, that he would give $10,000 for an engine that would do sixty miles an hour with a passenger train. Baldwin obliged with a twenty-five-ton job having a boiler larger and longer than usual, to supply the extra steam, a single pair of driving wheels, and the cylinder moved back to the waist of the boiler instead of being at the smoke-box. Its name was "Governor Paine," of course, and it is asserted that an engineer once took his life in his hands and ran a mile in forty-three seconds with it, or at the rate of eighty-three miles per hour. How he dared do it on that track one cannot imagine.

Simultaneously with the V. C.'s formal organization in 1845, its concomitant, its twin soul, the Vermont & Canada, was being chartered, to carry the line on to the Canadian border and the Ogdensburg connection. But here, among the subscribers and promoters of the new company, Paine encountered a group of Tartars—the well-known Smith family, plus Lawrence Brainerd, all of St. Albans, with none other than John Smith himself as the ringleader. To judge from the portraits of him that have come down to us, old John might have been the one who sat as a model for the Great Stone Face in the White Mountains. These simple villagers of St. Albans, who might never have ridden on a railroad train up to that time, could give Paine lessons in railroad promotion and strategy, and they did.

And so began the forty years' war in Vermont. The first move was made by Judge Follett of the Rutland & Burlington, who planted a secret agent in the enemy territory to buy up stock subscriptions to the Vermont & Canada, which the R. & B. regarded as a menace. But if the Judge expected to catch Messrs. Smith and Brainerd asleep, he was mistaken. The trick was discovered, and the state voided the subscriptions so purchased, because it was done "in a clandestine manner."

The charter of the Vermont & Canada mentioned as its northern terminus the town of Highgate, which bordered the Canadian boundary and the lower neck of Lake Champlain. From there it was to run south through St. Albans "to some point or points in Chittenden County" most convenient for meeting both the Vermont Central and the road later known as the Rutland & Burlington, then both just past the chartering stage. It was also to have the right to cross a bit of shallow water to South Hero Island in Lake Champlain, in order to reach a point most convenient for ferrying to Plattsburg, New York, for this had at first been mentioned as the eastern terminus of the Ogdensburg Railroad.

John Smith was elected first president of the road, and a brass plate bearing the word "Smith" might as well have been affixed to the presidential chair, for the family took a permanent lease on that post. Lawrence Brainerd was elected clerk. These two supplied most of the money for building the road, and they ran the company. They even moved St. Albans, county seat and all, three miles inland from the lake to a place where they owned a large area of cheap real estate, and there the company's headquarters and shops were located. At the south end of their line, they violated their charter by failing to enter Burlington and connect with the Rutland; instead, to spite the Rutland, they made connection with the Central at a point several miles east of Burlington, which was christened Essex Junction and which became notorious for its bleak waiting rooms and poor connections. Edward J. Phelps, a prominent Vermont attorney, sometime professor in the Yale School of Law and Minister to England under Cleveland, 1885–89, once boarded a "shuttle" train at Burlington, bound for Boston. Dismounting at Essex Junction, he waited dismally for the main line train. After much switching and shunting had taken place, he stepped aboard what he thought was the Boston train and in a few minutes found himself back in Burlington. He then wrote "The Lay of the Lost Traveler," one stanza of which ran:

With saddened face and battered hat
  And eye that told of black despair,
On wooden bench the traveler sat,
  Cursing the fate that brought him there.
"Nine hours," he cried, "we've lingered here,
  With thought intent on distant homes,
Waiting for that elusive train
  Which, always coming, never comes;
    Till, weary, worn,
    Distressed, forlorn,
And paralyzed in every function,
    I hope in hell
    Their souls may dwell
Who first invented Essex Junction!"

The Rutland & Burlington was doing nicely since some of the Fitchburg folk had taken an interest in it. As proof of this, the directors' report of January 12, 1848, shows that although building was going forward steadily, all bills were being paid regularly and there was $116,417 more in the treasury than was immediately needed. "Cash has accumulated beyond our immediate wants," the report said, "and to prevent any loss of interest, the Directors have loaned it in Boston from time to time with ample security"—which, with the possible exception of the plutocratic Boston & Lowell, must be a picture unique in the history of early American railroading. They were preparing for business in a big way: they had ordered 12 locomotives from Taunton and 238 cars. Still there was much delinquency among country subscribers. Follett admitted with "mortification" in 1849 that nearly all the balance due on subscriptions was from persons living along the line of the road. "Our friends, the city stockholders" were carrying the burden.

The Connecticut & Passumpsic Rivers had also started off well. With Erastus Fairbanks, the scale manufacturer of St. Johnsbury, and Addison Gilmore, Massachusetts magnate, as the two chief promoters, the enterprise was given such prestige that its bonds could be sold at par. It gave up the idea of building south of White River Junction, but pushed northward, and in November, 1850, reached St. Johnsbury, sixty-one miles up the river, where it halted for several years. Its coming to St. Johnsbury was a tremendous event, and many ads in the local paper referred to it. There was Aaron Farnham, the enterprising furniture dealer, for example, who not only showed guests "in his spacious ware rooms the most splendid assortment of FURNITURE ever exhibited in Caledonia County," but "will also conduct his friends to the pleasant upper piazza—where they can have a fine view of Depot and the cars as they arrive from the South, and the scenery around."

South of White River Junction the Sullivan County Railroad carried the rails along the Connecticut—most of the way on the New Hampshire shore—to Bellows Falls. From there the twenty-four-mile stretch to Brattleboro was covered by the Vermont Valley, which was put through in 1850–51; and when we find that our old acquaintance, Robert Schuyler, the New York banker, not only was treasurer of the company but built the road as contractor, we do not wonder at its beginning life under a financial handicap. Its condition at the age of two is indicated in the Vermont Central directors' report for 1853, in which, among the resources (!) of the Vermont & Canada, we find two rueful items:

Vermont Valley Railroad Stock, 135 shares, valued at $ .00
Boston & Vermont Telegraph Stock, 120 shares, " " .00

The Northern Railroad of New York (the "Ogdensburg Road") now rescinded its plan of making its eastern terminus at Plattsburg and decided upon Rouse's Point, at the outlet of Lake Champlain and almost on the Canadian border. This necessitated a change of plan on the part of the Vermont & Canada, and the latter came to the Legislature, asking permission to extend to Rouse's Point, bridging on the way the narrow neck of the lake as well as a shallow bay which intervened. This at once aroused the hostility of the other two railroads heading toward Canada, the Rutland & Burlington and the Connecticut & Passumpsic Rivers. The R. & B. was already furious at the Vermont & Canada's refusal to connect with it at Burlington, and it, too, now asked leave to push its line north from Burlington toward Canada. The idea of bridging the lake outlet was ridiculed as impossible—yet the opponents fought it lest it be made possible. The *Vermont Watchman and State Journal*, which favored the bridges, declared that the question was one of vital importance, not only to Vermont and New England but to the nation!

The opposition claimed that the bridge would hinder lake navigation toward Canada. A critic signing himself "Vermont" wrote a letter to the *Watchman* in which he asserted that the project of a ship canal between the foot of Lake Champlain and the St. Lawrence was assured, and this would mean ship navigation through to the Great Lakes, which must not be interfered with. By comparison with the importance of this matter, "questions of drawbridges and railroads . . . are of less consequence than the breath that is wasted in advocating them." To which the editor retorted that the bridge would in no way hinder the canal, and he delivered an uppercut at the navigators: "If you deny the bridge and cut off the Ogdensburg Railroad, you put an end to competition; you give a monopoly of the flour trade to the transportation companies—soulless companies, too, as much as either of your railroads." The real question, he said, "becomes simply this: SHALL THE LEGISLATURE OF VERMONT GO FOR AN *American Railroad* OR A *British Canal?*"

The vested interests battled fiercely in the legislative halls. Lobbyists from all quarters, including the New York side of the lake, swarmed into the Capitol. And finally, in the House, the bridge bill was defeated by 106 to 80. The *Watchman* listed the names of all representatives, how they voted, and what interest influenced them. The totals against the bill were "Rutland interest, 53; Passumpsic interest, 33; Vermont Central, 1 [why he voted wrong is beyond imagining], and unclassified, 19." As against this, the "Central interest" could muster only 42 votes and the Vermont & Canada 11, with 27 others supporting them. The Central had lost the first round, but it won a later one, and the connection to Rouse's Point was eventually built.

As it required money to build these bridges, which the Vermont & Canada didn't have, and as the money market was in bad condition, the Vermont Central took a lease on its sister road in 1849, a lease with a curious provision. The rental was to be 8 per cent on its cost, and if ever the "parent" company failed to pay the rent, the V. & C. would be entitled to take over its parent and operate it until all past due rents should be paid out of earnings. An action stranger still in that year was the appointment of Josiah Quincy, Jr., as treasurer of both companies, with practically unlimited power. His success with the Western Railroad was of course the reason for the choice. At a directors' meeting in August it was voted that Quincy's signature or endorsement as treasurer be binding upon the corporation, that he be authorized to pledge any of the company's bonds or scrip "as security for its debts or liabilities and . . . as security for any debts or liabilities which he shall incur in his private capacity for the use or benefit of the corporation." A little later they enlarged his powers so that he might do almost anything he liked. And in that same last week in August, at a directors' meeting of the Vermont & Canada, at which four directors—note their names: Charles Paine, John Smith, S. S. Lewis and Lawrence Brainerd—were present, it was:

*Ordered*, That the signature or endorsement of Josiah Quincy, Jr., as Treasurer on any notes or drafts, shall be binding on this Corporation, to all intents and purposes.

That such shrewd, tight-fisted men should grant such well-nigh unlimited powers to another seems almost beyond belief. Quincy afterward wrote in his defense that this was "the only condition on which I would remain responsible" for the company's financial affairs—which, by the way, were all to be conducted as nearly as possible in his office in

Boston. Between September 1, 1849, and November, 1850, he received $2,827,000 in Vermont Central bonds as collateral security for liabilities incurred by him in the name of the company. He drew a yearly salary of $5000 and expected to profit by speculation in the company's stocks and bonds. To this end, he subscribed for 10,309 of the 50,000 shares of stock issued in 1850, giving in payment very little cash but more than $309,000 in notes.

By November, 1851, he was no longer able to raise funds, either on his own private notes or on the company's, and certain irregularities had come to light which shocked the business world. He had made extensive use of the company's bonds for his private ends, had sold 1240 shares of stock belonging to the company and had sold 3462 shares which did not yet exist, which was equivalent to an over-issue in that amount. In justification, Quincy asserted that he had been made sole judge of what was best for the company, and that by the directors' act, he had a perfect right to use the name or the securities of the corporation in any manner he deemed advisable. As for the directors' explanation, one of them, Thomas Gray, said later, "The Directors understood so perfectly that we had given absolute power to Mr. Quincy to do what he pleased that we did not feel authorized to step behind his counter to look at the Corporation's books, or to ask what he was doing." Now they managed to obtain title to some property from him to cover part of his defalcation, though their final loss at his hands was figured at $295,205.

The insolvency into which its treasurer was forced ruined the credit of the Vermont Central, and in July, 1852, the trustees under the first mortgage bonds took possession of it. The stockholders now appointed an investigating committee—and high time, too—which uncovered more graft and bad management. S. F. Belknap had been given the contract to build the road upon promise to buy 5000 shares of stock, which he was unable to do. By 1849 he couldn't even pay his laborers and subcontractors, and the latter sued the company "as trustees for Belknap," threatening to discontinue work and forcing the company to cancel the contract. The committee found letters which proved that the directors were aware of Belknap's bad credit and financial condition. The resulting financial tangle was too complicated to explain here, but the committee estimated the company's loss through its relations with Belknap at fully $500,000.

President Paine came in for a scourging, too. He had been flying high at the expense of the company: $5000 a year salary for seven years—more than three times what any other railroad president in Vermont was getting—plus profits on car-building for the company at his shops at Northfield, and etceteras. In 1852 he was paid $43,619 "for incidental claims" over and above his salary, commissions and land damages. Other directors were amply compensated for the sale of securities and arranging of loans. The committee even accused Paine of obtaining company funds from the petty cash account for his private use. As a result of the inquiry, the stockholders overturned his regime in the spring of 1853; Paine was forced out and went immediately to Texas, where he was trying to promote a transcontinental railroad by the southern route when he died of dysentery at Waco a few months later.

All this had, for Vermont stockholders, somewhat clouded the great railroad celebration at Boston in 1851, when President Fillmore, the Canadian Governor-General and other eminences joined in *aves* to the completion of through service between Boston and Montreal—though the traveler had to deal with seven distinct railroads to achieve the journey, two of them being the Vermont Central and the Vermont & Canada. It was in those days that the long, jointed, through ticket was born and began to grow.

With the passing of Paine, the Smith-Brainerd crowd of the Vermont & Canada, through a minority group, gained virtual control. W. Raymond Lee, fresh from the presidency of the Central's hated rival, the Rutland & Burlington, was brought over to head the company, but remained only a year. The Central directors now signed a contract with Smith,

Brainerd & Company (two Brainerds and two sons of John
Smith, named W. C. and J. Gregory Smith, of whom we shall
hear again) for the construction and repair of Vermont Central cars in the shops at St. Albans—which meant the closing
and abandonment of the shops built by Paine at Northfield.
This ground-floor arrangement, with all its unpleasant possibilities, soon gave rise to internal dissensions and prolonged
litigation.

As we get deeper into the records of this era, the complica-
tions become more and more bewildering. The interlocking
of directorates and officials seems wholly incompatible with
the Donnybrook Fair that went on, unless you accept the
dictum that family quarrels are the most vicious of all. Corporations with joint officials are found belaboring each other,
boards of directors fought amongst themselves, contesting
the claims of the first and second mortgage bondholders, each
of which groups in turn fought the other two.

The Cheshire Railroad, which ran from Bellows Falls to
Ashburnham, on the Fitchburg, had, together with the Sullivan Railroad (Bellows Falls to White River Junction), at
first been the Vermont Central's connection with Boston; but
by 1853, when the Northern Railroad (White River Junction
to Concord, N. H.) acquired influence in Green Mountain
affairs—because its president, the ubiquitous Onslow Stearns,
was not only a director but also superintendent of the Vermont Central (and how he took care of it all is beyond us!)—
it is easy to see why Vermont Central–Boston traffic was now
passing over the Northern instead of the Sullivan and Cheshire. The original Cheshire stockholders had also bought
heavily of Vermont Central stock, in order to insure this business, and they were now much disgruntled. An agreement of
1854, defining the situation, shows the mixed condition of affairs. This pact, binding the signatories to exclusive interchange of traffic, was between the Northern of New Hampshire, the Vermont Central and the Northern of New York
(Ogdensburg), with the Sullivan as an unwilling party, a sort
of poor relation who had to come in because a director of the
Vermont Central also spoke for the Sullivan. The chief

signer for the Central, President W. Raymond Lee, also signed for the Northern of New York, while Onslow Stearns signed as president of the Northern of New Hampshire and director of the Vermont Central.

Meanwhile, civil war broke out in the Vermont Central–Vermont & Canada family. The rent-money for the V. & C. was duly paid by the Central trustees until December 1, 1854, when they defaulted on the $54,000 semi-annual installment, whereupon the Vermont & Canada demanded control of the Central property, as specified in the contract of 1849 in case of non-payment of rent. The trustees refused to hand it over, and the V. & C. went to court, which ordered the trustees to deliver the property, and this they did on July 2, 1855.

A violent quarrel was already raging on another sector of the home front. Four of the seven directors of the Vermont & Canada rebelled against the car-building contract with Smith, Brainerd & Company (the other three directors were Smith, Brainerd and one Clark, a local ally). Two of the dissenting directors lived in Boston, and it was not always possible for them to attend suddenly called directors' meetings; so all four "antis," to protect their cause, simply boycotted all board meetings. The minority three, finding themselves unable to have a valid meeting without a quorum, decided to act in their capacity as trustees for the first mortgage bondholders. Accordingly, in May, 1856, they petitioned the Court of Chancery for repossession of the railroad, on the ground that the directors of the V. & C. (including, of course, themselves) had not fulfilled the company's financial obligations, chief of which was the bill for 100 box cars built by Smith, Brainerd & Company. Before the other four directors knew what was happening, the road was back in the hands of the trustees. The four procured an injunction to prohibit the trustees from using the funds of either company to pay the Smith-Brainerd bill. But exactly one week later a Vermont court upset the injunction, and then the majority quartet saw that they could do nothing but compromise. The terms of the settlement were: payment of the bill for the 100 cars, cancellation—upon payment of a $35,000 penalty—

of an additional order for 200 cars, and the taking over of the Smith-Brainerd plant and materials; total cost to the road, $209,658.

And so on and on for twenty-seven years. Receivers were appointed for both roads in 1861. Old John Smith died in 1858 and was succeeded as president of the Vermont & Canada by his son Worthington, who reigned for ten years. Simultaneously, another son, John Gregory Smith, became president of the Vermont Central and held that post for twenty years, meanwhile doing other jobs with unbelievable versatility, as we shall see. During these incumbencies, the Vermont Central expanded rapidly. First, just to show the New Hampshire Northern that it had no monopoly on Boston business, the Central gathered in the Sullivan Railroad. J. G. Smith and his director friend Clark, having pushed the satellite Vermont & Canada to the international border, then built a continuation, the Montreal & Vermont Junction Railroad, on to St. Johns, Quebec, thereby establishing a new through line to Montreal. This new road was now leased to the Vermont Central for a mere 50 per cent of its gross receipts—not a bad bargain for Smith and Clark. Next, they took over the Stanstead, Shefford & Chambly, an unfinished road trending eastward through Quebec from St. Johns, which had been expected to serve as a connection to Montreal for the Connecticut & Passumpsic Rivers, for that road had reached the Canadian border with its track at Newport, Vt., in 1863. But in 1870 the Massanippi Valley Railroad, carrying the line on from Newport to Sherbrooke, Que., was completed and was promptly leased by the Passumpsic, thus giving it an entrance to Montreal via the Grand Trunk.

J. Gregory Smith—who was now swinging the Northern Pacific presidency with one hand and most of the Vermont railroads with the other—achieved still greater strokes in 1870, when, in behalf of the Vermont Central, he leased the Ogdensburg & Lake Champlain (formerly the Northern, of New York) and the Central's chief rival, the Rutland.

The last-named road had never fulfilled the dreams of its builders. In its earlier years its effort to form a through

route to Ogdensburg had been blocked by the refusal of the
Vermont & Canada—in flat violation of its charter—to connect
with it at Burlington.   For years it had to use boats on the
lake between Burlington and Rouse's Point, bringing 22,000
tons of freight that way in 1853; but at last, in 1860, the V. &
C. was forced to give it the connection—which, after all,
didn't seem to benefit it greatly.   In 1853 it was in the hands
of trustees and out again.   In 1863 two trustees for the second
mortgage bondholders took charge.   One of them was John
B. Page, Rutland banker and manufacturer,[2] who was likewise state treasurer at the time.   In 1867 he became governor,
and in one of those startling concatenations common to the
mid-century Vermont social scene, he reorganized the Rutland & Burlington that same year, shortening its name to Rutland, and not only remained as one of its two trustees but was
elected its president, which far-from-empty honor he retained
until 1883.

Page made valiant efforts to give his beleaguered road access to the outer world.   Unable to do anything with the
V. C. group, he had made an agreement with the Rutland &
Washington,[3] which ran from Rutland into New York State,
and its connection, the Rensselaer & Saratoga, for a through
western line.   The Western Vermont (which became the
Bennington & Rutland) and its lessee, the Troy & Boston,
fought this Rutland outlet, but to no avail.

Page and his fellow trustee, Birchard, leased the Vermont
Valley, collecting a handsome fee for doing so and giving
them a southern extension from Bellows Falls to Brattleboro.
At the other end of the road, a boat was built to ply between
Burlington and Plattsburg, whence the Montreal & Plattsburg
(bought by a group of Rutland stockholders) ran northwest

[2] For many years president of the Howe Scale Company.   At that time
Vermont was making nine-tenths of the scales used in America.
[3] The first railroad upon which a young man in his twenties named
Jason (later to be Jay) Gould tried his 'prentice hand.   With savings from
his activities in lumbering and tanning, he had bought its bonds at ten
cents on the dollar and became its president, treasurer, superintendent, its
Poo-Bah.   He sold it at a good profit and rapidly moved on to higher
levels.

# MORGAN'S
## *Newly Invented Rail Road Carriage.*

[*From the American (Boston) Traveller, of April 14th.*]

WE have the pleasure, herewith, of presenting our patrons and the public generally, with such views of Morgan's new Rail Road Carriage, as we hope will not only fully illustrate and explain this improvement in travelling vehicles, but arouse the attention of those who have given the subject of internal improvements but little thought, and silence the opposition of any who may have been disposed to look upon the contemplated Boston and Hudson Rail Road as a mere visionary scheme, or at best, a project to benefit a few interested towns. The ingenious inventor is a resident of Stockbridge, Berkshire Co. and has expended much labor and money to bring his machine to its present state of perfection. Having obtained leave of the city authorities he constructed a temporary rail road in Faneuil Hall, on which his application of friction wheels has been exhibited to very fine advantage. A weight of five pounds suspended over a pulley moved the carriage with its load, the whole weight being 2,850 lbs. —and when upwards of twenty persons in addition were mounted on the carriage, the whole was easily moved by a gentleman standing behind, with one foot. In the absence from town of Mr. Morgan, the carriage at Faneuil Hall is in charge of the new Rail Road Association, whose committee would take pleasure in making those who have not yet seen it, better acquainted with its principles, than they can be from examining a drawing or written explanation.

The engraving above, exhibits what may emphatically be termed a *Land Barge*, and 'to the Traveller will furnish an idea of all the convenience and comfort which belong to the best steam boats. It is constructed with a cabin, births, &c. below; a promenade deck, awning, seats, &c. above. We might as well mention here perhaps, as in another place, that the views are from the graver of our ingenious artist, Mr. Abel Bowen; who, we think, deserves much credit for their tasteful execution.

During the last six months, the Public have been called upon, in various parts of the Union, to witness the application of friction wheels to Railway Cars; and very striking experiments have been exhibited. The principle itself has been long known in Mechanics, its value fully appreciated, and found of essential benefit in the construction of some particular machines. It is, however, the mode of applying it, unincumbered with practical difficulties, to wheel carriages, which is new, and the Railway presents the most rational considerations for attempting its introduction under those circumstances which precluded its successful adoption on common Roads, become entirely changed by the arrangement. To understand, clearly, the nature of the improvement, a distinct idea should be first obtained, of the mechanical advantage gained by providing iron tracks for the wheels. Theoretically, a perfectly true and hard cylinder, rolling on a perfectly hard plane, would have no resistance; and though this is impossible in practice, the Railway approaches so near to it, that in estimating the friction to be overcome, the resistance at the axle of the Car is alone considered. The same carriage, with its load, which requires 125 lbs. to draw it on a common Road, being put on a Railway, needs but 15 lbs.; hence, it is easy to perceive, that as, in the first instance, 110 lb. is employed to overcome the obstruction at the rim, it is better to use all possible means of improving the surface of the road, than to resort to complicated methods for reducing the resistance which employs only 15 lbs. It appears, then, that on the Railway, the case is altered, and as *nearly* all the friction is found at the axle, every simple method to reduce it at that point is worthy of attention. How far the inventors of the several cars, which have come into notice, have succeeded in accomplishing this object, so as to stand the test of practice, will be determined by experience. The principle of compound leverage can be carried, without doubt, to an extent almost incredible, in reducing the resistance from attrition. Practical utility will alone be secured by such arrangement as shall require little complication, and no increased liability to get out of order.

The loading of Morgan's Carriage, is supported on a platform, suspended by iron rods from the upper part of four frames of cast iron, which enclose the wheels. These frames are unconnected with each other, and act independently, following their respective guides, on any curve which the rail assumes. These guides are substituted for the flanche, and by their peculiar arrangement, give much greater security, and less friction. It is optional as to the dimensions of the platform, as each system of wheels can be set at any distance required, or that the Railway will admit of. The whole load being suspended within one inch of the rails, combines, in a remarkable degree, commodiousness, safety and strength. It has been recently suggested, that a degree of comfort, in accommodations for travellers, not heretofore anticipated, may with ease be adopted.

The diagram annexed, together with the view above, will give an interesting idea of the method alluded to, and of the facility afforded by the new car for effecting this purpose. A. A.—*the Cabin.* B. B.—*the Births.* C—*the Wheels.* D:—*Captain's Office.* E.—*the Engine.* F.—*the Rails.*

## FLOOR PLAN OF MORGAN'S RAIL ROAD CARRIAGE.

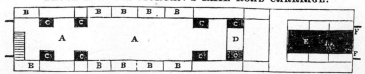

The rapid improvements since the introduction of Locomotive Engines, together with the general introduction of Railways, and the increasing estimation in which they are held, gives new encouragement to pursue, with confidence, those investigations, which shall insure the success of our great Western Railroad. To have asserted a few years ago, that it were possible to travel from Albany to Boston at the rate of 12 or 15 miles an hour, with greater comfort and less danger than we

A MASSACHUSETTS SUGGESTION FOR A SLEEPING CAR, 1829

*Jackson, courtesy Patrick T. Jackson: others from New York Public Library*

## RAIL PIONEERS AND THE FIRST RAILROAD

Gridley Bryant                      Patrick T. Jackson

A car of the Granite Railroad

Nathan Hale                       Thomas B. Wales

*Above*—First train on the Boston & Lowell R. R., 1835.
*Below*—Section of original stone-silled Boston & Lowell track, still preserved
in a park at Lowell.

*Pictures from Walter A. Lucas, Chas. E. Fisher, New York Central R. R., New York Public Library*

George W. Whistler                    William Gibbs McNeill
"Meteor", one of the first Boston & Worcester engines.
"Mud Digger," Western R. R.         "Brookline." Boston & Worcester, 1853

# ORDER OF ARRANGEMENTS

### FOR THE

# CELEBRATION

## AT THE OPENING OF THE

# WESTERN RAIL ROAD,

## AT SPRINGFIELD, OCT. 3, 1839.

A Salute will be fired, and the bells rung at sun-rise.

The Cars will arrive from Boston at 1 o'clock, P. M. A salute will give notice of their approach. Immediately after the arrival of the Cars, a procession will be formed at the Depot, under the direction of Col. H. Chapin, Chief Marshal, and his aids, in the following manner:

1. The Military.
2. The Directors, Engineers, and other officers.
3. The Governor, Lt. Governor, and members of the Council.
4. Members of Congress and of the Legislature.
5. The Clergy.
6. The Committee of Arrangements.
7. Invited Guests.
8. Citizens.

The procession will march down Main Street, and return to the Engine House, where a Dinner will be provided, at 2 o'clock, P. M.

TICKETS, for the Dinner, may be had at the Depot.

As our Public Houses will doubtless be full, persons who have extra beds to spare, are requested to leave their names with Charles A. Mann.

| | |
|---|---|
| GEO. ASHMUN, | E. EDWARDS, |
| HENRY SEYMOUR, | CHAS. STEARNS, |
| GEO. DWIGHT, | WELLS LATHROP, |
| THOS. WARNER, | CHAS. A. MANN, |
| J. W. CROOKS, | S. MERRICK, |

Committee of Arrangements.

George Bliss                                   Chester W. Chapin
*Below*—Handbill announcing opening of Western R. R. to Springfield, 1839.

Boston in 1840: Boston & Providence train in foreground, Boston & Worcester train at left.

Fall River R. R. train at Bridgewater, Mass., 1844. Note ox-drawn convoy of cars at right.

## NEW ENGLAND BRIDGES

1.—Canton viaduct, Boston & Providence. 2.—Boxed-in wooden truss bridge, Hartford & New Haven. 3.—A stone arch by Whistler, Boston & Albany R. R. 4.—Covered wooden bridge still in use, St. Johnsbury & Lake Champlain.

STOCK CERTIFICATES, 1850-75

to connect with the Ogdensburg & Lake Champlain and thus give the Rutland another western outlet. Page had taken over the Rutland & Whitehall, planning a rail line around the south end of the lake for use during the winter months while the boat could not run, when the Vermont Central dealt him a body blow by leasing the Ogdensburg road. Page and the Rutland had become a menace, and Smith decided to block and eliminate them. He suspected that Page was planning to absorb the Vermont & Massachusetts branch from Brattleboro south to a Fitchburg connection, perhaps even take over the New London Northern and have rails all the way to Long Island Sound. The only safe course was to gather them all in himself. So he made an offer to lease the Rutland, and as the latter's trustees were able to push the yearly rental price up to $376,000 for the Rutland alone, not to mention the leased lines, they accepted; it was more than the road could earn otherwise.

The lease was consummated on December 30. Before that time, Governor Smith—oh, yes, he had been governor, according to custom, in 1863–64—had also leased the New London Northern and the Vermont & Massachusetts connection with it.

The former is a railroad that we must pause to notice. New London, once a great whaling port, was the last city of any consequence on the Sound to get a railroad. The New London, Willimantic & Springfield, chartered in 1847, had its named altered to New London, Willimantic & Palmer, the last-named village, on the Western Railroad, becoming the new line's northern terminus when the track reached there in 1850. Then the Amherst & Belchertown was organized in 1851, to continue from Palmer through Belchertown, Amherst and Leverett to the Vermont & Massachusetts Railroad at or near Montague. In 1860 the N. L. W. & P. became the New London Northern, and in 1864 it bought the Amherst & Belchertown.

With the absorption of this road, the Vermont Central had a through line to the Sound, over which it could run trains from Canada, and with a boat connection, carry freight and passengers between Montreal and New York. But Smith did not rest with this: he wanted a better entrance to the metropolis. He had already picked up two more short roads, the Missisquoi and the Addison, and in 1872 the Central's advertising read:

> Comprising Vermont Central; Vermont & Canada; Ogdensburg & Lake Champlain; Rutland; Stanstead, Shefford & Chambly; Montreal & Vermont Junction; Montreal & Plattsburgh; Whitehall & Plattsburgh; Missisquoi; Addison; Sullivan; Vermont Valley; Vermont & Massachusetts (between Brattleboro and Grout's Corner); New London Northern and Ware River Railroads.

As if this weren't enough, in 1873 he took over the so-called Harlem Extension, embracing the former Bennington & Rutland and its end-to-end connection, the Lebanon Springs Railroad, which carried down to Chatham, N. Y., where the New York & Harlem completed the line into the city. This Rutland-Chatham rail, taken over by a group of New Yorkers—who, as it now developed, held three-quarters of the stock of the Vermont Central, sawed off on them by some person or persons unknown—had become altiloquently the New York, Boston & Montreal, and it fitted right into the Vermont Central picture.

Now the Central system had reached the greatest mileage of its history, but it was topheavy, under serious financial strain. Smith thought to overcome this by some financial necromancy: he created a new company, the Central Vermont, which became the receiver for the Vermont Central and Vermont & Canada, despite violent opposition from the victims, especially the Vermont & Canada. The directors' report of that company for 1873 said acridly:

> The charter of the Central Vermont Railroad Company, purporting to be granted for the benefit of the bondholders of the old Vermont Central Railroad, has been taken advantage of to organize a sort of "Credit Mobilier" in Vermont. . . .

We cannot ourselves understand, much less explain satisfactorily to you, how it has come to pass that your property
in the State of Vermont, wholly free of incumbrance,
should today be in the actual adverse possession of the old
receivers under the name and style of the Central Vermont
Railroad Corporation, who are now busily engaged in the
work of removing from the cars the old words, "Vermont
Central R. R.," and substituting therefor the new brand,
"Central Vermont R.R.," as if they supposed it were in the
power of paint to transfer the title of this railroad company
to its mere custodians.

The New York, Boston & Montreal concern soon faded
out, and it became increasingly clear that the leases of the
Ogdensburg and Rutland roads were bad deals for the Central. Both these lessors were having difficulty in collecting
their rent and wanted annulment, even suggesting amalgamation with the C. V. This did not suit the Central's taste, but
it was afraid to let them go, lest they be gathered in by an
increasingly dangerous New York competitor, the Delaware
& Hudson. Smith now accused Page of inveigling him into
the Rutland lease by misrepresenting its earnings—though the
records disproved both clauses of the charge—and tried to set
up a claim of excessive rent charges. Some of the most interesting and truthful comments on the situation may be found
in the directors' reports of the Vermont & Canada, which
could not collect and never did collect a cent of rent from
the Central Vermont for its property and was in litigation
with it continuously. The report for 1876 says that the legal
battle between the C. V. and Rutland had been compromised:

All claims against the Rutland of excessive rent, which
the President of the Central had declared under oath to be
$1,000,000, were abandoned; the Rutland lease was continued
upon lower terms, but still at a losing rent, and the Stock of
the Rutland party (i.e., the New York stockholders) in the
Central Vermont was taken *by the trust* at about half a million of dollars, and is now being paid for, it is stated, out of
the trust funds, including the earnings of your road, at the
rate of about $21,000 a month. The Vermont & Canada

opposed these proceedings as vigorously as possible, but in vain, Judge Royce, the Chancellor at St. Albans, promptly approved of the arrangement, and refused to allow any appeal from his decision.

The V. & C. was now claiming $1,000,000 in unpaid rent, but could get no satisfaction, and Smith was threatening to get a court order to have the road sold. He was not only president of the Vermont Central and the Central Vermont, and head of the committee of Vermont Central bondholders, but also one of the receivers of the Vermont & Canada, and he appeared to have the courts in his pocket. In short, the V. & C. hadn't the ghost of a chance.

The Rutland therefore continued under rental, but in 1877 the Ogdensburg and Harlem Extension leases were canceled. A new character had now entered the cast and menaced the Central—namely, the Portland & Ogdensburg, whose history must be briefly considered. It was largely promoted in St. Johnsbury, Vt., and Portland, Me., for Horace Fairbanks, the scale manufacturer of the former city, was most active in bringing it about. The idea of the Vermont section was first born in the form of three little charters, granted 1864–67, for end-to-end rails from the Connecticut River east of St. Johnsbury—where a junction was to be made with the Portland section—through St. Johnsbury and Montpelier to the northwest corner of the state, there to connect with the Ogdensburg & Lake Champlain. The Vermont companies (later consolidated into one) and the Portland company were organized in 1867. Ground was broken at St. Johnsbury in December, 1869: Thaddeus Fairbanks, inventor of the platform scale, and the oldest man in town, aged 92, tossed up the first spadefuls of earth. The Fairbanks Company and St. Johnsbury had given liberal support to the company, but Montpelier would do nothing, so a new and more direct route was taken, miles to the north of the capital.

The Portland company, though always cursed by poverty, managed to reach the Vermont border at Lunenburg in 1876, and promptly began a rate war with the Connecticut & Passumpsic Rivers for passenger business to Boston. Cut-rate excursions were run from St. Johnsbury and thereabouts on the same days, the Passumpsic's going via the Northern or the Boston, Concord & Montreal, the P. & O.'s via North Conway, N. H., the Great Falls & Conway and the Eastern. Excursion rates to Boston rapidly declined from thirteen dollars to five dollars. Meanwhile, the Vermont company was having its financial troubles, too, but in July, 1877, succeeded in completing its track to Swanton, on the V. & C., in the upper corner of the state, President Fairbanks—now inevitably governor of the state—driving the silver spike.[4]

The Swanton terminus still fell short by twelve miles of Rouse's Point and the Ogdensburg connection for the West. But the P. & O. Vermont Division was now at its last gasp. Receivers had taken over, only three months after the silver spike had entered the cross-tie, and two years later the bondholders took charge. In January, 1880, the latter organized the St. Johnsbury & Lake Champlain corporation to operate the road. By a desperate effort that company built its line to Rouse's Point in 1883, but Smith could not be expected to stand around idly and see this going on. The sixty-five year-old Master of Vermont rails simply bought, in behalf of his company, a large interest in the Ogdensburg & Lake Champlain and checkmated the St. Johnsbury by executing another lease of that line. Once more the St. J. was out of luck. On April 1, 1885, the Boston & Lowell assumed operation of it "as agent for the Boston, Concord & Montreal Railroad." Its subsequent history will be related later.

By this time another *coup* had taken place in Vermont affairs. In 1884 the Consolidated Railroad of Vermont (J. Gregory Smith, President) was organized, bought both the

---

[4] Governor Fairbanks was sternly opposed to Sunday trains, and none ran on the road while he was its head. Sometimes in winter, when it was absolutely necessary to use a snow-plow or a work train, the super sneaked it out, the engineer using neither bell nor whistle near St. Johnsbury and rolling out of town as quietly as possible. Thus they could sometimes get by without Fairbanks' discovering it. But if he did, somebody was haled up on the carpet and reprimanded. So says John S. Kendall in his *History of the St. Johnsbury & Lake Champlain Railroad.*

Vermont Central and the Vermont & Canada at forced sale and leased them for 99 years to the Central Vermont. In 1885 the dawn of a new era was seen when the Grand Trunk Railroad was granted a half interest in the Central Vermont in exchange for amounts due the former in a new through traffic arrangement. The Delaware & Hudson had now bought heavily of Rutland stock and had succeeded in getting rid of President Page, for he died in 1885. The lease to the Central continued until 1896, when the lessee ceased to pay the rent and the Rutland was again freed.

It may be interesting to pause for a moment and notice the passion for excursions which held Vermont in the seventies and eighties—excursions to Boston, Montreal, and, most popular of all, New York. Of course Vermont was not alone in this fad, originated by Yankees in the 1850's; but to judge from the handbills [5] the writer has seen, Vermont was a star patron and 1879 a banner year for such promotions. Advertising a "fall excursion" to New York in September, 1889, the bill announces, among other things, with many display lines, that:

This Excursion has been arranged expressly to
introduce the Novel Feature of Running Special
from Troy to New York
148 Miles without Stopping!
One of the longest runs in this Country, on the time
of the Famous
FAST LIMITED TRAINS
The Engine scooping Water from the Track Tanks while
*RUNNING AT FULL SPEED!*

In 1891 the long incumbency of John Gregory Smith as president of the Vermont Central and Central Vermont was terminated by his death, and his son, Edward C. Smith, succeeded him. But the day of native totalitarianism in Vermont

[5] In Mrs. Bella C. Landauer's collection in the New York Historical Society museum are many Vermont specimens of these long streamers which used to be tacked in bunches on posts and walls, for the public to carry away and peruse. The one quoted is among these.

was over. From 1896 to 1899 the Vermont Central and Vermont & Canada were operated by E. C. Smith and Charles M. Hays, president of the Grand Trunk, as receivers—whence it may be guessed that the great Canadian system was now dominant in Central Vermont affairs. In 1899 there was a reorganization, in which the Central Vermont Rail*road* became the Central Vermont Rail*way*, under the Grand Trunk aegis. E. C. Smith remained as president three years longer, then gave way to Hays; but in 1913 Smith came back to serve as president for fifteen years more. In all, this able representative of the Smith family was in Central Vermont service, from counsel to president, for fifty years. Quite naturally, he was also Governor of Vermont in 1898–99.

From those days to these, the Central Vermont lines have been a part of the Grand Trunk, and later of its greater successor, the Canadian National Railways, which system operates fine, fast passenger trains over it into New England and even through cars to and from New York.

As for the Rutland, a new figure, native-born Percival W. Clement, came into its history in 1887–88. He, with some assistance, bought control of the Rutland from the Delaware & Hudson, paying only fifty dollars a share for the preferred, and getting 10,000 shares of common thrown in, gratis. He became president in 1888—thus acquiring eligibility for the governorship, which, however, he did not attain until thirty years later—and set about building up the system. He was another who had been bitten by the Lakes-to-Boston germ. By 1899 the Rutland, under his direction, had built a track over the string of islands in Lake Champlain to Rouse's Point, thereby giving it a real connection with Montreal, as well as with the Ogdensburg & Lake Champlain, of which it bought control; while from Ogdensburg westward, as a finishing touch, a small fleet of its own steamers traversed Lake Ontario. In 1900 the Bennington & Rutland was purchased, quickly followed by the Chatham & Lebanon Valley (former Lebanon Springs), which gave the Rutland a highway for through traffic from New York to Montreal—while its main line to Bellows Falls served the Boston-Montreal trade.

Clement had now spent a pot of money and gained an impressive-looking but unprofitable system. But he was one of those men who seem to have all the luck. Enter a handsome physician with short beard parted in the middle, who had left medicine for big business. William Seward Webb, son of J. Watson Webb, famous New York editor and publisher, was born with means, studied in Europe, and before he was thirty, was eligible to marry a daughter of William H. Vanderbilt. His father-in-law made him president of the Wagner Palace Car Company in 1883, and of several small railroads; he even had the credit of building the Mohawk & Malone, an important New York Central appanage, and becoming its president.

It would seem that Dr. Webb now had all that was necessary to bring him ease and contentment; but he still had one gnawing, unsatisfied ambition—he wanted to be a state governor. Naturally, he first thought of New York. He built a handsome home at Lenox; he was prominent in society and good works; he took a hand in politics. But the New York politicians would have none of him: he was too much of a silk stocking. Observing that in Vermont, where his ancestors had long resided, railroad president and governor were practically synonymous terms, he bought heavily through brokers of Clement's Rutland stock, paying as high as 105 for it and enabling Clement to clean up, as report has it, a cool million. Webb became a director of the Rutland, created another great summer estate at Shelburne, Vermont, and was elected Rutland president in 1902. But though he was made a colonel on the governor's staff and inspector of rifle practice for the National Guard, Vermonters had a crusty preference for native sons, and Dr. Webb never reached the coveted goal.

But with him, Vanderbilt influence began to overshadow the Rutland, and in 1904 the president of the New York Central became also president of the Rutland, and the Central's trains to Montreal ran over what was practically its own track to the international border. The great railroad czar, Charles S. Mellen, was then becoming dominant in

New Haven. He wanted the Rutland, while the Central wanted the New York, Ontario & Western, on which Mellen had a hold. In the end they compromised, each trading half of each road to the other. This joint ownership of the Rutland continued until quite recent days, when it became so unprofitable that both big proprietors escaped from the responsibility. Thus, the present (1945) outlook for the Rutland is dark.

We cannot escape from this chronicle without mentioning the great flood of 1927, the most terrible in Vermont's history. A period of steady rainfall reached its climax on November 2 and 3, when eight inches of water fell, plunging the state into economic, social and physical tragedy. Highways, railways, bridges, villages, farms, public service systems were swept away, leaving only gashed and scoured countryside, strewn with twisted railway track and other ugly bits of wreckage. Dozens of the state's old covered wooden bridges, some of them used by railroads, were destroyed; even some iron and steel ones, too. So great was the devastation on the Central Vermont that the road was put into receivership on November 5, before the water had receded—a thing perhaps unique in railroad annals.

The deluge extended into New Hampshire and western Massachusetts, too, giving the Boston & Maine and especially the Boston & Albany, enormous repair bills. Looking at certain heaps and fields of bare rock along Westfield River in the Berkshires, one could scarcely believe that there had ever been a fine, well-ballasted, double-track railroad there. But the recovery work of engineers and their crews was heroic, incredible. On November 4, the B. & A. tracks were washed away, and just one week later a single track was again in operation; the second did not come into use until the thirtieth. The Rutland had its main line in fair shape by the twenty-first. But the Central Vermont, hardest hit of all, actually having to resurvey and find new rights of way in places where the terrain had been altered, did not get some of its lines back into service for four or five months.

Among the small Vermont roads not yet mentioned, there was one which was first chartered as the Montpelier & Connecticut River in 1849, but whose survey made the undertaking look so costly that investors were frightened away for twenty years. Reorganized in 1869–70 under its present name, Montpelier & Wells River, the thirty-eight-mile line was completed in 1873 to the latter village, where it joined the Passumpsic and the Boston, Concord & Montreal. Even into the twentieth century, the little road was still privately owned, as is the St. Johnsbury & Lake Champlain, though both are now operated by the Boston & Maine. And it is up in those parts that you may still see railroad trains passing through an occasional covered wooden bridge —a sight scarcely to be found anywhere else in the world.

# 13

## Concord and Discord in New Hampshire

A LARGE element of the population in New Hampshire was at first inimical to railroads. These people were particularly opposed to the heresy prevalent elsewhere that a railroad had a right to condemn property and take it for its own use. They believed that if a land-owner wanted an exorbitant price for his property, he should be permitted to hold it at that: land deals between individual and railroad corporations should be on the same basis as deals between individuals. For several years the state politicians catered to this element.

As already reported, a canal convention in Concord in 1825 had timidly mentioned railroads as a possible means of transportation. There had been meetings in 1830 and 1835 to talk of railroads, but nothing definite was done. The first corporation that ventured to ask for a charter in New Hampshire was the Nashua & Lowell, which received that favor in 1835, just as the Boston & Lowell Railroad was being completed. It was only five miles long, extending from Nashua to the state line, whence its sister railroad in Massachusetts carried on nine and a half miles farther to Lowell. The two companies were consolidated in 1836. Both were built largely with Boston money, but the New Hampshire portion could not have been built had it not been for a loan of $50,000, surprisingly enough, from the Legislature, which took corporation stock as collateral. The entire line went into operation late in 1838, with Onslow Stearns, who had been chief builder, as superintendent. Although it was a separate and distinct organization from the Boston & Lowell, the two operated as a continuous line, and freight and passenger trains with N. & L. rolling stock ran all the way into Boston over B. & L. tracks. Even at that early date the Nashua was being spoken of by its directors as "a link in a great chain of communication connecting the Seaboard and the Lakes."

A few miles farther up the Merrimac from Nashua was the village of Amoskeag, with a fine water power. The big Boston manufacturers who had transformed Lowell into a city now began developing it, and they predicted it would become the Manchester of America; they believed this so firmly that they presently changed its name to Manchester. It was clear that a railroad must soon continue up the valley: in fact, in 1835, a charter for a line all the way from Lowell to Concord had been granted, and the new Amoskeag Manufacturing Company promised to buy half the capital stock; but the creation of the Nashua & Lowell over a part of the course caused the alteration of this project into one covering only the 34½-mile stretch from Nashua through Manchester to Concord. This project, known as the Concord Railroad, was long delayed, too, partly because of the difficulty of buying land at fair prices. Many people were still hostile to railroads on principle, considering them overrated agencies, dangerous and monopolistic. The same arguments were brought up that had been used elsewhere—they would ruin innkeepers, stage lines, teamsters and horse breeders, alter the whole face of society.

But in 1837 progressive elements in the state succeeded in procuring the passage of an act which gave railroads the privilege of taking land by appealing to the Court of Common Pleas to appoint appraisers who would fix prices. Under this act the Concord Railroad went ahead with its promotion and surveys, the latter work being done by Loammi Baldwin the younger, McNeill and Whistler. Many, however, insisted that the act was unconstitutional, and fought it for seven years.

At a town meeting in Concord on January 30, 1837, it was "*Voted*, That the Act of the Legislature of New-Hampshire, passed January 14th, 1837, authorizing the town of Concord to hire money to be invested in the Concord Rail-road stock, be accepted by the town." Three men were appointed a committee to subscribe for the railroad shares, and to "hire" $30,000 on the town's credit. They subscribed for 800 shares at $50 each, the par value of the Concord's stock. But as three and four years went by, the failure of the company to get under way and the relentless fight being waged on the constitutionality of the appraisal law of 1837 so discouraged the town officials that in 1841 they donated 600 of the shares, on which one installment had been paid, to the Concord Literary Institution, which in turn sold them for $675. The remaining 200 shares were sold for almost nothing—all of which brought acute remorse in the years that followed, when the Concord became one of the best-paying railroad properties in New England—even in all America.

It is true that for a time it seemed that the rails could go no farther north than Manchester. But by a strenuous effort money was raised for a single track north of Manchester (it had been double south of there), and work, beginning in 1841, went forward so rapidly that the railhead reached Manchester by July 1, 1842, and Concord on September 7.[1] A station was erected at Concord which, like a number of others in New England, had a large second-story hall where

[1] The Concord bought its engines from Hinkley & Drury of Boston until 1849. Then the Amoskeag Manufacturing Co., a textile mill, permitted its machine shop to go into the manufacture of locomotives, and Amoskeag became one of the most famous in that line in New England. For years it made all Concord locomotives, and that road's track was used as a testing ground for its products. It was no uncommon thing, says the Concord Historical Commission, to see a train breeze into Concord or Nashua, drawn by a shiny new engine with the name of some western railroad on it and a couple of Amoskeag shopmen aboard, one holding the throttle.

concerts and lectures were given, regardless of the clangor of trains. There Adelina Patti, Ole Bull and others made music. Emerson and Holmes and many more literary and scientific lights lectured at $20 per night. For decades no Sunday trains were regularly scheduled in New Hampshire, but after the connection was built through to Vermont, an occasional rare special came through, carrying the Canadian mail when the fortnightly Cunard steamer had been delayed and reached Boston on Sunday morning. [2]

Opposition still held back other railroad projects. At a meeting at Lebanon in 1843 to discuss the project of a line from Concord to the Connecticut River, Professor Charles B. Haddock of Dartmouth College delivered an eloquent address, chiding the state for its backwardness and opposition to progress. "If we cannot maintain our position on the open field of generous and manly conflict," said he, "let us give up the State and go off in a body to Iowa or Oregon. Let it never be said that New Hampshire can live only within a Chinese wall that shuts out the enterprize and prohibits the intercourse of the rest of the world."

Having got her railroad, Concord was smugly against any railroad-building beyond, and the Democratic party, which had been in control in New Hampshire politics for several years, was opposed to the granting of any new charters. But now they began to feel an increasing pressure of public opinion in favor of railroads, a rising murmur that their attitude was retarding the state's progress. Conservative obstruction was still so strong, however, that they resorted to a curious stratagem in an effort to salve everybody's feelings. An act was passed in 1844, by the terms of which the state, exercising its right of eminent domain, took the

[2] It was the whistle of this train below Concord one Sunday forenoon, says Henry McFarland in his *Sixty Years in Concord and Elsewhere*, which brought Joseph A. Gilmore (then in trade) to his feet and out of the First Baptist Church to ascertain the price of grain in Liverpool; and when the Reverend Dr. Cummings went to the store on Monday morning to rebuke his parishioner, Mr. Gilmore saw him approaching—though pretending not to—and as he came within hearing, shouted to a teamster to hurry up to Dr. Cummings' house with that barrel of the best flour. After that, who could chide him?

land necessary for a railroad right of way, paying for it with money supplied by the corporation itself, and then leased the ground to the company for two hundred years —an arrangement which was corrected in later decades. But this law also stipulated that the railroads must report earnings annually to the state, and "in any and every year when their net receipts shall be found to exceed the average of ten per cent on their expenditures from the commencement of their operations, the excess shall be paid into the treasury of the State." That provision—if a railroad ever earned more than 10 per cent—was never carried out, but it led to trouble, as we shall see.

However, this law relieved the situation in the state, and railroad charters began to blossom. In that same year, 1844, a charter was granted to the Northern Railroad, to carry the rails on from Concord city northwest to the Connecticut River, where it would join hands with the Vermont Central in a Boston–Montreal–Great Lakes route. Next came authorization of the Concord & Portsmouth Railroad and the Manchester & Lawrence, the latter supported by Manchester industry on the ground that that growing city would be benefited by competition for the Boston traffic. From the state line just above Lawrence, this road's business entered Boston over the Boston & Maine.

The Manchester & Lawrence went into operation in 1849 and soon felt itself hampered because it had no entrance into the state capital, so it petitioned for the right to build track from Manchester to Concord—a request which was of course fought in the Legislature by the Concord Railroad. But a new solution now appeared. The Concord & Portsmouth, whose track was under construction and whose survey paralleled the Concord Railroad rather closely for the last few miles into Concord, received approval for a branch, which could be built so as to give a fairly direct course from Concord to Manchester—and thus the desired entrance for the Manchester & Lawrence. But the Concord, well served diplomatically and now acquiring influence in state affairs, succeeded in blocking this move, while cultivating the friendship of the new company, buying its stock and gradually becoming potent in its councils. The authorization for the Manchester branch had not named its other end, though Hooksett was what everyone had in mind. But with the promise of a $50,000 loan from the Concord to build it, the plan for the branch was now turned around, so that it left the main line at Candia instead of Hooksett, thus making a direct line from Portsmouth to Manchester instead of from Concord to Manchester.

The Concord now began to give the Manchester & Lawrence some hot competition. It installed two new fast express trains between Concord and Boston, the Boston & Lowell supplying the equipment for one of them, the Concord itself for the other. The southbound trip from Concord to Boston was made in an hour and fifty-five minutes, the northbound in two hours. The M. & L., checkmated all around, began to see that its best interest lay in an alliance with the Concord. In 1850 an agreement was made for joint operation of the two roads, but the M. & L. did not like the way this scheme worked out, and within six months was asking the Concord for amalgamation. The other partner was willing, but the State Senate forbade the banns. The M. & L. next pondered the idea of building the Hooksett-Manchester branch as its own, to gain the desired foothold in Concord, but this was seemingly made unnecessary in 1852 by a five-cornered agreement involving the Concord, M. & L., Nashua & Lowell, Boston & Lowell and Boston & Maine.

Once more the M. & L. was unhappy, believing that it was not getting its due, and by 1856 it again assumed a threatening tone. "Our line to Boston," said its directors, "has some natural advantages, which, under a more independent operation, would guarantee to us from our neighbors a little respect, which would be better than guaranteed dividends from them while they utterly refuse to fulfill their engagements with us." Again the M. & L. and Concord asked the state for permission to unite, and again they were refused. The Concord then leased the M. & L. in December, 1856, over the opposition of some stockholders who were also interested in the Nashua & Lowell and Boston & Lowell. Thereafter, the two roads had the same president and superintendent. In 1861 the lease was renewed for twenty years.

The Concord & Portsmouth had at last crept into Concord in 1852, but it was a hopeless organism. And yet, with greedy rivals all around and the Legislature a difficult problem, the C. & P. had its elements of menace. Accordingly, the Concord took it and its ramshackle equipment under lease in 1858 and gradually instilled into its directoral mind the Concord idea for a new order of things. In 1861 the lease was renewed, providing for a rental of $18,000 a year, plus 6 per cent on the cost to the C. & P. of tearing up its main track between Candia and Suncook and relaying it over the long proposed branch course from Candia to Manchester. The Concord, in turn, was to build a branch from Hooksett, above Manchester, to Suncook, so that in future all Concord and Portsmouth trains would travel via Manchester.

The consent of the Legislature to the elimination of that six miles of track must of course be obtained, and to get this, one of the most amazing tricks in railroad history was perpetrated. The claim was set up that the grades on the C. & P. between Suncook and Candia were so stiff as to be practically impossible. To prove this to the legislative mind, a party of solons was taken out by the superintendent—under Concord orders, of course—on a six-car train drawn by the weakest engine on the road. The super himself took the throttle as they neared the steepest grade. The firewood had been previously soaked in water, and he "worked the engine so as to reduce its effective force, which he knew well enough how to do," [3] until the old machine stalled just before reaching the summit. The lawmakers piled off and came forward; the superintendent met them before they

[3] So says the History Commission of Concord in its *History of Concord, New Hampshire* (Concord, 1903), from which the account of this episode is taken.

could reach the tender and see the water-soaked wood, spread
his hands hopelessly and said, "You see, gentlemen, what
kind of road this is. Best engine on the line can't draw this
train over the hill." All appeared to be convinced; the train
backed to Concord, and the Legislature gave permission for
the track between Suncook and Candia to be taken up.

Now to glance at some other feelers. First, the Concord & Claremont was chartered in 1848 to build from
Concord to the Connecticut River at Windsor. It managed to cover twenty-seven miles of the distance by 1850,
and then sank down exhausted. Second, from Contoocook-
ville, on this road, ten miles out of Concord, the Contoocook
Valley Railroad was thrust southwestward to Hillsboro
Bridge in 1849. Third, the New Hampshire Central was
constructed in 1849–50, northwestward from Manchester;
this road also was aiming at the Connecticut River, though
it got no farther than Henniker on the Contoocook Valley.
In 1853 the Legislature blessed the union of the Concord &
Claremont and the New Hampshire Central. However,
some curious and unexplainable juggling took place by
which the Concord acquired an operative interest in the
N. H. C. and for the second time did a demolition job,
removing several miles of track between North Weare and
Henniker. The work was done on a Sunday in 1858 by
a gang of men who came from Concord on four locomotives, and it caused great excitement at the time. The breaking
of the track forced southbound traffic from the Contoocook
Valley to travel around via Concord, thus giving the Concord
Railroad a larger share of the southward haul. Ownership of the N. H. C. had previously passed to one Corning,
and as was discovered later, from him to Joseph A. Gilmore,
then superintendent of the Concord and later Governor of
New Hampshire. The bifurcated road became the Manchester & North Weare, and when Mr. Gilmore sold it to
the Concord in 1868, he didn't lose any money on the deal,
you may be sure.

Long before this, railroad stockholders in southern New
Hampshire had begun to complain sourly of being pushed

around. There was even a grouchy little newspaper, *The Voice of the Stockholder*, launched in their behalf in 1854, but it didn't last long. Harping on a single string is painfully monotonous, and with no sports, movie or night-club columns to vary its zest, it soon faded out of existence.

Now let us return for a moment to 1844, when the law was liberalized and railroad projects north of Concord began blossoming. The first and strongest of these was the Northern, chartered to run from Concord "to the west bank of the Connecticut River in the town of Lebanon"—in reality, to White River Junction, across the river, where it met the Vermont Central. It was in fact a link in the Boston to Montreal-Ogdensburg highway which had been talked of for fifteen years or more. The charter placed the terminus of the Northern at the west bank of the Connecticut, because the state of New Hampshire claimed to own that entire river; it placed the boundary line between itself and Vermont along the western shore and got away with it, much to the annoyance of Vermont. A railroad along the west bank scarcely dared cross the mouth of a tributary stream lest New Hampshire accuse it of trespass and demand a New Hampshire charter.

Onslow Stearns was called from the Nashua in 1845 to be the building agent of the Northern. He became its president in 1852 and served until his death, twenty-six years later, meanwhile having his turn at being Governor of New Hampshire. Under his direction, the Northern was patriotic, buying more than half its rails from American rolling mills. Backed by ample funds right out of the coffers of State Street, Boston, the construction progressed with unusual rapidity for those days, and in June, 1848, the grand opening celebration was held, with Daniel Webster, that Professor Haddock of Dartmouth who had been such a railroad booster, and Erastus Fairbanks of St. Johnsbury, magnate of the Passumpsic and of the St. Johnsbury & Lake Champlain, among those present.

The Northern was a well-managed and fairly prosperous road from the start, its dividends increasing steadily from

4 per cent in its first year to 10 per cent in 1865–66. In the early fifties it took over the Sullivan, the Concord & Claremont and the Contoocook Valley. In 1851 it was one of the stars in a grandiose celebration staged at Boston, telling the world of the completion of the through rail route between that city and Montreal. That you had to traverse seven different railroads to negotiate the distance, no less than four of them between Boston and the Connecticut River, had no effect upon the enthusiasm. President Fillmore was there, and the Earl of Elgin, Governor-General of Canada, and New England's great showpiece, Daniel Webster. There were 400,000 guests in town during the three-day jubilee of parades, fireworks, decorated trains, whistle-tooting, banquets, and toasts drunk until many of the guests collapsed under the strain. And truly, if a roaring trade and increase in population are blessings, eastern Massachusetts did well to laud the rails, for that area had received material benefits from them far richer than did the stockholders of the railroads which played a major part in creating the prosperity. Boston in 1850 found itself with its population more than doubled in twenty years (61,392 in 1830, 136,881 in 1850). Smaller cities near by had done as well or better. Woburn had doubled, Lynn and Newton more than doubled, Waltham and Cambridge increased two and a half times, Roxbury nearly four times, Lowell more than five times. [4] Chelsea in two decades had leaped from 771 to 6701, and Lawrence from nothing to 8000; it doubled that in the next five years, 1850 to 1855.

Boston could well afford to build the Northern Railroad and those vast systems in the west which it, to a greater extent even than New York City, created. Other New England projects, such as the Boston, Concord & Montreal, chartered in 1844—the same year as the Northern—were bitter about it. Planned to run from Concord, skirting the

[4] From 6479 in 1830 to 33,383 in 1850. In 1848, in the eleven textile mills, a bleachery and a machine shop, 7915 females and 3340 males were employed, a total of 11,255, or more than one in every three of the city's population. The Merrimack Mills alone had 1775 employees, the Lawrence 1400, the Boott 1030 and the Hamilton 1020.

White Mountains, to Wells River much farther up the Connecticut, where it hoped to make a good connection for Montreal over the Connecticut & Passumpsic Rivers Railroad, then building, the B. C. & M. was regarded by the Northern as an impudently unnecessary competitor, to be put down, if possible. The B. C. & M.'s directors spurred local pride and support by commenting frequently upon its lone-hand fight for life against rivals and enemies; the project "met with no favor and could find no support in State Street," and "the corporation has had no aid from the monied interest of New England; for the most part the means have been furnished by the country through which the line passes." No subscription was too small; some came from the savings of laborers and factory girls; shares sold to farmers were paid for in ties, bridge timber, fence rails and firewood.

The company's only luxury was its English rails—they cost seventy dollars a ton in 1846, but dropped to thirty-eight dollars in 1852—and one cargo was lost by shipwreck on Minot's Ledge. Otherwise, the road was built in the most economical manner possible. Opposition both in and out of the Legislature, by both the Northern and the Vermont Central, delayed the project. Those two jealous worthies pledged $750,000 in aid to the young Connecticut & Passumpsic Rivers as a bribe to induce it to have nothing to do with the B. C. & M., though it had promised cooperation. Against all these untoward elements, the B. C. & M. progressed slowly. Not until the spring of 1848 was a twenty-mile stretch of track completed, so that the first passenger train, drawn by the locomotive "Old Man of the Mountains," all sky blue, from cowcatcher to cartail, could make a triumphal trip. From that spring's terminal, the line swerved eastward in a wide detour past Laconia and the shores of Lake Winipiseogee (now Winnepesaukee)—thus setting up some good summer business for the future—and then northwestward through Franklin and Haverhill (N. H.) to Wells River, which was not reached until 1853.

The White Mountains Railroad had been promoted, in close alliance with the B. C. & M., to run northeastward from Wells River to Littleton, with the eventual destination much deeper in the mountains. It was so poor from the start that it could buy no locomotives of its own, but borrowed from every railroad in the vicinity. One small machine, appropriately named "Boy," lent by the Passumpsic, was so weak that it could scarcely pull the lightest train uphill. The railhead of this line entered Littleton in 1853; and, to look ahead a bit, it reached Lancaster in 1870, Fabyans in 1874 and the base of Mount Washington in '76. The Profile & Franconia Notch, a little narrow-gauge connection, was built in 1878–79.

The Passumpsic turned against the Boston, Concord & Montreal—being particularly annoyed by its bid for White Mountain business—and tried to alienate the White Mountains Railroad, but in vain. Then it strove to prevent the B. C. & M. from touching the Vermont shore of the Connecticut; whereupon the latter bought a toll-bridge across the river, charter and all, and so gained an entrance to Wells River, building a new bridge to replace the existing one. Later, peace came about between the two roads, but for years the B. C. & M. was not prosperous, and many of the small stockholders sold out at a loss.

Certain eminent thinkers in Concord had resisted the building of railroads to northward, on the ground that they would make the town a way station and do it much harm. Now, with those roads siphoning business into the city, they were revealed as false prophets. At State Fair time, passenger trains were sometimes seventeen cars long, and this, mind you, without benefit of air brake or other safety device. The iron of the Concord Railroad grew hot under the heavy traffic. With many freight and some passenger trains destined for Boston clattering in from the two northern roads, and a few even coming from Vermont; with frequent specials, and with the regulars, which were often hours late, unequipped with any telegraph or signaling system, the Concord track was inconceivably cluttered, and it was only

by incredible luck that more accidents did not occur. The
Concord grew fat on the business. In 1865 it made an agreement with the Boston & Lowell by which the Manchester
& Lawrence was in effect almost a closed road. True, it
received its annual guaranteed rental from the Concord, but
little traffic. Cars came off the Northern with orders that
they should be routed over the M. & L., but the Concord
refused this, even when the Northern brakemen, under
instructions, tried to enforce the orders by violence. Nothing
was to be gained by such efforts, for the Concord held all
the trumps. And as to dividing the profits, the Concord and
Lowell arrogated to themselves much more per mile than
the Northern and B. C. & M. were allowed—which gradually drew the latter two together through sympathy.

The effect of all this was that in early years Concord stock
—par value fifty dollars a share—sold higher on the market
than any other in New England—at times as high as 145 per
cent. Under such circumstances its hierarchy could not
resist cutting melons and watering the stock issue, which,
from $800,000 in 1846, jumped to $1,200,000 in 1847 and
$1,500,000 in 1854, causing the shares to drop below par
in the following year for the first time in their history.
But in later years, as we shall see, they doubled and even
trebled in value.

Yet while directors luxuriated and stockholders cashed
dividend coupons, public sentiment seethed at this octopus
clutch on the heart of the state by a single railroad. In 1867
a law was passed which was aimed at the Concord's control
of the Manchester & Lawrence, but it didn't seem to take
effect; so in the following year David Currie, et al., residents along the line of the M. & L., brought suit to break
the lease and give them relief. Interestingly enough, the
attorneys who represented these suffering persons were
Eastman & Cross, attorneys for the Boston & Maine, which
was deeply concerned about the fate of the M. &. L. The
wheels of justice revolved with their customary celerity and
ground out a verdict five years later. By that time the two
roads were so entangled, with common ownership of roll-

ing stock and so on, that they were hard to pry apart. Then lawyers put their heads together and worked out some sort of hocus-pocus by which the Concord continued to operate the M. &. L. illegally for another fifteen years.

Meanwhile, strange things were occurring, in and out of the boardrooms. The Northern had been talking consolidation, under the name of the Great Northern Railroad, and President Josiah Minot of the Concord and some of his directors were leaning toward the idea when a situation developed which caused them to take hasty action: in 1870 they leased the Concord to the Northern for $150,000 a year, or 10 per cent on the common stock, for they saw that they were about to be ousted by a clique who wanted the consolidation, if it took place, to yield them some personal profit, but who were, first of all, in a jam (at least, their leading figures were) from which they sought escape.

In digging down to the foundations of this story, it should be explained that the conductors on the Concord, like those on many another road, had been doing a considerable business on the side. The railroads had begun a practice, which continued long afterward, of meeting competition by selling through tickets to a competitive point at a lower rate than to local places short of that. As an example, a traveler could buy a ticket from Detroit to Boston cheaper than one from Detroit to Concord or Nashua. Therefore, smart passengers for these local stops learned to buy tickets to Boston, and sold what was left of the ticket either on the train or after they left it. Conductors became "scalpers"— began buying these tickets and reselling them. They also bought produce and other commodities along the line, took them to the terminals in the baggage cars and sold them. For years no attention was paid to these well-known practices: they were a part of the conductor's perquisite.

But in 1866, Joseph A. Gilmore, who had long been superintendent of the Concord and who had also served as governor of the state in 1863–64, told the directors that the conductors were stealing $50,000 yearly from the company, and named one George Clough as a particularly heinous offender.  The company sued Clough for $100,000, alleging that he had not only scalped tickets, had not only failed to turn in the ten cents extra assessed on cash fares, but had often pocketed the full cash fare itself.  Spies on the trains watched him for two months but could not find that he held back any fares he collected.  He in turn said that his scalping had been done with Gilmore's permission, and his attorneys now began unearthing such damaging testimony that the suit threatened to become a boomerang.  It was alleged that Gilmore himself had not only taken thousands of dollars from the company but had used thousands of the company's tickets for his own ends.  The ticket-master testified that Gilmore, all through his incumbency, had given away railroad tickets for political and other purposes, and that when he was running for governor he sometimes got one hundred at a time.  "It would average three or four times a week," said this official.  "I was directed to make no account."  It was also alleged that Gilmore's animus at Clough arose from Clough's refusal to endorse some notes for the super, upon which Gilmore threatened, elegantly, "I'll learn George Clough to go back on me and refuse to sign my notes when I'm lying here sick."

Gilmore died before the trial took place, but by that time matters looked so ugly for his political confreres that they decided they must get control and squelch the trial.  They bought Concord stock, paying sometimes as high as ninety dollars a share (forty dollars above par), obtained control and ousted President Minot and his directors, putting themselves and their pals in.  They then brought suit to annul the Northern lease, and since three of the Supreme Court Justices were Concord stockholders of their own faction, they won.  They then proceeded to sell stock to the Northern and the Boston, Concord & Montreal, retaining good commissions on the deal, so that by 1873 the two northern connections had a joint stock control, though they did not operate the Concord.

An interesting sidelight here is that the Boston & Lowell, now beginning to evince an interest in New Hampshire,

tried to buy control of the Concord when the new directors came in.  In its earlier years, the Lowell was strictly
parochial in its thinking: its directors had more than once
remarked that the business of the Woburn Branch was more
important to them than anything or everything north of
Lowell.  In those years it devoted its best thought to
improving its equipment and service—acquiring, by reason
of the excellence and elegance thereof, the nickname of Old
Silk Stocking and such a reputation that it has been said
that the best recommendation you could give a new gadget
or appliance was to say that the Boston & Lowell was using
it.  In later years the Old Colony became another such
aristocrat.  But now the Lowell was finding isolationism
increasingly impracticable: it was even beginning to have
ideas of Manifest Destiny, not to mention such unease as
that caused when the Concord in 1876 leased the newly
built Nashua, Acton & Boston, leading from Nashua to a
connection with the Fitchburg, and so giving it another
entrance to Boston.  The Lowell had costly terminals in
Boston, and it needed plenty of business to keep them
profitable.

In 1868 some of the new Concord directorate were involved in another scheme, by which that road's destiny came
near being changed.  It was so rich a lode that many plots
were hatched for possession of it.  The stipulation in its
charter giving the state the right to purchase was now evoked.
A bill was introduced in the Legislature, creating a new corporation, the Concord Railroad—the same as the existing title,
but with the word "Corporation" omitted.  The bill provided
that the state should, by virtue of the charter power vested in
it, buy the railroad and all assets for $1,500,000 and turn it
over to certain favored grantees, organized as this new Concord Railroad, for $1,700,000—though its market value was
then well above $2,000,000.  The state would thus bank a
nice little profit of $200,000, as well as receiving an annual
income of $15,000 from the receipts of the company.
"Among the grantees named in this act were some who,
seven years before, had been active in tearing up the rails be-

tween Suncook and Candia." [5]    Fortunately, this measure did not become a law.

Concord stockholders were fretful under the interlocking directorates and presidencies with the two northern connecting lines and the belief that the Northern and B. C. & M. were getting more out of the alliance than they deserved. A suit was brought in 1879, in which these stockholders declared invalid the contracts made by directors of the Concord with themselves as directors of the Northern and/or the Boston, Concord & Montreal. As three of the directors under criticism were on the Supreme Bench of the state, while a fourth justice was a heavy stockholder in the Concord—leaving less than a quorum of the court actually non-partisan—it may be imagined that the court was in the very deuce of a state of puzzlement as to what would be, not the equitable, but the practical thing to do without making itself look like something out of *Gulliver's Travels*. It is small wonder it took them five years to decide.

But directors and connivers did not wait to hear court decisions. In 1880 the Boston & Lowell had leased the Nashua & Lowell for 99 years, and the following year the B. & L. and the Concord agreed upon a scheme of joint operation. This was brought on by a quarrel between the Central Vermont and the Northern when the latter sold the Sullivan County to the Connecticut River Railroad, which was now creating a considerable system up and down that valley. The Central Vermont made threats of construction which menaced the peace of mind of both the Northern and the Concord, causing the latter to lean toward the Lowell. But this partnership was short-lived: friction caused by the two northern connections brought about its dissolution within two years. During that time, however, the two roads had jointly bought control of the Manchester & Keene, leading to an important manufacturing and railroad center in southwestern New Hamp-

[5] Again we quote the Concord Historical Commission in its *History of Concord*, published in 1903—which should be information right from the grass roots. It is doubtful whether railroad politics in New Hampshire reached its lowest level at this time or twenty years later, when the great Concord–Northern–Lowell–Boston & Maine war was raging.

shire, and that line continued to be a part of the Lowell system after it separated from the Concord in 1883.

In May of that year the Legislature was asked for permission to consolidate into one system the Concord, the Manchester & Lawrence, the Boston, Concord & Montreal and the Northern (with its controlled Concord & Claremont). Knowing ones saw back of the petition the hand of the Boston & Lowell, seeking to gain control of the whole group. The better to make such consolidations possible, even the Boston & Maine and the Eastern now joined the others in urging a law which would eliminate or ease the existing prohibition against them. The result was the Colby Act, which would have permitted the desired amalgamation had not the Northern and the B. C. & M. still bickered over the question how much of the Concord pie each should get. The result was that the whole plan fell through.

The Lowell now offered to lease the Concord on a 10 per cent rental, but was refused. The Concord was too rich for that: didn't its stock go up to 107–214 per cent—in the following year? The Lowell thereupon threw a bomb by leasing both the Northern and the B. C. & M. in January, 1884, thus bottling up the Concord. Minority stockholders of the Northern quickly brought suit to invalidate the lease, alleging, first, that the Colby Act was unconstitutional, and, second, that the Boston & Lowell was not a New Hampshire corporation. But the Lowell calmly went still farther northward to buy control of and lease the St. Johnsbury & Lake Champlain. Thus the bugle was sounded, as George Pierce Baker says, "for one of the most bitter and most corrupt railroad 'wars' which ever took place in the halls of the New Hampshire legislature." [6]

The rather elaborate advertising books, *Summer Saunterings Along the B. & L.*, which the Lowell was putting forth annually in those years, were filled with alluring woodcuts of mountain and lake and happy vacationists at rest or play: they give no hint of the molten lava seething beneath the surface in

[6] *The Formation of the Railroad Systems of New England*, p. 119, Cambridge, 1937.

boardrooms and courthouses. The White Mountains had now been penetrated from all sides: the Lowell, the Boston & Maine, the Maine Central and the Portland & Ogdensburg were all competing for mountain summer business. Through the B. C. & M., the Lowell controlled the White Mountains Railway to the foot of Mount Washington, the Whitefield Railroad to Berlin, and the Pemigewasset Valley to North Woodstock. The Mount Washington rack railway, conceived by Sylvester Marsh of Littleton in 1858 and chartered—though one dissenting legislator sneered that they ought to give him the privilege of building a line to the moon—was constructed between 1866 and 1869, and "Old Peppersass," whose upright boiler and stack reminded one of a condiment bottle, began hauling goggle-eyed, half-frightened tourists to the windy summit. The road never paid any dividends, and until the Boston & Maine took it over, its higher officials drew no salaries.

Now that railroads had eliminated the necessity of days of driving in a carriage or jolting over rough roads in a rocking stagecoach in order to reach the mountains, not only the wealthy and more leisurely but the commonalty as well vacationed there. It was in those years that famous hotels had their heyday—Fabyan's, the Profile House, the Crawford House, the Summit House on Mount Washington, the Pemigewasset: Littleton, Bethlehem, North Woodstock, the Conways and other villages became tourist centers. And yet, in those pre-motor, pre-tourist-camp days, there were still many lovely solitudes left in the great hills.

The maps in the booklets mentioned, showing the Boston & Lowell as sweeping from Boston to Canada, seem to the present-day observer to prove that the Lowell was the logical company to control the traffic in the heart of New Hampshire. But this company received something of a shock when it learned that a group of twenty gentlemen, several of them directors or large stockholders in the Concord, had bought stock control of the Boston, Concord & Montreal and were fomenting rebellion. Nevertheless, the B. & L. went ahead to lease the Connecticut & Passumpsic Rivers. But on the very heels of that, early in 1887, came a paralyzing blow: the State Supreme Court, thumbing its nose at the Colby Act, handed down a decision in the case of *Dow, et als. vs. the Northern Railroad, et als.*, which declared the B. & L. lease of the Northern illegal and enjoined its operation after July 1. The New Hampshire courts were not of a mind to let a "foreign corporation" dominate their principal railroads.

The State Railroad Commission did not see eye to eye with the Law. In its annual report it said:

> This decision emasculated the Colby Act. It wrenched apart the Boston & Lowell system, which had been built up under that act. It compelled the unwilling owners of the Northern to . . . operate the road independently. It invited a contest in the courts for the Boston, Concord & Montreal, and it precipitated upon the legislature a railroad war more expensive, more demoralizing, and, in its results, more unsatisfactory to all the contending parties than any other that ever destroyed the substance and sacrificed the peace and dignity of the State.

The Boston & Maine, having a few miles of rail in New Hampshire, was incorporated there and so was not quite "foreign." It had consummated leases of the Eastern Railroad system and of the Worcester, Nashua & Rochester, and was therefore ready and waiting when the Boston & Lowell, shorn of a vital part of its mileage and shell-shocked by the court's decision, saw nothing else to do but give up the fight. In disgust and despair, the B. & L. directors sought peace of mind by leasing their system to the Boston & Maine for 99 years.

This did not necessarily mean that the B. & M. was in undisputed possession. After much "maneuvering for position," as the Railroad Commission put it, war broke out afresh. A syndicate of men—wholly unconnected with any other concern, of course (!)—bought stock control of the Manchester & Lawrence and promptly leased it to the Boston & Maine for 50 years. The Concord wanted it back, wanted the Northern, wanted its hold on the B. C. & M. confirmed. Both parties, with cohorts of lawyers and lobbyists in terrifying array, moved upon the State House. In June two bills, the Hazen and the Atherton, giving the B. & M. and the Concord precisely the same plums, were introduced, and all summer the conflict raged over them. Little branch railroads were promised to country members as bribes to get votes, and three of them were actually built. At last, in the autumn, the Hazen bill passed both houses, but the governor bluntly vetoed it. Then a measure was passed giving the B. & M. the right to lease the Northern only, but the governor bounced that one back, too. But he did permit the B. & M. to take over the Manchester & Lawrence, which was the only tangible result of the campaign. The Northern and the B. C. & M. were left where they were, said the Railroad Commission, "the one to be operated independently or under some makeshift arrangement, the other to be scrambled for in the courts." One could trust the lawyers, however, to rig up that "makeshift arrangement," and they did: by its provisions the Boston & Maine temporarily operated the Northern, while a truce was patched up with the Concord. By the terms of this armistice, the Concord was permitted to hold the B. C. & M. in peace, and in turn was to cease fighting the Boston & Maine's northward push. The result was that in 1889 the Legislature sanctioned the lease of the Northern by the Boston & Lowell, which then leased it to the Boston & Maine—and that road operates it to this day.

In the same year the solons blessed the union of the Concord with the Boston, Concord & Montreal, under the new name of Concord & Montreal—which was not greatly inappropriate, inasmuch as the new corporation had a line all the way from the Fitchburg Railroad in Massachusetts to two connections with the Grand Trunk in northern New Hampshire. Just before the union, Concord stock sold at $155.25 per share—about 310 per cent. In the amalgamation, the Concord was permitted to raise its capital from $1,500,000 to $3,000,000 by the simple expedient of making the par value

$100 per share instead of $50. To this were added the capital stock and bonds of the B. C. & M.—and still the new concern was profitable: so profitable that the politicians' chops were dribbling again, and the old charter right of the state to take over the road was talked of once more. Austin Corbin, New Hampshire-born capitalist who had made a reputation in the railroad world by rejuvenating both the Reading and the Long Island wrote to the governor in 1887, offering the state a half-million dollars for its interest in the Concord. Nothing was done about the offer at the time, but in 1891, when the Concord & Montreal asked for permission to add $3,000,000 to its capital (presumably because the dividend rates were too opulent) which would have made a total indebtedness in stock and bonds of $11,928,000, this seemed to be loading one small road pretty heavily, and Corbin again offered to take it over and pay the state a million for its interest. There was quite a stir about it in the state, and some pamphleteering; many thought the offer should be accepted and that the Boston & Maine might be seized, too, without any violation of ethics. But the state high court decided, after much pondering, that this would be taking property for less than it was worth, and could not equitably be done. That was the last appearance of the state-recapture hobgoblin.

Steadily the Boston & Maine was surrounding the Concord. It now had all the smaller roads, and the large ones, too, to east and south of it—yes, and to north and west of it: the Connecticut & Passumpsic Rivers, the St. Johnsbury & Lake Champlain, the Northern, the Sullivan, the Ashuelot (Keene to South Vernon) and most recent acquisition of all, the Connecticut River, running down to Springfield. The end was inevitable. In the early nineties the B. & M. was quietly buying Concord stock, and in 1895, the latter succumbed to destiny and was leased to the greater concern for 99 years. It had been one of the richest railroad properties in history. The dividends paid on its stock since its opening in 1842 had averaged more than 9 per cent per annum, so that every $100 invested at the beginning had been repaid fivefold. And the dividends would have been much larger if the capital stock had not been so egregiously increased.   At the end it was $7,170,000, of which nearly a quarter was held in the city of Concord.

## From Kittery to 'Quoddy

AS EARLY as 1828 a Maine legislative committee studied what information was available about the new form of transportation and reported their findings to an apathetic State Assembly. The public mind was not yet ready for any definite movement. The authorization of the first three short railroads out of Boston, however, reawoke the idea in Maine, and in 1832 its first two charters were granted. One went to the Calais Railway Company, which, after some years of toil in raising the needful cash, built and operated a two-mile horse railway between Calais and Milltown. The other was the Old Town Railroad, intended to connect Old Town with Bangor. The local enthusiasm over this project was so great that its shares are said to have sold at a premium before ever a spadeful of earth was turned. But so amateurish were both legislators and promoters at the time of these early charterings that the right of the corporation to seize land for its purpose was not assured, and a farmer could either chase the company's surveyors off his land with a pitchfork or have them arrested and jailed for trespass. The chartering had to be done all over again.

In 1833 the Bangor & Piscataquis Railroad and Canal Company, a rival enterprise financed in Boston, was chartered, with intent to run from Bangor through Old Town to some slate quarries thirty or forty miles up-country. The Old Town had done some grading and bridge pier building when, in 1835, it decided to sell out to the Bangor & Piscataquis. This company completed the road from Bangor to Old Town

in November, 1836, and on it that year appeared the first
locomotive in Maine, a Stephenson which stayed around for
thirty years thereafter, and of which, fortunately, we have a
crude photograph.

This road was not greatly successful and in 1848 was sold
to a new company for a fraction of its cost. In 1854 it was
extended to Milford and became the Bangor, Old Town &
Milford, having attained a length of twelve and one-half
miles. It was eventually taken over by the Maine Central.
This was the first steam railroad in the state, and the only one
until the Portland, Saco & Portsmouth was built in 1840-42.
There was another small affair built in 1841-42, the Machiasport, a lumber railroad connecting Machiasport and Whitney-
ville, and this continued to operate until 1890; it was a
friendly little affair, created solely for hauling timber, but it
would carry passengers free whenever they desired. Its trains
would even stop to pick up a woman or an elderly man. The
Calais & Baring was another lumber road, chartered in 1837.

The building of the Portland, Saco & Portsmouth, to connect Portland and Maine coast towns with the Eastern Railroad coming up from Boston; the taking over of the Eastern
by the Boston & Maine, and the leasing by the latter of the
P. S. & P. have all been described in Chapter VII. Portland
in particular was none too greatly interested in any line which
would tend to draw off the commerce of the state toward
Boston. Instead, knowing Canada's lack of good Atlantic sea-
ports, it hoped to accomplish the building of a railroad from
its own harbor to Quebec or Montreal, and thus become
Canada's seaport. The state lawmakers became interested in
the idea and in 1835 passed a resolution requesting Maine's
senators and representatives in Congress "to use their influence with the General Government to procure the aid of a
corps of engineers for the purpose of surveying a railroad
from Portland or some other point on the sea-board . . . to
some point on the border of lower Canada."

Look at the map of Maine, and you will see that it is more
than half surrounded by Canadian territory. It is no wonder
that so much of its early railroad planning had to do with

Canada. The national government saw the importance of Maine's request and sent a noted engineer, Colonel Stephen H. Long, to make the survey. After international consultations, Lord Almyer, the Governor-General, said that Canada would be happy to co-operate, and engineers were set to work on a survey southward from Quebec. In Maine there had been much argument over the question whether Portland, Wiscasset or Belfast would be the best terminus. Colonel Long, after several months of study and surveying, recommended Belfast, on the huge Penobscot Bay, and laid out a route from there to the border, near the headwaters of the Chaudière River. The Belfast & Quebec Railroad Company was actually chartered in 1836, and Belfast sought state assistance for the building of the line, but Maine's constitution forbade the lending of its credit for such a purpose, and so few people in Maine liked railroads that enough private money could not be found. The Panic of 1837 finally stopped all efforts. An attempt was made a few years later to revive the project, but by that time Quebec's interest in the matter had evaporated.

The failure of this plan suited Portland to a T. In 1839 it begged $4000 from the Legislature for a survey from Portland across upper New Hampshire and Vermont to Lake Champlain, the ultimate target being Montreal, whom many now began to see as the coming great city of Canada. The survey was made and some boosting was done, but Maine, still primarily interested in such things as lumbering, fishing, shipbuilding and shipping, had not yet warmed up to railroads; hence no money could be raised there—and certainly Boston could not be expected to co-operate. And so matters drifted along for a few years more.

The building of the Portland, Saco & Portsmouth, however, was highly educational, and thereafter, a greater interest in railroads began to be noticed in Maine. Industry was developing rapidly, and businessmen had begun to realize how the railroad tentacles thrust out from Boston were siphoning the commerce of New Hampshire, Vermont, and even of Maine itself to the New England metropolis. And now arose a pro-

moter, himself a vibrant enthusiast, who could stir the state
to action—a young Bangor lawyer named John A. Poor. He
had gone all the way down to Boston to see the Boston &
Lowell launched. He was an evangelist, not only for railroads, but for Maine. In 1865, when he was advocating the
broad-gauge railroad, he declared in an address: "The capacity of the human frame for labor is found to be greater
in Maine than in Massachusetts or any other State south or
west of it." He didn't say who had "found" it so, but there
isn't the slightest doubt that he really believed it.

Poor was one of the early proponents of Maine as the
natural sea-outlet for eastern Canada. He himself explored
possible routes between the coast and the international
boundary, following stream courses on foot through the
mountains and through what was then a savage, tangled wil-
derness. He made little headway with his gospel until the
early forties, when Portland and some interior towns began
to thrill again to the idea. Poor's plan had now crystallized
as a railroad from Portland to Montreal, and he urged upon
the former city the desirability of aiding the enterprise with
its cash. A preliminary survey by James Hall recommended
that the White Mountains be passed via the Androscoggin
River gulch and Dixville Notch. Hall figured the cost to the
border at $2,250,000.

Simultaneously, Montreal capitalists were being stirred up
by A. T. Galt—later Sir Alexander Galt—and were moving
toward organization to build the Canadian end of the line.
On February 10, 1845, the charter for the Atlantic & St.
Lawrence Railroad was granted in Maine. But several days
before this, word came to Poor that Boston emissaries had
reached Galt and persuaded him that their city was the logical
terminus. To tell the truth, Montreal didn't greatly care
which was chosen: all it wanted was a good seaport that was
open all winter, and it is easy to see that the big city of Boston would have some powerful reasoning on its side.

Poor did not lose a moment. He heard the news on the
morning of Wednesday, February 5, and he decided instantly
to start for Montreal, although a gale was blowing from the

northeast, and snow, "almost a coarse hail," was falling heavily. The stableman who supplied the horse and sleigh "would not stir an inch with me," so a friend named Cheney volunteered to accompany him. In fur coats and caps and under fur lap-robes they started at noon, "& such a storm," wrote Poor, "I never before encountered. . . . To face the storm with our eyes open was impossible, & the only protection to them was the covering of ice which hung in masses from our eyebrows." The snow was drifted so deep and hard that they went right over stone walls and woodpiles and never knew when they were in the road. "Five times we called up the people on the way to get our road, which as many times we lost." Reaching a tavern seven and one-half miles out, after three hours of driving, they warmed themselves and pushed on.

Where they stopped for the night is not clear, but early next morning they started again with two horses tandem and a veteran stage driver to pilot, shovel and break drifts. As they proceeded through South Paris and Rumford, they sometimes had two, three and four horses pulling the sleigh. Skirting the south shore of Lake Umbagog and nearing Dixville Notch, "the cold was most cruel & intense." A Captain Bragg guided them through the Notch. "Two young men volunteered to go ahead and break the path, & as they approached the Notch, they started out other horses & riders, so that we had 4 horses & 5 men to put us through this wonderful chasm. . . . The wind howled fearfully" through the gorge, "and the drifting snow darkened the air." The intrepid young men helpers "penetrated the drifts with an apparent relish for the excitement, & would accept no compensation."

Beyond the Notch, conditions eased a bit. Through Colebrook and Canaan they hurried on, driving into Sherbrooke, Que., on Saturday. Leaving there at 5 A.M. Sunday, they pounded "through an untrodden road, with 18 inches of snow," reaching Granby, forty-six miles distant, at 5 P.M. But they did not stop there. With a change of horses they drove all night, arriving in Montreal at 5:30 on Monday

morning, less than five days out from Portland. "The cold
was intense, some 18 below zero, & in crossing the St.
Lawrence [on the ice, of course] over 2 miles the mist of
frost entirely prevented our seeing three rods ahead."

You have only to look at Poor's portrait to know that nothing would have stopped the indomitable man from accomplishing his purpose. After a three-hour nap at a hotel, he
walked dramatically into a Board of Trade meeting, called to
consider the Boston proposition. Talking himself hoarse, assuring the Board that Portland had a charter and would soon
have the cash, he succeeded in getting postponement of action. About a week later, Judge William P. Preble, who was
to be the first president of the A. & St. L., arrived, also by
sleigh, with the charter; and with this evidence of good faith
and determination, the Montrealers were won over. A gentlemen's agreement was made with Portland, and the Canadian company was promptly chartered with the name in
reverse, St. Lawrence & Atlantic.

Back home, the war was being carried on merrily by the
Portland and Boston editors. The former asserted that Boston
harbor was silting up and would soon be unusable, also that
it froze every winter. It was noted that with the mercury
sixteen below zero, at Portland, the harbor was not frozen;
but with impish glee they quoted a Boston paper as saying,
"Our harbor is about as good, or rather, about as bad as
closed up. It is filled with ice and snow, and it is with the
greatest difficulty that a passage can be kept open for the East
Boston ferry." Boston editors could only sneer back, "We
would first inform the Maine editors that they and their
readers have not sufficient enterprise and public spirit to accomplish such an object." Portland proceeded to disprove
this during the following summer by raising a million dollars
and effecting an organization. A resurvey was made and a
route farther south than Dixville Notch was chosen, the one
actually occupied by the road today.

Here for the first time we find a rebellion against Stephenson's accidentally-fixed gauge, which has come to be our
standard. The track width decided upon by both companies

was 5 feet, 6 inches. There are two conflicting stories as to the reason for this. One is that A. C. Morton, the engineer in charge of building the Atlantic & St. Lawrence, wanted a broad gauge and persuaded the Canadian authorities to revoke their original plan to use the Stephenson gauge, as had been done on the first few miles of railroad in the Dominion. The other is that the British Government—Canada then being still a mere colonial possession—not only favored Portland over Boston as the terminus but specified the broad gauge, different from all other roads in the United States, in order to make troop and munition movements into Maine difficult for our government in case of war—which has a slightly romantic and illogical sound to our ears. Whatever the origin, that decision caused a number of other railroads in Maine to be built on the broad gauge, and brought on a very annoying tangle in the years to come. Poor may not have originated the broad gauge, but he was as stubbornly in favor of it as if he had.

On July 4, 1846, construction was begun on the Maine project. Judge Preble, with a silver-plated shovel, filled a barrow with earth and the governor wheeled it away, while the populace madly cheered at this charming condescension. That same year the Portland Locomotive Works was organized, largely by stockholders of the railroad. Its first engine, however, was built for the Portland, Saco & Portsmouth, after which it turned out a number for the A. & St. L. and other roads.

But after two years, only twelve miles of track had been built by the A. & St. L., and money was increasingly hard to get. With Boston frankly hostile to the project, there was no chance of selling any stock there. Near the end of 1848, only fifty miles of track was ready, and a connection was made at Danville Junction with the Androscoggin & Kennebec, then building. Progress had been even slower in Canada, where only the thirty miles from Montreal to St. Hyacinthe had been accomplished. C. S. Gzowski, a Polish exile, later Sir Casimir Gzowski, was chief engineer of the St. L. & A., and its general manager after 1852. But both companies received an impetus in 1849, with England's reduction to a minimum of import duties on grain, which threw open the English market to American breadstuffs.

The Atlantic & St. Lawrence now made a contract with private builders for the construction of the road to the Canadian boundary. The cost would be $26,000 per mile, to be paid one-half in cash, one-quarter in bonds and one-quarter in stock. The city of Portland lent its credit to the extent of $1,000,000 and a little later received permission to give additional assistance. But for two years more the thing dragged lamentably, and the railhead did not enter New Hampshire until July, 1851. Then it gained speed and reached the international border, north of Island Pond, Vermont, and 149 miles from Portland, in February, 1853. The Canadian company completed its track a little later, and the whole 292-mile line was theoretically open for use in July, 1853.

The promoters lost no time in bringing about the step which had long been contemplated. A new corporation, the Grand Trunk Railway of Canada, had been organized, and on August 5, it took a 999-year lease of the Atlantic & St. Lawrence (as well as its Canadian cousin), agreeing to pay all debts and 6 per cent dividends on the stock. Portland's loan was soon repaid, and that city profited handsomely by the investment. A year-round line of steamers to Liverpool was established, and large sums were spent in Portland for terminal facilities. Over a century has passed, but the Atlantic & St. Lawrence still has a corporate existence, most of its stock being held in Europe, though a small quantity of it still pays its comfortable 6 per cent to citizens of Maine.

The new Grand Trunk Company was rather supercilious about the plant it had taken over. In the annual report of 1854 the directors said that the line was supposedly open, but was unfit for use—

Particularly the section between Sherbrooke and Island Pond, and the locomotive and carriage stock was equally deficient, but according to the terms of the amalgamation, one train had to be run every day. This was done during the winter of 1853-4 with the greatest difficulty, as there were no snow fences, the line was not ballasted in many sections, and the old company had used some sort of a metal crosstie that was unsatisfactory.

They said that the amalgamated companies had thirty-four engines, of which four were scarcely worth repairing, while most of the others required extensive repairs. The report added that new locomotives for the company were being built in England, which would indicate that the Portland works had completely lost its influence; but this did not prove to be true, for later, more locomotives were ordered from Portland, and it built, all told, one hundred and fifteen of them for the Grand Trunk.

The building of that broad-gauge line launched a quarter-century of trouble. In 1836, citizens of Gardiner, up the Kennebec, had procured a charter for the Kennebec & Portland, to create a line from Portland up the river through Freeport, Brunswick and Topsham to their town. But Augusta, still farther upstream, said, "Why not to me, too?" and as she held the seat of government and was in a position to exert considerable pressure, the terminus had to be changed to the capital, in one of several recharterings of the company.

This project was still lagging in 1845, when two other charters were issued, following in general Poor's dictum as to the necessity for a rail connection between Portland and Bangor. One of the two roads, the Androscoggin & Kennebec, was to run from a junction with the Atlantic & St. Lawrence through Lewiston to a point on the Kennebec somewhere between Waterville—north of Augusta—and Hallowell, south of it. The Penobscot & Kennebec was to build from that rail end to Bangor. Both lines were being promoted by the same group, and were essentially one. Both had at first thought of Gardiner, Augusta or Hallowell as their junction point, but jealousies and bickering arose among Lewiston, Augusta, Waterville and Portland, with the railroad companies involved. The Androscoggin-Kennebec-Penobscot twin companies depended upon the Atlantic & St. Lawrence for their western-southern outlet and therefore made theirs a 5-foot,

6-inch track, like the greater line.  Augusta leaned toward
the Kennebec & Portland, which contemplated a 4-foot, 8½-
inch gauge, so that it might run cars through over the Portland, Saco & Portsmouth (also standard gauge) toward Boston.  The P. S. & P., by the way, had bought, or rather,
subscribed for (not always the same thing) one thousand shares
of K. & P. stock.  Portland, heavily interested financially in
the A. & St. L., preferred the broad gauge, which seemed to
promise it greater returns in traffic.  There were other bones
of contention, too many to list here, but it is enough to say
that, in the end, the Androscoggin & Kennebec didn't touch
Augusta, but passed to west and north of it, joining its Penobscot twin at Waterville.

Another group, among whom were some Augusta partisans,
made the situation hotter in 1848 by chartering the Somerset
& Kennebec, which was privileged to build north from
Waterville to Skowhegan and beyond, and south to Augusta,
*if* the Penobscot & Kennebec did not enter the capital.  This
was the best charter the company could get, says a local
historian, "from the railroad power which then controlled the
Legislature of the State" (meaning, no doubt, the broad-
gauge roads) "and prevented Augusta from being connected
with the upper Kennebec by rail during a long period of
years."  The Somerset & Kennebec did not get organized until
1852, and then wanted a charter amendment, assuring it of
the right to enter Augusta with no stipulations.  It was
backed by 2700 petitioners and opposed by 1500 remonstrants
from along the "upper route," as the Androscoggin-
Kennebec-Penobscot was called.  A major objection of the
latter faction was the probability that the Somerset would be
standard gauge, to make a continuous route with the Kennebec & Portland.  There was a terrific battle on the legislative floors; eminent lawyers on both sides volleyed and thundered.  One, W. B. S. Moor, for the upper route, threatened
in the extremity of his excitement to plant cannon at a certain
point (ever afterward known as "Moor's Battery") and "blow
the Somerset road to hell."

But the Somerset road won through at last, a significant

victory for the standard gauge. It was leased in 1853 and
when completed was operated by the Kennebec & Portland.
The latter in a reorganization in 1864 turned its name around
and became the Portland & Kennebec. That this road was
getting a foothold in state politics was proved in 1856, when
the Androscoggin & Kennebec and the Penobscot & Kennebec begged to be permitted to unite, but had to be content
with a lease of the latter by the former. For several years
these two competitors between Portland and Waterville carried on a traffic war, with the Legislature, the Boston & Maine
and the Eastern Railroads all putting in their oars. The A. &
K. had trouble also with a feeder line, the Androscoggin, a
vague little concern chartered in 1848, whose track left the
A. & K. at Leeds Junction and crawled northward with much
tribulation to Farmington, reaching that place in 1859. As a
connection with the A. & K., its track was broad gauge, and
it was fully expected that the A. & K. would take over and
operate it, but it didn't. When the little road proved unprofitable, the directors planned an extension southward to
the coast. They wangled a loan from the city of Bath, and
in 1861 completed a line to Brunswick, near Bath. This extension was made standard gauge, the same as the Portland &
Kennebec, with which it connected at Bath. Next the company planned to reduce its track between Leeds and Farmington to standard. The A. & K. procured an injunction
against this action, but the Androscoggin officials dodged the
process-servers (this was on a Saturday), and on the following day, when the Law was off the job, a force of men
changed the gauge to standard. Three years of litigation
over this episode ensued, the Androscoggin family finally
being sustained. It eventually passed into the hands of the
Maine Central.

And who was this Maine Central? Why, it was the consolidation in 1862—when the Legislature at last relented and
gave permission—of the Androscoggin & Kennebec and the
Penobscot & Kennebec; and what a relief it must have been
to get at least two of those confusing "Kennebecs" off the
record! The new corporation promptly announced that its

life's aim was peace, that all bickering with the "narrow-gauge roads"—as the broad-gaugers always contemptuously called the four-eight-and-a-halfs—was at an end. It established friendly relations with the Portland & Kennebec and the Androscoggin, and evolved deep-laid plans for expansion. By 1869 it was ready. It leased the Dexter & Newport that year, and in 1870 it took the Portland & Kennebec and its dependency, the Somerset & Kennebec, under lease for 999 years. This was as much consolidation as lease, for Richard D. Rice, who had so ably headed the Portland & Kennebec for several years, now became president of the Maine Central.

Even before the union, it had been secretly planned that the gauge of the two original units of the new system should be reduced from broad to standard. Most stockholders were now taken unawares by the news, and John A. Poor, long the foremost champion of the broad gauge, brought suit in equity, seeking to prevent the change and even praying for a receiver for the company, but failed in his purpose. The broad gauge was on the way out. In 1871 the M. C. took over the Belfast & Moosehead Lake, running from its main line southeast to Belfast, and Maine's greatest railroad system was well under way. The management did not await the settlement of Poor's suit—which was not finally defeated until 1872, a year after the suitor's death—but completed its change to standard gauge in 1871. This left only two important broad-gauge lines in the state, the Grand Trunk (which became standard gauge in 1873) and the European & North American; and three smaller ones, the Somerset, the Bangor & Piscataquis and the Portland & Oxford Central. Let us notice the minor ones briefly.

The Somerset, chartered in 1860 to build from Waterville up the Kennebec Valley, was supposed to pass automatically into the hands of the Maine Central, but though that company bought $50,000 worth of Somerset stock in 1868, it did not actually take over the road until thirty-nine years later. Meanwhile, in the seventies the Somerset fell a victim to a common malady of the Maine woods in those days and saw itself as a link in an international railway from the sea at

Wiscasset to Quebec, and a rival to the Grand Trunk. Three or four other companies, first and last, were chartered to become parts of this grand scheme; towns along the way pledged their credit; a Canadian company actually built track forty miles southward from Quebec—but the Panic of '73 halted all plans, and they never came to life again, the Somerset getting no farther north than Bingham.

The Bangor & Piscataquis was chartered in 1864 and organized three years later, with Hannibal Hamlin as its first president, to build from Bangor to Moosehead Lake, but it proceeded no farther than the Katahdin Iron Works. It later became a part of the Bangor & Aroostook.

The Portland & Oxford Central began in 1847 as the Buckfield Branch Railroad, to run from Mechanic Falls on the Atlantic & St. Lawrence to Buckfield. The stockholders lost their investment, and in 1857 the road passed into the hands of a Portland promoter, of whom Louis Clinton Hatch, in his *Maine, A History*, says, delicately but significantly, "The actions of the Hon. F. O. J. Smith in connection with this line would fill a volume." The Hon. Mr. Smith, known derisively the country over as "Fog" Smith, became what might be called notorious as a telegraph promoter,[1] entitling us to some vivid guesses about his rail manipulations. Under Smith the road became the Portland & Oxford Central, was reorganized twice under new names, changed to standard gauge in 1878, and in 1890 emerged as the Portland & Rumford Falls, running far up the Androscoggin Valley. A subsidiary company built an extension to the Rangeley Lakes.

Now we turn back to the Maine Central. So important a system naturally wanted a good outlet from Portland toward Boston. It was not satisfied with its service via the Eastern, and began negotiating for control of the Portland, Saco & Portsmouth. That road had been under joint lease to the Eastern and the Boston & Maine since 1847, but it had the right to cancel the contract upon payment of $100,000 to each of the lessees. The Maine Central offered it a higher rental; its two lessees took alarm, and the bidding among the three ran up to

[1] See Alvin F. Harlow, *Old Wires and New Waves*, 1936.

10 per cent per annum, where it stopped, everybody knowing that it would be ruinous to go farther. The P. S. & P., which leaned toward the Eastern, anyhow, thereupon paid off the Boston & Maine and leased itself to the Eastern. That road immediately began making overtures to the Maine Central, and a traffic agreement was presently effected. But it did not work satisfactorily, and as its next expedient, the Eastern began buying stock of the M. C., obtaining voting control by 1875.

And here it is time to notice a grandiose project which had become somewhat frayed and faded when the Maine Central got around to noticing it. But in 1850 something of a nation-wide sensation was created when the plan for the European & North American Railway was made public, with a promise to shorten the traveling time between the United States and Europe! There was to be a railroad—broad gauge, of course, for John A. Poor was in the project up to his ears—over which you would speed through Maine, New Brunswick and Nova Scotia to the farthest point of land at Canso. From there, fast steamers, "larger than any yet seen," would run to Galway, Ireland, in five days! From there, trains would dash across Erin to Dublin; then a quick crossing of the Irish Sea to Holyhead and a rail jump to London, and there you were—and another couple of hours or so would put you in France.

The promoters thought of the Androscoggin & Kennebec and Penobscot & Kennebec as covering a part of the route: east of Bangor they would have to build their own line. Delegates from the New England states, New Brunswick and Nova Scotia met in Portland on July 31, 1850. The Canadians promised grants of land and money. Orators expatiated. General H. A. S. Dearborn of Roxbury made the hit of the day when he told how Cato had shown the Roman Senate a cluster of figs taken from a tree in Africa only four days before. "And I," he declaimed, "shall see the time when the Rose of England, blending the colors of York and Lancaster and plucked from the gardens of Windsor, shall be twined freshly in America with the beautiful prairie flower, 'the Queen of the West,' and bound together with the Lilies of Canada, shall compose a fragrant wreath wherewith to crown the Statue of Concord in the Temple of Peace."

The applause for that passage rocked the building, and when he sat down, three cheers were given for the General; but curiously enough, the ecstasy was not great enough to induce many people to invest money in the project. Maine and the two provinces soon chartered their companies, but investors were scarce. Another convention was held in 1852, at which Poor made golden predictions, but the fact was that slowness in building the Penobscot & Kennebec was a detriment to the promotion. Then came the Panic of '57 to make money tight, and next the Civil War. Relations with England became strained, and lo! there was a new argument for the building of the railroad—military necessity, the defense of the frontier!  And this a project whose chief *raison d'être* only yesterday had been the cementing of international friendship!  Upon this ground, the company obtained a grant of 700,000 acres of land from Maine, while the city of Bangor in 1869 voted a $1,000,000 loan.  With this aid and a bond issue of its own, the company finally succeeded in completing the 114½ miles from Bangor to Vanceboro, on the international border, and there was a great celebration on October 17, 1871, with President Grant, the Governor of Maine, Lord Lingard, Governor-General of Canada, provincial authorities of New Brunswick and other luminaries present.  But John A. Poor, who would have been the happiest celebrant of all on that day, had died six weeks before.

The international road never approached the greatness predicted for it.  The Canadian extension got no farther east than St. John, and it was soon bankrupt, a subject for reorganization.  The Maine company scraped along until 1875 before going into the hands of trustees, of whom former Vice-President Hamlin was one.  It had leased the Bangor & Piscataquis, whose track it used as a main line from Bangor to Old Town, and when insolvency came, the B. & P. took back its property.  In 1877 the Maine Central agreed with the trustees to aid the company in altering its

gauge to standard, and in 1882 leased the E. & N. A. for
$125,000 a year and fixed charges. Simultaneously, the
Maine Central declared the first dividend in its twenty-year
history—2 per cent.

The E. & N. A. lease included the Bangor & Bucksport,
a little road which had a curiously chameleon-like history.
Originally built to broad gauge, it was drawn down to
standard gauge in 1877, and in 1879 reduced to three feet
width. Then when the Maine Central took full charge of it
in 1883, it was widened again to standard. The M. C. next
took over the incomplete Maine Shore Line, running from
Bangor through Ellsworth to Mount Desert Ferry, across
Frenchman's Bay from Bar Harbor. This road had the
charter right to extend from Ellsworth to Calais, on the
eastern boundary of the state, near the mouth of the St.
Croix, but that line was at last independently built in the
1890's as the Washington County Railroad to Calais and
Eastport, and the Maine Central acquired it in 1904.

Allusion has already been made to the Portland & Ogdensburg, which began construction in 1870 and was intended
to connect Portland with the outlet of Lake Champlain, at
the Canadian border, but which never quite got on its feet
financially. The Central Vermont did what it could to make
life difficult for the western end of it, and that portion
eventually became a separate company, the St. Johnsbury
& Lake Champlain, which passed through the hands of the
Lowell into those of the Boston & Maine. The Portland
& Ogdensburg thought it had scored a success when it
arranged with the Eastern for through traffic over the latter's Great Falls & Conway—which touched the P. & O. at
North Conway—while from a point farther north the P. & O.
hoped to collaborate in the building of a line to Montreal.
But nothing worked out as desired.

Next the P. & O. became interested in the Upper Coos
Railroad, a little project in northern New Hampshire which
the Boston & Maine had been aiding. The B. & M. would
have liked to take over the P. & O., but the city of Portland,
which had a stake in the road, preferred to see it go to the

Maine Central; and so the latter leased it in 1888 for a miserable 1 per cent per annum on its capital stock for the first three years, and after that, 2 per cent for 996 years. (We wonder if any of these railroad officials ever paused to conjecture what the world may be like at the end of 999 years!) An extension of the P. & O., built in 1889, connected it with the Upper Coos, which was leased in 1890.

During all these years since 1874, the Eastern had held a majority of the stock of the Maine Central. But the Eastern was not of the stuff that endures, and in 1884 it passed under lease to the Boston & Maine, carrying with it the leased Portland, Saco & Portsmouth and stock control of the Maine Central. Talk that now began to be heard of a lease of the Maine Central to the Boston & Maine aroused such a furor in Maine that the B. & M. quickly dropped the idea. The Maine Central pursued its independent way, maintaining its own offices and officials, leasing and buying here and there, until in 1899 a significant development appeared: Lucius Tuttle, president of the Boston & Maine, was also elected president of the Maine Central. The camel's head had got a little farther into the tent.

A railroad designed to put Rockland on the map by connecting it with Bath was first chartered in 1849, and lived in a state of suspended animation for two decades thereafter, finally reviving in the latter sixties under the name of Knox & Lincoln. Cities and towns along its route agreed to lend it aid in sums ranging from $50,000 to $400,000; even the village of Nobleboro promised $25,000. On top of that, several bought from $25,000 to $125,000 worth of stock, the last-named figure being that of the city of Bath, which also promised a loan of its credit up to $600,000. Bath and Bangor were two cities of modest size which were extraordinarily generous in their aid to railroads. But the cost of this line along the rugged coast, bridging many rock-bound estuaries and rivers, was far more than expected, and the communities all had to put up more money, so that by the time the road was completed in 1872, $2,395,000 worth of their bonds had been sold in its behalf, secured by first, second and third mortgages. An attempt to lease the road to the Maine Central found that company cold, and when the same expedient was proposed ten years later, it was defeated by popular vote in the bonded towns along the way. But unpleasant facts stared them in the face, and they decided to sell the property at a bargain price, if they could. A syndicate which included some Maine Central directors bought it for $1,300,000 in bonds and $200,000 in cash. Waldoboro at first shrieked, "No! We won't sell!" but, being small and alone, was forced to give in. In 1891 the property was leased to the Maine Central, which surprised nobody, and in 1901 was completely merged with it.

It was in 1907 that the Maine Central took over the Somerset and then the Portland & Rumford Falls when the latter began to talk big about building a through line between Portland and Quebec. The storm cloud from down Connecticut way which then threatened the M. C. will be discussed in another chapter.

The Portland & Rochester, originally chartered in 1846 as the York & Cumberland to build from Portland to South Berwick and there to connect with a road to Boston, had like some others "military importance" as an excuse for existence. Construction began in 1850. John A. Poor was briefly president and managed to push the track eighteen miles to the Saco River, where it bogged down. The bondholders took over in 1865, changed the name to Portland & Rochester and had visions of connecting with other roads at the newly proposed terminus, Rochester, N. H., to form a through line from Portland to New York. The city of Portland issued $700,000 in bonds to aid it, and it struggled on a few miles farther. In 1870 the city was persuaded to waive its first mortgage claim and permit $350,000 in bonds to be sold to the public. The next year a new issue was offered, but they couldn't be sold, until finally good old Portland heeded the cry of distress and bought them. The track crept on to Rochester, but the great western route did not develop, the Panic of '73 dealt it a fearful blow, and in the following year it couldn't even pay its interest. Portland now issued bonds to raise money to pay itself the interest on the mortgage held by itself, a device which would have delighted the author of *Pinafore*. The truth was that the P. & R. was a bottomless sink for money and had little excuse for being. At another reorganization in 1881, the stock held by the city passed into the strong box of the Boston & Maine, but an actual merger was not completed until 1900.

When in 1837 Canadian promoters talked of cutting through Maine with a railroad from St. Andrews to Quebec, the Down-Easters didn't like the idea of Britishers making a path across their dooryard. But by 1843, when the project took the form of a line from Halifax to Montreal, Maine folk had become more receptive, though they considered the 835-mile project beyond human power to accomplish. And sure enough, it didn't materialize for another forty years. A Canadian company calling itself the International Railway tried it in the seventies but stalled at the Maine boundary. In 1886 the Atlantic and Northwest Company bought out the International and immediately leased the latter's property in perpetuity to the Canadian Pacific Railway, which pushed the track across Maine to Mattawamkeag by 1888, used the Maine Central's rails from there to Vanceboro, and built its own line eastward through New Brunswick.

And this reminds us of another railroad, a remarkable piece of development which seems to represent the sturdy pioneer character of the Maine Yankee more than any other in the state—except perhaps one. The far northern county of Aroostook, a part of which Canada had once tried to ravish from us, was without rails save for two or three little branch lines from New Brunswick to Houlton, Caribou and Presque Isle, built between 1870 and 1880. Thus until 1892 the county, save for an extreme southern tip, was without rail connection with the outer world except through Canada. When the Canadian Pacific came streaking across the state in the eighties, Aroostookians thought they were about to fall into foreign hands again. Then a man arose who brought the gospel to them—Franklin W. Cram of Bangor, who had been general manager of the New Brunswick Railway from 1885 to 1890. He saw a future in Aroostook's lumber, pulp and agriculture, and he proceeded to create the Bangor & Aroostook Railroad, one of the soundest little rail developments in America. With the aid of Albert A. Burleigh, the company was financed, mostly with money from outside the state, chartered in 1891 and organized with Burleigh as president, for Cram at first modestly took the post of general manager. The American Express Company, angry at being thrown off the Canadian Pacific, loaned $600,000 at a critical moment to this new railroad, which it believed would injure the C. P.'s business. The Bangor & Piscataquis was taken over as a starter, and from its line at Brownsville the system was shrewdly extended into Aroostook County, covering it in strategic areas and helping to develop there the wonderful potato and pulp industries and others as well. A branch was thrown out to Moosehead Lake, and from Bangor a line was built down the Penobscot to tidewater at Searsport, where a great ocean terminal was developed.

The other railroad which is typically Maine is the Belfast & Moosehead Lake. It was promoted largely by the little city of Belfast and never got any farther than Bingham Junction on the Maine Central, thirty-three miles distant. It was taken under short lease by the Maine Central in 1871, and until 1925 Belfast enjoyed a comfortable little income of $36,000 yearly from the rental. Then the M. C. gave notice that it was going to abandon service, as the road was losing $40,000 a year. Belfast was stricken with horror, and saw itself, its lumber, fish and potato industries ruined. Businessmen got together, borrowed $5000 for operating capital from a local manufacturer, rented three old locomotives and some cars from the Maine Central and started out on their own. For a few years the profit and loss curve zigzagged up and down bewilderingly; then it settled to a steady progress upward, and in 1944 the road on which the M. C. was losing $40,000 annually had a

$50,000 surplus in its treasury—which proves something or other, if only we knew what. This, one of the two municipally owned railroads in the United States,[2] is a beautiful example of co-operation. It has no vice-presidents; the president and directors serve without pay; the secretary receives twenty-five dollars a year and the treasurer one hundred dollars. Directors' meetings are now being held in the back room of a drugstore, the druggist being one of the directors. One train crew does all the freight and passenger work, and the conductor dons overalls and helps in the yard and roundhouse between times. Co-operation and the absence of lost motion make the small community a much more efficient organism than the big city or a giant government like the United States. And here may be a hint that there are too much overhead and brass headgear and formalities about the big railroads.

[2] The other is the 336-mile Cincinnati Southern, from Cincinnati to Chattanooga, built and owned by the city of Cincinnati, but now under lease to the Southern Railway.

# 15

## Twentieth-Century Epilogue

A FEW more scenes and we shall have reached the final curtain. By 1900 most of the small railroads of New England had practically disappeared from the landscape. The fine-spun threads of many decades before had been and were being gathered and woven into a few great cables of traffic. At the turn of the century three or four powerful companies pretty well dominated the scene.

In 1880 the Boston & Albany rivaled the Concord as one of the most lucrative properties per mile in New England, and it was so much bigger than the Concord that its income was far greater. Physically, it had come to be essentially a continuation of the main line of the New York Central & Hudson River, as the big road was then called. Traffic flowed back and forth among Boston, Buffalo, Cleveland and Chicago almost as if the two were one concern. Nearly two-thirds of the B. & A.'s freight income came from interchange of business with the New York Central. Then a still closer alliance was formed on March 3, 1880, when the two companies signed a compact by the terms of which each considered the other's track as a part of its main line, whereon it had the same rights and privileges as if the two were actually one. The only exceptions were that the property and earnings of each were to be kept separate. The agreement was supposed to run only five years, but it was left undisturbed for twenty.

During that time the inevitable came to pass: the big fellow wanted more and more control. The Vanderbilts had long owned some stock in the B. & A. After 1887, Chauncey M. Depew, president of the New York Central, was on the board of directors of the B. & A.; this situation was presently reciprocated by putting President William Bliss of the B. & A. on the New York Central board. But not until 1899 was the question of a lease openly discussed. On the surface, there had never seemed to be less reason for a railroad to lease itself to another: B. & A. stock was quoted at $260 a share, and to the outsider there didn't appear to be a cloud on the horizon. But shrewd President Bliss saw beyond the horizon. He knew the fear that any railroad corporation, even a strong one, invariably knows when there is a still larger one impinging on its territory. The Central wanted an entrance into Boston, and there was the possibility that if the B. & A. refused it a lease, it might take over the rival, parallel and probably willing Fitchburg, and that would spell disaster. Also, there was the fact that no one could say that the B. & A.'s good income was necessarily permanent: it might be curbed for some reason yet unknown. A substantial dividend perpetually guaranteed to the stockholders would be a better form of insurance.

Yet when the proposal for a 999-year lease at 8 per cent per annum tax free on the stock, with a guaranty of interest and fixed charges, and $4,000,000 worth of B. & A. property reserved, reached the shareholders, there was a hullaballoo: a "protective committee" including many prominent citizens of Boston was formed to fight the deal. It was pointed out that the lessee under the contract would pay the B. & A. only $2,000,000 per year, whereas its net income for 1899 had been $2,310,000. The committee argued that if there must be a lease, the recompense should be high enough to raise the value of the stock to 300. But after a long and heated wrangle, the dissenters compromised. The term of the lease was reduced from 999 to 99 years; the $4,000,000 worth of property was to be purchased by the New York Central for $5,500,000; $2,500,000 more must be spent upon the B. & A. terminals in East Boston; the railroad must remain subject to Massachusetts laws and continue to make annual reports to the Massachusetts Legislature. With these stipulations, the lease was signed in July, 1900.

Much of the opposition had stemmed from a deep-rooted objection in the New England soul to letting any outlander rule its railroads. None had ever done so before. State Street, not Wall Street, had been the dominant force in New England rails, when there was any, outside of local capital. In fact, State Street, as we shall see, had for years financed and operated some of the greatest railroads outside New England. The first two or three years after the B. & A. lease were particularly unfortunate for the New York Central. The winters were unusually severe, and there were some serious tie-ups, even embargoes. Boston was angry, and of course there was the natural human tendency to blame the new regime. Engines and cars had all been re-painted with the name, "New York Central," but resentment was so strong that the Central, craving the good will of Massachusetts, now sought to mollify it by restoring the old name to the rolling stock until the ill feeling had died away. To this day the Boston & Albany maintains a suite of high-ceilinged offices in the big South Station in Boston, its president's office hung with portraits of past presidents, going back to those of the Western and the Boston & Worcester. To Boston the B. & A. is still very much alive.

The New York, New Haven & Hartford Railroad, between 1873 and 1893, had paid dividends of 10 per cent. After the nation-wide upset of 1893 they dropped to 8 per cent. The road's acquisition of a fleet of Sound steamers had not been of great benefit to it, but it was still financially stable. In 1903 its capital stock stood at $70,897,300 and its funded debt at $14,549,300. Here enters the "heavy" of the cast, the man who changed its whole life and plunged it into troubles from which it has not yet recovered. Charles S. Mellen (1851–1927), a Massachusetts Yankee, had, through various jobs with other roads, risen to the second vice-presidency of the New Haven in 1892. It is said that from that time onward, his career became a concern of J. P. Morgan, who procured for him the presidency of the Northern Pacific in 1897. In 1903 he came back to the New Haven as president, and things began to happen. He now had a national reputation; President Theodore Roosevelt consulted him about railroad affairs and quoted him extensively in messages to Congress.

Mellen seemed to be in agreement with certain political eminentissimos, believing that a railroad as well as a nation can spend itself into prosperity. He had practiced the technique on the Northern Pacific, and he now did it on the New Haven. He improved the rolling stock, built bigger and stronger bridges, added new track, constructed new stations or remodeled old ones and landscaped their surroundings; he installed new safety devices, electrified the road from New Haven to New York and joined with the Pennsylvania in creating the Hell Gate Bridge and tunnel loop in New York City, so that trains could run through between the Pennsylvania system and Boston. It must be admitted that he almost made over the road and greatly increased its business. But at what a cost! Look back at the capitalization and funded debt in 1903, as we have quoted it. After six years of Mellen's rule, the capital had been increased by 72 per cent, the funded debt by more than 1500 per cent—the outstanding stock and bonds in 1909 being $356,737,975.

This enormous increase was in great degree the result of Mellen's having set out to put his company in control of all the railroads in New England—and the steamships and trolley lines, too. Interurban trolleys had become a threat to the railroads in the 1890's, and to make all the six states a New Haven yard, it was necessary to have a thumb on the electrics also. Mellen bought recklessly with his company's money, taking over first the lines in Connecticut, then those in Rhode Island and Massachusetts. Not only that, but he bought control of the Boston & Maine, and with it the Maine Central, and began giving orders all the way to the New Brunswick border. The Boston & Maine, as we have seen, had taken over the Fitchburg and other lines covering much of New Hampshire and extending into Vermont; thus, including its stock interest in the Maine Central, it had a system, owned or controlled, of nearly 3000 miles. It had so far been conservatively capitalized: it was not staggering under a load of watered stock, debentures, first, second and consolidated mortgages, notes and refunding certificates. E. H. Harriman, upon first hearing of its chaste simplicity, is said to have exclaimed, "Great Scott! Is there anything like that still left out of doors?" It was still mostly Yankee-owned: in 1900, 93 per cent of its stockholders by number, owning 74 per cent of its capital stock, lived in Maine, New Hampshire and Massachusetts. After Mellen had done with it, it wore a different aspect.

Mellen succeeded in having his way with Massachusetts legislators, but Governor Curtis Guild loosed such a blast against him in 1905 and 1906 that he was alarmed and promised not to take over any more lines—though he broke his promise immediately. In 1908 the Massachusetts Supreme Court ordered the New Haven to divest itself of all corporate-owned stock covering lines in the state. It merely turned its trolley stock over to a dummy concern and "sold" its $16,000,000 stock in the Boston & Maine to a Connecticut coal dealer known to be worth less than a million.

Under Mellen, nothing was too good for the utilities. When the Fall River Line steamer *Providence* was built in 1905, it had a telephone in every room. When the still more luxurious *Commonwealth* appeared, it was popularly known as "Mellen's apartment houseboat." He had a private trolley car (they still keep it somewhere around New Haven) complete with sleeping quarters, kitchen and chef, in which he junketed over his vast electrical network. One of the strangest of his antics was the building of the New York, Westchester & Boston, a non-essential electric line out of New York alongside the New Haven up through New Rochelle and Larchmont, with a branch to White Plains. The Interstate Commerce Commission reported in 1915 that this road, then 18.03 miles in length, had cost the New Haven $36,434,173—$2,000,000 a mile! Also that it was being operated at a loss of $1,250,000 annually. A New York broker with the incredible name of Oakleigh Thorne —sounds like somebody right out of *East Lynne*—couldn't account for a trifle of $1,032,000 of New Haven money entrusted to him in the creation of this line.

One need not quote from muck-rakers who have excoriated Mellen and all big business in connection with those unpleasant years. The highly objective reports of the impartial Interstate Commerce Commission (XXXI, 1915) are severe enough. Scattered through this particular report we find such phrases as "sham methods," "financial joy-riding," "low state of financial morality," "attempts to control utterances of the press by subsidizing reporters," "profligate use of free passes," "regular employment of political bosses in Rhode Island and other States." The Commission quoted the testimony of one director who admitted that as each line was gathered in, "someone would ask the question in the board of directors if it were not in violation of law, and Mr. Robbins, general attorney for the New Haven, would state to the board that the New Haven charter permitted them to do anything." As to the Boston & Maine, its financial strength, manifest for half a century, "was converted into financial weakness in half a decade, after passing into the control of men who had the reputation of being eminent financiers. . . . The management of the Boston & Maine by the New Haven . . . began in illegality and in a lust for extended monopoly, and has resulted in great depreciation and impairment of credit."

There was one road in New England that Mellen could not buy—the Grand Trunk, controlling not only its original line to Portland, but the Central Vermont system, with one long tentacle reaching down across Massachusetts and Connecticut to the Sound at New London. Charles M. Hays, a doughty antagonist, was then its president. When he took over the headship of the conservative old road in 1896, there were locomotives with old-fashioned diamond stacks all over the place, and he proceeded at once to eliminate them. He went to the Southern Pacific presidency for a time, then came back to the Grand Trunk and threatened trouble. Early in 1912 a new company, the Southern New England, had been formed to build from Palmer, Mass., to Providence, and the keels of two new boats were being laid, to run between Providence and New York. Mellen, fearing for the effect on his Sound steamers, threatened to parallel some of the Grand Trunk's trackage in Vermont, but it paid no attention to him. Fate, however, intervened in Mellen's behalf. On April 15, 1912, the *Titanic* sank in mid-ocean with Mr. Hays aboard. The Providence line had been entirely his idea, and with his death there was no one left in the Grand Trunk offices with any enthusiasm for the project, and so work on it was abandoned.

But though Mellen was improving the New Haven equipment, a series of wrecks in 1912–13 brought down odium upon the road. Those who have been privileged to sit through that delightful bit of American folklore, *Life with Father*, whose period was that of the Mellen regime, will recall that in the first act, as the family are assembling for breakfast, the eldest son, Clarence, looking over the morning paper, announces, "Another wreck on the New Haven."

"I do wish," sighs his mother, "that those New Haven people would be more careful and not have so many wrecks. If they knew how it upsets your father—" And it did upset Father, evidently a stockholder.

Those disasters, together with the passing of dividends, brought public resentment to a head. Mellen was forced out of the presidency in 1914, and the Boston & Maine was freed from New Haven domination. For the first time, an outsider, Howard Elliott, born in New York, was called to the New Haven executive chair. The company had borrowed $44,000,000 from the government before we entered the First World War, and at the end of government war control, it owed Washington $60,000,000; another $30,000,000 was borrowed later. A terrifying situation to confront a new executive! But under Elliott and two incumbencies by E. J. Pearson, it slowly began to come back. By 1928 it was able to declare a 1 per cent dividend on the common stock—and then came the great depression, to deal it and all other railroads a terrific blow. But gain or lose, the New Haven has continued to serve its territory well, and there is no smoother sleep-inducing ride in all America than you can get between New York and Boston on one of its many night trains. There is now on foot an elaborate Plan (with a capital P) for its reorganization, set forth in a large, closely printed volume of such terrifying size and statistical aspect that this writer hasn't dared even to try to grasp it.

It has long been believed in the railroad world that Mellen, in his program of expansion, was little more than a puppet in the hands of Morgan—that the Dragon of Wall Street was the mainspring of all the trouble. But an eminent Boston banker, himself a railroad president, told the writer recently that he does not believe this: he thinks the splurge was largely a manifestation of Mellen's own ego. However this may be, an unfair stigma became, in the public mind, attached to the New Haven itself; as if an inanimate thing and some thousands of skilled and honest employees could be blamed for the acts of a dictator. But there have been some who, though they may have been critical, have remained loyal. Lucius Beebe, in his delightful *Boston and the Boston Legend*, says that despite the fact that the Mellen doings brought grief and consternation to half of the first families of Boston:

The road has always remained in the status of a household institution, to be tolerated, cherished and even petted. The loss of a topcoat aboard the Merchants' Limited by the writer's father approached the proportions of a *cause célèbre* for years, and communications between the aggrieved passenger and the company's offices were maintained through five presidencies of the line. To this day Fred Wright, the ranking Pullman porter on the run, and senior conductors in blue tail-coats argue possible hypotheses to explain the disappearance of this epic surtout, and annual reports on the investigation of the mystery have been regularly

turned in by New London station-masters. Most Boston
families maintain some similar tie of affection for the New
Haven. That the line recently inaugurated one of the
world's fastest trains in the form of a Diesel clipper which
slams its way across the countryside at one hundred and ten
miles an hour cannot induce Bostonians to regard the road
as anything but a delightful and perhaps vaguely irrespon-
sible household tradition.[1]

This paragraph reminds us that both the New Haven
and the Boston & Maine have long since installed Diesel
engines on a number of their trains, both passenger and
freight. The Boston & Maine almost fell into New Haven
hands in the early 1920's, but once more escaped. It has
evidently strengthened its tie with the Maine Central, for
since 1932 its eleven top-ranking officers, from the president down, have held precisely the same positions with the
Maine Central. No railroad in the country has explained
itself and its problems to the public and strengthened the
rapprochement between road and patron quite so cleverly
as the B. & M., in a remarkable campaign of newspaper
advertising.

Of the 250 or more charterings in New England since
1830—some, it is true, never materialized—a long process of
combination and elimination has reduced the number at the
present moment to about a dozen—and that includes the
Canadian Pacific, a mere bird of passage flitting across Maine,
and the Portland Terminal, which, with 128 miles of track,
is not to be sniffed at. It also includes the St. Johnsbury
& Lake Champlain and the Montpelier & Wells River, still
entities but leading sheltered lives, and the pert little Belfast
& Moosehead Lake, which seems destined to roll on as long
as the old Yankee spirit survives in Belfast—which, let us
hope, will be to eternity.

The Boston & Maine, with 1910 miles of its very own and
the 991-mile Maine Central system, a sort of Siamese twin,
has the greatest mileage in the six states. The New Haven,

[1] We accused Mr. Beebe of dramatizing the topcoat story, but he denies
it—though in the Gilbertian manner, "Hardly at all."

with 1867 miles and much double and quadruple track, is the other great system. The New York Central—or shall we say Boston & Albany?—is perhaps third in the list of greats, though the 603-mile Bangor & Aroostook, modest and sound as a nut under the presidency of a son of its founder, is a force to be reckoned with. In 1922 the Grand Trunk was taken over by the Canadian Government, to become a part of the Canadian National Railways. It operates the Central Vermont system and runs some fine Montreal–New York trains over its main line, while massive freight caravans thunder over its old track—where Poor once scouted through the blizzard—threading the White Mountains down to Portland. As hinted in Chapter XII, the future of the old Rutland, 407 miles of it, is shrouded in uncertainty.

At the end of the First World War, the railroads of New England, like those of other parts of the country, were handed back by the government to their owners in a dilapidated condition. Add to this the growing competition of the automobile and the unfair competition of trucks and buses, which do not have to maintain any tracks but run freely over public-owned highways—and New England's thickly settled area makes the competition of the motor vehicle all the more difficult to meet—and you have reasons which have for decades kept the railroads figuratively with noses to the grindstone, and have caused grave, but we hope unwarranted, fears for their future existence. During the second world conflict they have had some opportunity to catch up and to bank some well-deserved but long-delayed profits; but coincidentally, they—again we include all railroads of the nation—have demonstrated in this terrific emergency that profit is not their sole motive and that probably no business created by man can so magnificently rise to a crisis and overcome it as our rail transportation system. It has done many times as much and as varied work with fewer men and far less adequate equipment than in the days of peace.

# 16

## The Thin-Gaugers

A CONSIDERABLE number of narrow-gauge railroads
—that is, with two-foot and three-foot width of track
—have been born and died in New England, for they
are practically all dead now, and it is a pity that their homely
little history cannot be more thoroughly canvassed here,
since it is full of human interest. They were always quaint
and appealing little things, like human midgets leading lives
of their own, their toy engines going about their work as
fussily as a bantam hen, jumping the track and tumbling
about at frequent intervals, yet seldom killing anybody, and
in the long run performing much useful service for business
and society.

Narrow gauges came late in New England. A small book
on the subject published in 1875 mentions only two in that
area—the one on Martha's Vineyard Island and a three-mile
line at Worcester. But in that very year George E. Mansfield, living near Hyde Park, Mass., was building the narrow-
est railroad track the world had ever heard of. He had just
returned from Wales, where he saw a fourteen-mile, two-
foot gauge line doing a sound industrial job, and he saw
no reason why such a thing should not work in this country. As a preliminary experiment, he built near his home
a quarter-mile line with a mere ten-inch gauge: he used
strap iron rails on wooden stringers, the "ties" being bits of
one-inch plank. When he could persuade some of his neighbors to ride on the infant trains with him, they began to
think he might have an idea there.

Hearing talk of a projected railroad from North Billerica on the Boston & Lowell, to Bedford, 8-1/3 miles distant, Mansfield hurried up there and persuaded the local promoters, for economy's sake, to make it a two-footer, and so it became the first of that width in America. There had been a two-foot ore hauler built at Peekskill, N. Y., two years before, but it was strictly an industrial affair, not a common carrier. The Billerica & Bedford was organized in 1876 and opened for use in the fall of the following year. In the further interests of economy, its stock certificates, all locally sold, were type-set at a job printing shop and printed in red ink—an ominous portent, though no one seems to have noticed it. Two bunty little engines were bought, of the type designed by M. N. Forney (though built by Hinkley), which can best be explained to the uninitiated as a one-piece job, the small, stubby tender being fastened rigidly to the cab. In this case, too, the pilot and headlight were placed on the tender and the locomotive ran backward—evoking jeers and criticism, to which it was retorted that the engine crew could see ahead better, the cab was cooler in hot weather and could be closed in winter. Someone with a sense of humor and romance appropriately christened the two little engines "Ariel" and "Puck." They were sturdy pullers, too.

But some of the company's stock subscriptions were unsound, the road lost money and could never build a single passenger station on its line. Even before the road's completion, the contractors asked for an assignee to aid them in getting their pay. The company wriggled through that pinch, but early in 1878 it was thrown into bankruptcy: service was suspended on June 6 and everything was sold at auction. It was less than two years old.

Folks in several villages up in Franklin County, Maine—Strong, Phillips, Madrid, Rangeley and others—had been wanting a railroad for a long time, and when they heard of a two-footer down in Massachusetts, it sounded as if it might be just their size. The folding up of the B. & B.

did not discourage them; they thought that in their own area, rich in timber and entirely devoid of railroads, the idea would be more successful. The four towns mentioned above each promised a loan—to be paid when they saw the trains come in—and there was quite a bit of enthusiasm, but none of it reached the pitch of being willing to put up any money in advance to get the thing started. Boston was appealed to and promised to take $20,000 worth of stock if a like amount could be sold elsewhere—a tough stipulation. The man who had bought the B. & B. engines and cars for $9000 agreed to turn them in for $20,000 in stock if the new concern had no bonded indebtedness.

The company gladly accepted his offer but couldn't lay hands on so much cash. A Railroad Aid Society was formed, which used all sorts of devices for raising money: it staged plays, picnics, dances, suppers, lectures, anything for which a charge could be made. By March, 1879, $60,000 in subscriptions had been recorded, of which $3000 had been paid in cash! The company now organized as the Sandy River Railroad, with Abner Toothaker as president (Headaker would have been a better description of him in the next few years). The revised plan, necessitated by the shortage of cash, was for a line from the Maine Central at Farmington through Strong to Phillips, eighteen miles, omitting the continuation to Rangeley, which would have doubled the distance. Rangeley didn't like it but could do nothing.

Grading began in June, 1879. The two B. & B. engines, built to burn anthracite, were now converted to wood burners—wood being the cheapest of commodities in Franklin County—and renamed "Dawn" and "Echo." The cars were shipped to Farmington. But progress in tracklaying was slow, and it began to look as if they couldn't put the trains into Phillips by November 20, the deadline for saving that town's credit loan. Everybody along the way was urged to "give a day's work to the railroad," and merchants and their clerks, farmers, lawyers, preachers, all sorts and conditions of men, gave not only one but some of them several days, so that the goal was attained amid a tumultuous celebration.

Gradually more equipment was added, though its builders had to wait a long time for their money. In 1880 the directors, with $383.69 net in the treasury, even talked of extending from Farmington forty miles southeast to Gardiner on the Kennebec, but fortunately they did not attempt it. Instead, some of the stockholders helped in 1883 to organize the Franklin & Megantic Railroad, to build from Strong fifteen miles northward to Kingfield and open up a large area of virgin timber. In 1894 the Kingfield & Dead River was launched, to carry the rails on to Bigelow, and was operated by the F. & M. Neither ever prospered. In 1889 the Phillips & Rangeley was chartered, to carry out the original intention of the Sandy River. It, too, lost money consistently. It issued bonds from time to time and tried to pick up a bit of change by organizing and selling stock in two little branch lines, the Madrid and the Eustis Railroads, but nothing availed to change the annual balances from red to black.

Yet traffic from this spreading network of unprofitable little lines, all siphoned through the Sandy River from Phillips and Strong to Farmington, gave that trunk line increasing prosperity—so much that its president in 1898, Josiah S. Maxcy, a Gardiner banker, took over the Kingfield & Dead River and the Franklin & Megantic. The Sandy River even boasted a "saloon" or parlor car in those days. But, like its cousins, it was a tissue of amusing contrasts. Winter snow was the curse of all small northern railroads, and S. R. trains had been known to take two or three days to cover the eighteen-mile course from Farmington to Phillips, the passengers camping at night in the cars or at houses along the way. Game was plentiful in the woods, and all train crews carried guns. Once an engineer and fireman leaped from opposite sides of the cab to get a shot at a flock of deer they ran through, leaving the engine trundling along untended, until a brakeman crawled over the tender to shut it off. On another occasion a P. & R. train was skirting a millpond when the track dropped from under it: it was discovered that a colony of beavers had undermined the piles supporting it. [1]

President Maxcy, to cut down overhead, succeeded in 1908 in consolidating all these lines, which now sprayed out like the branches of a tree: one system, the Sandy River & Rangeley Lakes, was established, with a capital of $300,000. The new company for three years showed a small profit, but Charles S. Mellen, the terrible djinn of the New Haven, had his eye on it, and ordered the Maine Central, of which he had obtained temporary control, to buy it. Stock control was achieved by the M. C. in 1911 and some alterations begun. The Central advertised the Rangeley Lakes as summer resort country and boosted the passenger business considerably, one train in summer sometimes carrying as many as 400 persons. But the automobile was beginning to have its way, and as new roads were built, railroad business rapidly fell off and small branches began to be dismantled. In 1923 receivers were appointed. The revenue was now shrinking steadily, and in 1931 the steam passenger trains between Phillips and Rangeley were taken off and replaced by gasoline rail buses. Trucking companies were stealing the pulpwood business. In 1934 rails began to be removed from parts of what had been main line. On May 18, 1935, the road was sold at auction for $20,200, over the protests of certain mill owners along the line, and some of its steel was sent to Japan, to be used in killing our young men in the Pacific war. By the end of 1936 the largest system of two-foot gauge railroads in the United States had vanished from the earth. When H. T. Crittenden wrote his history of the road in 1941, there were still, among the fallen walls of the old roundhouse at Phillips, remains of the running gear of some of the locomotives—but this has probably been dug out since and contributed to the war god's scrap drive.

Bridgton, on the west shore of Long Lake in southwestern Maine, was a noted place of resort even before the railroads

[1] Incidents from "The Two-Footers" by H. T. Crittenden, *Bulletin No. 57, Railway & Locomotive Historical Society*, 1942.

came. Through most of the year it was accessible only by stagecoach, and in summer by steamboat through a chain of lakes. Agitation for a railroad from a point on the Portland & Ogdensburg began in 1879, but trouble flared when the Bridgton selectmen talked of a $40,000 bond issue to aid the project. The town became divided into "pros" and "antis," the latter led by steamboat and stage owners, and in 1881, when organization as the Bridgton & Saco River Railroad was effected, an injunction was granted against the proposed bond issue. Probably no small railroad project in history ever caused more community acrimony. The town detoured the injunction by voting to buy $36,000 worth of stock of the company, and early in 1883 another twenty-four-inch railroad was opened from Hiram Junction on the P. & O. to Bridgton, sixteen miles distant, two dinky little ten-ton locomotives doing all the work at first.

For nearly a decade the company was alternately in and out of the red, but by 1891, with a great increase in logging along the line, profits began to appear, and for the next ten years the company prospered in a modest way. It bought new equipment and in 1898 extended its track five miles farther, to Harrison at the upper end of Long Lake. When this was done, the company actually issued a neat advertising booklet, telling the world of the beauties of the Cumberland County lake region. Passenger traffic increased, and in 1921 the Maine Central (now operating the P. & O.) bought all the stock and improved the line and equipment. Dividends up to 11 per cent annually were being paid. But as the timber land was cut over, mills moved away and reaction came, and by the middle 1920's there was a deficit which steadily increased. Receivers were appointed in 1927, and in the following year citizens formed the Bridgton & Harrison Railroad Company to take over the road. The Bridgton News accused the Maine Central of having bled the road of $109,000 in dividends between 1912 and 1924, equivalent to practically the entire capital of the company.

In the first year of the receivership the B. & H. showed

a profit of $6000. The B. & H. corporation bought the property for $27,000 in 1930—and within four months abandoned service on the Harrison extension. The rest of the line managed to keep its nose above water. Summer business was particularly heavy from 1934 to 1936, but the rest of the year was a loss. Rail buses and motor units pulling freight cars were installed. The rapidly increasing cult of railroad fans discovered the road in 1937 and used it frequently thereafter for their characteristic outings, when they thronged the cab and took turns at holding the throttle. But the road was in a bad way, and all rolling stock that could be spared was being scrapped. In 1939 the town, which owned a majority of the stock, requested through the selectmen that the property be sold. The directors refused, factions formed and an imbroglio ensued. After two years of acrimony, the directors agreed to sell, but not to permit abandonment. The only offer to buy came from a junk dealer, and so the brawl continued for another two years, when the selectmen finally won the debate, and the Bridgton & Harrison, too, passed into limbo.

Wiscasset, Maine, with a better natural harbor than Portland's, could never understand why it was passed by as a great railroad terminus. In 1854 it chartered the Kennebec & Wiscasset, which was to connect it with Augusta, but not a foot of the line was ever constructed. A new company, the Wiscasset & Quebec, organized in 1873, bought the K. & W. charter, and it, too, immediately sank into slumber. In 1892 another company of the same name and with the same Quebec hallucination, dug up the old charter and planned a twenty-four-inch railroad. After two years of promotion, they mortgaged the road to a bank in Waterville for cash with which to get started, and the railhead crept northward on a hand-to-mouth schedule, progressing by 1900 some forty-three miles to a point across the river from Waterville. Poverty-stricken as it was, it had tried to give birth to two subsidiary lines. It began building piers for a bridge across to Waterville, but collapsed, bankrupt, and after a year's operation by receivers, was taken over in 1901 by a new corporation, the Wiscasset, Waterville & Farmington. The road was operated with a regular annual deficit until December, 1906, when a chain-store proprietor named Peck bought a controlling interest and apparently had it on the way to a more stable existence when he died in 1913, and its near-prosperity quickly faded. The thing changed hands a couple of times more and was finally scrapped piecemeal between 1934 and 1937. Its history had been even more depressing than that of most narrow gauges.

There were two other two-footers in Maine. One, the Kennebec Central, extending from Randolph to the National Soldiers' Home at Togus, five miles distant, began operations in 1890 and was heartily prosperous until a competing electric line was built to Togus. The railroad tottered on somehow until 1933, when it was dismantled. And there was the six-mile Monson Railroad, built in 1882–83 from a junction on the Bangor & Piscataquis to Monson, a slate-quarrying town. Slate was the road's chief reason for being: by 1940 its days as a common carrier were practically over, and it has survived since only as an industrial line.

We have mentioned the Bangor & Bucksport, which in one of its many incarnations was a three-foot gauger. And there is the Hoosac Tunnel & Wilmington, affectionately known to rail nuts as Hoot, Toot & Whistle, about the only narrow gauge left in the east which they can take possession of once a year and run the train to suit themselves. It is primarily an industrial line, running from the Fitchburg at the east portal of the tunnel up the Deerfield River a few miles into Vermont. One yard-wide railroad whose story differs radically from all the others is the Boston, Revere Beach & Lynn, which we have mentioned in Chapter VII. Opening in 1875, it was a success from the start, bringing woe and gnashing of teeth to the rival Eastern Railroad's household. Happy is the nation or railroad that has no history, and happy is this road that we can dismiss with a sentence or two.

Next most important to the Revere among the three-footers was the West River, which ran up the stream of that name from Brattleboro, Vermont. Originally planned in the 1840's as a standard gauge which was to cross the Green Mountains to Lake Champlain, the folks up the valley fought from 1867 to 1876 to get something under way and finally compromised on a narrow gauge to be called Brattleboro & Whitehall. After some optimistic and precarious financing, they began grading in 1878, and in the fall of 1880 the rails reached South Londonderry, thirty-six miles from Brattleboro, where they halted. The story of the road's highly checkered, fifty-six-year existence [2] is one of the funniest in all rail history, though most of the time the reality was anything but funny to directors, stockholders and passengers. Perhaps the stockholders, of which there were many up the valley, had the most fun, for on annual meeting day they all had a free ride down to Brattleboro and free dinner at the hotel. If one member of a family owned one share, the whole family horned in on the excursion.

This road seemed to have more than its share of derailments and bizarre mishaps. Snow caused the usual two- to five-day tie-ups, and once a train was eight days in toiling over the thirty-six miles of the line. At another time a landslide stopped everything and the mail which had left South Londonderry five days before finally came into Brattleboro on a hand car. Sometimes, when northbound trains failed to leave Brattleboro for a couple of days because of snowdrifts or broken-down engines, passengers from up the line who had bought tickets for home were boarded at the hotel by the railroad company. The anecdotes told of the road's troubles are too numerous to repeat here, but one of the choicest is told of the occasion when it took three engines, two snow-plows, three train crews and two days' time to transport four passengers from Brattleboro to the other terminus. The toils and endurance of the devoted employees are almost beyond belief in an age when so few people

[2] It has been well told by Victor L. Morse, first in the *Brattleboro Reformer* and later in pamphlet form.

want to do a hand's turn more than is barely necessary to enable them to get by on pay-day.

The Central Vermont had lent the company $150,000 early in the game. It foreclosed the mortgage in 1903, reorganized the concern as the West River Railroad, widened the track to standard gauge (charging the company $75,000 for the job) and made it a sort of Old Folks' Home for all the decrepit equipment it had lying around. Shopmen often toiled all night trying to patch up an engine so that it could take a train out in the morning, and then it might break down on the way. Fortunately, they had the telegraph. Once when a passenger engine broke down en route, a relief engine known as the "Scrap Heap" was sent to the rescue but collapsed on the way, and a third engine finally rescued the half-frozen passengers, who had burned all their firewood. There was one occasion when all the company's locomotives were off the track at once. The cars became so leaky that water sloshed around the floor in a rainstorm and passengers sat with umbrellas raised. The great flood of 1927 did much damage, but the Central Vermont had such appalling troubles of its own that it couldn't waste any thought on the West River. Valley citizens wangled a $200,000 loan from the state and put the road in good repair again. Then a man named Ashley, with an ambition to run a railroad, took a twenty-five-year lease, and with a rail bus and a decrepit engine proceeded to lose his life's savings. Finally, the staff was reduced to himself and his wife, she running the engine and he throwing the switches. In 1936–38 the road was dismantled, and the state managed to salvage $30,000 of its loan.

Talk of a railroad through Oak Bluffs, Edgartown and Katama on Martha's Vineyard Island, already a popular summer resort, began in the 1860's. After years of heated discussion, Edgartown gave the project some financial aid, and the three-foot line was completed in August, 1874, too late to get much of the summer's business. When the "Active," the only engine bought by the company, was brought to Woods Hole on a flat car to be transferred to a boat, the yard crew backed the car too abruptly against the string-piece of the pier and the "Active" shot off the car and dived into the harbor. They fished her out with a smashed pilot, and when she was sent back to be cleaned up, the shopmen swore they found seaweed in her cylinders. She was delivered to the Vineyard on August 22, amid great enthusiasm, and a booming business began. When General Grant visited the island the following week, a new era seemed to have dawned. There were financial troubles during the first three years while they were getting the road paid for, and Edgartown became pessimistic and sold its stock in 1877, just as the line began to be profitable. For a decade, it paid well, but Katama faded out as a resort, nullifying the value of the line south of Edgartown. In 1892 the big hotel at Oak Bluffs burned, and with it the railroad's pier, and in 1896 the trains ran for the last time. The "Active" finished its career working ignobly in a mill yard.

The other island off the coast, Nantucket, first built a three-mile narrow gauge from Nantucket town to Surfside, the south beach resort, in the spring of 1881, and carried 30,-000 passengers, they say, in that summer. It was extended from Surfside to Siasconset in 1884. This eleven mile line is affectionately remembered by old-timers, its friendly little trains obligingly stopping for you anywhere if you waved at the engineer. It passed out of existence in 1910.

# Operation by Trial and Error

THE fish-belly rail used by the Lowell never went any farther, and even the Lowell discarded it within a few years. The strap rail, which exhibited a fiendish tendency to come loose at the end, rise like a cobra, stab through the floor of the car and bite the passengers' legs or sometimes inflict even more serious injury—and as a final malignity, perhaps throw the train off the track—continued

*Strap-Rail Track, on Wooden Stringers*

in use by some roads even after 1840. A U-shaped rail was the next device, the U being upside down, with ears fastened to the sleeper by "chairs." But Robert Stevens, engineer, son of the railroad pioneer John Stevens, while crossing the Atlantic in 1830 had the inspiration which solved the rail problem for all time. He whittled out of wood a small model of a T-rail—he called it H-rail—which "could be spiked with hooked headed spikes directly to the bearing," and did not differ greatly from the rail of today, save that its top was rather more bulbous. But there was also a T-rail made without base attached, so that it had to be seated in a "chair," which itself was spiked to the tie. Strangely enough, wooden instead of iron chairs were sometimes used: the Vermont Central tried them for a time.[1]

Cast-iron rails sometimes broke as soon as put in use, and as America had no rolling mills in the earlier railroad years, all the rolled iron rails used in this country were imported from England and were usually of high quality. Stevens had difficulty in persuading British foundrymen to make rail after his pattern: at first they couldn't believe such a slender-waisted thing would stand up under the strain. But gradually they came around.

Meanwhile, iron works in Maryland and Pennsylvania had begun making U-, H and T-rails, but for a long time some of the leading railroads continued to buy most of their iron from England. In the Boston & Albany (New York Central) offices at Boston, the writer read many copies of letters from President Wales of the Western, beginning in 1838, ordering rails, oddly enough, from Baring Brothers, the London bankers, who placed the orders with various iron works. This arrangement was satisfactory all around. The American railroads were confident that they would get none but good iron if they ordered through Barings, while the manufacturers no doubt preferred to have the account handled by the bankers, who were familiar with the situation and knew how much credit those American chaps should be allowed. From Mr. Wales' letters, it appears that he often left it to Barings to choose the makers, and they distributed the orders among the Coalbrookdale, Ebbw Vale, and other sterling concerns. The Western Railroad, as is proved by these letters, was ordering rail from England well into the 1850's, long after America had begun rolling a pretty good article.[2]

[1] *Fifth Annual Report of the Railroad Commissioner of the State of Vermont to the General Assembly, 1860.* Rutland, 1860.

[2] An interesting letter of Wales to Barings, March 24, 1838, says, "As accidents happen to the best of vessels, I desire you would not ship more than 200 tons by one vessel, and only American vessels be used." Naturally,

The weight of rail steadily increased, and we find that in 1851 and 1852, old worn rails of English make were being re-manufactured into heavier rail—sixty pounds to the yard—at the Bay State Iron Works in South Boston and the Rensselaer Iron Works in Troy, N. Y. This practice continued for many years, for the iron in the English rail was of better quality than the American, and it was possible to remake it here more cheaply than good quality rail could be bought abroad.

Apparently, one might buy cheap rail, even from England, if desired, and some of the first produced in America was, as we have said, pretty poor stuff. E. B. Grant, in his pamphlet, *Boston Railroads* (1856), speaks of "a railway leading from Boston," whose history demonstrated the difference between good and bad iron. On one track was a lot of rails laid in 1834, most of which were still in excellent condition, although they had been in constant use for twenty-two years. In the same track were others laid in 1843, of which about half had been renewed; some laid in 1849, mostly renewed; and a few (his italics) *"of a lot laid in NOVEMBER, 1855, but taken up in FEBRUARY, 1856, utterly useless."*

America did not begin using steel rails until Civil War time; the Pennsylvania Railroad imported the first in 1863.

The subject of ties soon became an important one, too.[3]

---

Wales wanted to favor his friends and neighbors, the American ship-owners.

In 1939, one of those fine old English rails, a relic of the Hudson & Berkshire Railroad, was dug out of a creek bed between Chatham and West Stockbridge, and sections from it are preserved in the B. & A. offices at Boston. Its outer surface is furrowed a little by the contact of nearly a century with water and mud, but once cleaned and put in a dry place, it ceased to rust, and the cross-sections show that magnificent, fine-grained iron, with a polish like sterling silver, to be as sound and serviceable as it was when we were fighting the Mexican War.

[3] When American railroads shifted almost at the start from stone to wooden ties, while England still used stone, the English thought, wrote James H. Lanman ("Railroads of the United States," in *Hunt's Merchants' Magazine*, Vol. III, p. 284) that because of the "locomotive propensities of our population . . . constantly moving in masses from point to point," American railroads were "designed to be merely temporary, in order to be adapted to the changing political and statistical condition of the country."

Cedar resisted rot, but it was none too strong and the supply was limited. Some roads used oak, but oddly enough, we find no mention of it in Vermont in the early 1860's, where the State Railroad Commissioner listed a curious assortment of tamarack, hemlock, spruce, beech, birch and maple, with tamarack proving the most durable. Some of the others, he said, were being burnettized, a process named for its inventor and aimed at preserving wood with a solution of zinc chloride. Another process used to some extent in New England was kyanizing, so called because it was originated by J. H. Kyan, who used corrosive sublimate. Both processes were later supplanted by creosote.

There were no iron bridges in early decades of railroading. Most bridges, especially those of any considerable length, were of wood, though there were many fine stone arches, such as those of the Canton Viaduct on the Boston & Providence, built for the ages. Of the timber types, the Howe Truss, a wooden arch, was the favorite. This, as well as the lattice and other kinds, was usually covered over, to prevent the decaying action of the weather upon the trusses and sills. (You may still find a few covered wooden railroad bridges in Vermont.) But the wooden roof also menaced the bridge with destruction by fire from the engine sparks. Hence, most railroad payrolls had to include a watchman for each bridge, whose duty it was to inspect the structure—with pails of water in hand—after the passing of every train. Orders to locomotive engineers included the injunction, "Close ashpan while crossing bridges and shut off steam when possible to do so." The showers of sparks from the engine exhaust not only jeopardized the company's own property, but every fire in field, forest or building near a railroad track was apt to be attributed to "sparks from a passing locomotive," and damages were demanded. The balloon stack was a more or less futile attempt to overcome this trouble, and there were other devices—including one stack which somewhat resembled a saxophone—nearly all patented and too numerous to mention. Would-be "smoke consumers" appeared about 1840.

Wood continued to be burned on some roads until well

into the 1880's.  The Boston & Providence in early days
bought a large tract of forest in North Carolina, solely for
the purpose of providing itself with fuel, which was delivered
by coasting schooners.  An engine might have to be "wooded
up" every thirty or forty miles; hence, wood stations were
placed that distance apart, and farmers or others had contracts
to keep them supplied with good, heavy billets of the right
length.  The whole crew, with the possible exception of the
conductor, and even he in some cases, helped to toss the sticks
into the tender.  Not infrequently, husky passengers took a
hand, too, helping to get the train away as quickly as possible.
Some railroads in early days were so poor that old-timers long
afterward said they carried a saw and axes on the tender and
an extra man, so that they could stop and cut wood wherever
they saw a fallen tree, since they had no supply on hand and
no money to buy any.  New England sometimes saw trains
seized for debt at way stations, and once an official on board
pledged his gold watch to free a train.

Coal-burning locomotives appeared in considerable numbers in the fifties.  William Mason, the great engine-builder
of Taunton, produced his first one, for the Providence &
Worcester Railroad, in 1856.  But some of the more northerly roads used wood long after that.  The Maine roads, where
timber was still plentiful, were ordering wood-burners decades later.  Maine Central headquarters wrote to Baldwin,
who had built the "Governor Coburn" for them in 1870,
"The Coburn makes sad havoc with our wood-piles.  Can she
be improved in this particular?" [4]

[4]For some years the Boston & Worcester directors gave a page or two
in their annual reports to the "Doings of Engines." In 1867 they had
twelve coal-burning passenger engines (all named), two coal-burning
passenger-and-freight, eleven coal-burning freighters, five coal-eating
switchers, four wood-burning passenger engines, one freighter digesting
either wood or coal, one wood-burning yard roustabout and four wood-
burning "mixed" engines. The "Mars," with 32,215 miles during the year,
was the greatest voyager of the passenger locomotives, while the "Vulcan,"
passenger and freight, with 35,271 miles, was busiest of all. The "Buffalo"
switch engine averaged the greatest number of miles per ton of coal, 100.3,
its fuel cost per mile being only 9.5 cents, while the "Lion" ran only 41.8
miles per ton, and its fuel cost per mile reached the shocking figure of 21.9

Here it may be pertinent to quote the "Winter Rules for Enginemen" of the Boston & Worcester in 1835, when they were using the first little locomotives, whose pipes froze whenever the mercury dived toward twenty degrees. Remember, these rules were for men whose experience with locomotives had been limited:

To prevent the hose from freezing, use each pump alternately, first one and then the other, or what is better, use one pump all the time and shut the water off from the other.

As there is no means for filling the tenders at all depots, be sure, when the road is impeded by snow, to take warm water whenever it may be necessary, and heat it with your steampipes, blood warm; but where the track is clear, water at Framingham, as the cistern there is heated. If you get stuck in the snow, be careful *not to let your fire go entirely out*, but keep the engine warm and pour water in at the safety valve, otherwise the fire tubes contract and burst.

### In Short,

Keep your boiler full of water and the water hot. If this is done, no damage can ensue.

J. F. CURTIS, Supt.

Nov. 23, 1835

When the snow scraper is ahead, be sure to have it run the right end foremost.

It might be mentioned that there were times in dry seasons when the wayside tanks were empty, and trains had to stop near a brook or pond and form a line of crewmen and passengers, who dipped water in the leathern buckets which were kept hanging on the tender for the purpose, and passed them from hand to hand to the engine.

For ten or twelve years after railroads began operating in

---

cents. There was a wide difference in wood-burners, too—from 30.8 miles per cord to 50.8. Accounting had by that time become meticulous. The cost of oil and waste per mile for each locomotive is noted, the cost of repairs per mile, likewise the number of eight-wheeled cars drawn one mile, and finally, the cost per car-mile of fuel, oil, waste and repairs.

New England, it did not seem to occur to anyone that the engine crew might be sheltered from the elements. The engineer and fireman balanced themselves precariously, one foot on the locomotive and one on the tender, and took cinders, rain, hail, snow, sleet and terrific cold as it came— sometimes perhaps holding up a shingle to keep the rain or snow out of their eyes. One of the first engineers on the Boston & Lowell remembered standing for twelve hours at his post one day with the temperature far below zero. The first hint of a cab is said to have been a piece of canvas stretched between a couple of standards and the upright boiler of one of those "crabs" or "mud diggers" on the Western. Next it is rumored that a Boston & Lowell engineer named Wing rigged for himself a portable cab, probably of wood and canvas, which could be set up in winter and removed in summer: this was about 1847. By 1850 an engine without a cab was considered antique.

As locomotives became heavier and more powerful, the length of freight trains increased remarkably. In 1837 it was a matter of wonder that the little, nine-ton "Patrick" drew thirty-five cars, 201 tons weight, from Boston to Lowell, twenty-six miles in two hours and fourteen minutes; also that another machine built in the Lowell shop for the Stonington Railroad and only of ten tons weight, pulled forty-nine burden cars, total weight 276 tons, ten miles in fifty-one and one-half minutes. But Charles Brooks, the historian of Medford, writing of the Boston & Lowell in 1855, said, "The longest freight train drawn by one engine that has passed, loaded, over the road, numbered 163 baggage cars." He meant freight cars, of course, probably those early four-wheel affairs, none of them twenty feet long. But even so and even on the level B. & L., if we accept his statement that the cars were loaded and drawn by one engine, we find it hard to believe that the number of cars had been accurately reported to him.

And speaking of those early burthen cars, the first ones were little larger than a big wagon, but they grew in size steadily. The very earliest ones were open to the air, but that was soon corrected. For several years, all of them were brakeless. Fancy the difficulty of stopping a train with no brakes anywhere save on the engine! No wonder freight engineers were forbidden to run more than ten miles per hour. The Western Railroad, because of its steep grades, began to equip its freight cars with brakes from the very beginning, but some older roads were not so careful. When the Massachusetts Committee on Railways and Canals investigated an accident on the Western in December, 1840—a freight train had run away on a grade near Springfield and jumped the track into a terrific smashup—the report revealed that the Western and the Boston & Worcester were "using each other's cars indiscriminately," that there were a number of Worcester cars in this train, "and that the Worcester cars had no breaks on them. . . . Since this occurence, breaks have been attached to every car for passengers and freight, and a breakman to every two or three cars"—and the Committee did not think any such accident need happen again.

We doubt that the order for a "breakman" to every two or three cars was ever given the slightest notice by the railroads. Few companies, and certainly none of those in the state of near bankruptcy which was so common, could have afforded such a swarm of trainmen, even at a dollar-a-day salary. It was not until trains began to lengthen considerably that more than one brakeman was employed, and a freight conductor was in many quarters regarded as an unnecessary hanger-on. The brakeman was another chap who in early days had to take the weather and like it, for not until after 1850 were there any cabooses! Fancy sitting or standing on top of a train nipping along through a zero gale! No wonder the poor brakie so often took refuge on the locomotive, especially after cabs came in. As for his lunch, James H. French of Dorchester, an Old Colony veteran,[5] said that "frozen dinners in winter time were made eatable only by first stuffing the pails down the engine waste pipes."

By 1848–50, larger, eight-wheeled box cars were coming in, but many of the little old four-wheelers were still in service.

[5] Address before New England Railroad Club, Nov. 13, 1900.

The necessity for brakes had brought about the running board on top of the cars, but the brakeman's chore was a tough one, for every railroad had its own ideas as to height, shape and arrangement of cars. A typical freight train, a hodge-podge of sizes and painted in the wild variety of colors then affected by the railroads, was as multifarious in appearance as a zoo, and the brakeman was continually climbing up and down from one car to another. Some of the old four-wheelers were so much lower than the newer cars that three-link couplings had to be used, and they did not dare put one of those little cars, empty, near the front end of a long train, for it would be lifted right up in the air when the train started.

A. V. H. Carpenter, a Chicago businessman who wrote his memoirs in 1890, was born in Vermont, and in his callower years was stirred, by the building of the Vermont Central, with a yearning for adventure as a railroader. Armed with recommendations, he approached Governor Paine, president of the company, and won a dollar-a-day position as a freight brakeman. He had never climbed the side of a freight car in his life, but green as he was, he was sent forth on a winter day in 1849, with the mercury standing at thirty-six below zero, to grapple with the job on a run over half a dozen roads, all the way to Boston. Swathed in thick clothing, extra socks and boots, he mounted to his post. The ins and outs of the crew system, if it could be called a system, Carpenter regrettably does not explain. He had another brakeman with him as far as White River Junction. There the train was split and the other brakeman accompanied a part of it down the river valley, leaving Carpenter to escort twenty-five of those heterogeneous cars down the Northern Railroad to Concord. There was not even a conductor, but fortunately there was no local work or switching to be done. At Concord his cars were joined to a Passumpsic Railroad freight, which must have come over the same track just ahead of or just behind his; and, plus some other cars from here and there, the elongated caravan proceeded toward Boston with two conductors—one from the Northern, who now became, *ex officio*, the boss of the amalgamated train, while the Passumpsic conductor was reduced to the status of a brakeman, along with Carpenter.

Cattle cars in 1849 apparently did not have slatted sides; at least, they had a hole in the roof for ventilation, with a shutter which was turned back on the roof. Carpenter had made only two or three trips when he lost his lantern over the side one night, and in grabbing for it he fell through the trap-door of a stock car, down among the cattle. Fortunately, he escaped being trampled to death, but he had a rough time of it, and he couldn't get out. His cries brought rescue at the next stop, but when fished out, he was, as he says, "in no fit condition to appear in public."

It is evident that very early in the game it was found desirable to send loaded freight cars off their own parent tracks into alien territory. In the pioneer years there was no real system of keeping track of such wandering cars, and the owners might completely lose sight of them, but they got even by using as if they were their own the cars of other roads which fell into their hands, paying nothing for the rental, of course; nobody did. Cars might thus be used by non-owners for weeks, months, years—perhaps eventually be sidetracked as in "bad order." It was inevitable that such conditions should, after twelve or fifteen years, give rise to the functionary known as the car tracer and to a slowly evolving system of accounting for cars. Carpenter, after short terms of service at other jobs, became a tracer of lost freight and baggage and of stray cars for the Vermont Central. He says that the V. C.'s cars were not supposed to go west of the Hudson River, though one occasionally did. He even found on one occasion that employees of a certain New England road—which he does not name—had playfully stolen one of the Vermont Central's cars, lifting it onto trucks different from its own and painting it in the other road's color and design. But Carpenter was able to identify it by its earmarks, and he forced payment for it.

Foreign travelers were astounded to find the right of way unfenced and stock wandering over and along the railroad tracks at will. Trains sometimes had to stop and shoo herds off the track, for if one was killed, not only was there quite a pother about it, but a full-sized cow or horse was very apt to throw the light rolling stock of those days off the rails. "It is impossible to say," reported Captain Marryat (*A Diary in America*, 1839), "how many cows have been cut into atoms by the railroads in America." The Boston, Concord & Montreal directors of 1849 devote space in their report to mentioning an item, "damages of $22.76 for a cow destroyed by one of our locomotives in October last."

It might be interesting to glance at the salaries paid in those days. A stockholders' committee report of the Nashua & Lowell in 1850 shows that the superintendent and treasurer each received $1500 per annum; the superintendent's clerk, $800; the ticket master, $500; his assistant, $400; the master of transportation, $800; the roadmaster, $700; the station master at Nashua, $34 a month; baggageman, $1 a day; passenger conductors, $600 yearly; freight conductors, $540; engineers, $420 to $720; firemen, $1.25 a day; section hands, $1, and crossing watchmen, 67 cents a day. The superintendent's clerk kept the office accounts, paid all bills, made monthly settlements with other roads and with the freight master, settled with the passenger conductors and the Lowell ticket master once a week, settled with the stage drivers and kept the stage account (whatever that was); also copied in longhand all the superintendent's correspondence, made up the half-yearly accounts, ran a train as conductor in the absence of either of the regular conductors (sometimes one or two weeks at a time), made up the monthly accounts of receipts and disbursements for settlement with the treasurer, and occasionally wrote contracts for wood—and all for $66.66 per month.

The conductor was early established as the dictator of the train. "He will tell the Engineer when to START and when to STOP," said the Boston & Providence running rules of 1837, and he was to "report immediately upon his arrival at the Depots any disobedience of orders on the part of the Engineer." An early rule on all roads was that the engine bell must be rung, beginning eighty rods from a crossing. Another widespread rule was: "Trains will at all times move round curves slowly and with a good look-out; the engine bell will be rung at intervals until the engine has passed from the curve on to the straight line." The Boston & Maine as late as 1845 ordered that all wagon roads be crossed "carefully, so as to avoid frightening horses," and forbade a train passing another at a station to do so at a rate of more than four miles an hour. The red flag has not always been the danger signal, for on the Providence road in 1837, when brakemen were sent forward and back from a stalled train, they carried blue flags, while on the Eastern Railroad the flags were white.

An early rule found on several roads stipulated, when a train broke down between stations: "Let a Breakman get on horseback as soon as possible," and be dispatched to the nearest point for assistance. The Eastern, in 1838 when it ran only between Boston and Salem, decreed still more quaintly: "If at any time a train should not arrive at either depot in one hour from the time of its starting from the other, the Master of the Depot will immediately start on horseback to learn the cause of the delay." The Eastern then had the rule that no train should leave either end of the line when a train scheduled to be coming toward that end had not arrived. As business increased, this rule soon became impossible.

Naturally, the problem of meeting trains was the one which produced the most and the worst headaches during the first four decades, when New England railroads still scorned the telegraph. Among the rules on the subject were these: A delayed train, when the time was near for it to meet another one, "will not pass any Station unless it have time to reach the next Station ten minutes before the time assigned in the time table for the other Train to leave there." If a train arrived at a "turn-out" where it was to meet another train, and the other train didn't appear, "the Conductor, after remaining on the turn-out 15 minutes, will send a Brakeman forward with a flag, with orders to proceed as rapidly as possible." When another quarter-hour had expired, the train would proceed cautiously until it overtook the brakeman, then repeat the process. "Passenger Trains will *not* wait for Freight Trains," said the rules, emphatically. "Freight Trains *will* wait indefinitely for Passenger Trains." And a train which had been delayed until 6 A.M. of the next day lost all its rights and must keep out of the way of all others, which were to proceed as if the delinquent did not exist.

One of the earliest of all signals (hand-operated in those days, of course) was one which still endures—the highball. At the approach to an intersection or a drawbridge, a red or black ball was hoisted to the top of a pole if the way was clear, lowered to the ground if not. Failure by an incompetent engineer to observe the lowered ball caused the Norwalk bridge disaster in 1853.

Before railroads had been in operation long, it was found that the safety which had been boasted for them in comparison with stagecoaches was not necessarily a fact, especially on a single-track line. The Boston & Providence had been in operation no more than a year when it suffered a collision—with no fatalities, it is true, but seven seamen who were more or less injured recovered damages amounting to $11,350. That was an ominous portent for the railroads. Litigation became common, and though judges tried to persuade juries to hold the scales impartially, the tendency to penalize the supposedly wealthy corporation—though sometimes it owed more than its capitalization and was living from hand to mouth—was inevitable.

In that first Boston & Worcester collision in 1841, which was considered so terrible, though nobody was killed, one finds two of the prime causes of the earlier disasters—the lack of a telegraph or signaling system and the employment of green hands in the operation of trains. Whenever there was a large popular gathering and extra trains were called for, the early railroad managements were thrown into a dither, and trouble ensued. There was such an occasion on the Nashua & Lowell in 1841, when not enough engineers were available for the extra trains and they put on one engine a stage driver who had never before touched a throttle, under the impression, perhaps, that if he could drive a stage he could drive a locomotive. Again no one was killed in the resultant collision, but it cost the company $16,000, and the stockholders were still talking about it ten years afterward. Incidentally, a present-day observer does not so greatly wonder at their putting a novice on the job when he climbs into the cab of an old engine such as the *Daniel Nason*, now preserved in the New Haven shops in New York. Even in 1863, when this Boston & Providence locomotive was built, there were just three handles in the cab for the neophyte to learn the use of—the Johnson bar, the throttle and the injector. Compare it with the intricate maze of gadgets confronting the engineer of a modern steam locomotive, and you are likely to think that a boy of sixteen could learn to drive one of those old machines in one lesson. And so he could—after a fashion.

A series of accidents on the Western Railroad soon after it was completed was attended by some fatalities, and the State Committee on Railways and Canals was called upon to investigate. The higher valuation placed upon human life in those peaceful, pre-automobile-and-airplane days is indicated by the fact that the committee even went thoroughly into the case of a man who was killed while crossing the track at a road intersection—finding that he was not only deaf but that "it is supposed that his attention was attracted by a party coming from the opposite direction." They looked into the affair of the runaway train already mentioned which had so many "breakless" cars, and then took up the worst case, that of a fatal collision at Westfield. The hazards of those days, when trains were run on what was known as time-table rules—which were likely to be different on every road—plus written or verbal orders from the superintendent, and the care and common sense (if any) of the trainmen, are well illustrated in this instance.

It was October 5, 1841. The Western Railroad had been opened to the state line only the day before, and trainmen were still unaccustomed to the extension beyond Pittsfield. Time cards and a schedule of meeting places had been prepared and given to each conductor. The eastbound train

leaving Pittsfield at 10:05 and the westbound leaving Springfield at noon were to pass each other at Westfield at 12:25.
But fearing delay on the part of the eastbound train from
Hudson, Trainmaster Barnes at Springfield had written an
order reading:

> The train from Springfield at 12 M. for Hudson will have
> the preference.  Therefore, if the train from Hudson is de-
> layed, it will stay back and wait for the train from Spring-
> field.  If the train from Springfield is delayed, the train from
> Hudson will wait one hour behind its time, and then come
> on, keeping its time just one hour ahead of its true time, so
> as to arrive in Springfield at 1:48 P.M. instead of 12:48.
>
> > Springfield, Oct. 4, 1841.
> > For Mr. Lee, Conductor.
> > Show the above to Mr. Warren.

Lee, with the westbound train leaving Springfield at 7 A.M.,
was to meet Warren, eastbound, at Pittsfield at 10:05.  Both
were late, however, Lee reaching there at 10:25 and Warren
ten minutes later.  The crudity of pioneer railroading is seen
at its worst in the committee's description of what then happened.  When Warren arrived, "Lee, with his train, was taking in wood a short distance from the passenger-house."  He
presently returned to the station, became busy with passengers
and baggage, and not until his train was ready and the agent
was urging him to be off did he start, with the order in his
hand, to find Warren.  "A man who had been helping about
the baggage, and who he supposed belonged to Warren's
train," told him that Warren was "on the other side of the
train."

"Want me to give him that letter?" asked the stranger.

"Yes," replied Lee.

"I'll give it to him," offered the man, whereupon Lee
handed it over, saying, "Be sure to give it to him," and went
on his way.

Not until a number of unfortunate folk were killed did the
menacing importance of such orders begin to percolate
through men's brains.  When Lee came back from the state

line a few hours later, the stranger handed the envelope back to him with some remark to the effect that "he had not given or had forgotten to give it to Warren." Lee, says the committee, showed it to the agent at Pittsfield "and expressed his apprehension that there might be some difficulty, but that gentleman thought all would be right, as Moore and Warren would run cautiously." By that time, unknown to them, the disaster had already occurred. Warren, wholly unaware of the order, hurried his train eastward over the Berkshire summit and down the slope toward Westfield. His engineer protested and wanted to stop at Chester and wait for the up train, but Warren would not listen, and so the appalling thing happened.

Charles Minot had begun to dispatch trains on the Erie by telegraph in 1851, and was soon followed by other roads, but New England refused for twenty years and more to follow Minot's lead. This fact is all the more amazing because Yankees had been leaders in most other rail improvements and devices, either originating them or quickly taking them up when they appeared elsewhere. Telegraph lines spread rapidly over New England, whose commerce and journalism came to find them indispensable; only the railroads remained insensible to their value. As early as 1847 there was a wire from Boston through Salem to Newburyport, yet twenty-four years later one of the worst disasters in New England history occurred between Boston and Salem because the superintendent of the Eastern Railroad still stubbornly refused to use the telegraph. Here was the only phase of railroading in which New England rail men appeared hidebound. They clung to the thesis that the telegraph was a faddish and dangerous medium: the only sure way to transmit orders was by word of mouth or on paper. An advertising card of the New York, Providence & Boston (Stonington) Railroad, issued about 1870, actually boasts, "No Trains Run by Telegraph."

Nevertheless, in the decade 1840–50, partly because of the still moderate speed of trains and partly because the first few collisions had frightened trainmen into a more careful and cautious attitude, New England roads produced comparatively few fatalities. The Massachusetts Legislature found at the end of 1848 that the railroads of that state, from the beginning of their operation to date, had killed only twenty-two passengers and injured sixty-nine. The casualty list among employees was larger, for with the lack of safeguards which prevailed, early railroad men led a really hazardous life. Again in 1852, it was reported that in the past seven years, although the Massachusetts railroads had carried 55,357,000 passengers, only forty-two had been killed, twenty by their own carelessness in trying to jump on or off moving trains by standing on car platforms. But of employees, one hundred and twenty had been killed, thirty-two of them freight brakemen who were struck by the overhead structure of bridges. There were no fringes of leather thongs hanging over tracks then, to warn them of the nearness of bridges or tunnels.

For decades rapid expansion kept an oversupply of amateurs in the service, even in official positions, and there was a considerable percentage of fatality among them, due to inexperience. In 1839, James F. Curtis, superintendent of the Boston & Worcester, was, according to a contemporary newspaper account, "killed by putting his head from the car window near Boston," which clearly means that it struck against a building or bridge truss: everything was too close to the tracks in those days. And there was the case, some years later, of John Kauffer, engineer on the Androscoggin Railroad, who tried to thaw out a frozen petcock on his engine one winter day by blowing into it and was so badly burned in the mouth and throat when it back-fired that he died within a few hours.

The evidence is plain that for years many railroaders, high and low, didn't realize the gigantic potencies of the thing they had created; mentally, great numbers of them were still living in an age of stagecoaches, when their primitive operational forces were pretty easily controllable. As an example of the naïveté of early days, James H. French, the Old Colony veteran already quoted, was told by an old-timer in 1903 that when he was a section hand up-country half a century before, they never put out warning flags when they were replacing a rail, unless a regular train was nearly due: they never calculated on specials or delayed freights. They frequently went some distance to their lunch at noon, leaving a rail out and no flags to warn of it, simply because there was no train scheduled to pass at that time. Incredible as it may seem, a repair gang working on a bridge near Chester on the Boston & Albany one day in 1893 took some nuts and bolts out of the ironwork, and since noon arrived just then, knocked off for lunch, leaving it in that state. While they were eating, a train came along, the bridge fell apart, and many persons were killed or injured. That sort of thing could not happen in the twentieth century.

Probably the luckiest of all New England railroads in the matter of accidents was the Hartford & New Haven. One says "lucky" advisedly, remembering that it ran on strap rails until 1846; one cannot believe that the Most High had singled it out for special protection, as its directors seemed to believe. In their report of 1841, they demurely remind the stockholders:

> While accounts are almost daily reaching us of the destruction of life and property on other railroads, on ours no accident has occurred of any moment from its commencement to the present time. For this happy result we are indebted, under a kind Providence, in a great degree to the skill, prudence and care of our Superintendent of Motive Power, Mr. Wm. F. Hardy.

In the report of the following year, Mr. Hardy was deprived of credit:

> It is not less a subject of devout gratitude to the Almighty Disposer of Events, as well as of mutual gratulation to us that while the past year has teemed with melancholy accidents all around, the companies Rail Road has continued to be signally preserved, and the Board has no material accident to record.

Piety continued to grace the record in 1844:

With a deep sense of obligation to an overruling Providence, the Board again records the immunity from any serious disaster during the year of all the passenger and freight trains.

After that—although their immunity from wrecks continued until 1852, fifteen years after operations began—they apparently decided that God was getting too much credit, and they began ascribing the freedom from smash-ups rather more to good management. The Portland, Saco & Portsmouth directors in 1856, in the decade of disasters, were more objective: speaking of the year's passing without serious mishap, they added, "which is a cause for thanksgiving rather than boasting"; while the Somerset & Kennebec directors in 1861 manifested no piety at all when they remarked that the year's total freedom from accident "is chiefly attributable to the faithfulness of the Employees."

The decade of the 1850's was a calamitous one for the railroads. Tracks in the busier areas were far more densely populated with trains, and there had been little double-tracking. There were as yet no automatic signals or telegraph service; the power and speed of locomotives had been greatly augmented; time-tables were faster; engineers were becoming blasé, and in a free-and-easy age, they were like present-day teen-agers at the wheels of automobiles—they liked to see 'em eat up the rails. The first wooden bridges were beginning to decay, and they and the curves of the light pioneer track were not always proof against the surge of heavier locomotives and trains sometimes doing forty miles or more per hour. Boilers began to blow up, too, under the high-pressure urge for speed. In a Waltham cemetery is an epitaph to the memory of Michael Mitchell, a native of Ireland, "who came to his death on the 6th day of February, 1854, in Danbury, N. H., by the explosion of the locomotive Daniel Webster, of which he was engineer, aged 24 years."

"Thou didst not sink by slow decay,
Like some who live the longer."

Another factor was the public mania for speed, a rapidly developing psychosis which to this day has never ceased. Where railroads paralleled each other for a few miles, as they did in several places in New England, train races frequently took place, with the firemen stoking madly, cars careening in terrifying fashion, passengers half out of the windows, cheering, yelling defiance at the competitors and laying wagers. The *Illustrated American News* said editorially on January 29, 1853, "The public mind should be exorcised of the fiend which has possessed it, and which is impelling it on with heedless steps, inducing utter disregard of all considerations of safety."

That scathing editorial, from which we can quote only briefly, was published some three weeks after the calamity which fittingly ushered in the blackest year in New England rail history—the wreck caused by a broken rail on the Boston & Maine near Andover, in which President-elect Franklin Pierce's son, a boy not yet twelve years old, lost his life. Mr. Pierce and his wife were little hurt, but the boy, who was standing by a window, was killed, as were half a dozen others.[6] It was in that year that editors began referring to the disasters as "massacres."

W. E. Baxter, a visitor from England, remarked, "When I was first in America—in 1846—railway accidents were almost unknown, whilst in 1853 there were no fewer than 138, killing 234 persons, and wounding 496."[7] His figures covered

[6] Mrs. Pierce, a very devout woman in poor health and evidently something of a mental case, never recovered from the loss of her son, yet she was convinced that the bereavement had been an act of God, depriving the President of his child in order that he might have no abstraction, nothing to divert his mind from the responsibilities of his high office. She accordingly persuaded her husband to retain Benjamin F. Butler to defend the railroad against any damage suits resulting from the accident; and that wily limb of the law tells in his memoirs how he cozened the jury in the first suit into holding the railroad guiltless, after which there were no more suits brought over that affair.

[7] *America and the Americans*, London, 1855.

the whole United States, of course, but New England had more than her share of the trouble that year. One of her wrecks alone, that at the Norwalk bridge, cost fifty-two lives. The pages of the illustrated weeklies during the year were ghastly with horrifying pictures of wrecks, many in New England. William Chambers, another British tourist of the year,[8] was jolting up the Berkshire grade in a night train on the Western Railroad—in a day coach, of course: sleepers had not yet appeared in New England—when the train stopped about 1 A.M. for no apparent reason, since there was no station in sight. He saw the trainmen and several passengers climbing down an embankment with lanterns, and upon asking the reason, was told, "Only to take a look at some cars that were smashed this morning." He went outside, and by the lanterns' light saw below him a wrecked train, the locomotive on its side, cars crushed, the last one standing on end with its tail in the air. It was just a sight-seeing stop for the train crew. They clambered over the wreck, discussed it, came back aboard and the train went on.

Really criminal carelessness was seen in some of the accidents of that year. At the inquest held over some of the victims of a collision on the Providence & Worcester between Pawtucket and Whitinsville on August 12: "It appeared from the evidence that a brakeman was acting in the capacity of a conductor . . . that his train, with a single exception, had never been on time, and that the company had allowed him to run his train with a watch that would not run correctly." A few years before, in 1849, the Boston, Concord & Montreal directors, stressing the company's great care in operation, reported that an otherwise excellent trainman had been regretfully discharged simply because he let his watch run down!—also that they would tolerate no employee on the payroll who used liquor in any form or quantity. We wonder how long that rigidity endured.

Some further reasons why collisions occurred may be found in James H. French's memories of official time-tables:

[8] *Things as They Are in America*, 1854.

# THIS CAR FOR

| | |
|---|---|
| SO. LAWRENCE | KENNEBUNK |
| HAVERHILL MASS. | BIDDEFORD |
| EXETER | SACO |
| DOVER | OLD ORCHARD |
| SALMON FALLS | PINE POINT |
| NO. BERWICK | SCARBORO BEACH |
| WELLS BEACH | PORTLAND |

# CHANGE AT DOVER, N.H. FOR

| | |
|---|---|
| GONIC | WEST ALTON |
| ROCHESTER N.H. | SPRING HAVEN |
| FARMINGTON " | LAKE SHORE PARK |
| NEW DURHAM | BELKNAP POINT |
| ALTON N.H. | GLENDALE |
| ALTON BAY | GILFORD |
| LOON COVE | LILY POND |
| MT. MAJOR | LAKEPORT |

*Courtesy Warren Jacobs*

For information of travelers, these 11-by-14-inch cards were hung inside
passenger cars on the Boston & Maine in the 1850's.

Courtesy New Haven R. R. and Warren Jace

Not railroad presidents, but dignified Yankee conductors of Civil War times.
Conductor John Bradley, at bottom, devised rebuses for his checks,
to entertain passengers.

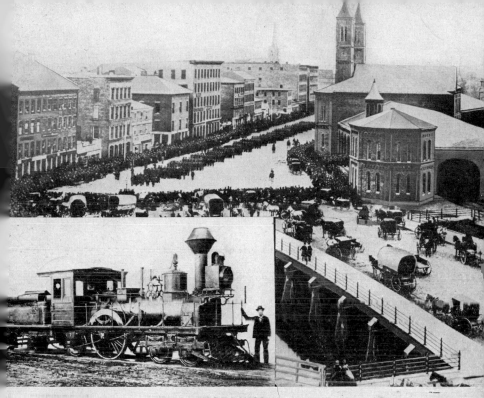

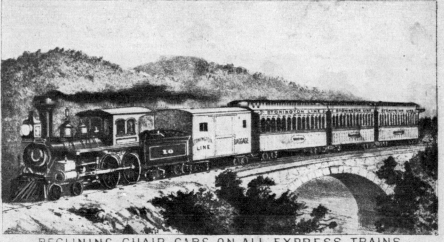

RAIL ROADS OF STONINGTON LINE ARE DOUBLE TRACK.

RECLINING CHAIR CARS ON ALL EXPRESS TRAINS.

*Courtesy New Haven R. R., Chas. E. Fisher, New-York Historical Society*

*Top*—A Rhode Island regiment leaving Providence Union Station
for the front., 1861.
*Left*—First locomotive of New York, Providence & Boston
(after cab was added).
*Bottom*—Ad. of Stonington R. R. (N. Y. P. & B.) about 1870. Note the
assurance "NO TRAINS RUN BY TELEGRAPH".

English-type railway carriages introduced on the Old Colony Railroad, 1866.

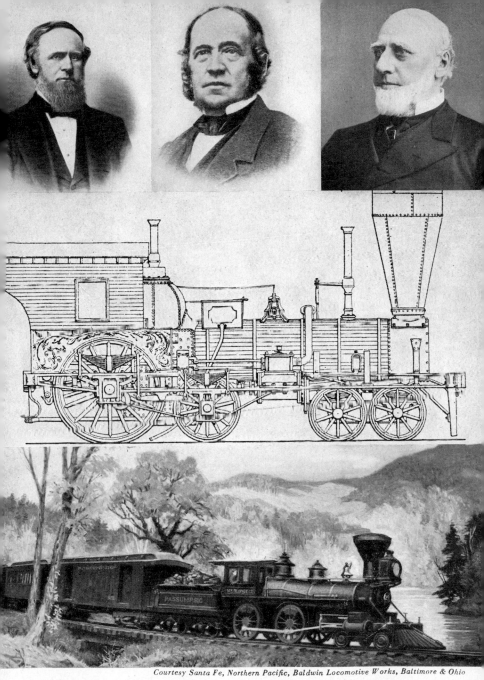

John B. Page
Pres. Rutland, West Shore

Henry Keyes
Pres. Passumpsic, Santa Fe.

J. Gregory Smith
Pres. Central Vt., No. Pac.

Locomotive "Governor Paine," Vermont Central, 1845.

The "W. K. Blodgett," Passumpsic R. R., driven by Daniel Willard, 1882.

Courtesy of Warren Jacobs

A TRAFFIC JAM ON CAUSEWAY STREET, BOSTON, IN 1884.
Here are four types of Transportation: Railroad, Elevated line (under construction), horse car, and horse-drawn bus.

*Courtesy C. B. Burr, Scientific American, John S. Kendall, N. Y. Pub. Library*

*Top*—New Haven, New London & Stonington's "Madison," 1860.
*Below*—Narrow-gauge engines.
*Left*—Bedford & Billerica.
*Right*—Profile & Franconia Notch.
*Bottom*—Nantucket R. R.

OUTSIDE CONNECTED PASSENGER ENGINE.

AMOSKEAG MANUFACTURING CO.

MANCHESTER N. H.

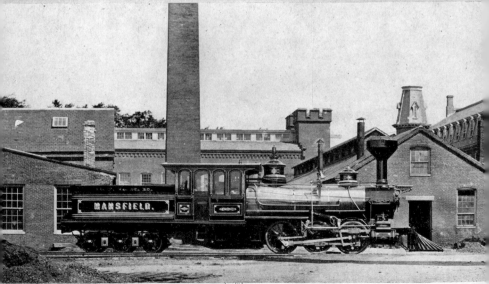

*Photos from Boston Public Library and Charles E. Fisher*

*Above*—Lithograph poster of the Amoskeag Locomotive Works.
*Below*—Mason's factory yard at Taunton, with one of his yard-engine types.

# PATRIOT, Extra.

## Terrible Accident
## On the Providence & Worcester Railroad!
## 13 Killed—Many Injured!

PATRIOT OFFICE, WOONSOCKET, }
2 o'clock P. M., Friday, Aug. 12. }

It is our melancholy duty to record a dreadful accident which occurred this morning, on the Providence and Worcester Railroad. A collision occurred between the Uxbridge (down) Train and the Providence (up) Train, about a mile this side of Pawtucket.

The Engine of the Uxbridge Train was driven a-top of the Providence Engine, and three Cars of that Train were almost entirely demolished.

From THIRTEEN to SEVENTEEN persons were killed, and many injured.— We have conversed with several passengers who were on board the Trains, and from them gather the following names of the dead:

### LIST OF KILLED.

Rev. Mr. Penny, of Manville, R. I.
John K. Perkins, fireman, of Uxbridge.
Mrs. Geo. Plant, of Whitinsville.
Peter Plant,            "
Thomas Brown,           "
Wm. Fullerlove,         "
Mrs. Richmond, of Worcester.

The names of the others killed we could not ascertain.

### INJURED.

Horsa Ballou, Pomfret, formerly of Woonsocket,—head badly cut.
I. H. Southwick, Superintendent of the Road, injured by splinters.
L. H. Perno, Providence, head crushed.

Frederick Wood, Westfield, Mass., severe gash on the head.

Mr. Goldthwait, of Uxbridge, arm taken off.

Mr. Chapin, Whitinsville, slightly injured.

Geo. Jepherson, brakeman, arm broken.

Rev. Mr. Bates, Northbridge, badly bruised.

John Brown, Whitinsville.

Geo. Plant, Whitinsville, badly hurt; wife and son killed.

Rowland H. Brown, and daughter, Whitinsville, badly bruised.

Francis Rist, Whitinsville.

We learn these particulars mainly from Messrs. Frederick Luke, of this village, and C. M. Wheelock, of Uxbridge, who were in the up train. Mr. Wheelock, who was in the baggage car, made a very narrow escape. He was considerably bruised by the trunks, which were thrown in every direction. Mr. Eliphalet Cook, of this village, also made a narrow escape. He was almost entirely divested of clothing.

The Uxbridge Train embraced an excursion party from Uxbridge and Whitinsville, and consisted of eight cars, all full of passengers. The people from these towns were the greatest sufferers.

We may issue another Extra this evening, with additional particulars.

*Courtesy New-York Historical Society*

*A Boston Newspaper Extra of 1853*

Instead of train numbers, conductor's names were used on some roads, and the schedule said that Brown would meet Jones at Jericho. Jones might die the day the time-table took effect and Brown be fired, but "Jones" and "Brown" met at the appointed place, day by day, notwithstanding. ... In the time-tables of some roads, the schedules merely gave the leaving time at the initial point, and not a figure or other indication to denote where the train went, or when it might be expected to get there, and yet the run covered the whole length of a single-track road!

One superintendent issued time-tables only to trains whose time was changed; and once a very important train which, because of uncertain connections, was required to keep clear of all other trains, happened to have no change in its schedule. Fortunately, its conductor learned of the new time-table and called at the office to ascertain why he was not supplied. He was informed that there was no change in his time. "No," said he, "but the time of every other train on the road is changed, and I've got to dodge 'em all."

The *New York Herald*, in a scorching editorial of 1858, captioned, "More Railway Murders," declared that the railroads of the country were "crazy, tumble-down structures over which the trains rush and sway at tremendous rates of speed, trusting to luck for the safe delivery of their passengers."

That was a bad decade for the railroads, morally and physically. Overproduction, a mania for building new lines, was bringing about a recoil—failure in maintenance, ruinous competition and rate wars. Stock jobbery in all its phases was being learned by men with tricksy tendencies: the year 1854 was notorious the country over for frauds in the over-issuance of railway shares, which had a depressing effect upon such stocks in general.[9] Most of the railways of New England escaped these evils, but there were a few, a very few, as we have seen, which unfortunately suffered from them.

Accidents had a sobering effect on many and spurred ef-

[9] "O me! How awfully bad the Railway Share-market looks!" wrote Thackeray, the novelist, to his friend, Willard S. Felt of New York, August 18, 1854.

forts at reform. The Norwalk bridge horror in 1853 brought about the immediate creation of the Connecticut Railway Commission. It also shocked the New York & New Haven Railroad into self-correction, so that by 1870 its directors could report proudly that during the year past, 9500 passenger and 2393 freight trains had passed over the road, not to mention gravel trains, and not one locomotive or car wheel had left the track. Nay, more: in fourteen years past, the road had carried 21,035,346 passengers, without loss of life or limb to any one of them.

Great changes in railway operation were then in the making, but one more dire disaster was needed to precipitate a general reform and bring about the use of the telegraph and other safeguards now regarded as indispensable. The logical place for this holocaust to occur was on the graft-ridden, badly managed Eastern Railroad. How it had escaped some fearful retribution of the sort for as long as it had is a mystery. The story is retold here only to illustrate the obstinate opposition to the telegraph which still prevailed, in no case so obstructively as in that of Jeremiah Prescott, superintendent of the Eastern, who manifestly was not big enough for his job. He seems never to have awakened from the belief that a railroad could be run in the same easy manner as a stage line.

As a result of the overbuilding of the 1840's and 1850's, the Eastern then had two almost parallel lines from Everett, a few miles out of Boston, to Lynn: one was known as the Saugus Branch; the other was the main line, which ran through Revere, where the old track branched off toward East Boston. The telegraph line which followed the railroad had offices in all the principal towns, sometimes actually in the railroad stations, though none at the smaller stops; but Prescott made no use of it. "If an engine broke down or a train got off the track," says C. F. Adams—then a Massachusetts State Railroad Commissioner—whose vivid description of this disaster we follow closely, "there was nothing done except patient waiting until things got in motion again; each conductor and station master had to look out for himself . . .

and need expect no assistance from headquarters." And this with a road nearly all single track!

During the unusually busy week ending Saturday, August 26, 1871, the ordinary summer volume of traffic had swollen enormously, and when Saturday was reached, "the confusion became so great that trains reached and left Boston with almost total disregard of the schedule." The staff in Boston that evening simply gave all their time and effort to getting trains made up and sent off, helter-skelter. Between 6:30 and 8 P.M., four trains were scheduled to depart—two Saugus Branch trains, at 6:30 and 7, a main line local at 7:15, and the Portland Express, main line, of course, at 8. In the prevailing confusion, all were late, and the second Saugus Branch train had become sandwiched in between the accommodation and the Portland express.

All four trains must run over the same track to Everett. There the first and third were to diverge to the Saugus Branch, the second and fourth to the main line. The rules were explicit that no northbound train might enter the Saugus Branch there before any southbound train then due should have arrived and passed off it. That evening a southbound branch train leaving Lynn at 6 was an hour and a half late because of some mechanical difficulty. Accordingly, when the first northbound branch train reached Everett, it must not enter the branch until the other train arrived. Believe it or not, there was no siding at Everett where trains could pass each other: the first Saugus train when it came blocked all the other trains behind it, each in turn being flagged.

In the words of Adams, "there was something ludicrous about the spectacle . . . a succession of trains standing idle because a locomotive had broken down ten miles off." There was a telegraph station at Lynn, and two instruments and operators in the station at Boston, but Prescott had never placed any reliance in the wire. "A simple message to the branch trains to meet and pass at any point other than that fixed in the schedule would have solved the whole difficulty; but no!—there were the rules, and all the rolling stock on the road might gather at Everett in solemn procession, but until the locomotive at Lynn could be repaired, the law of the Medes and Persians was plain; and in this case it read that the telegraph was a new-fangled and unreliable auxiliary."

The State Railroad Commission said in its report, "The employes of the railroad, both at Lynn and Boston, say that they think the telegraph operators at both places had either gone for the day or gone to tea; but at neither Boston or Lynn was any inquiry made for them, nor any endeavor made to telegraph inquiries or information."

At last, at 8:10, the belated train from Lynn rolled in, and by a four-times seesawing, the two Saugus Branch trains were released and went on their way, with the main line accommodation departing between them, and finally, the express. The conductor of the accommodation afterward vaguely thought he had been delayed there six or eight minutes; in reality, it was fifteen. Though he was clean off his schedule, "he took not a single precaution, so persuaded was he that everyone knew where he was." The non-arrival of the Lynn train at Boston had warned Prescott that there would be a blockade at Everett, and he had cautioned the engineer of the express to look out for trains ahead of him— this message being delivered to him orally from the platform just as he was moving out of the Boston station. He did not know that four trains instead of two had been held up at Everett: he thought the accommodation was far ahead of him.[10]

The result was that when the accommodation stopped at Revere, a few miles beyond Everett, the express was close behind it. The night was hazy, the visibility none too good. At Revere a track branched off to the shore, and a light on a mast indicated whether the switch was closed or not. Neither train crew knew where the other was. As the ex-

---

[10] Prescott's idea of train dispatching was to say to a departing conductor, "When you pass Smithers" (conductor of an incoming train) "tell him we're going to run an extra, leaving here at three o'clock. Tell him if he can pass it at Lynn, all right; if not, let him keep clear." He was superintendent in 1856 when a long freight train once waited all night at Salem for an extra passenger train, which in turn spent the night at Ipswich, waiting for the freight.

press came dashing along, the engineer was peering upward through the murk, looking for the switch signal light. The weak tail lights on the local were the company's regular equipment—just red-globed lanterns, with no reflectors. The engineer saw them too late.

Twenty-nine were killed in the crash and fifty-seven injured. There was great public indignation, and at a mass meeting at Swampscott, the eminent Phillips Brooks used the eminently silly phrase, "deliberate murder." Deliberate tolerance of incapacity and stupidity would have been a true bill. Adams asked Prescott whether the use of the telegraph might not have prevented the catastrophe. Prescott replied, No, he didn't think so; it might work well under certain circumstances, but for himself, he could not be responsible for the operation of a road running the number of trains he had charge of, in reliance on any such system.

The Eastern thereupon brought Charles F. Hatch from the Lake Shore to be general manager, and he installed train dispatching by telegraph. From there it spread gradually over New England. It is a curious fact that the telegraph had been in use in a desultory way for some fifteen years on the Old Colony. Along about 1857, that road's conductors began using it when they got off schedule, wiring the conductors of opposing trains to arrange new meeting points. The road's officials could not believe that one man, a dispatcher, could handle such matters as well as the conductors themselves!

New inventions for safety and efficiency were coming thick and fast at the time, and the Revere wreck had a salutary effect in bringing about a general rush to install them. A Boston editor, in a vitriolic editorial written just after this disaster, commented on the fact that the Boston & Providence was the only road in New England using "the patent atmospheric brake" (the Westinghouse, patented two years before) "which is under the complete control of the engineer," and which had enabled a train on that road, tooling along at a good speed a few days ago, to come to a stop within 400 feet when an obstruction was seen on the track. The use of the air brake now became a "must" on New England railroads—

for passenger trains only: freight cars were not equipped with it until long afterward. Engineers were at first highly indignant when it was thrust upon them. Some thought they ought to have more pay if they had the responsibility of braking the whole train: what were the brakemen going to do thereafter to earn their wages? Sam Parker, who drove the Old Colony's "Pilgrim," No. 10, grumbled, "Next thing, they'll be expecting us to climb over the coal, go through the train and take up the tickets." But he, like other engineers, quickly changed his mind and became delighted with the idea of controlling the whole train.

That slaughter at Revere also hastened the development of automatic and block signaling. Thomas S. Hall was a great pioneer in this work, though his system was supplanted a few years later by that of the Union Signal Company. Other inventions were coming in about the same time, notably Ezra Miller's improved coupling and car platform, which greatly decreased the telescoping of the wooden passenger cars, so dreadful a feature of previous collisions. Again, only a few years elapsed before Janney's coupler superseded Miller's. A little later, steel cars began to appear. Accidents happened, it is true, after Revere, we shall never be entirely free of them—but they did not occur, as did that and some others before it, because of bull-headed opposition to progress.

Another sort of naïveté, equally inconceivable to us today, was displayed in the affair of the Bussey Bridge, a two-span affair on the Boston & Providence Railroad, just outside Boston, which was rebuilt in 1876 by Edward H. Hewins, representing the Metropolitan Bridge Company. On a March morning in 1887 the bridge fell with a Dedham commuters' train, killing twenty-three and injuring more than a hundred. Then, when the State Railroad Commission investigated the disaster, they found that there was no Metropolitan Bridge Company and never had been any! Hewins, haled to the witness stand, testified that "it was his intention at the time to organize a bridge company, and he commenced under that name by himself until such time as the organization could be made." But somehow he never got around to it. The road and construction superintendents admitted that they knew the bridge was being built partly at two steel plants bearing other names, but they never inquired about the standing or even the existence of the Metropolitan Bridge Company and looked only to Hewins for responsibility in the matter. They had known him previously as manager of an iron works at Reading, "and his bearing impressed them as that of an able and upright man." Superintendent Folsom testified that he made inquiry of a man now dead regarding Hewins, "and received a favorable report, and thinks he may have inquired of one or two others." Finally, it came out that the railroad company employed no expert to pass either upon the original design or upon the bridge after it was built, "and in fact, consulted nobody in regard to it. . . . The design in many of its details proved to be bad."

Here was an example, which would be charming had so many lives not been at stake, of the old sweet confidence of man in man, of word being as good as bond, which was so characteristic of American life through more than three-quarters of the nineteenth century; and it was so because the conduct of the majority of men justified it. But inevitably there were exceptions to the rule, and they were becoming more common. Let it be emphasized, however, that the Chester and Bussey Bridge accidents were the last of their kind in New England. Such carelessness would be simply inconceivable today, or indeed, at any time in the past fifty years.

# 18

## Comfort and Elegance

IT IS remarkable how quickly the passenger car began to change its shape in New England. The coach-bodied type, with one to three small compartments and only four to six persons in each, was quickly seen to be inadequate, and a larger affair was devised, with end doors and center aisles, so that one could walk through the train in the modern manner. Yet these cars were still comparatively small, usually seating only twenty-four, and about as attractive as packing cases. Even on standard-gauge tracks, the manufacturers feared to make the cars as wide as they are now; hence aisles were narrow and seats were so small that they barely accommodated two persons by squeezing. Many seats were bare of upholstery, too, so that travel was anything but a pleasure. At first there were seats on the roof, but they were soon abolished. Crusty old Samuel Breck, whose picture of an early passenger train on the Boston & Providence has often been quoted, said of the cars, "Uglier boxes I do not wish to travel in." He was jammed into a corner by two laborers who smelled of fish and tar, and he saw all decency in travel at an end. That was July 22, 1835, and when some "bouncing factory girls . . . going on a party of pleasure to Newport," boarded the train, "Make room for the ladies!" bawled out the superintendent. "Come, gentlemen, jump up on the top; plenty of room there." "I'm afraid of the bridge knocking my brains out," said a passenger. Others made various excuses, and Mr. Breck flatly refused to move. It wasn't many years before these discomforts began to be eased a little.

If it can be conceived, those very first coach-bodied cars had neither lights nor heat, even in the worst of winter. But when the new, larger cars came in, this began to be remedied. On December 22, 1835, the *Boston Journal* congratulated New England travelers on the fact that "stoves in which anthracite coal is burned have been introduced upon the different routes leading from this city. A good improvement," which would "lessen the evil of travelling during excessive cold weather." On many lines the car stoves at first burned wood, requiring much attention and fuel space. The stove was originally placed squarely in the center of the car, blocking the aisle so that you had to walk around it, and necessitating the removal of one seat on each side. Those who sat near the stove sweated and roasted, while those at the ends, with doors constantly opening and closing, were cold.

In the beginning, there was only a candle or two at each end of the car, but these were soon replaced by two whale-oil lamps. The learned Dionysius Lardner, who was in this country in 1842, delivering his three lectures, on "The Moon," "Halley's Comet" and "The Steam Engine," said, "The vehicle is perfectly lighted and warmed." Other travelers did not entirely agree with him. The first car windows were immovable, though there was an occasional wooden panel between the windows which might be opened, provided it wasn't warped and stuck fast. Within a few years, theoretically hoistable windows were provided, though from that day to this it has required a man of brawn to move them. Dickens, traveling over the Boston & Lowell in 1842 (he described the cars as "like shabby omnibuses, holding thirty, forty, fifty people"), thought there were not enough windows, but a few years later some foreign travelers were complaining that the glare of sunlight through the many windows tended to give them a headache.

Around 1840 the railroads began introducing the iron-frame, reversible seat backs still in use, so that a seat could be made to face either way. They also began padding the seats and backs a little, but for several more years the backs were still very low, giving no support to the shoulders or head. At night (when trains began running after dark, which they didn't do in earlier years), Seymour Dunbar says (*History of Travel*, p. 1023), "A man hung his coat and waistcoat on one of the hooks along the wall, placed his feet on that part of the seat in front which was not occupied by the head of a fellow-sufferer, reclined his own head on that part of his seat not occupied by the feet of the man behind him, and so awaited the coming of the morning." The women could not even relax as much as this: they could only take off their bonnets and close their eyes.

The first roofs were just a single thin layer of plank, slightly curved upward and covered on the outside with oil-cloth. Inside, they were at first only six and a half feet above the aisles, but their height was rapidly increased, so that the Britisher Alexander Mackay (*The Western World*, London, 1849), to whom the Boston & Worcester car looked "like a small church on wheels," marveled that it "was so lofty that the tallest man present could promenade up and down the aisle with his hat on"—and he meant a tall beaver, at that. In the course of the first four or five years they began cutting a small hole in the roof for ventilation, but that lusty outdoor man, Dickens, still found the car atmosphere "insufferably close." British ceilings evidently continued low, for Sir Charles Lyell in 1849 found the opportunity of standing upright "when tired of the sitting posture" a distinct advantage of American trains over those of Europe. The original standard color for passenger cars seems to have been yellow, for William Chambers [1] speaks of the American car categorically as a yellow affair. There were a few exceptions, however: the Boston, Concord & Montreal, when it began operations in 1848, had painted not only its cars but its locomotives light blue, and the Housatonic a little later went in for bright red. But these were unusual variations. The Old Colony and the Boston & Maine clung to the yellow cars long after the other roads in New England had changed to the standard greeny-black.

Promenading through the train was an enjoyable and in-

[1] *Things as They Are in America.* London, 1853.

evitable feature of any railroad journey for the men. Passing from car to car was theoretically forbidden, but no one ever paid any attention to the rule. The practice was really hazardous, for the car platforms were at first so far apart that it was quite a jump from one to another, and the terrific jerks and jolts when the train slowed or accelerated made the act all the more risky. The Concord Railroad was a pioneer in introducing stuffed leather buffers between the cars in an effort to ease the jolts, but this relief came very, very slowly. The Creamer automatic brake, whose control was wound up with a spring and when released slammed on the brakes so that it literally "laid 'em in the aisles," added nothing to easy riding.

Locomotives, especially the passenger aristocrats, were glorious creations in mid-nineteenth century. The builders didn't feel that it was possible to put too many colors on them. A favorite hue for the wheels was vermilion, and sometimes there was a red stack, too, while blue, green, yellow, pink and intermediate tones rioted elsewhere. Brass hooping of the boilers, brass domes, sand boxes, wheel covers, steam-chests and cylinders entailed the expenditure of a terrific amount of elbow-grease to keep it all bright—for to go about with dull or tarnished brass would cause a dreadful loss of face. Sometimes figures or scenes in full color were painted on cab or tender—such as the Pilgrims' Landing mentioned in Chapter X. And of course locomotive speed soon became a prime consideration. There is a legend that in 1848 a Boston & Maine engine ran the twenty-six miles from Boston to Lawrence in twenty-six minutes: Beebe yarns it in his humorous fashion in his *Boston and the Boston Legend*. There was a famous race, too, in 1851, from Wilmington to Lowell, which was won by the Western Railroad's "Addison Gilmore," named in honor of the company's president, over the "Nathan Hale" of the Boston & Worcester. Notice the accompanying picture of the "Gilmore," with its delicate, daisy-pattern driving wheels and its gothic-windowed cab, and you get only a faint suggestion of what a really swanky locomotive of the period was like. If we could

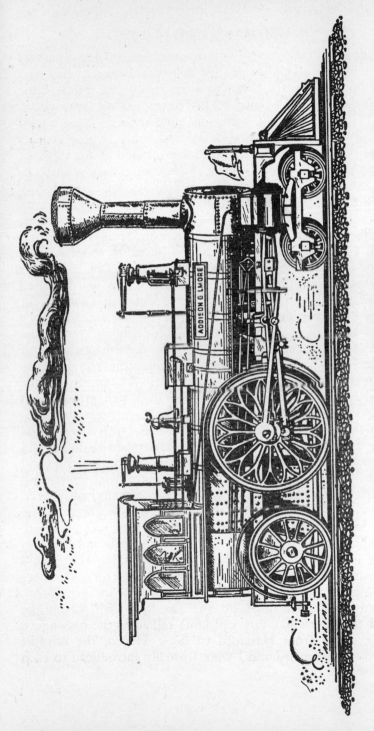

ADDISON GILMORE - 1851

Courtesy New York Central Railroad

reproduce it in its original colors, some present-day observers might refuse to believe us. Of course, these races and tests were only stunts, for there were no really fast trains in the earlier decades. Most of them had to stop nearly everywhere. The "Gilmore," by the way, was built in the Western's own shops by its master mechanic, Wilson Eddy, whose engines were so true and regular that they were called "Eddy clocks."

One longs for space to write of New England's great locomotive builders: of William Mason, Hinkley & Drury, McKay & Aldus, and John Souther, and of others, either less well known or wholly obscure, shopmen at Lowell, Lawrence, Manchester, Portland, Roxbury, Taunton, Springfield, Providence (where General Ambrose E. Burnside and associates founded the Rhode Island Locomotive Works in 1866) and elsewhere, who ably wrought their art. This word is used advisedly, and with special reference to Mason of Taunton, for it was he, according to the *Magazine of American History* (Oct., 1888, p. 589), who lifted engine-building "out of the range of mere mechanics to give [it] the dignity of a work of genuine art." For the first time, says the writer, the locomotive under Mason's hands began to possess beauty. The cylinders had always slanted downward; with grace and a suggestion of speed in mind, he made them horizontal, displaying a feeling for the level, flowing line which was the first suggestion of streamlining. He also arranged the domes and the stack so as to give balance and harmony to the design and gradually to develop the locomotive of the later nineteenth century into a thing of grace which has now vanished forever.

From the very beginning, the conductor was master of the train, but even he, great man though he was, was expected, according to the rules, to "examine the wheels and bearings of the cars at each end of the route," something that would be beneath the dignity of the modern conductor. For decades, neither he nor any other trainman wore a uniform. Dickens was entertained by the freedom with which the guard (as he was likely to call him) talked to the passengers. Going down from Hartford to New Haven, the novelist records: "The guard and I were formally introduced to each other (as we usually were on such occasions) and exchanged a variety of small talk." A conductor on the Boston & Worcester swapped comment with Alex Mackay on the car platform and offered him a "chaw" out of his tin box.

William Chambers called the conductor "a nondescript being, half guard, half clerk, with a dash of the gentleman. He is generally well dressed, sometimes wears a beard, and when off duty he passes for a reputable personage at any of the best hotels, and may be seen lounging about in the best company with a fashionable wife." Chambers' rather snobbish comment need not be accepted too categorically. A traveler too often judges a whole nation by a few specimens briefly seen. Captain Oldmixon, another British tourist, thought a conductor on the Fitchburg tried "a little knavery" on him.[2] The long, jointed ticket had already appeared: Oldmixon describes it as "a strip of paper in divisions, bits of which are plucked off as one advances and exchanged for small cards." Somehow his last coupon Fitchburg to Boston was lost or torn off too soon, and another conductor tried to collect from him again. It was probably just an error of some sort, and as the captain, after an argument, appeased the conductor by giving references and his word of honor, it was not such a serious matter, after all.

Inevitably, there were some unpleasant trainmen, but there were many of the other sort, typified by chivalrous John B. Adams, veteran conductor on the Western, who in 1852 was given a $200 silver tea set by a group of his patrons. "There is hardly a man," said a newspaper notice of the affair, "living upon the line of the railroad between Springfield and Albany who is not indebted to Mr. Adams for kind attention to his wife, mother or sister." And that substantial appreciation spoke well for the patrons, too.

Then there was the type like "Jolly Dave" Pratt, on the Grand Trunk, who genially teased his passengers about their propensity for doing the wrong thing: "Ladies and gentlemen, this is Lewiston Junction, not Danville Junction. Watch where you go." And they laughed and liked it.

[2] *Transatlantic Wanderings*, London, 1855.

This reminds us that some roads used to hang cards about eleven by fourteen inches in size—we picture two of them —inside the cars, one telling where the car went, the other where to change for other points: not a bad idea, even for today.

Around Civil War time, Conductor John Bradley of the New York & New Haven used to concoct rebuses to be printed on his checks, and you might see a whole car-full of passengers puzzling over them at once. One of them has been on this writer's desk for weeks, and he hasn't figured it out yet. And there was the rare precisian like Henry Banks, the first conductor on the Danbury & Norwalk, who would intone from the platform at leaving time: "Those who are about to proceed on the train will please take their seats." Approaching Norwalk, he would announce impressively, "The train will presently reach Norwalk bridge"; and after leaving Bethel, northward-bound, "We are now approaching the village of Danbury, which is the terminus of the road." Concord (N. H.) historians give a curious report of the conductor's method on the Concord Railroad. As the train drew into the capital city, "The conductor alighted in the grand manner from the head of the train, and announced the station at some window of each car as they all went by."

The passenger brakemen were expected to "keep the cars in good order"—which meant cleaning their interior daily— "examine the wheels and bearings at each stopping place, oil up and generally carry out the conductor's instructions." They also fired the stoves—which from one presently grew to two, one in each end of the car—helped the conductor to collect tickets if the train was long, and at the termini hauled the baggage on trucks between the station baggage room and the car door. Several of these duties were taken from the brakeman as years went by. In turn, the baggagemen were to "consider themselves and act as brakemen at all times"—which meant that they must help to twist the brake wheels as they neared a station, "but NOT SO AS TO SLIDE

THE WHEELS," everybody was warned, "which should never be done except in urgent cases."

An early Eastern Railroad admonition to baggagemen was, "They will see that the crates" (of baggage) "are taken on and off the ferry boat with as little jar as possible." That was early days, remember. Thirty years later, some of the favorite newspaper jokes were about "baggage smashers," baggagemen who took pride in wrecking the huskiest trunk consigned to their care. There was no baggage car on the passenger train—just a flat car next the tender, with the three containers, large boxes on wheels, which were filled with luggage or express matter and rolled on and off boats and flats. In the twentieth century, when the merchandise containers now so common and so indispensable began to be used on freight trains, someone tried to patent them. But someone else dug up an Old Colony stock certificate of long ago, and there were the containers right before your eyes, to prove that nobody in the twentieth century had "invented" them: they were just an old convenience of our forefathers which had been tossed aside and forgotten long ago.

Almost from the very outset, New England railroads appear to have taken care of a passenger's baggage, a practice differing widely from that of England, where for decades the traveler was expected to look after his own. To begin with, the railroads allowed twenty-five pounds free, then forty and in a few years sixty pounds. At first the passenger's name was chalked on the trunk or bag, and at the end of the run the travelers gathered around while a functionary called out each one's name and he claimed his articles. The baggage check appeared, though timidly, with the completion of the first railroads in 1835, when James Hendley of Boston cut the first ones by hand out of tin. Then J. W. Strange of Taunton produced a round check stamped out of brass. John Robbins of Boston entered the business in 1845 and became one of the leading manufacturers in the United States, making hundreds of patterns. The Fitchburg had a check of different shape for every station on its line. Lead was tried for check-making, but it was too soft to be popular. British travelers for years considered the brass baggage check one of the great inventions of the age. Mrs. Isabella Bird Bishop [3] and other tourists were delighted with the system, unknown in Europe. As she put it, the baggageman "attaches copper plates to your trunks." At the end of your journey, you just handed the check to a drayman, and in half an hour, there was your trunk in your hotel room. It was such a comfort, having your luggage entirely off your mind.

On some points, the conflicting reports are highly confusing. We are told again and again that no smoking was permitted anywhere on the train save in the baggage car, and anyone who *must* smoke had to go there. The first rules of the Eastern Railroad say of conductors, "They will permit no smoking in or on the cars." But Dickens, traveling over the Lowell in 1842, gives a different report; and reading his chapter brings up another point of divergence, that of the class cars. Both Dickens in 1842 and Sir Charles Lyell, years later, declared that the cars were all one class. But Dickens said, "There is a gentlemen's car and a ladies' car; the main distinction between which is, that in the first, everybody smokes; and in the second, nobody does. As a black man never travels with a white one, there is also a negro car. . . . In the ladies' car there are a great many gentlemen who have ladies with them. There are also a great many ladies who have nobody with them; for any lady may travel alone, from one end of the United States to the other, and be certain of the most courteous and considerate treatment anywhere."

Mrs. Bishop spoke with pleasure of the courtesy and consideration with which she was treated, and said that the cars were so comfortable and the company so agreeable that if it had not been for the tobacco spitting on the car floors, she would have preferred an American journey to an English one. But she, like Chambers and others, saw only one class of cars.

[3] *The Englishwoman in America,* London, 1856.

Even in the declassé cars, comfort was increasing slowly. By 1840, some of them had a toilet in one end. A few years later there was one in each end of the car, for men and women, as now. Seat backs grew higher, and the head-rest was often covered with "German oilcloth," as a protection against the Macassar oil with which so many men's hair was greased. Matting is mentioned as covering the floor of some cars, at which one shudders, recalling the tobacco spitting. Chambers noticed floors covered with "painted cloth," by which he may have meant an early form of linoleum. Cars were growing larger, too. In 1843 the Eastern's records showed that they had ten cars seating forty-eight persons and three seating eighty-four—as large as modern cars. They had the "butch" even in 1855, for Mrs. Bishop speaks of book, bonbon and peach vendors passing to and fro in the train.

The class cars were coming. A. V. H. Carpenter, who was railroading in Vermont and New Hampshire in the early fifties, said there were first- and second-class cars and emigrant cars then. The first class, he declared, might be considered fair second-class cars in 1890, when he wrote; the second class would then hardly be considered fit for emigrants, "and the Lord have mercy on the poor devils who had to content themselves with emigrant accommodations." John Macgregor [4] speaks grumpily of the "first class, full of second class folks," while the "second class is full of tobacco smoke, curling out as the door slams to let in the guard. A washing room is in the first-class carriage, and a tub of drinking water in the second class." Probably he didn't really mean a tub.

The fact is that the parlor car was coming in, and although we Americans to this day stoutly deny that we have first- and second-class cars as they do in Europe, the truth is that our Pullmans are our first class and our day coaches the second class. It has been said that the first parlor car in the country was built for the Eastern Railroad in 1846. It had individual swivel chairs, silk curtains, a red plush carpet and

[4] *Our Brothers and Cousins*, London, 1859.

silver-plated spittoons. But the Norwich & Worcester directors, in their 1841 report, spoke of the "Passenger cars, including four ladies' cars, believed to be superior to those on any other railroad in the country." What were these but parlor cars of a sort? Evidently some roads were making other differences in ladies' and men's cars besides the smoking privilege which Dickens observed on the Lowell. And some were introducing a combination: the Lowell in that same year, 1842, was buying some cars from Davenport & Bridges of Cambridgeport, which, said the *American Railroad Journal*, had a ladies' parlor in one end, "with luxurious sofas for seats, and in recesses may be found a washstand and other conveniences." Such cars cost $1700 each. The springs were better, the lighting was better, and the editor found it "difficult to imagine any improvements that could be desired," though he prophesied that "these down-easters will rig out some 'notions' ere long which will furnish board and lodging as well." He added that Davenport & Bridges were far behind with their orders.

In 1850 we learn that the Wason Manufacturing Company of Springfield was building first-class cars, which the *New York Herald* described as having mahogany doors and seat frames, velvet-cushioned seats, walls inlaid with satinwood, and silver-plated lettering (come, come, Mr. Bennett! Real silver?) on the outside—cost $4000 each and no wonder! Dean & Company, also of Springfield, were building baggage and second-class cars, the latter being "very plain," with uncushioned wood seats. In 1860 the first of Hapgood's sleeping cars—built by Osgood Bradley & Company of Worcester, the third of New England's great car-making plants—was exhibited at Springfield and began running on the night train on the Western. We note the steady rise in the cost of drawing-room cars, as they began to be called, in the New York & New England directors' reports—$5000 for the car "Queen City" in 1874, and $7656 for the "General Putnam" in 1875. In the nineties even the little Shepaug Railroad had to have a parlor car, "upholstered in light blue," which must have been the very deuce to keep clean.

But even the most elegant interiors could not protect the passenger from dust, smoke and cinders, which brought about the general wearing by both men and women, when traveling, of the "linen duster," a common sight on the trains in the nineteenth century. Ballasting was poor in early days, and dust flew in clouds in dry weather. W. T. Eustice, writing in the *New Englander* in 1851, "in behalf of passengers," urged the State Legislatures to:

> Grant no charter to a railroad without stipulating that said road shall be covered with a topping of coarse sifted gravel, not less than four inches deep. A railroad which cannot afford this expenditure should not be permitted in New England. Should this article be fortunate enough to meet the eye of a director in the New York & New Haven Railroad Corporation, we would suggest for their special consideration the policy of sodding the embankments, and by this outlay entitling themselves to the rich remuneration which they are receiving from the public. At Present, a ride over many of our railroads recalls the fable of Jupiter's journey in a cloud, except, alas! that we have dirt instead of vapor for our draperies.

The first vestibule—a thing whose absence is now unthinkable on passenger cars—came in 1853, though it was then known as Waterbury & Atwood's Mode of Ventilating Railway Cars and excluding dust, smoke and cinders. As advertised in the *American Railroad Journal* on July 1, 1854 (we reproduce the pictures), it is seen that the engine tender had large, hollow spaces on each side, which, as the train ran, sucked in air near the cab where it was untainted by smoke, passed it through a roof passage the full width of the baggage car, down at the rear end and through the passenger cars by means of vestibules, which were connected between the cars by collapsible canvas tunnels. The fresh air was thus supposed to be drawn through the whole train. It was installed on the Naugatuck Railroad, and E. F. Bishop, president of the road, said that he considered its use "necessary to every well-regulated railroad." Nevertheless, the air didn't circulate according to theory, and because it was thought of as a ventilating device only, it quickly passed out and the vestibule idea was not thought of again until 1887, when the first one was seen.

As evidence that New Englanders knew how to do things as smartly as anybody in America three-quarters of a century ago, let us cite the Boston Board of Trade excursion for its own members to San Francisco in May, 1870. They took the Western to Albany, the New York Central to Buffalo, and from there traveled mostly over Yankee-built rails, including the Pacific. There were eight cars in the special train—a baggage car, a smoking and club car with barbershop, and six of "the most elegant cars ever drawn over an American railway," specially built by the Messrs. Pullman for this trip and "combining sleeping and dining accommodations." There were two organs and two well-stocked libraries aboard. In the baggage car were large refrigerators full of meats, fruits and vegetables, and a Gordon jobbing press, on which a daily newspaper, *The Transcontinental* —four pages, 7¼ by 10 inches—was printed, a strikingly errorless job. The first number was dated Niagara Falls, May 24, 1870.

At this moment an earnest researcher is beginning work on a history of railroad stations, a labor of love which has long demanded attention. The small-city stations of early years are quaint-appearing things to us now; the trains ran right through their arched entrances at each end. Their huge wooden shutters were closed at night and in very cold weather. Sometimes a train came tooling along, found the doors unaccountably shut and crashed right through them, making no end of a mess. Why the engines didn't burn them all down, instead of just some of them—as an Eastern train did its East Boston station the very first time it was used—has always been a mystery to us.

Such stations were only for towns of considerable size: villages had to get along with almost anything or nothing. But the enclosed stations were all pretty well on the way out, by fire or otherwise, in 1870, and various nondescript affairs were appearing which were appropriate targets for public abuse as they grew old and the railroads were too poor to repair or replace them. Even some of the original ones were execrated. The first Western station at Pittsfield, for example—which, a local historian says, was "a wooden structure of Egyptian architecture," where "the passengers were landed in a damp and cellar-like recess and climbed by a tedious flight of stairs to the upper regions"—was fired, by engine sparks, as usual, one day in 1854. "The flames presented a beautiful spectacle" to the crowd which looked on, and the building "was never so much admired as during the last half hour of its life."

Leafing through old newspapers, one comes across hundreds of animadversions upon the railroad depots of the towns. The one built in the fifties at Skowhegan, Maine, by the Somerset & Kennebec, was spoken of thirty years later in the local paper as "the meanest passenger depot on the line of the Maine Central." There had been talk of a "new and elegant depot," but hopes were blasted: "The old rattletrap that has long disgraced the town is to be repaired." Toward the close of the century the *Providence Journal* began writing up decrepit stations in the vicinity—with illustrations—making good fun of the one at Fox Point and the N. Y. & N. E. shack at Woonsocket. Both appeared, externally and internally, something like barns, and it was asserted that in rainy weather passengers had to sit under umbrellas in their waiting rooms. J. L. Harbour, story writer and humorist, was sure that if the one at Woonsocket could be studied, marks of Indian warfare would be found on it. He offered to donate the fee of one of his lectures toward building a new one.

In villages the station might be just a building near the track, also housing a grocery store, saloon or other business: in numerous cases, this business and perhaps the building itself were the property of the railroad agent. There is record of a Connecticut agent who was notified by the company that they were sending a man to replace him on the first of the month (they thought he was growing too old), to which he retorted tartly that if they sent a new agent, they'd better send a new depot, too, as the one now in use belonged to the undersigned. Which reminds us (what a pity we are allowed only one volume for this history!) of that little town in a lovely spot up the Housatonic where two men named Gaylord and Merwin were rivals for the agency job and took it away from each other time and again, changing the name of the station each time from Gaylordsville to Merwinsville and back again, until the map-makers were so driven to despair that we have seen a map on which the name of the town is given as "Gaylordsville (Merwinsville)." Gaylord finally triumphed.

The railroad stations of Boston would make a pretty chapter if we had room for it. The Boston & Maine built its Haymarket Square Station in 1845, a severe, dignified affair, looking like a Greek temple. A year later the Fitchburg opened its granite Norman castle on Causeway Street, close by the Eastern's brick depot. The great upstairs hall in the Fitchburg station—they had them in many stations—was the scene of two notable concerts by Jenny Lind on October 11 and 12, 1850, when the room was packed to the doors with people not only from fifty miles around but some even from Portland, Montreal and Quebec. All these north-side buildings fell into disuse when the great North Station was opened in 1894.

The Boston & Worcester opened its station at Beach and Albany Streets in 1836. Old Colony trains began using it ten years later but in the following year moved to a building of their own on Kneeland Street. In 1881 the consolidated Boston & Albany opened its great new station on Kneeland Street, almost cheek-by-jowl with the Old Colony, which it completely overshadowed. One of the features of the big station which old-timers recall most fondly is the train-calling of the Negro, Henry Williams. William Dean Howells liked to go to the station and sit in the waiting room just to hear Henry intone the stations in the deep, velvety voice of his race. He put Henry into his pleasant little farce, *The Albany Depot*. At intervals in that playlet, "The

Colored Man Who Cries the Trains" punctuates the dialogue with something like: "Cars ready for College Farms . . . Longwood . . . Chestnut Hill . . . Brookline . . . Newton Centre . . . Newton Highlands . . . Waban . . . Riverside . . . and all stations between Riverside and Boston. . . . Circuit Line train now ready on Track Number Three."

The Boston & Providence, soon after its completion, built the station on Pleasant Street at the foot of the Common, which had its bell, just like small-town stations, to announce the imminent departure of trains. In 1875 a gorgeous new tall-towered structure at Park Square was opened with great fanfare, one of the guests at the celebration being none other than Kalakaua I, the new King of Hawaii—or the Sandwich Islands, as we called it then. The Old Colony moved into this station in 1890, but both this and Kneeland Street were abandoned in 1899, when the present South Station, still one of the great railway terminals of America, was opened.

There was a nineteenth-century union station at New Haven of which the various railroads and the city were inordinately proud when it was built in 1849–50. We venture to speak of it here because one of New Haven's own eminent citizens, the late George Dudley Seymour, satirized it so vivaciously, placing question marks after some of the vaunts made at the time of its creation—"Reflects the highest credit on the architect, the builders, the companies and the city," "Obliging servants always in attendance," etc. There was a "Parlor for gentlemen" and another for ladies, "furnished with a profusion of rich and costly sofas, divans, chairs, ottomans, mirrors," and what will you. A tower 140 feet high housed a gas-illuminated clock and a bell "to announce the arrival and departure of trains." A watchman perched up there at night, to sound the bell if he saw a fire anywhere.

But the tracks were sunk in the earth and the platforms were so narrow that the usually genial Oliver Wendell Holmes, bringing his son, the late Justice Holmes, back from a Civil War battlefield, spoke with unwonted acidity of New Haven, which he liked and admired, as "cursed with a detestable depot, whose niggardly arrangements crowd the track so murderously close to the wall that the *peine forte et dure* must be the frequent penalty of an innocent walk on its platform." In that narrow tunnel, dank, dark, filled with smoke and fumes, grim signs warned you to "Look out for pickpockets," and the thunder and clatter of trains were mingled with the fiendish bawling of hackmen waiting at the head of the steep stairs to kidnap the traveler.

A favorite story, told in New Haven itself, was that of the small boy who, arriving with his father for the first time in that dark, murky, sulphurous underground vault, with the hackmen up above yelling like demons, shrank close to his parent, clinging to his hand, and asked fearfully, "Papa, is this Hell?" "No, my son, it is New Haven."

In 1866 the railroads were forced by the city to make alterations in the building, and a few years later a new station was erected and the old one turned into a city market.

There was one thing at that station that was kindly, even fondly remembered by travelers—old Tommy Stuart, the Negro peddler who worked the trains there and in the succeeding station. One of Mark Twain's characters in *A Connecticut Yankee at King Arthur's Court* recalls Tommy's patter: "N-e-e-ew Haven! Ten minutes for refreshments—knductr'll strike the gong-bell two minutes before the train leaves—passengers for the Shore Line please take seats in the rear kyar, this kyar don't go no furder—*ahh*-pls, *aw*-rnjz, b'*nan*ners, *s-a-n-d*'ches, p—*op*-corn!"

Only ten minutes for refreshments: they were shaving the time pretty close as the century grew older. In 1850 Rutland trains from Boston to Burlington were stopping an hour for dinner at Bellows Falls!

Commutation and season tickets were an early phenomenon on the roads leading out of Boston, and it wasn't many years before the railroads were complaining that they were losing money on them. When, in 1845, the fare from Wakefield to Boston, 9.9 miles via the Boston & Maine, was 25 cents, packages of fifty "family tickets" were sold for $6.25 or 12½ cents each. In 1854 you could buy "Tickets at $10 per

# PASSENGERS
# Please Take Notice!

## THIS TRAIN
## Will stop at White River Junction

### TWENTY MINUTES FOR DINNER
### AND LUNCH,

Which will be served in the New and Elegant
Dining Hall and Restaurant at the Depot, immediately upon arrival there.

*Courtesy Mrs. Bella C. Landauer Collection, New-York Historical Society*

month to and from Boston to any station on the South Shore
Railroad. One ride each way per day." In 1855 the Fitchburg figured out that it cost 1.11 cents to haul a passenger one
mile, whereas season short-haul tickets were often sold for
a cent or less per mile and some as low as 7.9 cents.

Not many, we dare say, are aware that the bargain-price
excursion is distinctly a New England invention. Josiah
Perham (1803–68) was a Maine Yankee—we were going to
say typical, but not quite, for he was too adventurous. He
made a small fortune in trade, then lost it in bad invest-

ments in 1842. Climbing to his feet again, he was bankrupt once more in 1849. Looking about him for something to do, he bought a "Panorama of the Great Lakes," and by an ingenious device caused the picture to move across a screen. When he showed it in Melodeon Hall at Boston, it attracted such attention that people came from miles outside the city to see it. That gave him an idea: if the railroads would grant low round-trip fares, both they and he would do a big business. They saw merit in the suggestion, and for years afterward Perham was an excursion promoter, sharing profits with the railroads. Then he went on to larger things, as we shall see later.

The season-ticket business was the greatest headache. After the commuter had bought a season ticket and the conductor had become accustomed to him, he was never disturbed or asked to show his ticket. A Boston & Providence stockholders' committee in 1857 found that no check was ever kept on such matters. Fortunately, the original sales of season tickets were on record, and from this book the committee drew up a list of more than 150 persons whose tickets had expired anywhere from one to sixteen months before but who had just blithely gone on riding. Nobody in the office had the faintest notion whether they had ceased to ride or "were still passing daily over the road." One of the committee recognized several as being constant passengers. The superintendent argued that "it was impossible for the conductor to know all the commuters," and that "commuters dislike to be obliged to show their tickets, and would find fault with such a requirement," but neither excuse seemed valid to the committee. They promptly set about collecting some of the back pay and got $300 from one passenger for fares for himself and son for a year, $240 from another, and so on. Some delinquents, however, were inclined to be tough: one gave a note for $150, "and this note is believed by the Committee to be worthless."

Before ticket-numbering began, no one knew how many times the same ticket was sold, for there was no accurate method of accounting for them. There were many stations without ticket offices, and many persons just got on the train anyhow without buying tickets, so that the conductors collected many fares—an invitation to crookedness, for there was no check on them. A conductor had no cash fare receipts to issue, with a stub for his own record, so the only way he could be sure of being honest with the company was to keep its money carefully in one pants pocket, his own in the other.

It was hard to decide which was worse—the season ticket or the free pass. From the very outset, directors and officials regarded themselves and their families as divinely set apart to ride free. Stockholders, a somewhat lower order, might ride gratis to the annual meetings, but no more. Simply by showing his stock certificate to the conductor, a stockholder could get a free ride at annual meeting time and have some fun, too, for such meetings were no cut-and-dried affairs. In those days, Zeke Scoggins the butcher and Deacon Micajah Green, owning one share apiece, spoke their minds as freely as the biggest frog in the puddle, and if the company was losing money, the proceedings might take on a tinge of the uproarious.

But no sooner was a railroad organized than its directors realized that state legislators must be taken into consideration. They were frequently called upon for loans, and on the negative side, they might easily pass a law that would ruin you. They must be kept in good humor, and there was nothing better for that than an annual pass. Then there were the newspaper chaps: they could do you a lot of harm by criticism, or they might, if kept in good humor, give you some fine editorial boosts. So passes went to the city papers, and then, first thing anybody knew, the little sheets out in Billerica and Hopkinton were demanding them. Next the big merchants and industrialists who were heavy shippers began to wonder why they shouldn't be shown a little courtesy—for there is no one more eager to get something free than your rich man who can easily afford to buy it. Drovers escorting shipments of cattle to market and returning home came into this category. But when the big shippers were gratified, the next biggest began demanding passes, and so on down, until, as the B. & P. stockholders said plaintively, there seemed to be no end to it. The hotel proprietors appeared as a menace, too: if you didn't give them passes they would knock your road and talk their guests into going by another route. And of course the employees of the company . . . well, Charles W. Felt, in his pamphlet, *The Dead-Heads*—published in 1875, when the thing had become a scandal yet nobody did anything about it—listed among those who received passes (besides directors and officials), employees whether on actual duty going to and from work, on private errands or on vacation—and of course, always their families; employees of all other roads, ditto, ditto; post-office and telegraph employees; civil engineers and their assistants; steamboat owners and officials; news dealers, stage proprietors and drivers; hotel and stable keepers; getters-up of picnics, agricultural shows and side-shows generally; railway guide publishers and editors; real estate agents and drummers; projectors of new railways, and persons whom the old conductors knew that it was for the interest of the road to pass occasionally.

To these a Northern railroad stockholders' committee added railroad commissioners, United States marshals, agents for patent boxes, spark arresters, trunk frames, wheels, rubber springs, etc., persons looking for lost luggage, referees and witnesses in suits to which the railroad was a party, engine builders, persons examining wood, persons having claims of damage to settle, persons visiting those accidentally injured by the train, and some others whose "pull" the stockholders simply couldn't account for. Add to these shipwrecked seamen and persons whom the conductor regarded as objects of charity, and you have just made a beginning. If the conductor knew the parties, he didn't even look at their passes. Conductor Asa Moore, in the Old Colony investigation of 1850, said, "Eight or ten times as many more pass over the road free, than the number the conductors are required to return or do return."

Meanwhile, the Boston & Providence report said acridly,

"The unfortunate stockholder, who receives no dividends, is generally made to pay for his ticket when travelling on his own road."

In the suit of the Concord Railroad vs. George Clough, tried at Concord, December, 1868—January, 1869, Mason W. Tappan, counsel for the defendant, said: "The cars were filled with 'dead-heads'—everybody almost was riding on free passes—so much so that when the list of bank directors, lawyers, politicians, insurance agents, substitute brokers, merchants, clergymen, etc., all over the State who rode free was being put in, the Hon. Chairman remarked, in view of the vast throng that was presented, that it would probably save time to put in a list of those who *paid their fares! . . .*"

In the Vermont Senate on November 13, 1874, Senator Albert Clarke of St. Albans delivered a courageous speech which must have created a sensation. At that time, not only were state legislators and officials in Vermont riding on passes, but even judges! Senator Clarke charged that you might see trains on which a quarter to a half of the passengers were riding free. He ironically commended the "thoughtful impartiality" of a judge whom he named who would not try a certain case involving a railroad until he had returned his pass.

But even then there were some Vermont roads that were just plain stingy. We have before us a ticket of the Montpelier & Wells Railroad, "Good only during session of 1874," which agrees that

Mr. Anthony S. Nichols,
A Member of the Vermont Legislature,

By Purchasing a Regular Ticket at Montpelier for each Trip to any Station on the Road, may RETURN FREE to Montpelier, on each exhibition of this Ticket to the Conductor.

We hear of Commodore Vanderbilt traveling up into the White Mountains on one occasion, with a party of twenty, all riding on his one personal pass, while he walked through the cars with the conductor, pointing out to him those who were entitled to ride free. General Grant was an ardent traveler in that harum-scarum postwar era and never thought of paying any fare for self, family or friends; nor for a long time did any railroad functionary dare ask him for ticket or pass. But he finally ran against a snag, as Edward Hungerford relates in his *Men and Iron*. When the Grand Central Station in New York was opened in 1871, gatekeepers were installed, with rigid orders to see every ticket before the passenger was admitted to the trainshed. Up came General Grant one day with no less than eighteen friends, headed for Boston with no tickets. The New Haven gatekeeper —for each road had its own—stopped him. Grant was amazed and argumentative, the gatekeeper adamant. Finally the soldier in Grant recognized the justice of the other man's position: he retreated to the ticket window and came back with nineteen tickets. It was not quite the dawn of a new era, but it might have been called the first cock-crow before the dawn. The good old open-handed days—when the hand was open both to give and to receive—gradually succumbed to a sterner age—not entirely free from guile, it is true, but more businesslike.

# 19

## More Yankee Ingenuity

AMONG the many things pertaining to the railroad in which New England pioneered was the express service, definitely a Yankee creation. Colonial post riders had begun the carrying trade in New England, delivering anything, even up to a yoke of oxen, as a sideline of their own—so Hugh Finlay, postal inspector, found and reported in 1773. They even stuffed boots, tools, anything they were asked to carry, into the letter portmanteaus. Finlay heard at Newport, R. I., that "there were two post-offices, the King's and Peter Mumford's"—Mumford being the post rider to Boston, reputed to be deriving considerably more revenue from his carrying than the King did.

We have glanced at some of the early shipments by merchandise train—oysters, for example, which later were traveling by express. It soon became apparent to some men in New England that there should be some sort of parcel or small shipment service, not to mention a way of sending letters, money and valuable papers, which would avoid the unconscionable rates then being charged by the Post Office. Stage drivers at first carried things in their tall hats. Benjamin P. Cheney, who began life as a Massachusetts stage driver and later became an express and railway magnate, used to attribute his middle-aged baldness to the early years of friction caused by a top-hat full of packages.

Business presently grew too heavy even for a beaver hat. At times the drivers carried thick packages of paper money or bonds, merely thrust under the coach-seat, though some of them equipped themselves with bags or boxes. They were purely informal messengers, not legally licensed to carry and under no bond, but although there were 106 stage lines running out of Boston in 1832 and several times that number of drivers, this writer has in years of newspaper research found no recorded instance of a driver's absconding. Every morning a wallet containing $30,000 to $40,000 in notes would be handed by a clerk from the Suffolk Bank in Boston to a stage driver for delivery to a Providence bank. He gave no receipt for it—yet it was always delivered, and so far as we can discover, without a dollar missing. When the first short railroads were built, they co-operated with the drivers of the stage lines which they were displacing. For example, when the Eastern Railroad ran only from Boston to Salem, the stage drivers coming down from Portsmouth, N. H., had passes, and when they left their stages at Salem, they would take the train into Boston to carry letters and parcels committed to them in the back country, make collections, and do other errands for clients along their route.

There were thousands of letters and parcels which went absolutely free in those days when everybody was everybody's neighbor. "Who goes to Hartford or New York or New Haven," asked an editor, excoriating the mail service, "without carrying letters, unless he takes his start so suddenly that no body knows of his going?" Even a total stranger, seen with his luggage at a city railroad station or steamboat dock, was sure to be accosted by numerous persons, some of them total strangers, and asked to carry letters or parcels, sometimes packages of money, to be left somewhere, though not infrequently he was asked to make delivery into the very hands of the addressee—and such was the neighborliness of the times that many men did this without a murmur.

The railroad conductors took up where the stage drivers left off and added considerably to their incomes by their work as carriers—of which, by the way, one never finds a word of complaint on the part of the railroads. On some roads the trainmen augmented their pay by buying fruits, vegetables and poultry at country stations and selling them at good profits to Boston provision dealers, who would often be waiting to meet the train and get their goods. The cost of transportation was nothing, so the profits were comfortable. The railroad company was not unwilling that the baggage cars should be so used, if they were not already full.

A curious transition stage toward the real express is seen on the Boston & Lowell. Soon after it opened in 1835, Silas Tyler carried packages in a little four-wheeled car attached to passenger trains, and in this business he seems to have been a sort of partner with the railroad company. Tyler sold out in 1836 to W. C. Gray, who added a bank messenger service to the parcel carrying. The Boston & Worcester had been open less than six months when David T. Brigham procured a contract from it, whereby, for a fee of eight dollars a week, he was permitted to have a seat in the Belvedere car and to carry a small box for express matter. But he found that the conductors, among them a fellow named Harnden, were carrying on so much competition that he soon gave up the experiment. In that same year, Dean and Davenport began carrying letters and packages between Boston and Taunton, they themselves being the messengers. In 1838 R. W. Whiting advertised in the Worcester papers that he would go to Boston in the morning and back in the afternoon, not only to carry packages, bundles, etc., but to "transact any other business that may be committed to his care." He, too, did not long endure.

In that same year a slender, delicate, undersized young man named William F. Harnden, after serving for a while as a conductor on the Boston & Worcester, had sold tickets in the Worcester station, but found the job too confining and wanted something more active. Several persons contend for the honor of having suggested the express business to Harnden, but it is just as likely that Harnden himself, who was no fool, had seen enough of the carrying by others to believe that somebody was going to make a real business out of it someday, and decided to have a try at it. He has come to be known as the founder of the express business, though this is not quite true. But he was the first to carry express between cities as far apart as New York and Boston, and he did not, like the others, fade out quickly, but stuck to it until he extended his system to other cities, and even to Europe. He really deserves a page in history, though he was not an originator.

He consulted the Providence railroad people and the boat line from there to New York, obtaining exclusive rights on the boats but not on the railroad, for two men named B. D. and L. B. Earle had a "franchise" there. Acting as bank messengers, they had begun shuttling back and forth over the road as soon as it was opened, and they had had so many letters and other packets offered them by outsiders that they decided to go into business for themselves, and so organized Earle's Express, which presently touched not only Providence but Bristol, Warren, Stonington and New London. Henry Prew, a deliveryman in their service, worked up to a partnership, and as Earle & Prew the concern operated on the Old Colony and thereabouts until the end of the century. The Earles, therefore, predecessors of Harnden, may with equal justice be spoken of as the founders of the express business.

On February 23, 1839, the Boston newspapers carried the first advertisement of Harnden's "Boston and New York Express Package Car," the first use of the Express in connection with business. Harnden traveled via Worcester, and for several months after he began business, a medium-sized valise carried all that was entrusted to him. In 1840 he began running "crates"—those freight containers already mentioned, which were shifted from flat car to steamboat deck and back again. He set up a New York office in a corner of a stationery store, and his brother Adolphus—a diminutive fellow like himself—served as agent there when he was not tripping back and forth opposite William as a messenger. But on January 13, 1840, when the steamboat *Lexington* burned on the Sound with a loss of 121 lives, Adolphus Harnden was among the dead. His valuables were lost, but when his body washed ashore, 148 letters were found in a pouch which clung to him, giving Washington a hint as to the business which was slipping away from Uncle Sam because of exorbitant postal rates.

A major weakness of Harnden's was his inability to see the possibilities for express expansion in his own country. He was obsessed with the thought of pushing his business across the ocean to Europe, and he spent much money on that dream, but when Henry Wells, his agent at Albany, urged that messengers be sent to Buffalo, to Chicago, even to the Mississippi River, he retorted, "If you choose to run an express to the Rocky Mountains, do it on your own account. I choose to run an express where there is business. Put a people there, and my express will soon follow." A few years later Wells took up that challenge, and the American Express Company and Wells, Fargo & Company were the outcome.

In a typically friendly letter to a vacationing employee on May 5, 1840, Harnden casually takes notice of the birth of a great rival, saying that "Burke & Co.'s Express commenced running yesterday. They did not have quite a hatfull of packages." Here enters one of the real colossi of the business—Alvin Adams, Vermonter, beginning life all over again at thirty-six. Left an orphan at eight, he started out on his own at sixteen, and after holding various office jobs became a produce merchant in Boston, where the Panic of '37 left him a bankrupt, though it is said that when he got on his feet again, he paid every dollar he owed. He studied the experiences of other expressmen, who were just going into the business, and foresaw in the future an express service that would handle much heavier freight than any then offered it. The cloud of depression still hung over the land when, on May 4, 1840, he and P. B. Burke launched their little venture between Boston and Worcester. Burke was soon discouraged, and after a few weeks with no more than a "hatfull" per trip, he withdrew into the obscurity whence he came, thereby losing his chance for fame and fortune. Each partner had put in $100, and Adams bought Burke's share, paying for it at the

rate of $10 a month. The name promptly changed from
Burke & Company to Adams & Company, and thus humbly
began a business which fourteen years later was capitalized at
more than a million dollars, and thirty years later was worth
no one could say how much.

Samuel S. Leonard started a Boston-Worcester express that
same year. Some railroads didn't care how many expresses
used their lines, for each one added its pittance to the road's
income. Leonard and Adams were sharp rivals at first, with
Adams—a big, alert, good-looking man, tactful, daring and
far-seeing—usually getting the better of the other through his
keenness and diplomacy. As time went on, and he quickly
extended his express to New York, to Philadelphia and in
twenty directions over the country, even to New Orleans in
1847, he ceased to trouble himself with such small fry as
Leonard, and the latter finally sold out to the giant Adams
Express Company in 1862.

The Postmaster-General gave mournful attention to the expresses in his report of those days, telling Uncle Sam how
much business they were taking away from him. In 1841 he
listed eighteen operating out of Boston, and omitted a dozen
or so at that. Besides Harnden and Adams, he mentioned
Earle's Express to Providence, Davenport to Taunton, Hatch
to New Bedford and Martha's Vineyard, Kingsley to Fall
River, Leonard to Worcester, Gray to Lowell, Gillis to Nashua, Niles to Dover, N. H., Dow to Haverhill, and two,
Law and Potter, to Salem, as well as two more, P. C. Hatch
and Conant & Walker to Portsmouth, N. H. Among those
he overlooked was "Colonel" Favor, sole owner and staff of
Favor's Eastport Express, operating on the steamer *Admiral*
between Boston and Eastport, Calais and St. John, N. B.
Short, narrow Court Street in Boston swarmed with expressmen then—Harnden at No. 8, Adams at No. 9, Favor at No.
10. The P. M. G. failed to discover four others in a back
room at No. 8, all having the same agent. By 1844 there were
said to be forty expresses operating out of or near Boston.
By 1870, Stimson, the express historian, guesses their number
at 300. Nine-tenths of them were coat-pocket or one-man

expresses, just a sort of messenger service. There might be three or four over the same route, say, from Boston to Quincy. One ran only to Harvard University.

Harnden's frail body succumbed to overwork and he died in 1845. His company was really succeeded by Thompson, Livingston & Company, though there was a Harnden's Express which pursued a more or less shadowy existence for twenty years longer. Adams had long since taken in William B. Dinsmore, a Bostonian, as a partner, and in 1854 they absorbed Thompson, Livingston & Company and three other concerns, to reorganize as the Adams Express Company, with a capital of $1,200,000.

Of those four expresses in that little back room at No. 8, two of them in 1857 combined to form the Eastern Express Company, which by 1875 had 570 miles of steamer lines and 380 miles of rail, covering Maine and parts of New Hampshire and even reaching Nova Scotia and Prince Edward Island. In 1879 it was taken over by the American Express.

In 1842, Benjamin P. Cheney, another of the swarming expressmen in that back room, organized, with two partners, Cheney & Company's Express, which threw lines up into New Hampshire and Vermont and presently by stagecoach to Montreal. Before 1850, Liberty Bigelow organized an express on the Fitchburg Railroad, and this eventually became Fiske & Company's Express and then Cheney, Fiske & Company, operating from Boston to Burlington, Vt. Cheney, another of those big, husky express pioneers and keen, unconquerable Yankees who did so much toward making the nation what it is, soon combined all his lines under this name, extended to Ogdensburg and into parts of Canada. Early in the 1850's he reorganized his holdings east of Lake Ontario as the United States and Canada Express, with its major termini at Boston and Montreal. He sold this to the American in 1882 and reorganized his holdings elsewhere in Canada as the Canadian Express Company, with a capital which rapidly mounted to $1,500,000. He was now a stockholder in most of the big express companies, and a railroad magnate as well: he took part in financing both the Santa Fe and the

Northern Pacific, and was instrumental in placing Wells-Fargo service on both of them.

Thus the process of combination and expansion went on until half a dozen giant express companies controlled the business for the entire country—and all of them had their germs in New England.   Of their promoters:

> Nine out of ten of them were either born New England Yankees or the sons of New England parents, and first saw the light no farther west than "York State."   Shrewd, conservative, tough-fibered and with a passion for work, most of them stayed on the job until death stilled their hands, although nearly all of them lived to great ages—some to 70, 80, even 95. . . .
>
> That their fortunes were not even greater was due to the conservatism of most of them, their dislike for speculation. They were mostly without ostentation; they did not hurry to Fifth Avenue and strive for a foothold in New York society, as did new millionaires in other lines of business. . . .   One reason for this was that the majority of them cared little for such vainglory; another was that they were close-mouthed, not overanxious to let the public know how rapidly money was pouring into their tills.   For even during the early '60's the word "monopoly" was being muttered regarding them.[1]

[1] Alvin F. Harlow, *Old Waybills*, 1934, p. 68.

# 20

## New England, Mother of Railroads

N O COMPARABLE area in the United States has
done so much toward creating and operating the
vast railroad system of the nation as has New England. Her sons not only built and ran her own intricate railway system—practically never calling on an outsider for aid—
but promoted a number of the great roads of the middle and
far west, including the first three great transcontinental lines;
financed them for the most part, and as presidents, superintendents, general managers, directors, operated them for
many years. Modest New England has never boasted of this,
and so far as this writer can discover, the story has never been
assembled until now. A considerable search has been made,
but undoubtedly some names which should be there will be
omitted from the list, and for this, apology is made in
advance.

Glancing first at the engineers, McNeill and Whistler were
the only outsiders among the pioneers. James F. Baldwin,
James Hayward, James M. Fessenden, William Raymond Lee,
William Henry Swift, Samuel M. Felton, Alexander C. Twining and Edwin M. Johnson, who have been mentioned in our
pages, were all home products. Some of these distinguished
themselves in other ways: Fessenden being for some years
member of the Massachusetts State Railroad Commission;
Hayward not only building the first line of the Boston &
Maine, but becoming its president; Lee serving the Vermont
Central, the Rutland and the Northern (New York) as president; Swift (1800–79), a native of Taunton, heading both

the Western (Massachusetts) and the Philadelphia, Wilmington & Baltimore, and acting as chairman of the board of the Hannibal & St. Joseph from 1846 to 1877; Felton also being president of the P. W. & B. (for fifteen years) and of the Pennsylvania Steel Company, and serving as Hoosac Tunnel Commissioner, Union Pacific Railroad Commissioner and director in other great railroad companies (his son, of the same name, was president of many roads).

Of the home-born promoters and executives of New England's own railroads, we have spoken at length—of Gridley Bryant, Thomas H. Perkins, Nathan Hale, Theodore Sedgwick, Patrick T. Jackson, Thomas B. Wales, Josiah Quincy, Jr., John A. Poor, George Bliss, Chester W. Chapin, Ginery Twitchell, George Peabody, David A. Neal, Charles Paine and the Smiths of Vermont, John B. Page, Alvah Crocker, John W. Brooks, James Brewster, Joseph E. Sheffield, Onslow Stearns, the Bordens, E. H. Derby, F. B. Crowninshield, Charles P. Clark, Charles S. Mellen, Lucius Tuttle and others. The activities of some of these extended far beyond New England: Page, for example, in addition to heading the Rutland, was also one of the promoters of the West Shore, which menaced the Vanderbilts in the eighties, and was one of its early presidents; Mellen's other presidency besides the New Haven was the Northern Pacific; Twitchell, in addition to the Boston & Worcester and the Boston, Barre & Gardner, also headed the Santa Fe and served three terms in Congress; Bliss, after leaving the Western, was president of the Michigan Southern (now a part of the New York Central's main line) and held that post until he had pushed the track into Chicago in 1852—and he was also president of the Chicago & Mississippi and a director of the Rock Island, being instrumental in building 600 miles of the through line from Boston to the Mississippi River.

Joseph E. Sheffield (1793–1882), another of those mentioned above, was a Connecticut Yankee, born poor at Southport, clerking in a store in his teens, then becoming wealthy in the cotton trade, prominent in the New York & New Haven organization and the chief owner of the New Haven

& Northampton Railroad. As contractor—in collaboration with his friend, engineer Henry Farnam—he built 170 miles of the Michigan Southern, of which Bliss was then president, carrying it into Chicago. He then built by contract 182 miles of the Chicago & Rock Island, including its bridge across the Mississippi. He found the necessary cash—$5,000,000—for doing this job and took his pay for it in Rock Island stock and bonds, which he divided equally with Farnam. He gave so liberally—about a million dollars, all told—to the scientific department of Yale College, which had been made a separate school, that in 1861 it was christened the Sheffield Scientific School, and still bears this name.

The story of how Massachusetts—more specifically Boston—became interested in those midwestern roads is an interesting one. The initial impetus was given it by John W. Brooks—born at Stow, Massachusetts, in 1819—whom we have seen first as a young assistant surveyor on the Boston & Maine and thirty years later as Hoosac Tunnel Commissioner. In between these episodes was the most notable activity of his life.

In 1845 there was no rail connection between the seaboard and the new, booming, overgrown village of Chicago. Going west from Albany, you jolted over a series of disjointed rails to Buffalo, took a smelly little lake steamer to Detroit, then a ramshackle train to somewhere out in the woods and continued in a stagecoach through prairie mud to Chicago. In the wild 1830's, when several midwestern states embarked on a program of state ownership of transportation, Michigan had bonded herself and launched a railroad from Detroit toward Lake Michigan, but it got only part way when the bubble burst. The state was bankrupt, and there for the next decade the fragment of railroad lay, its wooden stringers rotting under the cheap strap-iron rails.

Restless, ambitious, vibrant with nervous energy, Brooks went out to Detroit in 1844, saw and learned the story of the stranded railroad, and was fired with an ambition to complete it. He went back to Boston in the hope of raising the necessary money, but he was only a pink-cheeked youngster of twenty-six, with almost no acquaintance among men of means, and they smiled at the suggestion of entrusting two or three million dollars to him. Unsuccessful there, yet not disheartened, Brooks went down to New York and discovered a big bank holding a bushel or so of Michigan bonds, on which it couldn't even collect interest. Of course it was eager to see the state sell its public works and restore its credit: therefore, the suggestion of a purchaser was warmly welcomed. Brooks next hurried back to Michigan to obtain the necessary legislation. In Detroit he met and took into alliance a Yankee lawyer, James F. Joy (1810–96), born in Durham, N. H., a Dartmouth graduate and emigré to Detroit, where he was doing right well. The state was willing to co-operate if it could get $2,000,000 for the 145 miles of railroad, and a bill was passed by the Legislature, authorizing the sale and incorporating the Michigan Central Railroad Company. Six months' time was allowed Brooks for promotion and organizing; then he was to push the track through to Lake Michigan within three years, laying the whole distance from Detroit with sixty-pound T-rails.

Still hoping to finance the company in his native state, Brooks now rushed—if travel by such means could be called rushing—back to Boston, with something more impressive to offer, which presently won the ear of bankers and moneyed men. His principal catch was John Murray Forbes (1813–98), who had gone into business at fifteen and by twenty-four had made a small fortune in the China trade. At thirty-three his enormous business ability and energy were so emphasized by his varied talents and personal charm that Ralph Waldo Emerson later wrote of him, "Never was such force, good meaning, good sense, good action, combined with such domestic lovely behavior, such modesty and persistent preference for others. Wherever he went, he was the benefactor . . ."[1] with much more of the same sort.

Still it was no easy task for the youthful Brooks to sell his idea to these men, who thought nothing of risking a cargo by sail and sea to China but were distrustful of the American

[1] *Letters and Social Aims*, p. 101.

interior. At last, however, Forbes became his chief investor, the two other important ones being John E. Thayer, the banker, and David A. Neal, the wealthy Salem sea captain, second president of the Eastern Railroad. In later years the Thayers of State Street became perhaps the leading railroad banking house of New England, though there were others with millions invested.

Brooks barely got under the wire in time with the organization of his railroad; and thus he, more than any other one man, paved the way for the great participation of Boston in the building and ownership of the vast western railroad systems. Forbes was elected as first president of the Michigan Central, and in 1849 the line was completed to New Buffalo on Lake Michigan, from which traffic crossed to Chicago by boat. But when the Michigan Southern, under that other Yankee genius, George Bliss, came tooling through toward Chicago, Forbes and Brooks saw the danger of its competition, raised some more cash and threw a line out from Kalamazoo around the foot of Lake Michigan, reaching Chicago almost simultaneously with the rival road in 1852. When the Panic of 1857 threatened the very existence of the Michigan Central, Forbes went to England and procured the means to save it.

In C. F. Adams' opinion, the Michigan Central, "founded on individual enterprise and private capital, unhampered by the necessity of perpetually looking to a Legislature for assistance," became what the Western should have been—"the nucleus around which Boston capital centered and the base from which it expanded." No sooner had it reached Chicago than Brooks and Joy—now the company's attorney and a large stockholder—decided that there must be a connection with the Illinois Central, which bisected the state fifty miles to westward. While Joy was in Springfield attending to this chore, he ran across some men who were building a little line from Burlington toward Galesburg. He talked them into giving him an option on their project, conferred with Brooks and hastened to Boston for money. Again he met with skepticism and had to go to New York and pick up $150,000;

then, with that recommendation, he persuaded Forbes, the Thayers and others to come in. Back in Chicago, he and Brooks managed to increase the nest-egg to $500,000, took over the Burlington charter, organized the Chicago, Burlington & Quincy Railroad and proceeded to build the first 130 miles of that now mighty system. Joy became its first president. After a few years he dropped his law practice to give his whole time to railroads and other business, including the building—with Brooks—of the ship canal around the Sault rapids on the United States side. During his presidency of the C. B. & Q., it reached out to Omaha and to Kansas City, where it built the first bridge to span the Missouri at that place. He also headed the Wabash, St. Louis & Pacific, and, among other things, in 1867 succeeded to the presidency of the Michigan Central, following Brooks, who had taken over from Forbes. Joy added considerably to the M. C.'s mileage.

But the story must also be told of how Bostonians missed one of the great opportunities of the century, one which would have given their city a through line to the middle west, perhaps across the continent. In 1853 the desultory chain of little roads between Albany and Buffalo had been assembled into the New York Central, with a capital of $23,000,000; but the stock was never at par, and C. F. Adams says that in Civil War times it ranged around 80. Chester W. Chapin, president of the Western and one of the smartest of American railroad men, found that control could be bought for about $9,000,000. He saw what a valuable thing its ownership would be for his railroad and for Boston, and he repeatedly brought the matter to the attention of his leading stockholders and the moneyed men of Boston, but without effect. He was a Springfield man, a sort of foreigner, not a banker, and therefore he did not touch their imagination. Why they could not see the importance of the idea without having it hammered into their heads will always remain a mystery. Boston capital already controlled the Michigan Central and had a large stake in the Michigan Southern; it was even reaching out beyond Chicago. The New York Central and one link more would have completed a Boston-owned line from the Massachusetts capital to Lake Michigan and the Mississippi River. The great New York Central would have been a feeder for Boston instead of New York and would have put New York's nose decidedly out of joint.

Chapin did not easily give up his idea. Failing to interest the capitalists himself, he employed a Berkshire attorney, James D. Colt, later a justice of the State Supreme Court, to present the case in, he hoped, more elegant language than he could muster. Chapin himself promised to raise $1,000,000 in and around Springfield if Boston would produce the rest. But sending Colt was a mistake: he was a lawyer, not a financier, and he and State Street didn't even speak the same language. "To carry it through," says Adams, "would have required a great command of money, and that confidence which comes only from the habit of long acting together." And so opportunity knocked at the door for the last time. In 1867–68, Commodore Vanderbilt, who had drifted into railroads almost accidentally, took over the New York Central— and that was that. Boston had lost the greatest chance in its history—strangely, unaccountably, for the New England imagination had long since reached out across the continent to the shores of the Pacific.

Perhaps the biggest story in this volume comes at the very end—namely, that it was New Englanders who, within a matter of three decades, had promoted, built and were operating the first three great transcontinental lines that spanned our nation—the Union Pacific, the Northern Pacific and the Santa Fe–Southern Pacific. In the first two cases, even the conception took place in the brain of a Yankee. Asa Whitney (1797–1872), born at North Groton, Connecticut, was the first man to dream of a transcontinental railroad. While on a business trip to China in 1840, he was struck by the idea that a cross-continent rail line would save thousands of miles of sea voyage between our eastern ports and China. He laid the plan before Congress in 1844, but because he asked nothing for himself, the belief prevailed that he was secretly planning some huge speculation. He was ignored. For seven years he carried on a newspaper campaign, but in vain. He even went to England—upon invitation—to present the suggestion that the line be built through Canada, but he was ahead of his time. He finally retired, was almost forgotten, and when the last spike in the Pacific Railroad was driven amid great ballyhoo in Utah in 1869, no one thought of inviting seventy-two-year old Asa Whitney to be present.

Whitney had scarcely given up his idea and retired to a country home near Washington before Thomas Clark Durant (1820–85), a Massachusetts man, who was born at Lee in the Berkshires but who had gone to New York and prospered there, began experimenting with it. In the early 1850's he was scouting up the Platte Valley with an engineer named Peter Dey, and Dey had as assistant a young cadet from Vermont, just out of Norwich University in his native state, whose name was Grenville M. Dodge (1831–1916). One day on a hotel porch in Council Bluffs, young Dodge talked with a lank, big-footed lawyer from Illinois, who quizzed him in a high-pitched voice about the proposed railroad. More than a decade later that lawyer, who had become President, called Dodge from his army service in the Civil War to become chief engineer of the Union Pacific, which Congress had created in 1862 and on whose survey Dodge had worked when it was just a prophecy. With the rank of major general, Dodge took over the construction task in 1865.

Durant, now a Wall Street broker, had put the company on its feet, though groggily, when no one else would touch it—he assumed a huge personal responsibility. He next made a contract with one Hoxie to build track at $50,000 a mile, though Congress had guessed the cost at $16,000 to $48,000. The few subscribers who had come in were suspicious of the Hoxie contract, and many refused to pay any more installments on their stock. The project seemed on the verge of collapse when in 1865 a new agency appeared, the Credit Mobilier, organized to take over the construction job. Two of its foremost figures were brothers, Oakes Ames (1804–73) and Oliver Ames II (1807–77), Massachusetts shovel manufacturers. Oakes was also a member of the House of Representatives and of its Pacific Railroad Committee.

Trouble flared between Durant and the Ameses. Durant, a hard-boiled go-getter, did not believe that the railroad would ever prosper, and wanted to take his profit out of its construction, as so many others had done. The Ames brothers opposed this philosophy. The worst feature of the Credit Mobilier was its interlocking ownership with the railroad. Durant, its president, was vice-president of the Union Pacific, and his faction wanted the Credit Mobilier to clean up a big profit on the building. But Oliver Ames was acting president of the railroad in 1866–68, during the construction period, and he and Oakes kept honest Dodge slogging ahead with the work, which he was doing for an average figure of $27,000 a mile—a little more than half what Hoxie had asked. It should be understood that both Durant and the Ameses had pledged every cent of their fortunes to the project. Oakes vowed to put it through, "if it takes my last shovel." By high-pressure salesmanship and giving a $1000 Union Pacific bond with every $1000 purchase of Credit Mobilier stock, many shares had been sold. But everybody concerned was in a desperate situation. They were at the mercy of politicians, and the railroad had bitter enemies, both in Congress and out of it. Politicians had set impossible figures for construction costs; they were now threatening rate regulation which might be ruinous; they must inspect every mile of track, and this might be disastrous if they were not kept in good humor. One government inspector demanded a $25,000 bribe before he would approve the road.

Congressmen had to be kept in good humor, and in his extremity, Oakes Ames made a serious mistake: he placed blocks of Credit Mobilier stock with such prominent members of Congress as Colfax, Blaine, Garfield, Dawes, Schofield, Boutwell, Bingham and others—"where it would do the most good," as he frankly said later, a phrase which had a damning sound when repeated publicly. The story broke during the campaign of 1872 and was good political ammunition. A virtuous Congress (the majority of whose members had received no Credit Mobilier shares) proceeded to put Oakes Ames in the dock. A member who had received some of the stock testified that no one connected with the railroad or the Credit Mobilier had ever asked him to do anything in behalf of either corporation, and no evidence to the contrary was produced. Nevertheless, Ames was expelled by the House, though the investigating committee declared in its report that "his purpose was not to secure positive beneficial legislation, but to prevent possible detrimental legislation"—in other words, he was simply defending the road against malignancy. Some members who had voted against him apologized to him afterward, saying that they did so through fear of their constituents. This episode has been a favorite subject for muckrakers in recent years, but more objective historians, such as Professor Robert E. Riegel of Dartmouth, have decided that Ames has been unduly pilloried. He returned home greatly broken by his experience, but though his neighbors greeted him as an honest man maligned, he died within a few months. From a strictly ethical standpoint, his action was indefensible, but the difficult position in which he was placed, with the nation's sorely needed project at stake, should be taken into consideration. The only ones who profited by this deal were the government—which got its transcontinental railroad with comparatively little cost to itself—and a few market riggers.

Speaking of stock jobbers, when U. P. stock was at its lowest, Jay Gould and his ribald partner, Jim Fisk, began picking it up. We mention this because it may as well be confessed here that Fisk was a New Englander. But as he was never a real railroad man—just a gambler—he may be dismissed with this brief notice.

Oliver Ames II continued as director of many railroads—Union Pacific, Atlantic & Pacific, Kansas Pacific, Denver Pacific, Colorado Central, Old Colony and others. Oliver III, son of Oakes, had a terrific struggle to recoup his father's wrecked fortune, but he succeeded. He served terms as president of the Union Pacific, the Sioux City & Pacific and the Fremont, Elkhorn & Missouri Valley, and he was director of many roads. His most spectacular feat was his getting the better of Jay Gould—buying Central Branch, Union Pacific stock at 25 cents a share and selling it to Gould at $250 a share.

As lieutenant-governor of Massachusetts for four terms and governor for three terms (1887–90), he was sharply criticized for arranging the sale of the state's interest in the New York & New England Railroad at some loss—and of its heavy holdings in Troy & Greenfield and Hoosac Tunnel at less than a third of their theoretical value—but time proved the wisdom of all these measures.

While Dodge was pushing the Union Pacific westward, the Central Pacific was driving eastward across the Sierras to meet it in that flamboyant ceremony in Utah in 1869. Of the four Sacramento shopkeepers who promoted it, it was Stanford, then California governor, who scintillated at the golden-spike driving, but the really great genius of the quartet was Collis P. Huntington (1821–1900), the Connecticut Yankee who at the age of fifteen began peddling clocks and worked thus through the South and West to California in 1848. With the Central Pacific completed, he proceeded to build the Southern Pacific eastward to New Orleans, completing it in 1881. Then he took over the Oregon & California, and as the man who practically put California in bondage to the railroad, he became one of the best hated men in the state. He later built the Chesapeake & Ohio and controlled forty-four railroads before he died.

As builder of the Southern Pacific, he was one of the New Englanders who created our second great transcontinental line, though it was under two managements. It is true that Cyrus Holliday, who had the inspiration for the Atchison, Topeka & Santa Fe, was a Pennsylvanian, but the engineer who built the line, seized the Raton Pass, and went far beyond Holliday's dream, was Albert A. Robinson, one of that army of Vermonters who have done more than their share in creating our railroad empire. When Holliday felt the reins slipping in his own hands, he called upon Henry Keyes, the Newbury, Vt., merchant, who had taken over the presidency of the Connecticut & Passumpsic Rivers and made it the first railroad in Vermont to pay dividends. Keyes assumed the Santa Fe presidency in 1869 but died in the following year. Then came Ginery Twitchell, fresh from a ten-year term as president of the Boston & Worcester. By this time State Street had become interested in the Santa Fe—especially the banking brothers, Joseph and Thomas Nickerson, and the firm of Kidder, Peabody & Company. Thomas Nickerson became president in 1874, and in the following seven years, with the assistance of engineer Robinson, the line was driven through to El Paso and the connection with the Southern Pacific.

Nickerson resigned the presidency in 1880, but only because he had too many other irons in the fire. He was building a Santa Fe subsidiary, the Atlantic & Pacific, westward from Albuquerque to California, and beyond that the California Southern (he was president of both). Moreover, he and Boston associates had organized the Mexican Central that year, and he became its first president. And thus these indomitable baked-bean and blueb'ry-muffin eaters drove Mexico's first great railroad, the Mexican Central, through to the city of Mexico, and the Santa Fe system to the Pacific Ocean at the Golden Gate. Engineer Robinson eventually became president of the Mexican Central (serving from 1893 to 1906), as did another New Englander, S. W. Reynolds.

C. F. Adams remarks, "The three combinations, the Chicago, Burlington & Quincy, Union Pacific and Santa Fe, all of which in whole or greatest part originated in the private enterprise of Boston, and having been constructed by the city's capital, were controlled from thence, represented in 1880 no less than 10,000 miles of railroad and $340,000,000 of securities." He does not mention the Mexican Central, which had just begun to be built, nor for some reason does he include the Michigan Central or Michigan Southern. The general offices of the Burlington, Union Pacific, Santa Fe and Mexican Central were all in Boston for several years—and we might include other small "foreign" roads, too, such as the Cleveland, Canton & Southern. The Union Pacific offices had been removed to Boston from New York in 1869, and it had not seen its last Yankee executive with the passing of the Ameses. In 1884, Charles Francis Adams (1835–1915), whom we have quoted so often in these pages—the worthy

representative of a great American family and long a Massachusetts State Railroad Commissioner—became president of
the Union Pacific and served until 1890.

As for the Santa Fe presidency, it was for decades a private
fief of New England. Thomas J. Coolidge, another Boston
capitalist, briefly succeeded Nickerson, and then in 1881 came
another of the Santa Fe's great men, William Barstow Strong
(1837–1914), a native of Brownington, Vt., who, beginning as a station agent, became its president. Within eight
years, with Albert A. Robinson, the Vermonter, as his vice-
president and general manager, Strong built most of the Gulf,
Colorado & Santa Fe system—extending his company into
Oklahoma and Texas- and the Chicago, Santa Fe & California,
which made Chicago its eastern terminus. He took over the
Santa Fe as a 2200-mile system, and when he resigned in 1889,
he left it with 6960 miles. After him there was a period
when the road, being out of New England hands, fell into
incompetence and receivership. But it was rescued by one
of the great modern railway executives, Edward P. Ripley
(1845–1920), born at Dorchester, Mass., who was first in the
drygoods business, then in railroads. He became general
manager of the Burlington in 1888, third vice-president of
the Chicago, Milwaukee & St. Paul in 1890, and on January 1,
1896, he was made president of the Santa Fe, filling that chair
most ably for twenty-four years. He sold the company's
interest in the St. Louis & San Francisco and swapped off some
other non-paying track, but built much more, including the
Belen cutoff across Oklahoma and the Texas Panhandle and
a southern connection between the Gulf, Colorado & Santa
Fe and the mother road. The Santa Fe had 6435 miles of
track when he became its head; he increased it to 11,291 miles.
Ripley was one of the chief promoters of the World's Columbian Exposition at Chicago in 1893. He was regarded as one
of the highest authorities in all railroad affairs, and when he
spoke, his utterances were publicly accepted as those of the
American railroad system as a whole. He resigned the presidency on January 1, 1920, and died a month later.

The third mighty transcontinental line was conceived in

the restless brain of Josiah Perham (1803–68), born in Wilton, Maine: we have already mentioned him as the pioneer of the modern excursion. He was an early advocate of a cross-continent railroad and hatched the idea of having it "owned by the people," its $100,000,000 capital to be distributed among a million stockholders. When he tried to get a charter for the People's Pacific Railroad in Massachusetts, it was refused, but he was more successful in Maine. The Union and Central Pacific Railroads, then building, fought him so hard that he was driven to seek a northern route. With the aid of Thaddeus Stevens he obtained a charter for the Northern Pacific Railroad, and President Lincoln signed it on July 2, 1864. Perham and a few others put all the money they could spare into the company, and he was elected its first president. He soon found that his idea of a vast popular distribution of the stock was not to be realized, but enough shares were sold to create a faction hostile to him, and he was compelled to yield the presidency to another Easterner, that bold spirit, John Gregory Smith of the Central Vermont, whose activities we have already observed. Smith pushed construction vigorously, being as usual charged with self-seeking and shady practices; but when friction with Jay Cooke, who was largely financing the road, forced him out in 1872, he had built 500 miles of track across Minnesota and Dakota.

The collapse of Cooke's banking house, which precipitated the Panic of '73, left the Northern Pacific flat. The directors elected Lewis Cass, son of the old New Hampshire general and statesman, as president, but the real mainspring of the company was Frederick Billings (1823–90), born in Royalton, Vt., who had made a small fortune in law in San Francisco. He thought he had retired because of ill health, but he became interested in the Northern Pacific and organized the company's land department, advertised widely, sold lands to settlers at reasonable prices, and so created the great northwestern farming area. After the crash he formulated a plan of reorganization, fought it through with directors and legislators, and put the company on its feet again. In 1879 he became president and began building track westward from Bismarck and eastward from the Pacific Coast. He cut overhead to the bone, cast off encumbering branches and induced a banking syndicate to take on a $40,000,000 bond issue, supplying enough cash to complete the gigantic task. But a shrewd and none-too-scrupulous promoter named Villard, who was building a road along the Columbia River, saw a threat to his plans in the N. P. and succeeded secretly in obtaining practical control. Billings, always harassed by ill-health, resigned in 1881, but to him should go the credit for the completion of the line two years later.

Other New Englanders followed: Thomas Fletcher Oakes (1843–1919), Boston-born, became vice-president of the N. P. in 1881, president in 1888, and after the Panic of '93, was receiver for two years. His colleague in the receivership was Henry Clay Payne (1843–1904), born at Ashfield, Mass., who had already built up Milwaukee's railway and light system, had been president of the Milwaukee & Northern, and was later president of the Chicago & Calumet Terminal and some interurban electric lines. Another Yankee Northern Pacific executive was Jule M. Hannaford, born at Claremont, N. H., who was its president from 1913 to 1920 and headed the Northern Pacific Express Company from 1906 to 1913.

We have only just begun on the catalogue of great New England railroaders. There was Henry B. Plant (1819–99), native of Branford, Conn., who got his start in a small way as an expressman, became superintendent of Adams' southern division, and when the outbreak of the Civil War forced the division of the Adams Express Company into two parts, was president and chief stockholder of the lower half, known as the Southern Express Company. When he died—still president—he owned 38,000 of its 50,000 shares, which had been paying 8 per cent dividends ever since it was organized, thirty-eight years before. At foreclosure sales in 1879–80, he bought the Atlantic & Gulf and the Charleston & Savannah, and on that foundation built the great Plant System which, within twenty years, included fourteen railroads, with 2100 miles of track, steamship lines and hotels. He created a new town, Plant City, in Florida; he found Tampa a village of a few hundred population and made it a city, giving it, at a cost of $2,500,000, the most flamboyantly oriental hotel to be found outside Xanadu.

Melville E. Ingalls (1842–1914), born in Harrison, Maine, and serving as lawyer and Massachusetts legislator in 1867 and 1868, was made receiver of the Indianapolis, Cincinnati & Lafayette in 1871. He reorganized the company, became its president in 1873, paid off its debts, consolidated it with other lines, and in 1880 formed the Cincinnati, Indianapolis, St. Louis & Chicago, the first "Big Four." His genius attracted the attention of Vanderbilt, who controlled the Bee Line, and in 1889 their interests were merged in a new Big Four, the Cleveland, Cincinnati, Chicago & St. Louis, with Ingalls as president. He held that position until the New York Central assumed control of the properties in 1905, then was chairman of the board until he resigned in 1912. He was also president of the Kentucky Central, from 1881 to 1883, and of the Chesapeake & Ohio, from 1888 to 1900.

The activities of Thomas H. Hubbard (1838–1915) of Hallowell, Maine, extended beyond the boundaries of the United States. He helped to reorganize the Wabash and was a director for twenty-six years. He became president of the Houston & Texas Central in 1894, vice-president of the Southern Pacific in 1896 and president of the Mexican International in 1897. He sold out of these companies around 1900 and bought into others, including a corporation which owned the Guatemala Central Railroad. Hubbard extended this line and in 1912 sold it to International Railways of Central America. From 1902 until his death he was head of a banking concern which participated in building railways in the Philippines.

Charles Parsons, who was born in Alfred, Maine, in 1829, was the Yankee who walked into a directors' meeting of the Rome, Watertown and Ogdensburg one day in 1883 and informed Samuel Sloan, president of the Lackawanna, who was in the chair, that the Lackawanna no longer controlled the R. W. & O.: he rather guessed that he, Parsons, would take over. He gathered in the Utica & Black River three years later and made the R. W. & O. a real system covering northern New York with 600 miles of track, but was forced to yield control to the New York Central in 1891, when that big neighbor had become disturbed by his activities. He then reorganized the little New Jersey Central and sold it, was briefly president of the New York & New England in 1892 and 1893, then bought and rejuvenated the South Carolina & Georgia Railroad and was its president until he sold it to the Southern in 1899.

Charles Morgan (1795-1878), a Killingworth, Conn., farm boy, first grocery clerk, then merchant, then in steamboats, fought Commodore Vanderbilt for the Forty-niner business via the Isthmus of Nicaragua (Vanderbilt threatened to ruin him, but didn't), and then founded the Morgan Line between New York & New Orleans, which at a recent date was still going strong. In 1869 he bought the New Orleans, Opelousas & Great Western, which had stalled eighty miles west of the Crescent City, christened its terminus Morgan City, and built it westward under the unique name of Morgan's Louisiana & Texas Railroad. A year before his death he bought control of the Houston & Texas Central and then had a water-rail line from New York to the heart of Texas.

Alpheus B. Stickney (1840–1916), born at Wilton, Maine, was first schoolteacher, then lawyer, then railroad builder, his first achievement being the creation of the St. Paul, Stillwater & Taylor's Falls. In 1879 he was building the St. Paul, Minneapolis & Manitoba (subsequently the Great Northern). In 1881 he organized and built the first section of the Wisconsin, Minnesota & Pacific and was made vice-president of the Minneapolis & St. Louis. In 1883 he promoted and began building the Minnesota & Northwestern and was its president until its union with the Chicago, St. Paul & Kansas City in 1887, when he became president of the consolidated road, whose name was changed to Chicago Great Western in 1894. Stickney continued as president until 1900 and chairman of the board until 1908.

Amasa Stone (1818–83), a farmer boy from Charlton,

Mass., became a carpenter and helped his brother-in-law, William Howe, to devise the Howe truss bridge, so widely used in the nineteenth century. In 1849 he and two others procured the contract to build the Cleveland, Columbus & Cincinnati Railroad, and Stone became successively superintendent and president. He built by contract the Chicago & Milwaukee, as well as the Cleveland, Painesville & Ashtabula, and was president of the latter from 1853 to 1869. When it was merged with the Lake Shore & Michigan Southern, he became president of that road, too.

Shall we name a few more? Philo Hurd, for example (1795–1885), of Brookfield, Conn., was a leading promoter of the Naugatuck who later completed the railroad from Indianapolis northward, eventually a part of the Lake Erie & Western. He was then vice-president of the Hudson River Railroad, and after Schuyler's defalcation, president of the Harlem in the latter fifties. Eleazar Lord (1788–1871) of Connecticut, who entered the ministry but gave it up because of eye failure and went into business, was first president of the Erie, fixed its six-foot gauge, and is said to have tided it over some of its darkest early days. Gordon Lester Ford (1823–91) of Lebanon, Conn., president of the New London, Willimantic & Palmer (1852–56), and first operator of the Amherst & Belchertown, was later president of the Brooklyn, Flatbush & Coney Island. George H. Nettleton, born in 1831 at Chicopee Falls, Mass., began as an engineer's rodman, and before the end of the century was president of the Kansas City, Fort Scott & Memphis; Kansas City, Clinton & Springfield; Kansas City, Memphis & Birmingham; Kansas City & Memphis Railway & Bridge Company, and Kansas City Belt Railway, not to mention another small one or two.

Austin Corbin (1827–96), of Newport, N. H., at first a lawyer, was the resuscitator of both the Long Island and the Philadelphia & Reading (he took charge of the Reading in 1886 and had it on its feet, with a good color in its cheeks, in two years), developer of steam transportation from New York to Coney Island, and short-term president of the New York & New England. His brother, Daniel C. Corbin (1832–

1918), was one of the creators of Spokane, Washington, builder of the Coeur d'Alene Railroad and Navigation Company, and also of the Spokane Falls & Northern and the Spokane International, which drove through the Rockies to a connection with the Canadian Pacific. Isaac Hinckley was one of the early superintendents of the Boston & Providence and Providence & Worcester and later president of the Philadelphia, Wilmington & Baltimore (1865–87) and of several small lines in Delaware and Maryland which subsequently merged with the Pennsylvania; he was likewise president of the Eastern Railroad Association in its first eleven years of existence.

Horace F. Clark (1815–73) of Southbury, Conn., attorney and ante-bellum Congressman, became director of the New York & Harlem, president of the Lake Shore, Michigan Southern & Northern Indiana, and also of the Union Pacific, and was director of others, his holdings being so important that the term, "a Clark stock," was applied to that of the railroads in which he was chiefly interested. Edmund Rice (1819–89), of Westfield, Vermont, who began as a farmhand and country store clerk, went to St. Paul in 1849 and became known as the "father of the Minnesota railway system," being promoter and president of the Minnesota & Pacific and its successors, the St. Paul & Pacific and St. Paul & Chicago, which latter was sold to the C. M. & St. P. in 1872. Samuel Vaughan Merrick (1801–70), of Hallowell, Maine, was a promoter of the Pennsylvania, its first president from 1847 to 1849 and a director for long afterward, and was also president of the Sunbury & Erie.

Chauncey Rose (1794–1877), native of Wethersfield, Conn., organized and built the Terre Haute & Richmond (later Terre Haute & Indianapolis, now a part of the Pennsylvania's St. Louis line), and was its first president (1847–53); he was also promoter of the Evansville & Terre Haute and its extension to Chicago. William P. Burrall (1806–74), from Canaan, Conn., was president of the Housatonic from 1839 to 1854, vice-president of the Hartford & New Haven from 1856 to 1867 and president from 1867 to 1872, and under his management that road became one of the best-paying lines in the country; he was vice-president of the New York, New Haven & Hartford from 1872 to 1874, and president of the Illinois Central from 1853 to 1855, continuing as its advisory counsel until his death. He was succeeded as head of the Illinois Central by William H. Osborn (1820–94), a Salem, Mass., man who had reorganized the I. C. after the Schuyler scandal and was its president from 1855 to 1865 and director for twenty-two years; he was also president of the Chicago, St. Louis & New Orleans from 1877 to 1882, and he combined this road with the I. C. to give it a track from Chicago to the Gulf. Edward F. Winslow (1837–1914) of Augusta, Maine, who built the first fifty miles of the St. Louis, Vandalia & Terre Haute (now Pennsylvania main line), was vice-president and general manager of the Burlington, Cedar Rapids & Northern from 1874 to 1880, then president of the New York, Ontario & Western, and formed the company to build the West Shore; in 1879 he was vice-president and general manager of the Manhattan Elevated Railway, and still had time in a long life to be president of the St. Louis & San Francisco and vice-president of the Atlantic & Pacific.

We have touched upon J. P. Morgan, greatest of railroad bankers, born in Hartford, but we have not mentioned Charles A. Prouty, born in Newport, Vt., long head of the Interstate Commerce Commission, nor the other Ripley, William Z., economist and so great an authority on railroads that the Rock Island in 1917 made him, a mere college professor, a director. He became administrator of labor standards for the War Department in 1918, chairman of the National Adjustment Commission of the United States Shipping Board in 1919 and 1920, and special examiner on consolidation of railways for the Interstate Commerce Commission, from 1920 to 1923.

There are dozens more in our notebooks. Naming the presidents only, omitting the other important jobs that they held, there are: Edwin H. Abbot of Beverly, Mass., president of the Wisconsin Central; William H. Baldwin, Bostonian, Southern and Long Island Railroads; John F. Barnard of

Worcester, Ohio & Mississippi; George T. Benedict of Vermont, New Orleans, Texas & Pacific; E. B. Phillips of Massachusetts, Fitchburg and Lake Shore; James H. Benedict of Norwalk, St. Joseph & Grand Island, also Chicago & Atlantic (Chicago & Erie); Timothy B. Blackstone of Branford, Conn., Chicago & Alton; D. W. Caldwell of Littleton, Mass., New York, Chicago & St. Louis (Nickel Plate); W. W. Crapo of Dartmouth, Mass., eighteen years president of the Flint & Pere Marquette; A. L. Hopkins of Massachusetts, Peoria & Pekin Union; H. H. Hunnewell of Watertown, Mass., Kansas City, Fort Scott & Gulf; Charles J. Ives of Wallingford, Vt., Burlington, Cedar Rapids & Northern; James T. Harahan of Massachusetts, Illinois Central; Edson J. Chamberlain of Vermont, Grand Trunk; John H. Clifford, a Providence lawyer, Boston & Providence; Gardiner Colby of Maine, builder of the Wisconsin Central and benefactor of Colby College; Austin H. Loveland of Chatham, Mass., builder and head of the Colorado Central; Henry C. Nutt of Montpelier, Vt., Atlantic & Pacific; Thomas W. Pierce of Dover, N. H., who built and was president of the Galveston, Harrisburg & San Antonio; Walter Peirce of West Swansey, N. H., Sharpsville & Shenango; Homer E. Sargent of Leicester, Mass., Fargo & Southern; Orland Smith of Lewiston, Maine, Cincinnati, Washington & Baltimore; another Asa Whitney (1791–1874), of Townsend, Mass., locomotive builder, builder of the Mohawk & Hudson inclined planes and president of the Philadelphia & Reading; John F. Wallace of Fall River, great bridge builder, chairman of the Chicago Railway Terminal Commission, first president of the American Railway Engineering and Maintenance of Way Association; and Henry W. Corbett of Westboro, Mass., one of the builders of the Northern Pacific and the Oregon & California.

Only the other day, as it seems, one of the greatest of twentieth-century railroad presidents died. Daniel Willard was born on a farm at North Hartland, Vermont, in 1861; he taught school at sixteen and seventeen, entered an agricultural college and helped to pay his way by cleaning the cow-stables and cooking his own meals, but he was forced out by eye trouble after six months and took a job as track laborer for the Central Vermont at eighteen, working up to a fireman's place and then to engineer for the Connecticut & Passumpsic Rivers. He was fifteen years with the Soo Line, served briefly with the Erie and in 1904 became vice-president of the Burlington, later adding the vice-presidency of the Colorado & Southern and the presidency of the Colorado Midland. In 1910 he went to the Baltimore & Ohio as president and stayed for thirty-one years—trying to resign time and again after seventy, but failing. In the First World War, he was Colonel of Engineers, chairman of the Advisory Committee of the Council for National Defense and chairman of the War Industries Board, and he sent to Russia the corps of American railroad men who did such yeoman service. His directorates, board chairmanships and honors, American and foreign, were too numerous to be recited here. When he left the B. & O. presidency at eighty-one, after having carried the company through strike, storm and stress, he was regarded as the topmost railroad man in America. He died a year later, June 6, 1942.

The story of Daniel Willard is the story of America and of more than 90 per cent of the railroad executives mentioned here. Almost none of them had means to begin with: they came up the hard way. All these men held other high positions which lack of space forbids our listing. Nor can we mention hundreds of other New Englanders who were directors, vice-presidents, general managers, superintendents, general passenger and freight agents, chief engineers and so on, of railroads all the way from the Atlantic to the Pacific and from Canada to South America. In this, the greatest railroad-building nation in the world, the six northeastern states have reason to be proud of the fact that from their purses and counting rooms came the daring cash to build some of our greatest railroads, and from their farms, country stores, shops and offices have come a number, out of all proportion to the area of the region, of the men who have dreamed, designed, financed, built and operated our vast railway system and the equipment that has rolled over it.

# Acknowledgment

WITHOUT the vast files of old newspapers and periodicals and the quantities of railroad material—original documents, monographs, time tables, pictures and what not—of the New-York Historical Society and New York Public Library, and the co-operation of my good friends on the staffs of both institutions, this book could not have been written. These were supplemented by the library of the *Railway Age*, where Walter A. Lucas and Miss Edith C. Stone, the librarian, were particularly helpful; by the library of the Engineering Societies of New York, by the Boston Public Library, Boston Atheneum, the library of the Old State House in Boston and that of Yale University. Richard H. Johnston, librarian of the American Association of Railroads at Washington, supplied a compilation difficult to obtain otherwise.

Certain individuals have contributed aid which could not have been obtained from the libraries: notably such men as William T. Gaynor of the New York Central, who has made this book one of his personal concerns, and who has aided and encouraged in more ways than can be listed here, no request of mine being too troublesome for him to comply with, if he possibly could; Warren Jacobs of Boston, Secretary of the Railway and Locomotive Historical Society, one of the kindliest of men, whose great collection of notes, documents and relics and whose brain full of railroad lore are at the service of any who seek assistance; and Charles E. Fisher of Boston, President of the Railway and Locomotive Historical Society, who practically never has to say, "I don't know," to a question about railroads, especially those of New England, and whose seemingly boundless collection of locomotive photographs and information about them were at my service.

Add to these Sidney Withington of New Haven, gentleman and scholar, who has assisted in many ways; John S. Kendall of St. Johnsbury, Vermont, who has lent material and donated photographs; C. B. Burr of Derby, Conn., who gave other photographs out of his vast collection. Among railroad collaborators, there were P. V. B. Lockwood, advertising manager of the New York Central, H. L. Baldwin, publicity director of the Boston & Maine and the Maine Central, Leslie G. Tyler of the publicity department of the New Haven Railroad at New Haven and D. W. Norris and his staff of the same company at New York, also Ben Deacon and Mrs. Helen L. Henriques of the Canadian National and M. K. Wright of the Baldwin Locomotive Works, all of whom contributed photographs generously from their files, more than I could use. For portraits of Yankee rail men who wrought greatly outside of New England, I had only to turn to Lee Lyles of the Santa Fe, William S. Murphy of the Union Pacific, K. C. Ingram of the Southern Pacific and L. L. Perrin of the Northern Pacific, to get every picture I wanted.

Other friendly aides have been Carlton Parker of Newton Centre, Mass., Messrs. G. A. Kirley, William L. Oldroyd, Ira G. Rasp, L. G. Morphy, R. G. Henderson and V. E. Gaudreau, all of the New York Central (Boston & Albany) staff in Boston, Allan Forbes and Patrick T. Jackson of Boston, Henry F. McCarthy of the New Haven and the staff of the *Scientific American* in New York. Thanks are also due to Lucius Beebe and his publishers, D. Appleton-Century Company, for permission to quote from his *Boston and the Boston Legend*, and to Edward Hungerford and the New England Railroad Club for permission to quote briefly from their publications.

# Bibliography

To list all the original documents and pamphlets which supply material for a history of New England railroads would require another volume in addition to this. Therefore, some of the categories are summarized below, there being a few notable exceptions which are mentioned later:

Proceedings of mass meetings and conventions to promote railroads.
Prospectuses of proposed railroads.
Surveys, preliminary and final.
Petitions for charters and amendments to charters.
Acts of incorporation.
Governors' messages and addresses.
Boards of directors' reports.
Reports of stockholders' investigating committees and replies to same.
Petitions by railroads for state loans, with debates and speeches on same and remonstrances by opponents.
Hearings before state railroad committees and commissions.
Lawsuits, reports of trials, attorneys' speeches, etc.
Circular letters to stockholders.
Statements by railroads to the public.
Reports of public meetings of protest.
Proceedings of railroad conventions and association meetings.
Reports of state railroad and canal committees and commissions.
Guide books, time tables, advertising pamphlets, etc.
City, county and town histories and gazetteers, other than those separately listed.
Correspondence and minutes in some railroad files.

## BOOKS, PAMPHLETS AND MAGAZINE ARTICLES

Abbott, Lyman. "The American Railroad," Harper's Magazine, XLIX (1874), pp. 375-394.
Adams, Charles Francis. Chapters of Erie and other Essays. Boston, 1871.

—. *History of Braintree, Mass., and the Town of Quincy.* Cambridge, 1891.

————. *Notes on Railroad Accidents.* New York, 1879.

————. *Railroads: Their Origin and Problems.* New York, 1878.

————. Chapter by, on "The Canal and Railroad Enterprise of Boston" in Justin Winsor's *Memorial History of Boston,* Vol. IV, pp. 111-150. Boston, 1881.

————, ARTHUR T. HADLEY, GEN. HORACE PORTER, M. N. FORNEY AND OTHERS. *The American Railroad.* New York, 1889.

ALDRICH, LEWIS CASS. *History of Franklin and Grand Isle Counties, Vermont.* Syracuse, N. Y., 1891.

ALEXANDER, E. P. *Iron Horses.* New York (1941).

ANGLO-AMERICAN, AN (pseud.) *American Securities.* London, 1860.

ATWATER, EDWARD E. *History of the City of New Haven.* New York, 1887.

BACON, EDWIN M. *The Connecticut River and the Valley of the Connecticut.* New York, 1906.

BAKER, GEORGE PIERCE. *The Formation of the New England Railway Systems.* Cambridge, 1937.

BALLOU, ADIN. *History of Milford, Mass.* Boston, 1882.

(BARRON, C. W.) *The Boston Stock Exchange.* Boston, 1893.

BAXTER, JAMES PHINNEY. "Reminiscences of a Great Enterprise," *Maine Historical Collections and Proceedings,* 2nd ser., III, p. 247.

BAXTER, W. E. *America and the Americans.* London, 1855.

BAYLES, RICHARD M., ED. *History of Providence County, R. I.* New York, 1891.

BECK, CHARLES. *On the Consolidation of the Worcester and Western Railroads.* N.p., n.d.

BEEBE, LUCIUS. *Boston and the Boston Legend.* New York, 1935.

BIRD, F. W. Hoosac Tunnel pamphlets, all pub. at Boston: *The Road to Ruin,* 1862; *The Hoosac Tunnel, Its Condition and Prospects,* 1865; *The Hoosac Tunnel, Our Financial Maelstrom,* 1866; *The Last Agony of the Great Bore,* 1868.

BISHOP, MRS. ISABELLA BIRD. *An Englishwoman in America.* London, 1856.

BLISS, GEORGE. *Historical Memoir of the Western Railroad.* Springfield, 1863.

BOSTON BOARD OF TRADE. *Annual Reports*, 1855–61.

————. *Report of a Select Committee of, on the Controversy between the Boston & Worcester and Western Railroads*. Boston, 1862.

BOSTON & MAINE RAILROAD. *A Statement Showing the Result of the Management for the Last Ten Years*. Boston, 1866.

BOSTON TERCENTENARY COMMITTEE. *Fifty Years of Boston*. n.p., 1932.

BRADBURY, JAMES W. "Railroad Reminiscences," *Maine Historical Society Collections and Proceedings*, 2nd ser., VII, pp. 379-390.

BRADLEE, FRANCIS B. C. *The Boston & Lowell, the Nashua & Lowell and the Salem & Lowell Railroads*. Salem, 1918.

————. *The Boston & Maine Railroad*. Salem, 1921.

————. *The Eastern Railroad*. Salem, 1922.

BROOKS, CHARLES. *History of the Town of Medford, Mass.* Boston, 1855.

BUCKINGHAM, J. S. *The Eastern and Western States of America*. London (1842).

BUTLER, BENJAMIN F. *Butler's Book.* Boston, 1892.

CABOT, MARY R. *Annals of Brattleboro, 1681–1895.* Brattleboro, 1922.

CARPENTER, A. V. H. *Glimpses of the Life and Times of A. V. H. Carpenter*. Chicago, 1890.

CARPENTER, E. W., and MOREHOUSE, C. F. *History of Amherst, Mass.* Amherst, 1896.

CAULKINS, FRANCES MAINWARING. *History of Norwich, Conn.* n.p., 1866.

*Challenge, The* (Great Flood of 1927 in White River Valley, Vt.). Randolph, Vt., 1928.

CHAMBERS, WILLIAM. *Things as They Are in America*. Philadelphia, 1854.

CHANDLER, CHARLES H. "An Historical Note on the Early American Railways," *Transactions of the Wisconsin Academy of Sciences, Arts and Letters*, XII (1898), pp. 317-324.

CHAPIN, CHARLES W. *Sketches of the Old Inhabitants and Other Citizens of Old Springfield of the Present Century*. Springfield, 1893.

CHAPMAN, HENRY SMITH. *History of Winchester, Mass.* (Cambridge) 1936.

CHASE, EDWARD EVERETT. *Maine Railroads*. Portland, 1926.

(CLARK, T. C.) "Railway Engineering in the United States," *Atlantic Monthly*, III (1858), pp. 641-656.

CLARKE, ALBERT. *The Free Pass Evil*. Speech delivered in the Vermont Senate, Nov. 13, 1874. Boston, 1907.

CLEVELAND, FREDERICK A., and POWELL, FRED WILBUR. *Railroad Promotion and Capitalization in the United States*. New York, 1909.

COBURN, LOUISE HELEN. *Skowhegan on the Kennebec*. Skowhegan, 1941.

COE, HARRIE B. *Maine. A History*. New York, 1928.

CONCORD, HISTORY COMMISSION OF. *History of Concord, N. H.* Concord, 1903.

CONNECTICUT RAILROAD COMMISSION. *Report for 1879* (for story of New York & New England Railroad). N.p., 1880.

COPELAND, ALFRED M. *Our County and Its People. A History of Hampden County, Mass.* Boston, 1902.

CRANE, ELLERY BICKNELL, ED. *History of Worcester County, Mass.* New York and Chicago, 1924.

CRITTENDEN, H. L. "The Two-Footers," *Bulletin 57, Railway & Locomotive Historical Society*.

CROCKER, GEORGE GLOVER. *From the Stage Coach to the Railroad Train and Street Car. . . .* Boston, 1900.

CROCKETT, WALTER HILL. *Vermont, the Green Mountain State*. 5 vol. New York, 1921–23.

*Cumberland County, Maine, History of*. Philadelphia, 1880.

CURRIER, JOHN J. *History of Newburyport, Mass.* Newburyport, 1909.

CURTIS, JOHN GOULD. *History of the Town of Brookline, Mass.* Boston, 1933.


(DAGGETT, JOHN) *Remarks and Documents Concerning the Location of the Boston & Providence Rail-Road through the Burying-Ground in East Attleborough*. Boston, 1834.

———. *A Sketch of the History of Attleborough, Edited and Completed by his Daughter*. Boston, 1894.

DANIELS, WINTHROP M. *American Railroads: Four Phases of Their History*. Princeton, 1932.

DAVENPORT, C. N. *The Vermont Central Ring—Bribery and Corruption, Argument before Special Masters in Chancery*. St. Albans, 1875.

(DAVIS, WILLIAM T.) *Professional and Industrial History of Suffolk County, Mass.* 3 vol. Boston, 1894.

*Dictionary of American Biography.*

DRAKE, SAMUEL ADAMS. *History of Middlesex County, Mass.* Boston, 1880.

DUNBAR, SEYMOUR. *A History of Travel.* 4 vol. Indianapolis, 1915.

DUTCHER, L. J.. *History of St. Albans, Vermont.* St. Albans, 1872.

EATON, LILLEY. *General History of Town of Reading, Mass.* Boston, 1874.

(EDDY, CALEB) *Historical Sketch of the Middlesex Canal, with Remarks for the Consideration of the Proprietors.* Boston, 1843.

(EUSTICE, W. T.) "The Railroad Enterprise: Its Progress, Management and Utility," *New Englander*, Aug., 1851, pp. 321-344.

EVERTS, LOUIS N. *History of the Connecticut Valley in Massachusetts*, Philadelphia, 1879.

*Evidence showing the manner in which Locomotive Engines are used upon Rail Roads, and the Danger and Inexpediency of permitting rival Companies using them as the same Road.* Boston, 1838.

FAIRBANKS, EDWARD T. *The Town of St. Johnsbury, Vermont.* St. Johnsbury, 1914.

FELT, CHARLES W. Pamphlets: *The Dead-Heads, or Who Rides Free on the Railroads, No. 1,* 1874; *No. 2,* 1875; *St. Ennial Dead-Heads,* 1876; *The Eastern Railroad,* 1873; *No. 2,* 1874; *Nuts for Butler to Crack, No. 1,* 1876; *No. 2,* 1878; *Our Steam Railroads and Suburban Travel,* 1883.

FISHER, CHARLES E. *Story of the Old Colony Railroad.* N.p. (1919).

FLINT, HENRY M. *Railroads of the United States*, etc. Philadelphia, 1868.

FORBES, CHARLES S. "History of the Vermont Central–Central Vermont Railway System," *The Vermonter*, Nov.–Dec., 1932.

FORBES, JOHN MURRAY. *Letters and Recollections of John Murray Forbes*, edited by Sarah Forbes Hughes. Boston, 1899.

GENERAL RAILROAD ASSOCIATION. *Journal of the Proceedings at their Second Convention, Springfield, Nov. 10, 1852.* New Haven, 1852.

GENERAL RAILROAD CONVENTION. *Journal of the Proceedings of, held at Springfield, Aug. 24 and 25, 1852.* New Haven, 1852.

(GRANT, E. B.) *Boston Railways. Their Condition and Prospects.* Boston, 1856.

GREGG, W. P., and POND, BENJAMIN. *The Railroad Laws and Charters of the United States.* Boston, 1851.

GREEN, MASON A. *Springfield, 1636–1886. History of Town and City.* Springfield, 1888.

GRIFFIN, S. G. *A History of the Town of Keene, N. H.* Keene, 1904.

HADLEY, A. T. *Railroad Transportation. Its History and its Laws.* New York, 1885.

HALE, EDWARD EVERETT. *Memories of One Hundred Years.* New York and London, 1902.

HALE, NATHAN. "Massachusetts Rail-Road," *North American Review,* April, 1829, pp. 522–537.

———. *Remarks on the Practicability and Expediency of Establishing a Railroad on one or more Routes from Boston to the Connecticut River.* Boston, 1827.

———. *Remarks on the Practicability of Railroads from Boston to the Hudson River and from Boston to Providence.* Boston, 1829.

HANEY, LEWIS HENRY. *A Congressional History of Railways in the United States.* 2 vols. Madison, Wis., 1906, 1910.

HATCH, LOUIS CLINTON. *Maine. A History.* New York, 1919.

HAUPT, HERMAN. *Reminiscences of Herman Haupt.* N.p., 1901.

———. *Reply to a Communication from Members of the Legislature of Massachusetts of 1868.* Boston, 1868.

———. *Rise and Progress of the Hoosac Tunnel.* N.p. (1862).

———. *Statement of, presented to the Joint Special Committee on the Troy & Greenfield Railroad and Hoosac Tunnel.* N.p., 1864.

HAYES, LYMAN S. *The Connecticut River Valley in Southern Vermont and New Hampshire.* Rutland, Vt., 1929.

HAYWARD, JOHN. *A Gazetteer of Massachusetts.* Boston, 1847.

HAZEN, HENRY A. *History of Billerica, Massachusetts.* Boston, 1883.

HAZLETT, CHARLES A. *History of Rockingham County, N. H.* Chicago, 1915.

HEALY, KENT T. "Development of Transportation in Southern New England," *Connecticut Society of Civil Engineers,* 1934, pp. 95–120.

HENDERSON, HARRY, and SHAW, SAM. "Cracker-Barrel Railroaders" (Belfast & Moosehead Lake R.R.), *Collier's*, Jan. 13, 1945.

HILL, BENJAMIN THOMAS. "The Beginnings of the Boston & Worcester Railroad," *Worcester Society of Antiquity Collections*, VII, pp. 527-576.

HOLLAND, JOSIAH GILBERT. *A History of Western Massachusetts.* Springfield, 1855.

Hoosac Tunnel pamphlets. In addition to those separately listed here, the author has seen more than 100, including engineers' estimates; advance pamphlets for and against; petitions of Troy & Greenfield Railroad for charter and state loans; remonstrances of Western Railroad against such charter and loans; speeches in Massachusetts Legislature; reports of court trials and attorneys' addresses; reports of committees, railroad and legislative; boards of directors' reports of Troy & Greenfield, Troy & Boston, Fitchburg, etc.; reports of 27 hearings before Committee on Railways regarding railway consolidation (Jan.-March, 1873); committee reports of Boston Board of Trade; reports (one of 730 pp.) of Troy & Greenfield and Hoosac Tunnel commissioners; "Hoosac Tunnel Papers" (1866); petitions of contractors for relief and additional remuneration; engineers' reports of progress; committee hearings on Hoosac Tunnel and Troy & Greenfield Railroad in 1887; correspondence, etc.

HOUGH, HENRY BEETLE. *Martha's Vineyard, Summer Resort, 1835-1935.* Rutland, Vt., 1936.

HUNGERFORD, EDWARD. "Vermont-Central, Central-Vermont," *Bulletin, Railway and Locomotive Historical Society*, Boston.

———. *Men and Iron. The History of New York Central.* New York, 1938.

HUNTINGTON, E. B. *History of Stamford, Conn.* Stamford, 1868.

HURD, D. HAMILTON. *History of Cheshire and Sullivan Counties, N. H.* Philadelphia, 1886.

———. *History of Norfolk County, Mass.* Philadelphia, 1884.

———. *History of Rockingham and Stratford Counties, N. H.* Philadelphia, 1882.

———. *History of Worcester County, Mass.* Philadelphia, 1889.

HURD, DUANE H. *History of New London, Conn., etc.* Philadelphia, 1882.

HUTT, FRANK WALCOTT. *History of Bristol County, Mass.* New York, 1924.

INTERSTATE COMMERCE COMMISSION OF THE UNITED STATES. *Reports*, 1887–1944, especially XXXI (1915), pp. 32-131 (New Haven Railroad).

JACKSON, JAMES R. *History of Littleton, N. H.* 3 vol. Cambridge, 1905.

JACKSON, WILLIAM. *A Lecture on Rail Roads delivered Jan. 12, 1829, before the Massachusetts Charitable Mechanic Association.* Boston, 1829.

JACOBS, WARREN. "The Story of the Boston & Albany," *New York Central Magazine*, Aug., 1928.

JOHNSON, DAVID N. *Sketches of Lynn.* Lynn, 1880.

JOHNSON, EDWIN FERRY. *Memoir of Edwin Ferry Johnson.* Philadelphia, 1880.

JOHNSON, EMORY. *American Railway Transportation.* New York, 1908.

JOINT STANDING COMMITTEE ON RAILROADS. *Report of the, on the Resolution to inquire whether any Railroad companies have Combined to prevent the Construction of any other Railroads.* New Haven, 1857.

JONES, A. D. *Commercial, Mechanical, Professional, and Statistical Gazetteer and Business Book of Connecticut, 1857–58.* New Haven, 1857.

KENDALL, JOHN S. *History of the St. Johnsbury & Lake Champlain Railroad.* N.p. (1940).

KENNEDY, J. H. "The American Railroad. Its Inception, Evolution and Results," *Magazine of Western History*, VII, VIII, IX, X and XI (1887–89).

KISTLER, THELMA M. *The Rise of Railroads in the Connecticut Valley. Smith College Studies in History.* Northampton, Mass., 1937–38.

KNIGHT, J., and LATROBE, BENJAMIN H. *Report upon the Locomotive Engine, and the Police and Management of several of the Principal Rail-Roads of the Northern and Middle States.* Baltimore, 1838.

LAMB, WALLACE E. *The Lake Champlain and Lake George Valleys.* New York (1940).

LANE, WHEATON J. *Commodore Vanderbilt.* New York, 1942.

LANGTRY, ALBERT P., ED. *Metropolitan Boston*, III. New York, 1929.

LEBANON SPRINGS RAILROAD, *Acts relating to the.* New York, 1863.

LEWIS, ALONZO. *Annals of Lynn, Essex County, Mass.* Continued by James R. Newhall. Boston, 1865.

LINCOLN, GEORGE, AND OTHERS. *History of Hingham, Mass.* (Cambridge) 1893.

*Litchfield County, Connecticut, History of.* Philadelphia, 1881.

LOCKWOOD, JOHN H. *Westfield and its Historic Influence.* Springfield, 1922.

LORING, LEWIS P. "Early Railroads in Boston," *Bostonian* (mag.), I (1894), pp. 299-309.

MCADAM, ROGER WILLIAMS. *The Old Fall River Line.* Brattleboro, 1937.

MCCLINTOCK, JOHN N. *History of New Hampshire.* Boston, 1889.

MCDUFFEE, FRANKLIN. *History of the Town of Rochester, N. H.* Manchester, 1892.

MCFARLAND, HENRY. *Sixty Years in Concord and Elsewhere.* Concord, N. H., 1899.

MACGILL, CAROLINE, AND OTHERS. *History of Transportation in the United States before 1860.* Washington, 1917.

MACKAY, ALEXANDER. *The Western World.* 3 vols. London, 1849.

MCLIN, WILLIAM HELLEN. *The Twenty-four Inch Gauge Railroad at Bridgeton, Maine.* Bridgeton, 1941.

*Manchester. A Brief Record of its Past and a Picture of its Present.* Manchester, 1875.

MARRYAT, CAPTAIN FREDERICK. *A Diary in America.* London, 1839.

MARSHALL, BENJAMIN T., ED. *A Modern History of New London County, Connecticut.* 3 vols. New York, 1922.

MARTIN, JOSEPH G. *A Century of Finance. Martin's History of the Boston Stock and Money Market.* Boston, 1898.

MASSACHUSETTS BOARD OF RAILROAD COMMISSIONERS. *Special Report on disaster . . . Mon., March 14, 1887 . . . Boston & Providence Railroad . . . Bussey Bridge . . .* Boston, 1887.

MASSACHUSETTS COMMITTEE ON RAILWAYS AND CANALS. *Inquiry into Accidents on the Western Railroad, Senate Doc. No. 55* (1842).

MASSACHUSETTS RAILROAD ASSOCIATION. *Reports made to the*

*Directors of, on the Practicability of Conducting Transportation on a single Set of Tracks.* (Boston, 1829.)

*Massachusetts Railroads, 1842–1855.* Boston, 1856.

MERRILL, GEORGIA DREW. *History of Androscoggin County, Maine.* Boston, 1891.

MORGAN, FORREST. *Connecticut as a Colony and as a State.* 4 vols. Hartford, 1904.

MORSE, JARVIS M. *A Neglected Period of Connecticut History, 1818–1850. Yale Historical Publications, Miscellany,* XXV.

MORSE, VICTOR M. *The Story of the West River Railroad.* Brattleboro, 1939.

MOTT, EDWARD HAROLD. *Between the Ocean and the Lakes, The Story of Erie.* New York, 1901.

NEW ENGLAND ASSOCIATION OF RAILWAY SUPERINTENDENTS. *Reports,* etc. Boston, 1850.

NEW HAMPSHIRE. *Report of the Commissioners . . . to ascertain the State's Interest in the Concord Railroad . . . and in the Boston & Maine Railroad.* Manchester, N. H., 1889.

NEW YORK & NEW HAVEN RAILROAD. Many pamphlets on the Schuyler affair. New York and New Haven, 1853–55.

*New York, New Haven & Hartford Railroad, A Brief History of, during the past Twenty Years.* New York, 1926.

NORTH, JAMES W. *History of Augusta, Maine.* Augusta, 1870.

NUTT, CHARLES. *History of Worcester and its People.* New York, 1919.

*Old Colony Railroad, History of.* Boston (1893).

OLDMIXON, CAPTAIN. *Transatlantic Wanderings.* London, 1855.

ORCUTT, SAMUEL. *A History of the old Town of Derby, Conn.* Springfield, 1880.

———. *A History of the old Town of Stratford and the City of Bridgeport, Conn.* (New Haven) 1886.

———. *A History of Torrington, Conn.* Albany, 1878.

OWEN, HENRY WILSON. *History of Bath, Maine.* Bath, 1936.

PALMER, COURTLANDT, Pres. New York, Providence & Boston Railroad. Unpublished correspondence, New York Public Library.

PATTEE, WILLIAM S. *History of Old Braintree and Quincy.* Quincy, 1878.

PEARSON, HENRY GREENLEAF. *An American Railroad Builder, John Murray Forbes.* Boston, 1911.

*Penobscot County, Maine, History of.* Cleveland, 1882.

PERKINS, JAMES W. *The New York & New England Railroad Company.* (A documentary history, printed but not published. Not more than half a dozen copies bound.) Boston, 1874.

POOR, HENRY VARNUM. *History of the Railroads and Canals of the United States.* New York, 1860.

———. *Poor's Manual of the Railroads of the United States.* New York, 1868–1924.

———. *Sketch of the Rise and Progress of the Internal Improvements of the United States.* New York, 1881.

POOR, JOHN ALFRED. *The First International Railway and the Colonization of New England.* New York, 1892.

———. *The Railroad.* Boston, 1867.

POTTER, C. E. *History of Manchester, N. H.* Manchester, 1856.

POWELL, MAX L. *The Twenty-Seven Years' Litigation between the Vermont Central and Vermont & Canada Railroads.* Montpelier, Vt., 1909.

QUINCY, JOSIAH, JR. *Letter to the Shareholders of the Vermont Central Railroad.* Boston, 1852.

———. *Public Interest and Private Monopoly.* Boston, 1867.

———. *The Railway System of Massachusetts, Boston City Document No. 109.* Boston, 1866.

RANN, W. S., ED. *History of Chittenden County, Vermont.* Syracuse, N. Y., 1886.

RICHARDSON, FREDERICK H., and BLOUNT, F. NELSON. *Along the Iron Trail.* Rutland, Vt. (1938).

RINGWALT, JOHN L. *Development of Transportation Systems in the United States.* Philadelphia, 1888.

ROWE, HENRY K. *Tercentenary History of Newton* (Mass.) Cambridge, 1930.

*Rutland County, Vermont, History of.* White River Junction, Vt., 1882.

(SEDGWICK, THEODORE) *Brief Remarks on the Rail Roads proposed in Massachusetts.* By "Berkshire." Stockbridge, Mass., 1828.

SEYMOUR, GEORGE DUDLEY. *New Haven.* New Haven, 1942.

SHUTE, JAMES M. *Rejected Papers in Relation to the Hoosac Tunnel.* Boston, 1868.

SMITH, MRS. E. VALE. *History of Newburyport, Mass.* Newburyport, 1854.

SMITH, H. P., and RANN, W. S. *History of Rutland County, Vermont.* Syracuse, N. Y., 1886.

SMITH, J. E. A. *History of Pittsfield, Mass.* Springfield, 1876.

STACKPOLE, EVERETT S. *History of New Hampshire.* 5 vols. New York, 1916–18.

STARR, J. W. *One Hundred Years of American Railroading.* New York, 1928.

STIMSON, A. L. *History of the Express Companies and the Origin of the American Railroad.* 3rd Edition. New York, 1881.

STONE, ARTHUR F. "Early Days of the Passumpsic Railroad," *Vermonter,* XL (July, 1944).

SUMNER, WILLIAM H. *A History of East Boston.* Boston, 1858.

(SYLVESTER, NATHANIEL BARTLETT) *History of the Connecticut Valley in Massachusetts.* Philadelphia, 1879.

TANNER, H. S. *A Description of the Canals and Railroads of the United States, etc.* New York, 1840.

TEELE, A. K., ED. *History of Milton, Mass., 1840–1887.* N.p. (1887).

TEMPLE, JOSEPH H. *History of the Town of Palmer, Mass., 1716–1889.* Palmer, 1889.

THOMPSON, FRANCIS M. *History of Greenfield, Shire Town of Franklin County, Mass.* Greenfield, 1904.

TRAYSER, DONALD G. *Barnstable: Three Centuries of a Cape Cod Town.* Hyannis, 1938.

TRUMBULL, J. HAMMOND, ED. *Memorial History of Hartford County, Conn.* Boston, 1886.

TUCKER, WILLIAM HOWARD. *History of Hartford, Vermont.* Burlington, Vt., 1889.

TUTTLE, CHARLES W. "Hon. John Alfred Poor of Portland, Maine," *New England Historical and Genealogical Register,* XXVI (Oct., 1872).

VARNEY, GEORGE J. *Gazetteer of the State of Massachusetts.* Boston, 1886.

VOSE, GEORGE L. *Notes on Early Transportation in Massachusetts.* New York, 1884.

——. *Sketch of the Life and Times of George W. Whistler.* Boston and New York, 1887.

WADLEIGH, GEORGE. *Notable Events in the History of Dover, N. H.* Dover, 1913.

WALDO, GEORGE C. *The Standard's History of Bridgeport.* Bridgeport, Conn., 1897.

WALL, CALEB A. *Reminiscences of Worcester.* Worcester, 1877.

WEBSTER, DANIEL. *Argument in behalf of the Boston & Lowell Railroad, before the Railroad Committee of the Massachusetts Legislature.* Boston, 1845.

WELLS, FREDERICK P. *History of Newbury, Vermont.* St. Johnsbury, Vt., 1902.

WIGGIN, EDWARD, and COLLINS, GEORGE. *History of Aroostook County, Maine.* Presque Isle, Me., 1922.

WILLIAMSON, JOSEPH. *History of the City of Belfast, in the State of Maine.* Portland, 1877.

WITHINGTON, SIDNEY. *The First Twenty Years of Railroads in Connecticut, Connecticut Tercentenary Publication.* New Haven, 1935.

WOODWARD, CHARLES G. *The New London, Willimantic & Palmer Railroad Company.* Hartford, 1941.

*Ye People's Interest in Ye Concord Railroad, etc.* Concord, N. H., 1892.

## PERIODICALS

*American Railroad Journal,* 1832–86.
*American Railway Review,* 1859–61
*Hunt's Merchants' Magazine,* 1839–60.
*New England Railroad Club Proceedings,* 1894–1943.
*Railroad Age Gazette,* 1856–1908.
*Railroad Gazette,* 1870–1908.
*Railroadians of America,* annual publication.
*Railway Age* (with changes of title), 1876–date.
*Railway Chronicle,* 1873–1915.
*Railway and Locomotive Historical Society, Bulletins,* 1921–date.
*Railway Times,* 1849–67.
*Railway World,* 1875–date.
Daily and weekly newspapers of New England and New York, 1828–date.

# Index

Abbot, Edwin H., 430
Adams, Alvin, 407, 408, 409
Adams, Charles Francis, 24, 26, 31, 35, 39, 48, 114, 117, 119, 134, 200, 203, 373, 374, 376, 415, 416, 417, 422
Adams, John, Pres., 32, 34
Adams, John B., 385
Adams, John Quincy, Pres., 10, 34, 35, 216
Adams Express Co., 408, 409, 425
"Agricola," 36
Agricultural Branch R.R., 142, 232
Albany, N. Y., 6, 7, 22, 36, 43, 58, 66, 70, 71, 72, 77, 116, 117, 119, 122, 124, 125, 126, 127, 128, 131, 133, 134, 136, 137, 177, 179
Albany & West Stockbridge R.R., 117, 122, 124, 125, 126, 130
Allen, Andrew J., 42
Allyn's Point, Conn., 204, 218, 220, 221, 222
American Express Co., 327, 409
American Railroad Journal, 63, 181, 186, 187, 390, 391
American Society of Civil Engineers, 42
American Traveller, 3, 28, 34, 56, 79
Ames, Oakes, 418-420
Ames, Oliver, II, 418-20
Ames, Oliver, III, 421
Amherst, Mass., 254
Amherst & Belchertown R.R., 275, 428
Amoskeag. See Manchester, N. H.
Amoskeag Locomotive Works, 287
Andover, Mass., 121, 143, 144, 155
Andover & Wilmington R.R., 143-146, 147
Andrew, John A., Gov., 246
Androscoggin R.R., 318, 366

Androscoggin & Kennebec R.R., 314, 316
Appleton, Nathan, 80, 147
Aroostook War, 46, 326
Ashuelot R.R., 306
Atchison, Topeka & Santa Fe R.R., 409, 412, 417, 421, 422, 423
Atlantic & Pacific R.R., 420, 422, 430, 431
Atlantic & St. Lawrence R.R., 311-315, 316, 320
Attleborough, Mass., 107
Augusta, Me., 316, 317

Baggage check, first, 387
Dalton, George Pierce, 257, 302
Baldwin, James F., 44, 48, 61, 411
Baldwin, Loammi, 22, 23, 24, 44, 83, 239
Baldwin, Matthias, 263, 354
Baldwin, William H., 430
Baltimore & Ohio R.R., 27, 34, 134, 432
Bangor, Me., 159, 162, 308, 311, 316, 320, 321, 324, 327
Bangor & Aroostook R.R., 320, 327, 338
Bangor & Bucksport R.R., 323, 346
Bangor, Old Town & Milford R.R., 309
Bangor & Piscataquis R.R., 308, 319, 320, 322, 327, 346
Banks, Henry, 386
Banks, N. P., Gov., 246
Baring Bros., 124, 168, 351
Barnard, John F., 430
Bath, Me., 318, 324
Baxter, W. E., 369
Bay State Iron Works, 351
Bay State Steamboat Co., 218
Beacon Hill, 18
Beebe, Lucius, 336, 382

Belfast, Me., 310, 319, 327, 337
Belfast & Moosehead Lake R.R., 319, 327, 337
Belfast & Quebec R.R., 310
Belknap, S. F., 237, 269
Bellows Falls, Vt., 260, 266, 271, 274, 281, 396
Benedict, George T., 431
Benedict, James H., 431
Bennington, Vt., 259, 276
Bennington & Rutland R.R., 253, 274, 276, 281
Berdell, Robt. H., 202, 203, 204
Berkshire County, 25, 37, 42, 48, 49, 53
Berkshire Hills, 7, 44, 134, 283
Berkshire & Hudson R.R., 49
"Big Four" R.R., 426
Billerica & Bedford R.R., 340, 341
Billings, Frederick W., 424, 425
Bird, Frank W., 245, 246, 247, 250, 251
Bishop, Alfred, 180, 183, 184
Bishop, E. F., 391
Bishop, Isabella B., Mrs., 388
Bishop, William D., 190
Blackstone Canal, 23, 46, 78, 103
Blackstone, Timothy B., 431
Bliss, George, 118, 124, 126, 129, 130, 136, 138, 412, 413, 415
Bliss, William, 191, 192, 193, 330
Boat Train, 217, 218, 219, 223, 230, 231, 234
Boott, Kirk, 80
Borden, Nathaniel B., 225, 226
Borden, Thomas, Capt., 218
Boston, loss of trade pre-eminence, 4-8, 14-16, 19, 62, 63; and migration, 8, 9; first tramway in America, 18; ponders interurban railroads, 20, 28, 31; interest in Granite Railway, 32-34; considers canal to Hudson River, 16, 20, 23-25, 28; discusses steam railroads, 38-42; demands legislative action, 42; considers city aid to railroad to Albany, 53; urges state-aided corporation, 55, 56; organizes booster association, 57; debates single- and double-track problem, 58-61; turns toward private ownership, 65; four companies chartered, 70; promotes first railroads, 71-79; builds first three rail-

roads, 80-115; enthusiasm over first trains, 97, 98, 99, 108; railroads historical milestone for, 114, 115; slow to buy stock in Western R.R., 120-122; never appreciated the Western, 134; annoyed by Western and B. & W. squabbles, 139-141; refuses to promote Eastern R.R., 150; its Causeway Street as "railroad row," 159; its railroads spur Connecticut, 171, 172; through rail line to New York, 184, 185, 190, 191, 192, 194; its promoters develop New York & New England, 198-204; connection with New York by Old Colony and Fall River Line, 218-219; by other boat lines, 219-223, 228-230; railroads to haul ice for Boston, 237; aids Rutland & Burlington, 265; great railroad celebration of 1851, 270, 294; city chief builder of Nashua & Lowell, 285; backs Northern R.R. (N. H.), 293; refuses to aid Boston, Concord & Montreal, 295; fights Portland's plan to get Grand Trunk terminus, 311, 313; incensed by lease of Boston & Albany to New York Central, 330, 331; affection for New Haven R.R., 336, 337; promises to aid Maine narrow gauges, 341; Board of Trade excursion to San Francisco, 392; railway stations, 394, 395; origin of excursions, 398; of express business, 405-409; expresses in 1870, 408; finances Michigan Central R.R., 414, 415; and the Burlington, 416; fails to see importance of New York Central, 416, 417; builds Santa Fe R.R., 422; and Mexican Central, 422; Union Pacific offices moved to Boston, 425; headquarters of western roads in, 425
Boston Advertiser, 9, 27, 33, 39, 68, 77, 83, 98, 99, 104
Boston & Albany R.R., 37, 137, 141, 142, 191, 192, 193, 194, 206, 258, 283, 329, 330, 331, 351, 352, 367, 394
Boston, Barre & Gardner R.R., 257, 412

Boston Board of Trade, 139; excursion, 392
Boston, Clinton & Fitchburg R.R., 232
Boston, Clinton, Fitchburg & New Bedford R.R., 233
Boston, Concord & Montreal R.R., 279, 284, 294, 295, 297, 299, 301, 302, 303, 304, 305, 306, 360, 370, 381
*Boston Courier*, 24, 43
Boston, Hartford & Erie R.R., 196, 200-204
Boston, Hoosac Tunnel & Western R.R., 255, 257
Boston & Lowell R.R., 71, 72, 75, 76, 80-93, 99, 103, 113, 129, 143, 144, 145, 147, 156, 159, 254, 255, 279, 285, 286, 290, 291, 297, 299, 300, 301, 302, 303, 304, 305, 311, 323, 339, 350, 356, 380, 388, 390, 405
Boston & Maine R.R., 118, 137, 143-148, 154, 155, 157-161, 194, 249, 255, 258, 283, 284, 290, 297, 301, 302, 303, 304, 305, 306, 309, 318, 320, 321, 323, 324, 326, 332, 333, 334, 335, 337, 361, 369, 381, 382, 394, 396, 411, 413
*Boston Patriot*, 20, 25, 53, 98
Boston & Providence R.R., 55, 77, 78, 84, 95, 103, 104-113, 129, 144, 194, 219, 233, 353, 354, 360, 362, 363, 376, 379, 395, 398, 400, 429, 431
Boston, Revere Beach & Lynn R.R., 163, 166, 346
*Boston Transcript*, 97, 98
Boston & Worcester R.R., 77, 78, 84, 86, 87, 93-104, 110, 111, 113, 116, 118, 126, 128, 135, 138-142, 171, 232, 331, 354, 355, 357, 362, 366, 381, 382, 385, 394, 405, 412, 422
Bradley, John, 386
Brainerd, Lawrence, 263, 264, 268
Brattleboro, Vt., 63, 70, 71, 239, 240, 253, 259, 266, 274, 275, 346
Breck, Samuel, 379
Brewster, James, 172, 412
Brewster, N. Y., 200, 205, 208, 210
Bridgeport, Conn., 125, 133, 134, 177, 178, 179, 183, 207
Bridgewater, Mass., 217, 223, 224
Bridgton, Me., 343, 344
Bridgton & Harrison R.R., 343-345

Bristol, R. I., 224, 229, 230
British type railway cars, 230, 231
Brookline, Mass., 78, 114, 142
Brooks, Charles, 81, 356
Brooks, John W., 147, 248, 250, 412, 413-416
Brunswick, Me., 318
Bryant, Gridley, 17, 18, 22, 23, 25-27, 32-35, 412
Bunker Hill Monument, 17, 23, 159
Burke & Co.'s Express, 407
Burleigh, Albert A., 327
Burlington, Vt., 72, 260, 261, 267, 274, 396
Burlington, Cedar Rapids & Northern R.R., 430, 431
Burnettizing, 353
Burnside, A. E., Gen., 384
Burrall, William P., 429
Burt, William L., Gen., 255, 256
Bussey Bridge disaster, 377, 378
Butler, Benj. F., Gen., 167, 369

Caldwell, D. W., 431
Calais R.R., 308
California Southern Ry., 422
Cambridge, Mass., 47, 78, 114, 294
Canadian Express Co., 409
Canadian National Rys., 338
Canadian Pacific Ry., 326, 327, 337
Candia, N. H., 290, 291, 292, 301
Canton Viaduct, 105, 106, 110-112, 113, 353
Cape Cod R.R., 226, 227, 228
Carpenter, A. V. H., 358, 359, 389
Central New England & Western R.R., 210
Central Pacific R.R., 421
Central R.R. of New Jersey, 426
Central Vermont R.R., 195, 276-284, 301, 323, 334, 338, 348, 424, 432
Chamberlain, Edson J., 431
Chambers, William, 370, 381, 385, 388, 389
Champlain Canal, 8, 15, 63, 72
Champlain & Connecticut River R.R., 260
Champlain, Lake, 8, 15, 46, 71, 259, 260, 264, 266, 267, 281, 306, 323, 347
Chapin, Chester W., 138, 139, 140, 141, 176, 191, 193, 412, 416, 417

Charles River R.R., 198, 206
Charlestown, Mass., 18, 78, 91, 159, 237, 238
Chatham, N. Y., 37, 127, 130, 276, 352
Chelsea, Mass., 159, 294
Cheney, Benj. P., 403, 409
Chesapeake & Ohio R.R., 421, 426
Cheshire R.R., 260, 271
Chicago, 115, 412, 415, 416, 423
Chicago & Alton R.R., 431
Chicago, Burlington & Quincy R.R., 416, 422, 432
Chicago & Erie R.R., 431
Chicago Great Western R.R., 427
Chicago, Milwaukee & St. Paul R.R., 423, 429
Chicago, Rock Island & Pacific R.R., 412, 413
Chicago, St. Louis & New Orleans R.R., 430
Chicago, Santa Fe & California R.R., 423
Cincinnati, Washington & Baltimore R.R., 431
Clark, Charles P., 194, 206, 207, 211-213, 412
Clark, Horace F., 429
Clarke, Albert, 401
Clement, Percival W., 281, 282
Cleveland, Canton & Southern R.R., 422
Cleveland, Columbus & Cincinnati R.R., 428
Cleveland, Painesville & Ashtabula R.R., 428
Clifford, John H., 431
Clinton, De Witt, 5, 6, 29
Clough, George, 298, 299, 401
Cocheco R.R., 157, 160
Colby, Gardiner, 431
Colby Act, 302, 304
Colorado Central R.R., 420, 431
Columbian Centinel, 78
Concord, N. H., 19, 46, 73, 74, 75, 92, 148, 260, 271, 285, 286-294, 296, 358
Concord R.R., 148, 286-292, 296, 297-307, 329, 382, 386, 401
Concord & Claremont R.R., 292, 294, 302
Concord Historical Commission, 287, 291, 301

Concord & Montreal R.R., 305, 306
Concord & Portsmouth R.R., 289, 291
Connecticut & Passumpsic Rivers R.R., 240, 259, 261, 265, 267, 273, 278, 279, 284, 296, 303, 306, 358, 421, 432
Connecticut River, 7, 14, 15, 16, 23, 40, 46, 48, 63, 72, 118, 176, 184, 186, 193, 194, 221, 239, 240, 260, 289
Connecticut River R.R., 138, 193, 194, 241, 301, 306
Consolidated Ry. of Vermont, 279
Contoocook Valley R.R., 292, 294
Cooke, Edmund Vance, 161
Cooke, Jay, 424
Coolidge, T. J., 423
Copley, John Singleton, 18
Corbett, Henry W., 431
Corbin, Austin, 306, 428
Corbin, Daniel C., 428
Cram, Franklin W., 327
Crapo, W. W., 431
Crawford House, 303
Credit Mobilier, 418, 419, 420
Crittenden, H. T., 343
Crocker, Alvah, 236, 237, 239, 240, 242, 247, 412
Crowninshield, F. B., 224, 225, 412

Daggett, John, 107
Danbury, Conn., 177, 178, 200, 205, 208, 386
Danbury & Norwalk R.R., 178, 208, 386
"Daniel Nason," engine, 363
Danvers, Mass., 156, 157, 158
Davenport & Bridges, 151, 390
Davis, John, Gov., 99
Dean & Davenport, 405
Dearborn, Benj., 21
Dearborn, H. A. S., Gen., 321
Dedham, Mass., 109, 110, 206, 377
Delaware & Hudson R.R., 61, 277, 280, 281
Depew, Chauncey M., 330
Derby, Conn., 184
Derby, E. Hasket, 224, 236, 237, 412
Dickens, Charles, 11, 176, 185, 381, 384, 388, 390
Dighton & Somerset R.R., 228
Dinsmore, William B., 409

Dixville Notch, 311, 312
Dodge, Grenville H., 418, 419
Dorchester, Mass., 34, 114, 216, 223, 357, 423
Dover, N. H., 146, 160
Drew, Daniel, 201, 202, 203, 204
Dude Train, 232
Dunbar, Seymour, 381
Durant, Thomas Clark, 418, 419
Dwight, Timothy, 34, 170

Earle & Prew, 406
East Boston, 149, 150, 151, 152, 330, 373, 392
Eastern R.R., 143, 145, 148-169, 279, 302, 304, 309, 318, 321, 323, 324, 346, 361, 365, 373-376, 387, 388, 389, 392, 394, 404, 415
Eastern Express Co., 409
Eddy, Wilson, 384
Edgartown, Mass., 348, 349
Elgin, Earl of, 294
Elliott, Howard, 335
Engine cab, first, 356
Erie Canal, 3, 5, 6, 8, 16, 29, 41, 62, 63, 75, 132, 133
Essex R.R., 156
Essex Junction, Vt., 264, 265
European & No. American Ry., 319, 321-323
Eustice, W. T., 391
Evans, Oliver, 20
Evansville & Terre Haute R.R., 429
Everett, Mass., 157, 159, 374
Everett, Edward, Gov., 120, 125
Exeter, N. H., 146
Express service, first, 405, 406

Fabyan's, N. H., 303
Fairbanks, Erastus, 265, 293
Fairbanks, Horace, 278, 279
Fairbanks, Thaddeus, 278
Fairfield County R.R., 177
Fairhaven Branch R.R., 227
Fall River, Mass., 218, 221, 228, 229
Fall River Line, 219, 222, 230, 234
Fall River R.R., 217, 218, 223, 224, 225, 226, 228
Fall River, Warren & Providence R.R., 233
Farmington, Conn., 318

Farmington, Me., 341, 342
Farnam, Henry, 181, 182, 413
Favor's Eastport Express, 408
Felt, Charles W., 165, 400
Felton, Saml. M., 238, 248, 261, 411
Fessenden, James M., 94, 117, 150, 152, 411
Fillmore, Millard, Pres., 270, 294
First baggage checks, 387
First charter, 49
First engine cab, 356
First express service, 405, 406
First parcel room, 225
First sleeping car idea, 56, 57
First tramways, 18, 24-34
First vestibuled cars, 391
Fisher, Charles E., 97, 101
Fishkill, N. Y., 197, 200, 201, 202
Fisk, James, Jr., 420
Fitch, John, 21
Fitchburg, Mass., 192, 233, 236, 237, 238, 239, 240, 250, 260
Fitchburg R.R., 137, 159, 236-258, 260, 261, 262, 265, 271, 275, 300, 305, 330, 332, 346, 385, 387, 394, 397, 431
Fitchburg & Worcester R.R., 232, 242
Flint & Pere Marquette R.R., 431
Follett, Timothy, 260, 263, 265
Forbes, John M., 414, 415, 416
Ford, Gordon L., 428
Forney, M. N., 340
Framingham, Mass., 96, 101, 103, 232
Franklin R.R., 63, 71
Franklin & Megantic R.R., 342
Fremont, Elkhorn & Missouri Valley R.R., 420
French, James H., 357, 366, 370

Galt, Alexander T., 311
Galveston, Harrisburg & San Antonio R.R., 431
Gardiner, Me., 316
Gardner, Mass., 240
Gauges, 32, 313, 314, 317, 318, 319, 321, 339-349, 428
Gaylordsville, Conn., 394
Georgetown, Mass., 157, 158
Ghost Train. See White Train.
Gilmore, Addison, 138, 265
Gilmore, Joseph A., 288, 292, 298
Gould, Jay, 207, 274, 420

Grand Junction R.R., 160
Grand Trunk Ry., 273, 280, 305, 315, 316, 319, 334, 335, 338, 385, 431
Granite Ry., 25-27, 32-35, 76, 106
Grant, E. B., 109, 352
Grant, U. S., Pres., 227, 230, 322, 349, 402
Grattan, Thos. Colley, 229
Gray, W. C., 405
Great Falls & Conway R.R., 160, 166, 279, 323
Greenfield, Mass., 136, 192, 240, 241, 242, 243
Greenport, L. I., 218
Guild, Curtis, Gov., 333
Gulf, Colorado & Santa Fe R.R., 423
Gzowski, Casimir S., 314

Haddock, Charles B., 288, 293
Hale, Edward Everett, 39
Hale, Nathan, 28, 33, 39, 40, 53, 55, 57, 62, 68, 83, 94, 95, 98, 100, 117, 139, 412
Hall, Basil, Capt., 44, 45
Hall, James, 311
Hall, Thomas S., 377
Hamlin, Hannibal, 320, 322
Hampshire & Hampden (Farmington) Canal, 7, 23, 180, 181
Hannaford, Jule M., 425
Hannibal & St. Joseph R.R., 412
Hapgood's sleeping cars, 191, 390
Harahan, J. T., 431
Harlem & Port Chester R.R., 193, 205
Harnden, Adolphus, 406
Harnden, William F., 405-409
Harriman, E. H., 333
Hart, William T., 205
Hartford, Conn., 14, 19, 80, 118, 119, 120, 134, 171, 175, 176, 179, 197, 205, 214, 384
Hartford & Connecticut Valley R.R., 193
Hartford & Connecticut Western R.R., 214
Hartford & New Haven R.R., 118, 119, 121, 138, 172-176, 180, 182, 183, 189-191, 367, 429
Hartford, Providence & Fishkill R.R., 197-200, 205
Harvard University, 10, 409

Hatch, Charles F., 163, 376
Hatch, Louis C., 320
Haupt, Herman, 244-248, 249
Haverhill, Mass., 65, 143, 145, 157, 158
Hawthorne, Nathaniel, 10, 152
Haymarket Square Station, 147, 394
Hays, Charles M., 281, 334
Hayward, James, 55, 72, 81, 146, 411
Hewins, Edward H., 377, 378
Hinckley, Isaac, 429
Hingham, Mass., 113
Hinkley & Drury, 287, 340, 384
Hitchcock, Samuel J., 180
Holliday, Cyrus K., 421
Holmes, Alexander, 230, 248
Hooksett, N. H., 290
Hooper, Samuel, 163, 164, 165
Hoosac Tunnel, 24, 137, 142, 163, 233, 239, 242-252, 256, 257, 258, 346, 412, 413, 421
Hoosac Tunnel & Wilmington R.R., 346
Hopkins, A. L., 431
Houlton, Me., 326
Housatonic R.R., 125, 136, 173, 176-180, 194, 208, 382, 394, 429
Houston & Texas Central R.R., 426, 427
Howe Truss Bridge, 353, 428
Howells, William Dean, 394
Hubbard, Thomas H., 416
Hudson, N. Y., 50, 117, 119
Hudson & Berkshire R.R., 117, 123, 127, 130, 137
Hudson River, 6, 15, 23, 36, 37, 46, 55, 63, 123, 133, 137, 170, 194, 359
Hungerford, Edward, 402
Hunnewell, H. H., 431
Huntington, Collis P., 421
Hurd, Philo, 428
Hyannis, Mass., 226, 227

Illinois Central R.R., 187, 429, 431
India Point, 105, 110
Ingalls, Melville E., 426
Interstate Commerce Commission, 333, 334
Island Pond, Vt., 315
Ives, Charles J., 431

Jackson, Andrew, Pres., 117, 144
Jackson, Patrick T., 80, 81-93, 105, 412

Jackson, William, 54
Jacobs, Warren, 18, 107
Johnson, Edwin F., 190, 411
Journal of the Franklin Institute, 58
Joy, James F., 414, 415, 416

Kalakaua I, 395
Kansas City, Clinton & Springfield R.R., 428
Kansas City, Fort Scott & Memphis R.R., 428
Kansas City, Memphis & Birmingham R.R., 428
Kansas Pacific R.R., 420
Keene, N. H., 301, 306
Kendall, John S., 279
Kennebec Central R.R., 316
Kennebec & Portland R.R., 316, 317, 318
Kentucky Central R.R., 416
Keyes, Henry, 421
Kidder, Peabody & Co., 422
Kingfield & Dead River R.R., 342
Kipling, Rudyard, 209
Knox, Henry, Gen., 16
Knox & Lincoln R.R., 324
Kyanizing ties, 353

Lafayette, Marquis de, 17
Lake Shore & Michigan Southern R.R., 163, 376, 412, 415, 416, 428, 429, 431
Langdon, James R., 261
Lardner, Dionysius, 22, 380
Lawrence, Mass., 115, 147, 148, 155, 156, 289, 294, 382, 384
Lawrence, Abbot, 120
Lawrence, Samuel C., 166
Lebanon Springs R.R., 208, 276, 281
Lee, Mass., 48, 49, 50, 119, 122
Lee, William Raymond, 106, 110, 270, 272, 411
Leonard, Samuel S., 408
Lewiston, Me., 316
Life with Father, 335
Lincoln, Abraham, Pres., 418, 424
Lincoln, Levi, Gov., 16, 17, 23, 31, 43, 46, 49, 51, 53, 99, 119
Lind, Jenny, 394
Lingard, Lord, 322
Littleton, N. H., 296, 303

Liverpool & Manchester R.R., 61, 83
Locks and Canal Co., 80, 81, 85, 86, 126, 145, 151
Long, Stephen H., Col., 310
Long Island R.R., 218, 220, 306, 428, 430
Lord, Eleazar, 428
Loring, Louis P., 85
Lothrop, Thornton K., 163, 164, 168
Loveland, Austin H., 431
Lowell, Mass., 11, 70, 71, 72, 73, 74, 75, 81, 89, 92, 115, 144, 151, 155, 232, 294, 382, 384
Lyell, Charles, Sir, 10, 11, 215, 381, 388
Lynn, Mass., 115, 149, 151, 157, 163, 164, 166, 294, 373-375

McAdam, Roger W., 221
Macgregor, John, 389
McKay & Aldus, 384
Mackay, Alexander, 381
McLeod, A. A., 194, 210, 214, 234
McNeill, William Gibbs, 87, 95, 105, 106, 108, 110, 121, 221, 286, 411
Maine Central R.R., 143, 161, 162, 169, 303, 319, 320, 321, 343, 371, 325, 326, 327, 332, 333, 337, 341, 344, 354, 393
Maine Shore Line, 323
Makepeace, Royal, 49, 57, 61, 68, 72
Manchester, N. H., 147, 148, 286, 287, 289, 290, 292, 384
Manchester & Keene R.R., 301
Manchester & Lawrence R.R., 148, 289, 290, 297, 298, 302, 304, 305
Manchester & North Weare R.R., 292
Mansfield, George E., 339, 340
Mansfield & Framingham R.R., 232
Marblehead, Mass., 154
Mark Twain, 396
Marsh, Sylvester, 303
Martha's Vineyard, 227, 231, 232, 339, 349
Maryland, ferryboat, 205, 206, 208
Mason, William, 354, 384
Massachusetts Central R.R., 254, 255, 257
Massachusetts R.R. Corpn., 56, 71
Massachusetts Rail-Way Association, 57
Maxcy, Josiah S., 342

Medford, Mass., 82, 356
Mellen, Charles S., 282, 283, 331-336,
  343, 412
Meriden, Conn., 172, 175
Merrick, Samuel V., 429
Merrimac River, 3, 19, 80, 143, 145,
  148, 154, 286
"Meteor" engine, 100, 102, 103
Methuen, Mass., 148
Mexican Central Ry., 422
Mexican International Ry., 426
Michigan Central R.R., 249, 413-416,
  422
Michigan Southern R.R., 412, 413, 422
Middleborough, Mass., 217, 226, 228
Middlesex Canal, 3, 17, 72-74, 80, 86
Middletown, Conn., 171, 172, 207, 213
Mill Dam Foundry, 97
Milton, Mass., 26, 223
Minnesota & Northwestern R.R., 429
Minot, Charles, 365
Minot, Josiah, 298, 299
Mohawk & Hudson R.R., 63
Monson R.R., 346
Montpelier, Vt., 46, 261, 278, 284
Montpelier & Wells River R.R., 284,
  337, 401
Montreal, Que., 273, 274, 309, 310, 311,
  312, 313, 314, 323, 338, 394
Montreal & Vermont Junction R.R.,
  273
Morgan, Charles, 427
Morgan, J. Pierpont, Sr., 173, 210, 211,
  332, 336, 430
Morgan, R. F., 37, 45, 56
Morgan's Louisiana & Texas R.R.,
  427
Mount Desert Island, 164, 323
Mt. Washington R.R., 296, 303
Mowbray, George H., 249, 251

Nantucket, Mass., 226, 231, 349
Nantucket R.R., 349
Nashua, N. H., 18, 72, 92, 286, 293,
  300
Nashua & Lowell R.R., 285, 286, 290,
  291, 301, 360, 362
Naugatuck R.R., 183, 184, 194, 200,
  391, 428
Neal, David A., 154, 155, 412, 415
Needham, Mass., 99, 100

Neponset River, 105, 216
Nettleton, George H., 428
New Bedford, Mass., 4, 131, 217, 226
New Bedford & Taunton R.R., 217
New Britain, Conn., 172, 193
Newburgh, Dutchess & Connecticut
  R.R., 201, 205, 214
Newburyport, Mass., 148, 149, 150,
  152, 158, 159, 365
New Canaan, Conn., 194
New England Terminal Co., 208, 209
New England Transfer Co., 205, 207
New Hampshire Central R.R., 292
New Haven, Conn., 7, 8, 80, 119, 121,
  133, 134, 171, 173, 176, 177, 178, 180,
  184, 209, 213, 384, 396
New Haven & Derby R.R., 184, 193
New Haven & New London R.R.,
  184, 190
New Haven & Northampton R.R.,
  181, 182, 187, 412
New Haven Steamboat Co., 176
Newington, Conn., 173
New London, Conn., 172, 184, 195,
  218, 334, 337
New London Northern R.R., 275
New London, Willimantic & Palmer
  R.R., 275, 428
New Orleans, Texas & Pacific R.R.,
  431
Newport, R. I., 218, 224, 229, 379
Newton, Mass., 95, 96, 97, 98, 100,
  101, 199, 294
New York & Albany R.R., 124, 132
New York & Boston Air Line, 190,
  205, 207, 214
New York, Boston & Montreal R.R.,
  276, 277
New York Central R.R., 186, 189, 199,
  210, 254, 258, 282, 283, 329, 338, 351,
  392, 416, 417
New York, Chicago & St. Louis R.R.,
  431
New York & Erie R.R. (N. Y., L. E.
  & W.), 137, 142, 186, 197, 200-202,
  206, 428, 432
New York & Harlem R.R., 134, 138,
  179, 181, 187, 189, 192, 193, 200, 208,
  276, 278, 428, 429
New York & New England R.R., 192,
  194, 195, 196-214, 233, 234, 390, 420

New York & New Haven R.R., 138, 180-183, 184, 186-191, 373, 386, 412
New York, New Haven & Hartford R.R., 184, 191-195, 196, 200, 205, 207, 210, 211, 232, 233, 331-337, 363, 401, 430
New York & Northern R.R., 200, 208, 210
New York, Ontario & Western R.R., 283, 430
New York, Providence & Boston (Stonington) R.R., 112, 121, 184, 194, 220, 221, 222, 223, 229, 233, 234, 356, 365
New York, Westchester & Boston R.R., 333
Nickerson, Thomas, 422, 423
Nobleboro, Me., 324
Noddle's Island, 149
Norfolk County R.R., 198, 199
Norris, William, 97, 98, 99, 111
North Adams, Mass., 251, 252
North Conway, N. H., 160, 279
North Station, Boston, 159, 394
North Woodstock, N. H., 303
Northampton, Mass., 7, 47, 138, 171, 180, 181, 182, 183, 192, 240, 241, 253
Northern Pacific R.R., 273, 332, 410, 417, 423, 431
Northern R.R. (N. H.), 260, 261, 271, 272, 279, 289, 293-295, 297, 298, 301, 306, 358, 400
Northern R.R. of N. Y., 266, 271, 272, 411
Northfield, Vt., 260, 262
Norwalk, Conn., 177, 178, 208
Norwalk bridge disaster, 181, 186, 362, 370, 373
Norwich, Conn., 46, 172, 204, 220, 221
Norwich University, 418
Norwich & Worcester R.R., 173, 204, 206, 220, 390
Nutt, Henry C., 431

Oakes, Thomas F., 425
Ogdensburg, N. Y., 46, 72, 79, 137, 233, 260, 273, 274, 281, 293
Ogdensburg & Lake Champlain R.R., 264, 267, 273, 275, 278, 279, 281
Ohio & Mississippi R.R., 431

Old Colony R.R., 35, 162, 194, 215-235, 236, 248, 300, 357, 367, 376, 381, 387, 394, 395, 400, 420
Old Colony & Fall River R.R., 226-228
Old Colony & Newport R.R., 228
Old Town, Me., 308, 309, 322
Old Town R.R., 308
Osborn, William H., 430
Osgood, Bradley & Co., 99, 390
Otis, Harrison Gray, 53, 57, 91
Oyster Bay, N. Y., 208, 209

Page, John B., 274, 275, 277, 280, 412
Paine, Charles, 260, 261-263, 268, 270, 271, 357, 412
Palmer, Mass., 47, 275, 335
Palmer, Courtlandt, 223
Parcel room, first, 225
Parsons, Charles, 210, 426
Payne, Henry Clay, 425
Peabody, George, 150, 154, 155, 412
Pearson, E. J., 335
Peirce, Thomas W., 431
Pennsylvania R.R., 134, 205, 208, 244, 246, 332, 429
Penobscot & Kennebec, 316, 317, 318, 321, 322
Peoria & Pekin Union R.R., 431
Perham, Josiah, 397, 424
Perkins, Thomas H., Col., 23, 25, 31, 35, 148, 412
Phelps, Abner, Dr., 28, 31, 32, 57
Phelps, Anson G., 183, 186, 187
Phelps, Edward J., 264
Phelps Committee, 31, 32, 38
Philadelphia & Reading R.R., 194, 210, 233, 234, 306, 428
Philadelphia, Reading & New England R.R., 211, 214
Philadelphia, Wilmington & Baltimore R.R., 248, 412, 429
Phillips, Me., 340, 341
Phillips & Rangeley R.R., 342
Phillips, E. B., 431
Pierce, Franklin, Pres., 369
Pierce, Walter, 431
Pittsfield, Mass., 44, 47, 49, 119, 122, 135, 180, 364, 365, 393
Pittsfield & North Adams R.R., 136
Plainville, Conn., 182, 183

Plant, Henry B., 425
Plant System Rys., 425
Plattsburg, N. Y., 264, 266, 274
Plymouth, Mass., 35, 215, 216, 217
Point Judith, R. I., 221
Pomeroy, Lemuel, 124, 126
Poor, Henry·V., 186, 187, 188
Poor, John A., 310-313, 316, 319, 321, 322, 325, 338, 412
Porter, Asa R., 231
Portland, Me., 80, 148, 154, 159, 161, 162, 164, 165, 278, 309, 310, 311, 313, 314, 315, 316, 317, 318, 320, 325, 326, 334, 338, 384, 394
Portland & Kennebec R.R., 318, 319
Portland Locomotive Works, 314, 316
Portland & Ogdensburg R.R., 166, 278, 279, 303, 323, 324
Portland & Oxford Central R.R., 319, 320
Portland & Rochester R.R., 325
Portland & Rumford Falls R.R., 320, 325
Portland, Saco & Portsmouth R.R., 145, 146, 152, 154, 159, 161, 166, 309, 310, 314, 317, 321, 324, 368
Portland Terminal R.R., 337
Portsmouth, N. H., 14, 15, 145, 146, 148, 152, 154, 290, 404
Potter, Gene, 211-213
Poughkeepsie Bridge, 194, 211
Pratt, Dave, 385
Preble, William P., 313, 314
Prescott, Jeremiah, 162, 373-376
Presque Isle, Me., 326
Profile & Franconia Notch R.R., 296
Profile House, 303
Prouty, Charles A., 430
Providence, R. I., 7, 43, 46, 70, 77, 78, 80, 103, 104, 105, 109, 110, 112, 113, 171, 172, 184, 186, 197, 205, 218, 221, 222, 230, 335, 384
Providence, Warren & Bristol R.R., 229, 233
Providence & Worcester R.R., 219, 230, 234, 354, 370, 371, 429
Provincetown, Mass., 226, 227
Pullman cars, 162, 210, 231, 256, 258, 336, 389, 392

Quincy, Mass., 17, 26, 32, 34, 216
Quincy, Josiah, 10, 16, 42
Quincy, Josiah, Jr., 78, 120, 121, 122, 124, 130, 131, 140-142, 268, 269, 412

Railroad Gazette, 191, 192
Railway and Locomotive Historical Society, 97, 101
Rainhill Trials, 55, 61
Rangeley, Me., 340, 341
Revere, Joseph W., 105
Revere disaster, 162, 163, 165, 365, 373-376, 377
Reynolds, S. W., 422
Rhode Island Locomotive Works, 384
Rice, Edmund, 429
Rice, Richard D., 319
Riegel, Robert E., 420
Ringwalt, J. A., 18
Ripley, Edward P., 423
Ripley, William Z., 430
Robinson, Albert A., 421, 422, 423
Robinson, William, 89-91
Rochester, N. H., 325
Rockland, Me., 159, 324
Rogers, Henry H., 227
Rome, Watertown & Ogdensburg R.R., 426
Roosevelt, Theodore, Pres., 332
Rose, Chauncey, 429
Rotterdam Jct., N. Y., 256, 258
Rouse's Point, N. Y., 266, 268, 274, 279, 281
Roxbury, Mass., 78, 294, 384
Rutland, Vt., 136, 260, 276
Rutland & Burlington (Rutland) R.R., 253, 260, 261, 263, 264, 265, 267, 270, 273, 275, 277, 278, 280, 281-283, 396, 411
Rutland & Washington R.R., 274
Rutland & Whitehall R.R., 79, 259, 275

St. Albans, Vt., 263, 264, 271
St. Johnsbury, Vt., 266, 278, 279
St. Johnsbury & Lake Champlain R.R., 278, 279, 284, 293, 302, 306, 323, 337
St. Joseph & Grand Island R.R., 431
St. Lawrence & Atlantic R.R., 313

St. Louis & San Francisco R.R., 423, 430

St. Louis, Vandalia & Terre Haute R.R., 430

St. Paul & Pacific R.R., 429

Salem, Mass., 4, 148, 149, 151, 152, 153, 154, 158, 159, 165, 365, 404

Salem & Lowell R.R., 155, 156

*Salem Observer*, 62

*Salem Register*, 152

Saltonstall, Leverett, 78

Sanborn, John, 167, 168

Sandwich, Mass., 226

Sandy River R.R., 341-343

Sargent, Henry, Col., 38, 76, 149

Sargent, Homer E., 431

Saugus Branch R.R., 157, 374, 375

Sawpits Village, N. Y., 179

Schuyler, Robert, 180, 186-189, 266, 428, 430

Searsport, Me., 327

Sedgwick, Theodore, 44, 45, 50-53, 55, 66, 82, 412

Seward, William H., Gov., 131, 133

Seymour, George Dudley, 395

"Shadrack," 3, 9

Shanly, Walter and Francis, 251

Sheffield, Joseph E., 180, 181, 182, 192, 412

Shepaug R.R., 390

Sherbrooke, Que., 273, 312, 315

Shore Line R.R., 185

Shute, James M., 250

Sioux City & Pacific R.R., 420

Skowhegan, Me., 317, 393

Sleeping car, first suggestion of, 56, 57

Smith, Edward C., 280

Smith, F. O. J., 320

Smith, J. Gregory, 253, 271, 273, 275, 279, 280, 424

Smith, John, 263, 264, 268, 271

Smith, Orland, 431

Smith, Worthington, 273

Somerset R.R., 319

Somerset & Kennebec R.R., 317, 319, 368, 393

South Berwick, Me., 146, 154, 160, 161, 162, 325

South Braintree, Mass., 217, 223, 224, 225

Southbridge, Mass., 199

Souther, John, 384

Southern R.R., 328, 427, 430

Southern Express Co., 425

Southern Pacific R.R., 334, 417, 426

South Londonderry, Vt., 347

South Reading Branch R.R., 156

South Shore R.R., 223, 397

South Station, Boston, 331

South Vernon, Vt., 241, 306

Spokane Falls & Northern R.R., 429

Sprague, William, Gov., 197, 198

Springfield, Mass., 37, 80, 117, 118, 119, 122, 125, 128, 130, 135, 138, 176, 179, 182, 190, 191, 193, 194, 205, 214, 221, 306, 357, 384, 390, 417

Stamford, Conn., 179

Stanstead, Shefford & Chambly R.R., 273

State Street, Boston, 201, 293, 295, 331, 415, 417, 422

Stearns, Onslow, 229, 256, 271, 272, 286, 293, 412

Stephenson, George, 18, 21, 26, 62, 83, 313, 314

Stephenson, Robert, 83, 86, 87, 97, 100, 309

Stevens, John, 21, 350

Stevens, Robert, 350, 351

Stickney, A. B., 427

Stockbridge, Mass., 37, 38, 49, 122, 125

Stone, Amasa, 428

Stonington, Conn., 113, 121, 172, 184, 218, 220, 221, 222, 228

Stonington R.R. *See* N. Y., Providence & Boston.

"Stourbridge Lion," 61

Strange, J. W., 387

Strickland, William, 22

Strong, Me., 340, 341

Strong, William B., 423

Stuart, Tommy, 396

Sullivan, John L., 45, 46

Sullivan County R.R., 266, 271, 273, 301, 306

Suncook, N. H., 291, 292, 301

Swift, William H., 121, 138, 221, 411

Taunton, Mass., 77, 217, 224, 228, 233, 354, 384, 387

Terre Haute & Indianapolis R.R., 429

Thames River, 46, 185, 186, 191, 220
Thayer, John E., 415, 416
*The Albany Depot*, 394
Thomas, Seth, 183
Thompson, Livingston & Co., 409
Thoreau, Henry D., 328
Toothaker, Abner, 341
Tredgold, Thomas, 21, 29
Trevithick, Richard, 20
Troy, N. Y., 70, 242, 253, 259
Troy & Bennington R.R., 252
Troy & Boston R.R., 252, 253, 255, 256, 257, 274
Troy & Greenfield R.R., 137, 242, 245, 248, 252, 253, 254, 257, 421
Tuttle, Lucius, 258, 324, 412
Twining, Alexander C., 119, 121, 172, 174, 178, 180, 411
Twitchell, Ginery, 139, 412, 421
Tyler, Silas, 405

Union Pacific R.R., 412, 418-421, 422, 423, 429
U. S. & Canada Express Co., 409
U. S. Railroad Administration, 232
Upper Coos R.R., 323, 324

Vanceboro, Me., 322, 326
Vanderbilt, Cornelius, 111, 189, 200, 201, 203, 204, 401, 417, 427
Vanderbilt, William H., 192, 208, 256, 282, 426
Vermont & Canada R.R., 263, 264, 266, 267, 268, 270, 272-274, 276-278, 280
Vermont Central R.R., 253, 261-263, 264, 266, 267-274, 275, 276, 278, 280, 289, 293, 295, 351, 358, 359, 411
Vermont & Massachusetts R.R., 95, 137, 239, 240, 241, 242, 248, 253, 254, 275
Vermont Valley R.R., 187, 266, 274
Vestibuled cars, first, 391
Villard, Henry, 425

Wabash, St. Louis & Pacific R.R., 258, 416
Wagner sleeping cars, 191, 256, 282
Waldoboro, Me., 325
Wales, Thomas B., 105, 111, 121, 122, 130, 351, 412

Wall Street, 118, 142, 201, 207, 331, 336
Wallace, John F., 431
Walpole, Mass., 245
Waltham, Mass., 96, 238, 241, 294
Warehouse Point Bridge, 176
Washburn, Emory, 32, 36, 123, 130
Washington, George, Pres., 5
Washington County R.R., 323
Wason Mfg. Co., 390
Waterbury, Conn., 183, 197, 200, 205
Waterbury & Atwood ventilation, 391
Watertown, Mass., 96, 114, 241
Waterville, Me., 316, 317, 318, 319, 345
Watson, Elkanah, 45
Webb, J. Watson, 111, 282
Webb, W. Seward, 282
Webster, Daniel, 17, 32, 75, 81, 156, 216, 217, 293, 294
Wellesley, Mass., 94, 95
Wells, Henry, 407
Wells, Fargo & Co., 407, 410
Wells River, Vt., 295, 296
West River R.R., 347, 348
West, Thomas, 145
Westborough, 96, 100, 102, 103
Western R.R. (Mass), 101, 116-141, 174, 190, 221, 245, 247, 268, 275, 331, 351, 356, 357, 363, 382, 384, 385, 392, 393, 412, 416
Western Vermont R.R., 253, 274
Westfield, Mass., 47, 363, 364, 365
Westfield River, 122, 283
West Shore (N. Y., W. S. & Buffalo) R.R., 255, 256, 258, 430
West Stockbridge, Mass., 47, 123, 127, 177, 352
Whistler, George W., 86, 87, 91, 121, 122, 127, 130, 135, 136, 221, 286, 411
Whistler, J. A. McNeill, 87
White Mountains R.R., 296, 303
White Plains, N. Y., 181, 192, 333
White River Jct., Vt., 262, 266, 271, 293, 358
White Train, 209-213
Whiting, R. W., 405
Whitney, Asa (1791-1874), 417, 431
Willard, Daniel, 431, 432
Williams Bridge, N. Y., 180, 181
Williams, Henry, 394

Williamstown, Mass., 47, 243, 252
Willimantic, Conn., 197, 199, 200, 207, 209
Wilmington, Mass., 143, 147, 155, 382
Wilson, James H., Gen., 205
Wilson's Point, Conn., 177, 208, 209
Winans, Ross, 135, 136
Winchester, Mass., 85, 93
Winslow, Edward F., 430
Winsted, Conn., 183
Wiscasset, Me., 310, 320, 345
Wiscasset, Waterville & Farmington R.R., 345, 346

Wisconsin Central R.R., 430, 431
Woods Hole, Mass., 227, 232
Wooldredge, John, 164, 165, 167, 168
Woonsocket, R. I., 200, 393
Worcester, Mass., 7, 12, 36, 40, 46, 47, 53, 77, 78, 91, 94, 99, 101, 102, 104, 115, 118, 123, 125, 139, 172, 339, 390
Worcester, Nashua & Rochester R.R., 304

Yale University, 170, 182, 192, 264, 413
"Yankee," engine, 97, 99, 100, 102, 126
York & Cumberland R.R., 325

WEST RIVER P. 347
BEN CHENEY 409
NO WOODSTOCK?

OLD COLONY RA